How to Do Ev
with Your Web 2.0 Blog

D0932567

About the Author

Todd Stauffer is the author or co-author of more than three dozen books on computing and the Internet. He's been a television host, radio host, speaker, magazine writer, and editor mostly on technology topics, although he's occasionally written about cars, travel, and politics. He's the publisher of the *Jackson Free Press,* a newsweekly in Jackson, Mississippi, where he lives with writer/editor Donna Ladd and an embarrassing number of cats.

About the Technical Editor

Jim Bumgardner is a senior technical guru at Yahoo! Music, a teacher at Pasadena's Art Center College of Design, and the creative mind behind CoverPop .com and CrazyDad.com. An expert in graphics and music software, Jim makes mashups, software toys, and experimental user interfaces using Flash, JavaScript, PHP, and other tools.

How to Do Everything with Your Web 2.0 Blog

Todd Stauffer

New York   Chicago   San Francisco   Lisbon
London   Madrid   Mexico City   Milan   New Delhi
San Juan   Seoul   Singapore   Sydney   Toronto

The *McGraw·Hill* Companies

Cataloging-in-Publication Data is on file with the Library of Congress

005.276
5 T 2992

How to Do Everything with Your Web 2.0 Blog

1234567890   FGR FGR   01987

ISBN: 978-0-07-149218-8
MHID: 0-07-149218-6

Sponsoring Editor	**Technical Editor**	**Composition**
Roger Stewart	Jim Bumgardner	International Typesetting and Composition
Editorial Supervisor	**Copy Editor**	
Jody McKenzie	Claire Splan	**Illustration**
Project Manager	**Proofreader**	International Typesetting and Composition
Vastavikta Sharma, International Typesetting and Composition	Shruti Pandey	**Art Director, Cover**
	Indexer	Jeff Weeks
	Kevin Broccoli	
Acquisitions Coordinator	**Production Supervisor**	**Cover Designer**
Carly Stapleton	George Anderson	Pattie Lee

To Mom. Thanks for your constant help and encouragement.

Contents at a Glance

Contents

Acknowledgments

I would like to begin by thanking Roger Stewart and Carly Stapleton at McGraw-Hill for being extremely friendly and considerate taskmasters during the initial writing of the book, which took a great deal longer than any of us expected. Thanks also to Jim Bumgardner for an extremely helpful technical edit and to Jody McKenzie, Vastavikta Sharma, and Claire Splan for shepherding this book through its edit phase. Editing technical books can sometimes be a thankless job. This is a great crew and I'm so pleased at the additions they've made by way of their edits, questions, and encouragement.

I'd also like to thank my co-workers at the *Jackson Free Press,* who have had to put up with my absences through this and other writing projects. I'd especially like to thank Stephen Barnette, co-founder and advertising manager, for making the revenues roll and the trains run on time at our little newspaper.

Finally, thanks to Donna Ladd, my partner in life and work, for doing everything she does at the newspaper and for helping me make the time to get this book done. I'll try not to hold it against her that the moment I finished the last chapter, she promptly kicked me and my stacks of papers out of the spare room so that she can get to work on her own book.

Introduction

Got a blog? Want one? Feel like you need one but you're not sure where to start? Whatever the case, I'd suggest flipping through this book and seeing what you might be able to learn on this little journey through the latest and greatest in blogging. Yes, "Web 2.0" is at least 25 percent marketing term and 25 percent Internet hype, but it's also a way of thinking when it comes to creating, designing, and updating a weblog (or similar community site) on the Internet. It's about a simpler approach to Web design and it's about designing sites that encourage interaction with others.

If you don't yet have a blog, but you do feel you have something to say, then dive right in. You've got plenty of options for getting started, ranging from free tools to nearly free blogging services to inexpensive blogging applications that you can load on your own Web hosting computer. You'll get started quickly and, with the help of this book, you can reach out to many of the other "Web 2.0" services on the Internet for image sharing, video, audio blogging, and so on and incorporate those services into your blog quickly.

If you've already started blogging, I think you'll find some valuable discussion in this book on how to take your blog to the next level, including the creation of a sense of community for your blog, building more traffic to your site and, if you're so inclined, there's even some discussion on how to make a little money from your blogging.

All in all, though, this book is about using and incorporating the latest tools and ideas into your blog—not just to make it "buzzword-compliant" but to make your corner of the Internet that much richer—and to make the ideas and experiences you share with others that much more vivid and compelling. "Web 2.0" can be a fun journey for both the user and the creator. Here's hoping you'll find this book handy as you become a little bit of both.

Who Should Read This Book?

This book is designed to appeal both to Internet users who have not yet begun to blog (or, for that matter, people who have never published any sort of Web site) as well as for those who have started to blog, but would like to expand their blogging expertise and explore new tools and ideas.

If you're just getting started or if you're considering a new blogging tool, you'll see a discussion of four of the major tools, and I'll touch on some of the others, as well. In particular, I'll focus on some of the reasons you might choose one blogging tool over another, and help you make a choice that can grow and change with your blog over time.

You needn't have any web publishing experience, although I do assume that you're at least somewhat familiar with the Web and the Internet. As long as you know how to launch a Web browser and visit a Web site, you should be able to get into blogging very easily; it's considerably simpler than, say, creating Web documents from scratch. (That said, we'll touch on design and hand-coding of site templates in Chapter 4.)

Once you've gotten a blog started (or if you already have a blog that you'd like to augment) then you'll find chapter after chapter on the different "Web 2.0" services that you can add to your site, from image posting and video hosting to creating online discussions, allowing groups of authors to publish ideas, and building a community of readers using newsletters and other tools. We'll even look into a few different ways you can try to make some money from your blog.

How This Book Works

After an introductory chapter (Chapter 1) that encourages you to think about the different ways you can create and manage a blog so that you can choose an appropriate blogging tool, Chapters 2 and 3 introduce you to four different blogging tools that we'll concentrate on throughout the rest of the book. Chapter 4 then shows you how you can delve deeper into the design of your blog and customize it a little (or a lot) to make it truly your own.

From there you can pick and choose the topics you'd like to check out and the features you want to add to your blog—don't worry about reading the chapters from start to finish, but enjoy jumping around from topic to topic, including headline feeds (Chapter 5), photos and multimedia (Chapter 6), integrating your blog with tagging and "social bookmarking" services (Chapter 7), wikis and online collaboration (Chapter 8), communicating with users (Chapter 9), and ways to grow your blog's traffic and potentially monetize it (Chapter 10).

Throughout the book you'll see a few different special features, including:

- **Notes**   These generally point you to important information or clarify something in the main text. I'd recommend reading most of these.

- **Tips**   They're designed to help you extend or learn more about a particular topic that's covered in the main text. You'll find that they're often Web addresses for more information or just nuggets of wisdom that you can internalize and cherish—or ignore.

- **Sidebars**   These are boxed sections of text within the chapters that I felt compelled to write, but you may not feel all that compelled to read. If it's a topic that you don't know anything about or that you want to explore, feel free to read away; if it's something you already know or if your brain is pretty much full and you don't want to top it off, go ahead and skip it.

Of Course I Have a Blog!

Let's not let this book be the end of a fruitful relationship. Plug www.toddstauffer .com into your Web browser and you'll be whisked into iToddCentral—my blog, where we can discuss this book or any Web 2.0 blogging topics in more depth. I'll also try to keep up with the latest news on the tools covered in this guide, as well as new services, interesting tweaks, or answers to your questions. If you get a chance, stop by, sign up, and say hello!

Chapter 1

Plan Your Web 2.0 Blog

How to…

- Figure out "Web 2.0"
- Make some key choices about online community
- Make decisions about the technology that you'll use for blogging

The word "blog" means different things to different people. I'm a techie guy, so I think of a blog as a website that uses a certain type of *content management system* (CMS), which is software designed to make it easier to publish on the Web. Most of the "blogging" CMS applications help you create a website that's loosely based on the way a personal journal or diary is organized, comprised of individual *entries* that are organized by date and time. (The original term was *web log*, which is suggestive of a personal log or diary. The term since has been shortened through general usage to *blog*.)

If you've spent any time on the Internet, you've probably seen tons of sites just like that. But, it's certainly not all that blogs can be. Indeed, what blogs *aren't* might be easier to define—they aren't the sort of brochure-style website that people have tended to put up in years past. Because the blogging software is designed to enable you to create content for your website without knowing arcane little codes and commands (or at least *fewer* of them), the theory is that you'll spend more time creating and updating the content—the words and pictures—on your site. And the more entries you write—again, in theory—the more you'll be able to interest an Internet-based audience in what you have to say.

People use blogs for all sorts of reasons, from keeping a diary-like account of their day-to-day lives to pitching products and services. Some people who have blog-style websites focus on politics or on making a difference in a social context. Others create and maintain blogs to get back at their ex-girlfriends or boyfriends—or to woo new ones. Some have blogs in order to write about rumors and scandals; some keep blogs to cover the latest gizmos and gadgets. Some blog about history or hobbies or local nightlife or world peace—you get the idea.

Meanwhile, if one of the main characteristics of the blogging phenomenon is that it makes publishing on the Web an easy proposition, it stands to reason that you don't need to read two or three chapters in a book to get you started with blogging. You don't. As we'll discuss in Chapter 2, getting started with blogging can be as simple as logging onto a website and setting a few preferences.

And, of course, things can also get *much* more complicated than that.

So, while the startup process might be simple, there is certainly something to be gained from planning your blog ahead of time—you'll be less likely to do it again at some point in the future. Different blogging platforms have different strengths, and which you choose can depend on what you ultimately would like to do with your blog. For instance, for a truly "Web 2.0" blog, you'll probably want some interactive features, which may range from offering your readers the opportunity to comment on your entries to enabling readers to search through photos and multimedia archives that you've stored on services such as Flickr and YouTube. Or you might even want to offer sophisticated community tools to your users to get them to stop by your site often just to chat or argue or make friends (and enemies).

In this chapter, we'll look at some of the basic terminology of "today's" blogging, Web 2.0-style, and we'll discuss some of the decisions you'll want to make as you plan to implement a blog.

NOTE *The term "blog" can be both a noun and a verb. As a noun, it refers to the website itself, as in, "Have you checked out my blog lately?" As a verb, it means the process of adding to your blog, as in "I'm going to blog about that play I saw last night." People who get known for their blogging (another oft-used form of the verb) are often called "bloggers," and the sort of imaginary space in which "things are talked about on blogs" is sometimes referred to as the "blogosphere," as in "The left-wing blogosphere is fired up over the announcement of a new nominee for the Federal bench."*

What's This "Web 2.0" Stuff?

The term "Web 2.0" was coined by Dale Dougherty in a brainstorming session with book publisher Tim O'Reilly at a conference in late 2005, and while it wasn't perfectly well-defined at the time, it was meant to suggest the *next generation* of Web applications that were turning the Web from a sort of static experience into a more active—maybe "useful"—one. (In computer software parlance, the "2.0" version of a product represents a generational step-up from the original "1.0" version of that product.)

Since that time it's been a very popular moniker that generally encapsulates the idea of "all the fun stuff happening on the Web these days," even if people don't totally agree on its meaning. In that original brainstorming session, the term was "defined" when the participants listed examples of web applications that they thought of as fitting the Web 2.0 mold, such as Google's Adsense advertising program, Flickr (www.flickr.com, an online photo-sharing site), and Wikipedia (see Figure 1-1), all sites that make interaction with us, the users, the primary goal.

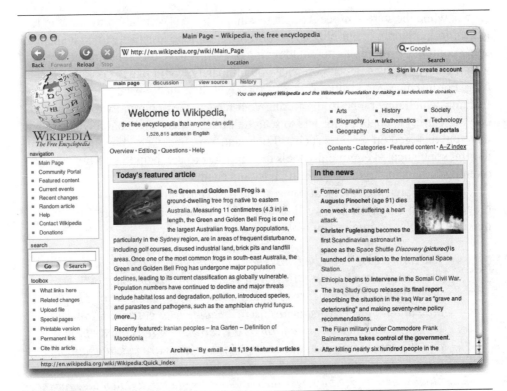

Wikipedia is an extremely popular Web 2.0 site where user-generated articles make up the entire content of the site's encyclopedia-like entries.

As things have developed, "Web 2.0" is really being slapped on to a lot of different situations. The way we'll use it in this book is in the sense that a "Web 2.0" blog and the associated add-ons you can implement may experience a more *interactive* one for people who read your blog. (So much so, in some cases, that they become "visitors" instead of "readers" because they're active participants on your blog.) As I'll talk about more in a moment, the Web 2.0 aspect of your blog is that it enables you to create a sense of community for those who visit, giving them the tools to talk back, or add their own creative sparks, or otherwise participate and get to know others who also visit your site.

Blogs themselves tend to be thought of as Web 2.0, even though they pre-date the term "Web 2.0" itself. The fact that blogging software makes it easy for you to frequently update the content on your website is a Web 2.0 feature, and the fact that many blogging systems have reader-commenting features built in add to a sense of interactivity that can help you build an online community. Many blogging CMS tools also have syndication tools built in that allow other people to "subscribe" to your blog's headlines (or full entries) and read them in special applications or publish automatic links to your work on their own web pages.

Another way to integrate Web 2.0 concepts into your blog is to take advantage of the many Web 2.0 applications that are appearing on the Web. Picture and video-sharing sites such as Picasa, Flickr, YouTube, and Yahoo! Video are Web 2.0 applications and communities in their own right, while, at the same time, offering you enhancements for your blog. Rating sites such as Digg.com and Technorati.com can help others find the entries that you post; social bookmarking sites such as del.icio.us or Spurl.net allow you to share your bookmarks (and links to your blog) with others in order to find like-minded folks and build online relationships.

Another usage of the term "Web 2.0" refers to a slightly amorphous *design* sensibility—one of simplicity and a form-follows-function approach. If you'd like a Web 2.0-looking blog, then you'll want to search for blog-site templates (or to design one yourself) that offer a simple, clean look that tends to pervade the current crop of Web 2.0 applications (see Figure 1-2). It's not mandatory—you should feel

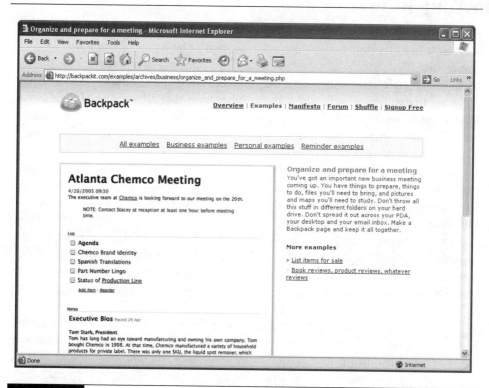

FIGURE 1-2   Backpack (www.backpackit.com) offers a simple design with familiar Web 2.0 elements that visually add to the fact that this is really a Web-based application, and not just a website.

free to express yourself when it comes to creating your blog, particularly if it's a personal site. However, following a few simple guidelines when it comes to design can help to build community. It makes your site more navigable and useful because the simpler designs of today's Web 2.0 sites tend also to be more familiar to users. (I'll delve much more deeply into design issues in Chapter 3.)

NOTE *It's worth saying here that design sensibilities change all the time, so the Web 2.0 approach to design—particularly some very frequently used items such as rounded corners on boxes and glass-like shadows under logos—may well change soon after you get your hands on this book (if they haven't already). Hopefully, though, the underlying simplicity will remain a part of Web design, as that Web 2.0 notion is really a return to some of the fundamental form-follows-function theories that are part of the original vision for the Web.*

Plan Your Blog

Perhaps the most important thread that runs through most of the blogs that are on the Internet is this: they seek to create and/or be a part of *some sort* of community. The blog format itself—those dated entries—can give your family, friends, customers, constituents, or like-minded strangers a window into the topics you want to explore online. And with the other tools that are discussed in this book—wikis, social networking, photos, video, audio, and so on—you can add a number of different features and entry points to make your site more interactive and compelling for the people you want to have visit.

But in order to get there from here, you'll need to do some planning. The first step is to pick the content management system that you want to use for your blog. As you might imagine, there are many different options. Which you choose is important, even when you're getting started, because you'll probably find yourself becoming attached to that CMS as you become familiar with it and dig deeper into its features. When you do, you'll probably find that it has the design flexibility to handle your needs and your style of blogging. So, to help make that determination you'll want to decide on the "style" of blog that you intend to create.

NOTE *You'll often hear people say that they're "married" to a particular blogging application; the metaphor can be quite apt. If you're just getting started, you should take a week or two to "date" a few different blogging applications first before marching down the aisle with one particular one. It's generally easy to move a few blog entries and comments from one system to another, but the more customization you do, the more you'll probably want to stick with that blogging application through the good times and bad!*

1

What's Your Style?

When planning your blog, you'll want to consider the reason that you want a blog in the first place. As mentioned, a great reason to start a blog is because you want to start a Web community, whether for personal reasons—diary-like entries that talk about your day or that focus largely on a hobby or topic of interest—or for business or organizational purposes. Organizations are finding that blogs are a great way to communicate with people they need to reach, whether it's to sell products and services, build community among a base of donors or supporters, or to spread news and opinion.

In one sense, most blogs are pretty much the same. In almost all cases, the most recent entry you've made appears at the top of the web page that's generated by the blogging software, with previous entries appearing beneath it in chronological order. Once you get past a certain number of entries (or, say, into your second month of entries) the blogging software will usually create an automatic *archive* of your entries that a reader can browse through or search at their leisure.

From there, however, *how* you blog—including the type of content and the style of the presentation—can vary pretty dramatically. Here are a few different examples of blogs and consider some of the tools or features they offer that support the style of blog that they represent.

- **Personal Diary**   Often a personal blog can be simple—at least at first blush—when it comes to design and features. With a personal blog, you may or may not want to allow others to comment on your entries. You will likely want to offer a subscription feed so that people can see when you've added new items. And if you're a photographer or you have a hankering for home video, you may want to take advantage of Web-based services to displays those multimedia files for your visitors. Figure 1-3 shows a nicely presented personal blog.

- **Views and Reviews**   Another popular "style" of blog is one that takes a top-down approach to some particular topic—views from an expert, a pundit, a maven, or perhaps even a self-proclaimed demagogue. Whether or not you want to allow comments is up to you (some of the most famous online pundits don't) but you will want to keep the opinions and links to others coming fast and furious. With these blogs, I'd suggest taking advantage of the many different ways that your readers can rate or social bookmark your entries so that you get them publicized, passed around, and in front of larger and larger audiences.

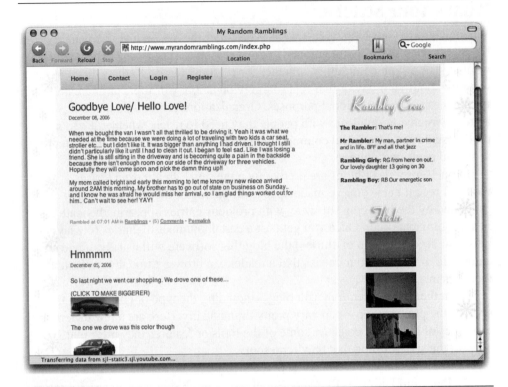

A personal blog will often have a simple design, but might highlight photos, video, or other multimedia features.

- **From the Desk Of ... Blog** Some of the best blogs in a commercial sense can either create a community around a company or product or actually create a market for a product by bringing customers together to read and participate in the blog. If you're setting something like this up, you may still want to offer comments, although *moderating* those comments might be more important to you in this setting. It may be important to you to be able to *tag* or categorize entries on your blog so that visitors can more quickly find items that are important to them. And, while you may have photos and videos linked to your blog as well, you might find that social bookmarking or rating tools are more important to you, if only because you want to get your blog seen by more people in order to entice them into learning more about you or your company or product. You may even want a content management system that can integrate with online merchant tools so that you can sell your product directly to consumers.

- **Organizational Outreach Blog**   A blog can be as useful for a non-profit organization as it can for a for-profit business—sometimes more so, if only for their value in what we might call "online outreach." A church, school, charitable organization, or politician's website should be designed specifically to inform visitors about news and developments they would find interesting. You may not care as much, in this case, about commenting features, but you may want to offer tools for receiving feedback in other ways. Photos may be important, as might wiki tools, which help you create reference-style sites as shared information resources.

> **NOTE**   A wiki *is a website that enables its visitors to add content and edit the pages right in the browser window. Wikipedia is one huge example of a wiki, but using the same principles you can publish your own wiki that you and your readers can build, change, and grow.*

- **Internal Organizational Blog**   Depending on the size of your company or how dispersed it is geographically, you might find that a blog that's specifically designed for internal news and discussions is a handy tool. In this case you may want to look for a blog that focuses on collaborative tools. In my day job, I'm a newspaper publisher, and we use both blogs and wikis extensively for brainstorming, "group memory," and planning.

- **Community Blog**   This is really a catchall category, and the topic can be anything from local news and events to a topic-focused blog that's designed for a particular audience. The truth is that a lot of popular blogs can easily be said to fit this category, from political sites such as DailyKos.com and RedState.org to one of the sites I run, www.jacksonfreepress.com (see Figure 1-4). Any topic-oriented or even personal site can become a community site, particularly if you offer your readers ways to post not just comments, but also their own entries (either as authors of their own blogs, in "forums" or in special open blogs on your site). It's with these sorts of sites that you may really see user-generated content take off, particularly if you give your users tools that they need to express themselves.

You can probably come up with a few more twists, but most of the blogs out there fit one or more of these general categories. Each in its own way is destined to create some sort of community (assuming you keep at it and have some success getting visitors), no matter how limited. So, depending on your motives and ambitions for your site, thinking about the style of site you want to build will certainly have an impact on your planning.

Forums enable user entries   Blog entries with comments

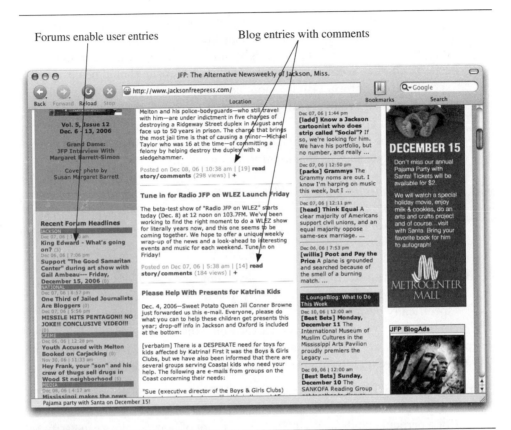

At www.jacksonfreepress.com, visitors comment on stories and add their own stories in the forums, all in the interest of publishing more information, news, and opinion about our hometown.

It's worth saying at this point that not all sites—not even all community sites—are ideally presented using blogging software. For instance, sites such as ePinions.com or the multitude of independent technical support or product-focused sites on the Web are often better presented using *forum* software or a similar solution such that people can create their own posts and garner responses in a more structured online environment (see Figure 1-5). Sometimes this can be accomplished in a blog, but more specialized software might be a better fit.

Blogs tend to be designed best for "one-to-many" or "few-to-many" discussions, where you have one person or a few people—the authors—who post blog entries and invite comments from visitors. In some cases, an "open blog" can make sense, where anyone (or anyone who has, say, been registered for the site) can post an entry for others to read and comment on. But if the core purpose of a

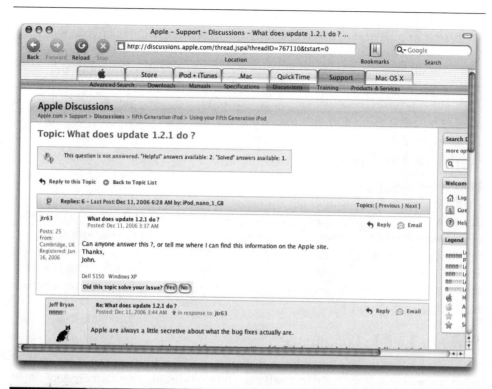

FIGURE 1-5   Apple's Discussions site is designed for users seeking the help of other
users for product advice or user-generated technical support.

site you're envisioning is to give visitors the freedom to post their own content that
others can respond to, just know that there might be a better tool for that.

> **NOTE**   *Some blogging CMS software* is *designed to allow registered users to
> create their own blogs on the site, essentially making it possible for you
> to run a site that is a collection of individual blogs. That's different in my
> mind from the purpose of a forum or some other specialized site where
> the point is not that anyone could run their own blog—which is still a
> one-to-many format, even if you have many people who are set up as
> "authors"—but rather that people can post questions and answers or
> quick topics of interest in order to get a conversation going.*

It's also worth pointing out that you don't have to have a blog as the only
type of presentation on your website. As you'll see in later chapters, it's possible
to mix and match a blog with static pages that are used for other items, or with

photo galleries, forums, wikis, and all sorts of other Web applications. And while this book will pretty much assume you're using your blog's index page as the home page of your personal or professional site, that isn't necessary either. Many people install blogging software and offer their blog as a subsection of their overall website, preferring to have a static "home" page and then linking to their blog (even if their blog is hosted on a different computer or via a blog service). Consider which is best for you and you'll be able to easily make any of these combinations happen.

Will You Enable Comments?

Most of the blogging CMS applications and services that are available will also enable you to turn on a feature that allows your readers to comment. Your first decision will be how important this to you—it may not be at all. Allowing readers to comment on your entries is certainly the first step in making your site more interactive, and it is one possible component of a thriving online community. But there are also some pretty successful blogs that don't allow comments on individual stories, relying instead on e-mail or other systems for garnering reader responses (see Figure 1-6).

Why *Not* Enable Comments?

Although I'm generally a fan of blogs that allow comments, there are some good reasons *not* to enable them. In scientific and Internet circles, there's a concept referred to as the "signal-to-noise ratio" that harkens back to communications systems such as radio and radar. In Internet-based discussions, the concept refers specifically to the percentage of good conversations or feedback you get ("signal") versus how many unproductive or even unreasonable comments you get ("noise"). While Internet communities can be great for creating ongoing discussions and even for building consensus among widely scattered groups, enabling comments can also invite *trolls*, or people who comment on your stories simply to start fights or to garner negative attention.

NOTE   *The "signal-to-noise" concept as it relates to communication was first put forth in a paper called "A Mathematical Theory of Communication" by Claude Shannon, published in 1948. Visit http://en.wikipedia.org/wiki/ Claude_E._Shannon for more information and to find links to the paper, if you're interested.*

Many bloggers have another problem—*spam*. You may be familiar with spam e-mail messages promoting products or websites you aren't interested in. On blogs, spam refers to comments that are added to blogs (sometimes by people, sometimes automatically by "robot" programs on the Internet) with a similar

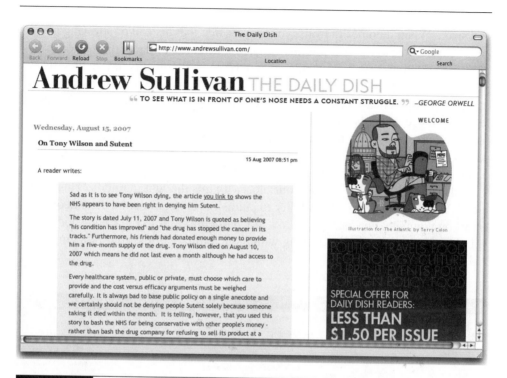

FIGURE 1-6   Andrew Sullivan (www.andrewsullivan.com), a popular political pundit
in the U.S., doesn't allow comments on individual entries, but does
respond publicly to reader e-mail.

purpose of either promoting someone else's website or someone else's products,
often having little or nothing to do with the topic of your blog.

NOTE   *One way for websites to gain positioning in popular search engines such
as Google or MSN.com is for them to have many, many links to those
sites. The number of links that exist on the Internet leading to a particular
site is one of the criteria that is weighed when a search engine places that
site high in its rankings. So, in order to place a nefarious or unscrupulous
website high in search engines, some people will turn to spamming blog
comments, thus adding a link to their site from that blog to their own
site in an effort to fool those search engines into ranking them higher.
Many of those links in comments are actually pointing to splogs, or spam
blogs which are designed to come up high in search engine results, thus
resulting (theoretically) in more traffic and higher revenues for their ads.
Not everyone is blogging just to become popular and adored!*

As a blogger, you have a number of ways to deal with both problems—trolls and spam. When it comes to trolls, you may decide that instead of allowing all comments to post to the site automatically, you need to moderate discussions by using blogging software that allows you to see all comments before they're posted. (Most of them make this possible.) If the volume of your comments makes that impractical, then you might have to moderate in other ways, such as requiring those who wish to post comments on your blog to *register* with your blog first, providing a username and password (and often requiring a valid e-mail address), so that you can communicate with troublesome visitors and disable their commenting privileges if necessary (see Figure 1-7).

I also think it's fair to go into your blog with this thought in mind: "This is my blog." You don't have a responsibility to publish every comment that someone enters on your site, nor must you allow any particular user to run roughshod over your blog with their opinions. Along with moderation options, your blogging

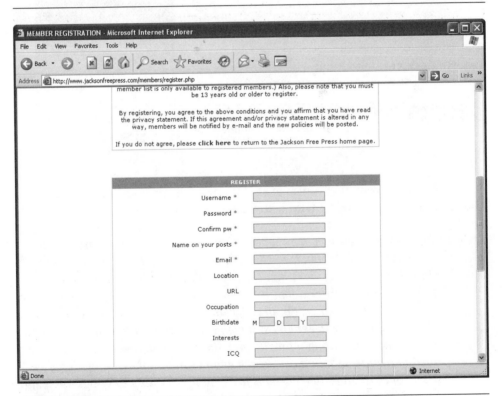

FIGURE 1-7   In order for someone to add a comment on www.jacksonfreepress.com, they must enter some basic information so that they become a registered user of the site.

software will likely also have "blacklisting" options that enable you to stop certain types of visitors from register and/or posting—for instance, anyone with an offensive word in their e-mail address, or visitors from a certain IP address. You might also be able to use a blacklist function to stop certain comments from appearing if they have particular keywords in them.

In a famous case in 2007, popular blogger Kathy Sierra, who wrote about web design issues (headrush.typepad.com), gave up much of her public blogging after receiving death threats and other nasty messages in her blog comments. Obviously, if something like that happens on your blog, you should feel more very comfortable with the idea of moderating comments, adding barriers to entry for registrations and, if necessary, turning off the comment feature completely.

> **TIP**
>
> *On the Jackson Free Press website that I run, we deal in local political issues often, which can lead to trolls who insult others or otherwise comment in order to pick fights. Our solution is a posted "user agreement" that generally tells people they're allowed to post any opinion that they have, but that they can't insult people directly on the site, nor can they use hate speech or insult groups of people when expressing their opinions. It takes vigilance, but we've found that people with a multiplicity of opinions, even on politically charged issues, can have civil conversations when you set a few ground rules.*

As for spam, asking your users to register can help cut down on spam, since certain types of automatic spamming systems can't get past the registration system. Another popular solution is a system called CAPTCHA, which stands for *Complete Automated Public Turing test to Tell Computers and Humans Apart*. If you've done some Internet banking or participated in online forums then you may have started to see this system gain popularity. Its most typical form is a small graphical box that requires you to type in the letters that you see—those letters are often misshaped, italicized, or on a graphical background that makes them a little more difficult to discern than they might otherwise be. When you type in the correct letters, your other input—whether it's a bank account password or a blog comment—is accepted by the system (see Figure 1-8).

> **NOTE**
>
> *The problem with CAPTCHA systems is that they tend to cut down on the usability of your site for people who use browsers designed for the vision impaired. Newer CAPTCHA and Turing Test systems are being developed to try and overcome that (using tests such as simple math problems), so keep on the lookout when you're implementing such a test for your blog.*

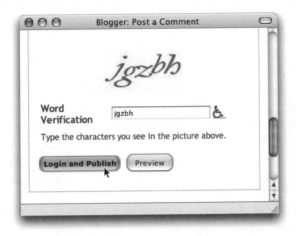

FIGURE 1-8   CAPTCHA systems are one way to cut down on comment spam.

In order to use registration, CAPTCHAs, or other spam- and troll-deterrent systems, your blogging software will need to have them built in, so that will be a consideration when we take a look at specific solutions in Chapter 2.

Comment "Weight"

If you *do* opt to allow comments on entries that you post to your blog, then there's another consideration to make that might affect both the blog software you choose and the choices you make when designing your site—how much *weight* should comments have? By comment weight, I simply mean the relationship between your entries and the comments. You might consider implementing one of the following approaches:

- **Equal Weight**   When comments on your site have equal weight to your entries, it simply means that they appear just below the entry and are displayed on your entry pages by default. This is the way I've set up the main entry pages on my newspaper site (see Figure 1-9).

- **Entry "More Equal" Than Comments**   In this case, you might find that you want to separate your comments slightly from your entries. This is a common approach on many commercial magazine sites, for instance. While getting to the comments generally doesn't require another click and/or another page to load, there may be other ways in which the comments are

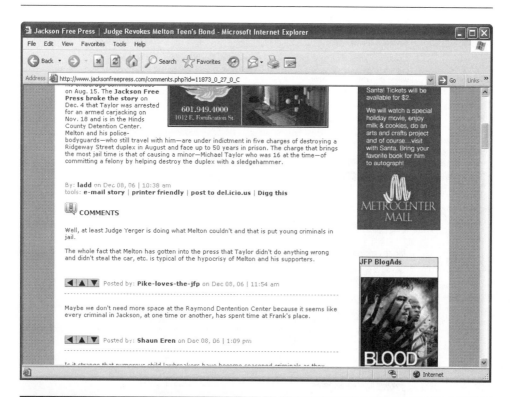

| FIGURE 1-9 | Here, comments flow directly after the entry ends and appear in the same general font and type size. |

slightly less important than the entries, such as a design that puts them in a smaller font, in a scrolling area on the page, or beneath a "disclosure" triangle of some sort, such that you can view or hide the comments quickly (see Figure 1-10).

■ **Comments Are Unequal to the Entry**   In this case, you might require your readers to click a special "view comments" hyperlink that loads another page or, perhaps, a floating window in order to view the comments. As shown in Figure 1-11, a pop-up window for comments is the default approach taken by Blogger (www.blogger.com), for instance, one of the most popular entry-level blogging tools available.

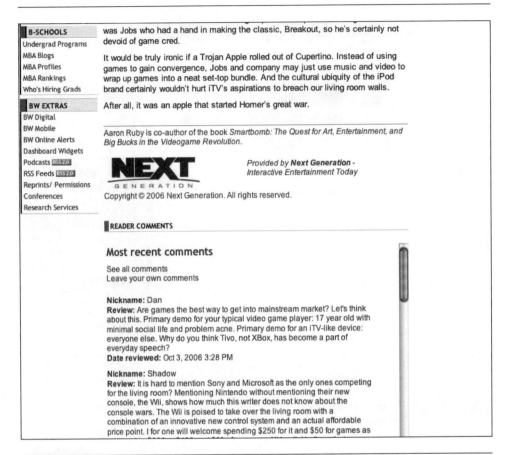

FIGURE 1-10   In this case, comments are presented as a little less equal to the main entry.

■ **Comments Are Completely Separate from the Entry**   In this final case, the comments on a particular entry are stored in a separate system—often an online forum or some sort of open blog where readers can create their own entries that link back to your original entry. I see this a lot on larger daily newspaper sites where they may not want readers commenting directly on stories, but where they want to offer some level of interactivity. For most of us standard-issue bloggers, this approach can stifle conversations online; for high-traffic political blogs or for blogs where you don't have the time or inclination to moderate, this might be a potential solution to encouraging at least some discussion about your writing.

FIGURE 1-11   Blogger, by default, uses a pop-up window to show comments on a given entry.

NOTE   *Many blog CMS applications allow you to offer both a "clean" version and a "comment" version of your blog entry; sometimes the "clean" version, sans-comments, is called the "more" page. Likewise, many blogs offer "printer-friendly" pages that don't include comments so that the entry can be more easily printed without wasting paper. (Printer-friendly pages often also have fewer of the site's interface elements and graphics in order to make the entry a little easier to read on paper.)*

Most blog CMSs incorporate another option that you might want to consider whether or not you are enabling comments on your blog—the *trackback*. With trackbacks, the idea is that you could read something on my blog that peaks your interest and then comment on it on *your* blog. Once you've gotten the entry typed up and posted, you then return to my site and add your response's Web address (or *URL*) to my entry. Now, when others read that entry on my blog, they can click the trackback link to see what you had to say about it on your blog.

NOTE *URLs, or uniform resource locators, are the standard method for finding a particular site or page on the Web—URL is the official name for addresses such as http://www.yoursportsite.com/todaysgame.html. URLs can be used for more than web pages, making it possible to link to an e-mail address, an FTP address (file transport protocol, for downloading files), and others. We'll discuss creating links to other Internet resources in some depth in both Chapter 2 and Chapter 3.*

The trackback feature is a pretty cool one, but it seems to me that it's used quite a bit *less* than you might think, perhaps because more people prefer to carry on conversations on the same site where an original entry of interest was posted, instead of trying to move from blog to blog in order to discuss a given topic. (You'll notice when you're reading a blog where trackbacks are mixed with regular comments, the trackbacks tend to make relatively little sense in context and can interrupt the flow of a conversation.) That said, trackbacks are a fun way to build links between different blogs, which, in turn, can develop additional traffic for your own blog, as well as potentially increasing your ranking in search engines. If you have the option of offering a trackback feature to your readers, it might be a good thing to implement.

One Author or Many?

Another important decision to make about your blog is whether you're likely to be the only author who will contribute to the main entries of the blog, or if you'll have multiple authors. In a very basic sense, deciding that you'll have multiple authors may eliminate a few blogging CMS choices, since some of them don't support multiple authors at all. Others simply don't support multiple authors *all that well* in that they're limited in flexibility. And making the decision to support multiple authors may mean you want to shop for your tool more carefully, depending on how you want those authors to be part of the blog and how technically savvy those users are—some blogging systems are easier to learn than others.

Here's a look at some of the different authoring systems that can be set up:

- **One-to-Many**   In this instance, you've got one blogger—you—and others can comment or perhaps contribute in forums. No one but you appears in the spotlight. Nearly any off-the-shelf blogging tool is designed to accommodate this structure.

- **Few-to-Many**   In this case, you've got a few different authors, and all of you are enabled for adding items in the main blog section. Again, readers might be able to reply in comments to your main stories and/or add their own insights via a forums function. Or not.

■ **Tiered Blogging**   In what I call "tiered blogging," you've got a main blog
that might be managed by a few people, and then you have a secondary
blog (or blogs) to which another group of authors can contribute. In this
scenario, you may find it useful to occasionally "promote" a blog entry
from your secondary blog(s) to your primary blogs. We use a system like
this at the Jackson Free Press online site, which is really a collection of
many different blogs on one page. As shown in Figure 1-12, our JackBlog
is actually a collective blog that's contributed to by a number of authors
who we authorize as "community" bloggers on the site. Our main blog
(called "Noise") is managed by our editor and staff for breaking news and
stories they feel would be of interest to our readers. Sometimes, though,
when a JackBlog author has something really hot or interesting, we'll
"promote" it to Noise, moving it over so that it gains more prominence.

Noise (the "official" blog of our newspaper)   JackBlog ("community" bloggers)

FIGURE 1-12   On the Jackson Free Press site, two different blogs have authors that can
sign into our system. Some are employees who can add to our main Noise
section; others are "community" bloggers who can add to the JackBlog.

■ **Tiered Blogging with Diaries**   I borrowed the tiered blogging concept from something I'd seen done by popular political sites such as DailyKos and MyDD (as well as some popular sports sites such as SundayMorningqb.com) that use software called Scoop as their CMS. Scoop introduces the idea of the *diary*, which is a reader blog that any registered user can have on the site. Diaries are entered and voted on; the most popular rise to the Top Diaries category. The Top Diaries, then, can be promoted to the main blog, where the greatest readership is possible (see Figure 1-13). At the same time, some Scoop sites have one main blog author and some have many. It's a flexible system that encourages user-generated content and can make a site extremely popular for community building.

Main blog   Top diaries

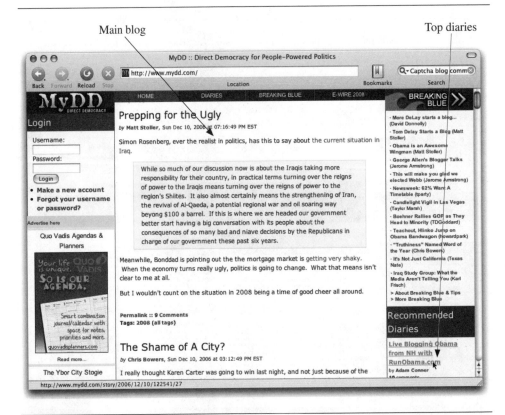

FIGURE 1-13   Sites that use a "diary" system allow all of their users to have their own blogs, and give them a fighting chance at being seen by a wide audience.

So, you can get pretty serious about the number of people that you allow to blog on your site. In some cases, it'll depend on the flexibility of the blogging tool that you choose, so I'll point out what sort of multiple author scenarios each blogging CMS can support when we look at the popular ones in Chapters 2 and 3. If you opt for a system that I don't take a look at there, you might want to ask yourself what sort of author support you're going to want and whether or not the CMS you're evaluating supports that mix.

Do You Need Sophisticated Categories and Tagging?

Most blog CMSs allow you to place your entries in categories, which can then be accessed in some way by the reader. For your personal blog, you might have categories such as Life, Love, Movie Reviews, Poem, Tech—whatever it is that you like to cover and want to blog about. When your user goes to your site, they might notice that they really like what you have to say on a particular topic, so they click a category link or choose it from a menu so that they can see what else you've blogged about within that category.

Some blogging CMS software will limit you to one category per entry, while other software will enable you to enter multiple categories per entry. While this may not be the primary reason for you to choose a CMS, bear it in mind. More categories may end up giving your readers additional ways to organize and enjoy your content.

A more recent approach to the whole "categories thing" is *tagging*, which, put generally, is a system where you can assign categories "on the fly." While categories are generally assigned ahead of time, a tag is usually something that you can add as you're creating a blog entry, and it need not be predefined or, for that matter, you need not have ever used that tag before or ever use it again.

Say you're writing an entry about a movie that stars actor George Clooney, you might place it in the category Movie Reviews. If it's about *Good Night and Good Luck* and your system supports multiple categories, then maybe you'd put in the categories Journalism and Movie Reviews. That would give readers two different ways to access this story if they opted to view your blog by its categories, since you've classified it in both.

With tagging, you could be considerably more freeform. You might assign the piece the tags Movie, Review, George Clooney, Journalism, TV, Jeff Daniels, McCarthyism, and so on. Each of those tags, if entered or selected by one of your readers, would cause this entry to display as well as any others that you've written and tagged in that same way. (So, if you're a George Clooney fan, then they'll see all of those entries, regardless of whether your entry is a movie review, a gossip tidbit, or coverage of George Clooney's public politicking.)

If there's a problem with tags, it's that your readers don't necessarily know what they are, and they can quickly get out of control of if you use a lot of them. So, blog CMS tools that support tags also generally support a way to list those tags, either as a straight list or as something called a *tag cloud* (see Figure 1-14). With most tag clouds, you don't just see the most popular tags, but the tags that you use most often appear larger and/or bolder, reflecting the popularity of that tag in your entries. A reader can now just click a popular tag to see the entries that you've organized using that keyword.

NOTE *There's more on tagging and the theories behind doing it well in Chapter 7.*

Tag cloud

FIGURE 1-14 A tag cloud (shown in the left-hand sidebar) is a visual representation of the tags that you use to categorize your entries.

Flexibility and Extensibility

Yet another consideration when choosing a blogging CMS is how important it is to you that the CMS be *extensible*—that is, how easily can it accept new features or integrate new capabilities by its original authors or by third parties?

Many of the blogging systems that are available for you to try offer modules, plug-ins, and other snippets of code that are written either by the folks who publish the software (particularly if it's commercial software) or by eager programmers who want to add to the blog software's functionality (particularly if the CMS is of the open-source variety). If the software you start with has most or all of the features you think you'll want, then even if it lacks some of the bells and whistles of extensibility it still might be a good choice. If you think you might want to continue adding features to your blog, then you might decide to choose a CMS that has an active developer community.

As an example, the software that I've used for the first five years for the Jackson Free Press website is called pMachine Pro, published by a company called pMachine, Inc. (www.pmachine.com). pMachine, Inc., stopped active

Open Source vs. Commercial Software

Open source software is software that is published in a way that the source code can be accessed by the general public and, depending on the license, can be altered and made freely available in that altered form. (Things can get more complicated than that because there are various intellectual property licenses under which open source software can be published, but the term generally refers to software that can be used and altered for no exchange of money as long as you contribute your changes back to the public *if* you change it.)

Commercial software, whether or not it is actually for sale, can generally not be altered and re-distributed, although there are some exceptions. In a more general sense, open source software is often freely available on the Internet, while commercial software often costs something to use and upgrade.

Depending on the actual software in question, both open source and commercial options can be high-quality options that you shouldn't hesitate to use for your blog; just because something is open source doesn't mean it's an inferior product by any stretch of the imagination.

development of pMachine a few years ago, and it never gained a massive third-party developer audience, although there were some folks who created little *hacks* to the code (some of which I continue to use). pMachine (now called EllisLab, Inc.) now offers another application called ExpressionEngine, which is in the running as the basis of the the next iteration of the Jackson Free Press website. That software is designed to support *modules* and *plug-ins*, making it easier for programmers to add features to the CMS' capabilities.

By the same token, the software that I use for my personal blog at www .toddstauffer.com, is WordPress, an open source option that also has a vibrant developer community. WordPress is arguably the most popular server-side solution for blogging, and hundreds of plug-ins are available for WordPress to extend its capabilities and/or to make working with it more convenient or powerful.

Here's a quick look at some of those different ways that a CMS solution might be extensible:

- **Plug-ins** Plug-ins are generally small snippets of code that are designed to add one or more features to a given blogging CMS. For instance, a CMS might not natively support the ability to encode e-mail addresses on your page so that you can keep an e-mail address from being "harvested" for spam purposes, but a plug-in might be available for the CMS that adds this capability. WordPress is fairly well known for the sheer number of plug-ins available for it.

- **Modules** A module is generally more complicated than a plug-in, adding a whole new set of functionality. Expression Engine, for instance, relies on modules to add features such as wikis and forums. Drupal and Joomla, two popular open source CMSs, use modules for all sorts of features such as calendars, user profiles, messaging between users, and all sorts of fun stuff.

- **Hacks** Generally, what differentiates a hack from a plug-in is the fact that the CMS wasn't designed to support the hack without a change in its code. (In this sense, "hack" doesn't suggest maliciousness the way it might in the "computer hacking" of the movies.) Some CMS applications are designed to accept plug-ins; some aren't. And even some of those that do accept plug-ins might need to have their code tweaked a bit in order to get them to do what you want. Of course, hacking your CMS in this way could cause you to break something else in the program and/or make it impossible to upgrade the software in the future, so it's a risk that programmer types are generally more willing to take than are the rest of us.

■ **Templates**   The popular blogging CMS apps generally have lots of
   templates available on their sites and elsewhere on the Internet, for free
   and for sale, so that you don't have to do the site design yourself—or so
   that you have a more professional jumping-off point for your blog's design.
   As we'll see in Chapter 4, many of the blogging CMSs enable you to
   change the look and feel of your pages with some ease—some more than
   others. Depending on the system, you might need a little help from external
   templates.

Hosted or Serve-it-Yourself?

I'll ask this question again in later chapters as we discuss different solutions, but
I wanted to make sure we're on the same page as to what it means. You've got
two basic approaches to building your own blog—you can sign up for a *hosted*
solution, or you can install your own *serve-it-yourself* solution and take care of it
on your own. Signing up for a hosted solution is generally easier (especially if you
don't already have your own website and you're not terribly interested in jumping
through a hoop or two to get one), while installing a serve-it-yourself solution can
be more powerful.

   Popular hosted blogging CMSs include Blogger.com, Typepad.com, Vox.com,
Squarespace.com, and others. With these services, you simply access the site, go
through a registration process and, in some cases, enter your payment information
to cover the monthly fee. (Some are free, some require payment.) These are hosted
services—somebody else worries about the Internet server, setting up the Web
addresses and all that sort of stuff. You're given a URL for your site, some online
tools for editing your blog (and, perhaps, for editing the template and making
some minor changes to the functionality), and you're ready to go. We'll cover
some specific hosted solutions in Chapter 2.

   With a serve-it-yourself CMS (we'll specifically cover WordPress and
ExpressionEngine in Chapter 3) you'll need to do a little legwork. First, you'll
need some sort of web hosting account from an Internet Service Provider. You
might already have something along those lines from the Internet Service Provider
that you use for Internet access, or you may need to shop for a web hosting
account that will support the specifications of your blogging software.

In fact, there are a few things to look out for when you've chosen a CMS and you're looking for an ISP to host it:

- *Does it support the CMS' scripting language?* Most of the blogging CMSs we'll discuss are written in a scripting language called PHP, so your web hosting account will need to offer support for PHP in order for them to run. You should read the fine print as well, because different web hosts support different versions of PHP (such as PHP 4 or PHP 5), and that can be important when you're installing your CMS.

- *Does your host offer database support?* Again, many of the solutions we'll discuss use MySQL databases for storing your blog entries, information about your users, and so on. If that's true with the CMS that you choose, you'll need to have a web hosting account that supports MySQL. In addition, you may want to check on how *many* databases you're allowed to have, how large they can be, and so on. If you later decided to implement a wiki, a forum, or some other database-driven application your website, you may find that having support for just one or a few individual databases isn't enough.

- *Does the web hosting account offer enough storage space?* Web hosting accounts will generally come with a fixed, assigned amount of storage space for your website's files—anywhere from a few megabytes to tens or hundreds of gigabytes. Just like the hard disk in your computer, this storage space is necessary to store the documents, templates and images that you'll use to display on your blog. So, it's interesting to know not only how much space you have, but also whether or not that space is shared with other features offered by the web host, such as e-mail accounts, databases, and log files. You may find that a very inexpensive host gives you what sounds like an impressive amount of storage—say, 50 megabytes—but that you quickly fill it up if your website files, database, and e-mail accounts must all share that space.

- *What is the allowed throughput?* If your blog gets popular—or if you load it down with bells and whistles such as video and images that you serve up from your web hosting account—then it's possible you'll be sending a lot of data from your ISP to your visitors. If that's the case, you'll want to know what the limit it. (I've recently moved my newspaper blogging site to a server that allows up to two *terabytes* of throughput per month—it's overkill, for now, but at about 75,000 visitors per month and 500,000 pages served, I found that my previous limit of 30GB per month was insufficient.)

TIP
Many web hosts offer features that will install popular blogging tools such as WordPress from within their control panels. This isn't always advised, as the installations aren't always the latest versions or can occasionally be a bit more difficult to customize. But, if you feel that you're strongly allergic to the installation processes discussed in Chapter 4 for server-side solutions (or if you want to try a number of different blogging tools that are offered by your host), that "one-click" install can be a convenient option.

As you're shopping, you should consider other options such as the reputation of the hosting company, whether or not the hosting company offers the support options that you need, whether the host offers your favorite blogging package already installed or included, or whether the hosting company is actually specifically set up to host a particular blogging package (there generally are a few that specialize in a particular CMS). But just as you should plan to choose your CMS tool with an eye toward growth, it's not a bad idea to do the same with your hosting company, just in case your blog really does take off in popularity!

Chapter 2

Choose Your Blog Tool

How to…

■ Determine the type of blog application you'd like to use

■ Choose between a hosted or serve-it-yourself blogging solution

■ Choose an Internet hosting service

■ Get up and blogging with Blogger

■ Get started with a Typepad blog

As you might imagine (or, as you may already know from experience), the Internet offers countless options when it comes to choosing a tool for your blog. Some of them are very similar, but many have particular strengths and weaknesses. Some allow you to get started very quickly; others take some configuration and setup. Which tool you choose can ultimately affect everything that you can get done with your blog—and everything you can't. And when you run up against a limitation that becomes a deal-breaker in terms of enabling you to do everything you want to—particularly in the Web 2.0 arena—that can be frustrating. And since not all blogging tools make it easy to migrate from one tool to another, choosing the one you'll be content to use for a long time is ideal.

That ideal is, of course, difficult to make happen in practice. I have two blogs that I spend a great deal of time with: www.jacksonfreepress.com and www .toddstauffer.com. I'll talk about the Jackson Free Press blog in Chapter 3, since it's a more complex beast. But suffice to say that while I've been writing this book, I've also been moving that blog (it's actually a collection of multiple blogs all organized into a sort of "portal" site that supports our weekly newspaper) from its current platform to another after nearly five years using one blogging application. It did everything I needed it to for a long time, but now I'm moving on.

I also have a problem in that I'm hard to please, and never content once I choose. Along with migrating the JFP to a new platform for pretty good reasons, I've also recently moved much of my every-so-often technology blog (it was called "MacBlog") to its new URL—www.toddstauffer.com, now called "iTodd Central"—where I can blog about a wider range of stuff than just Macs, such as my personal experiences with technology and gadgets. And in the process of that migration, I've experimented with a number of systems—TypePad, WordPress, and ExpressionEngine, all of which I'm discussing in this book. Oddly, though, in the past I've gravitated back to the simplest option, Blogger, partly for its ease-of-use and partly just because I have fun using different tools for different blogs. Mostly, though, for the type of blog that www.toddstauffer.com is, I like the way that Blogger presents entries for a single-user's blog—but I'll get into more of that as the chapter wears on.

(And, having said all *that,* I've got to admit that in the course of writing this book I've moved to WordPress for www.toddstauffer.com. I've really been pleased with the updates that have happened recently, with the latest versions offer a lot of Web 2.0-style features in a very easy-to-manage package. Who knows what I'll be using if and when you next visit!)

In this chapter, I'd like to take a look at some of the basic decisions that go into choosing a blogging tool so that, ideally, *you* won't have to do what I do and move around from one to another to find the perfect one. If your goal is to get up and running with your blog quickly, then it's important that you make a good decision. The right blogging application may help you blog more often (because you enjoy the experience) and give you the ability to extend the features on your website as your audience grows. (If you don't mind a little experimentation, though, play with all of the tools I'm discussing and perhaps even some others; it can be a fun experience to see what's similar, what's different, and what you find appealing.)

Then, after we've discussed how you make your choice and some of the other factors to consider, later in the chapter I'll take an in-depth look at two of the most popular hosted options, Blogger and TypePad. Then, in Chapter 3, I'll discuss two major serve-it-yourself options, WordPress and ExpressionEngine.

How Do You Make the Choice?

In some cases, the blogging software you choose may simply be a matter of personal taste—you may enjoy the demo, you might appreciate the simplicity, or you might have seen some other blogs using the same software and decided that's what you want to go with. To dig a little deeper, though, especially when we consider the Web 2.0 possibilities of a given blogging tool, you may want to ask a few questions:

- What kind of blog are you going to run?

- Do you prefer full-entry blogging or blurbs?

- How flexible is the templating system?

- How are comments and trackbacks supported?

- How modular are the add-ons for the system?

- How well-supported is the blogging software by its user and/or developer community?

Let's explore each question in turn in this section.

What Kind of Blog Are You Going to Run?

As was discussed in Chapter 1, there are different types of blog-based communities, which we can break down essentially along the lines of *one-to-many*, *few-to-many*, and *many-to-many*. (Actually, I've run quite a few *one-to-few* blogs, but that's not the goal here, is it?) Which type of blog you intend to run can have a huge impact on the software that you choose. As we go through some of the options in Chapter 3, I'll try to identify whether or not a particular tool works well for community-oriented sites or if it's best for a one-to-many format. The deeper you go into the many-to-many paradigm, the deeper you're reaching into Web 2.0 territory, which is always nice, but often more complicated.

Do Your Prefer Full Entries or Blurbs?

One of the hallmarks of the Blogger tool is the fact that all blog entries appear in their entirety on the main page of your site (see Figure 2-1). There's no "read more"

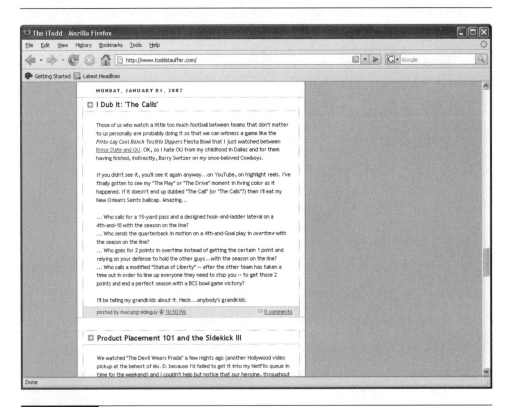

FIGURE 2-1   Blogger sites post an entire blog entry on the front page.

or "continue" link so that you can show a preview of a blog entry and then have your readers click a link in order to continue with that entry.

That's a weakness for certain types of sites for a few different reasons. First, it causes your readers to do a lot of scrolling if they're looking past an entry or two to see what else you've written. Second, it means fewer *pageviews* on your site, which can be important if you're trying to make money from advertising. (Each time a new page on your site is loaded, that's a pageview, so having "story" pages, comment pages, and so on can be one way to keep readers on your site and show them a few more ads.) And third, it just means there's a lot more on the page to scroll through, whereas shorter blurbs make it easier for your reader to quickly scroll through your front page and decide what to read.

The Blogger approach can also be a strength—for a personal blog or one with shorter "quick-hit" entries, it's a lot easier to just read that one page. And if your blog is a component of a larger web strategy, then the one-page blogging approach might be ideal. For instance, if your site sells widgets instead of ads, then you probably want your life-with-widgets blog to be as straightforward as possible. Or, if you're blogging for a non-profit, or running a "boss" blog for your organization or company, then the full-entry approach is simpler for your constituency to read. Fortunately, many of the blogging systems beyond Blogger give you the flexibility to do either—you can blurb an entry and ask readers to click a "more" link to read the whole thing, or you can simply post the entire entry in a part of your form so that it shows up on the main page (see Figure 2-2).

How Flexible Is the Templating System?

The Web 2.0 design mentality tells us that plain pages make sense when you've got good content. But that doesn't necessarily mean you want a blog that looks like everyone else's, and sometimes the best designs actually require more flexibility. So, you need to know a little something about the templating system for your blogging software.

But let me back up for a second. Here's how most blogs work:

1. Blog entries are added using a "back-end" interface of some kind, usually based on Web forms—entry boxes and check boxes. You might also use an application on your computer to add items to your blog.

2. Those entries are stored in a database, which is almost always online. It can either be a database that's hosted by the service that provides you the blogging application, or a database you create on a web-hosting computer that you own or lease. (That goes for a "shared" hosting environment, as well, which refers to the standard sort of personal Web hosting account.)

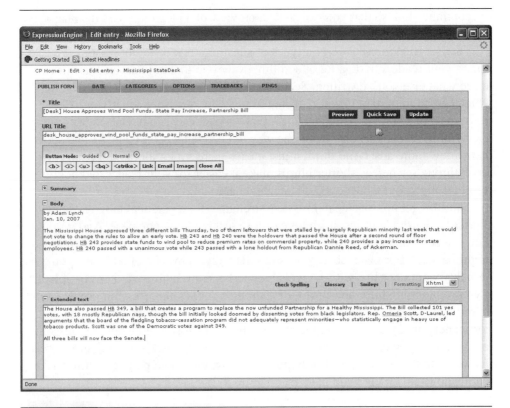

FIGURE 2-2   In ExpressionEngine, as with the majority of blogging systems, you
can decide how much of your post appears on the main page ("body" in
EE parlance) versus how much appears only when the user clicks "read
more" ("extended text") or something similar.

3. When the blogging software is ready to "build" your page, it accesses the
    database and drops the resulting content into a *template*. The template
    will generally be designed in HTML (HyperText Markup Language) with
    special database *calls* within the template itself. The calls will be little
    snippets of code that tell the blogging application "I'd like you to show the
    five most recent entries here" or "I want you to grab the ten most recent
    comments and place them here."

4. The template will also likely rely on a CSS (Cascading Style Sheets) file
    that can be used to make decisions such as what fonts the text can be in,
    how paragraphs are indented, and many other stylistic choices that will
    affect the "look and feel" of the blog pages that are produced.

5. With all of that information gathered, the blogging tool does one of two things to make the pages available to your readers. Some tools "publish" pages whenever you add a new entry, creating "static" HTML documents that can be read by your visitors' Web browsers when they visit your blog site. Other blogging tools generate pages "on the fly" when a visitor views them by retrieving the blog entries from a database and then displaying that content using a template that you've created and stored as part of the blogging system.

I want you to understand this process because not all templating systems are built alike. Blogger, for instance, offers two different ways that you can make changes to your blog—a drag-and-drop Page Elements interface and a "classic" template that uses special codes mixed with HTML. We'll discuss both in Chapter 4, but for now I want to use the "classic" template approach as an example. When you're accessing the administrative control panel of your Blogger site, you can dig into the template by clicking the Template tab, then clicking Edit HTML. Now, on that page, click the option Revert to Classic Template and after confirming your decision, you'll be at a page where you can add items directly to the HTML of your main page's template (see Figure 2-3).

Whenever you click the Publish or Re-publish links that you find available to you within the Blogger interface, your site is rewritten by combining the text from your blog entries (stored in a database) with the decisions you've made about your template.

Here's an example of the code that Blogger requires in order to access the recent postings on my Blogger-based blog, toddstauffer.blogspot.com:

```
<div class="post"><a name="<$BlogItemNumber$>"></a>
    <BlogItemTitle>
    <BlogItemUrl>
            <a href="<$BlogItemUrl$>" title="external link" class="title-link">
            </BlogItemUrl>
    <h3 class="post-title">
    <$BlogItemTitle$>
    </h3>
    <BlogItemUrl></a></BlogItemUrl>
    </BlogItemTitle>
    <div class="post-body">
    <p>
    <$BlogItemBody$>
        </p>
</div>
```

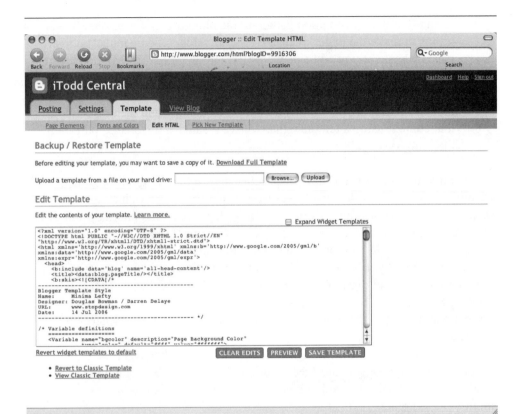

FIGURE 2-3 With Blogger, you can edit the template for your site directly.

Without getting deep into what this all means (that's what Chapter 4 is for), notice the special commands that Blogger employs, including `<BlogItemTitle$>`, `<BlogItemURL$>`, and `<BlogItemBody$>`. Those are the commands (called *tags*) that Blogger uses to access the database and substitute the content from the database you create when you write and store blog entries that include titles and body text.

NOTE *With Blogger, you don't have to dig this deep; as I'll discuss in Chapter 4, the drag and drop approach that's taken by Blogger and other tools (such as TypePad and WordPress) makes some basic design choices very easy to make. What I'm showing here, however, is the abstraction between the design of a page, which you can alter quite a bit, and the commands that are used by the blogging software to access items stored in a database—like titles, entries and author information—and display that information on your blog.*

Some blogging systems offer template tags that are considerably more complex than Blogger. With ExpressionEngine, for instance, the templating system offers a slew of different commands that you can use to mix and match the data that's stored in the database with HTML and CSS so that you can put a variety of items on your blog pages. Here's an example of a fairly basic call for showing blog entries on the main page:

```
{exp:weblog:entries weblog="default_site" orderby="date"
sort="desc" limit="5" disable="member_data|trackbacks"}
<div class="entry">
{date_heading}
<h3 class="date">{entry_date format=' %l, %F %d, %Y '}</h3>
{/date_heading}
<h2 class="title">{title}</h2>
{summary}
{body}
{extended}
<div class="posted">
Posted by <a href="{profile_path=member/index}">{author}</a>
on {entry_date format='%m/%d'} at {entry_date format='%h:%i %A'}
<br />
{categories}
<a href="{path=site_index}">{category_name}</a> &#8226;
{/categories}
<a href="{title_permalink={my_template_group}/index}">Permalink</a>
</div>
{paginate}
<div class="paginate">
Page {current_page} of {total_pages} pages

{pagination_links}
</div>
{/paginate}
</div>
{/exp:weblog:entries}
```

Believe it or not, I've cut some stuff out of that! Notice, however, some of the calls inside that code snippet such as {summary}, {body}, and {extended}, which are the ExpressionEngine's weblog codes for displaying different portions of a blog entry. (If I wanted, in this case, to show only the summary portion of a blog entry, then I'd leave off the {body} and {extended} tags.) Also notice the code that appears between the {paginate} and {/paginate} tags, for example, which are used to determine how multiple blog entries will be broken up over multiple pages.

ExpressionEngine has its own language, really, for displaying the data that it stores in a database in thousands of different ways, depending on how you structure the calls. This is extremely flexible, but it has something of a learning curve if you decide to dig into the code and customize it beyond the most basic levels.

The third approach to templating is a system like Drupal (www.drupal.org). While Drupal is an extremely powerful content management system, it comes "out of the box" configured as a blog, albeit with a very structured look (see Figure 2-4). Unlike some other blogging tools, Drupal requires some complex *themes* in order to change the look and feel, and to get a remarkably different-looking Drupal site you need to get educated about the ways in which themes are built, because Drupal's fundamental design is based on "modules" of content. The typical Drupal blog has a center section for your blog content and sidebars that host all sorts of modular content, including information about your visitors (both members and non-members), recent comments, other statistics, and so on.

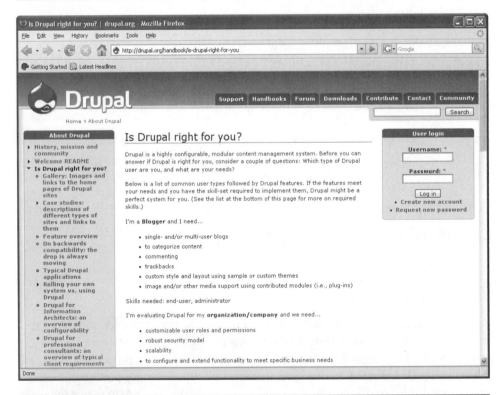

FIGURE 2-4 Drupal's blog design is blocky—in fact, there are a lot of blog and content management applications that tend toward this "block" format— but it offers very strong user tools and a very active community that builds add-ons and modules.

Drupal's strength is its ability to integrate any number of third-party modules, which can make it relatively easy for you to publish a website that supports Web 2.0 stuff such as user-created groups, community calendar listings, integrated forums, wikis, and so on. But because of the complexity and diversity of options, some sort of system is required to get those modules to play well together. That system is the Drupal theme, which makes it possible for all these different modules to stick to guidelines in terms of how they present information.

So, in order to create a new look for your Drupal site, you've got to build (or modify) a theme, which is considerably more complex than altering your template in Blogger or TypePad, and somewhat more complex than altering the various templates in blogging software such as ExpressionEngine or WordPress. Again, it's a new "language" of sorts, and it isn't rocket science, but it does require some tinkering under the hood. Some folks out there have done some remarkable stuff with Drupal (see, for example, The Onion, at www.theonion .com), but it takes some doing.

NOTE   *The complexity of Drupal is a little outside the scope of this book. In Chapter 3, I'll cover WordPress and ExpressionEngine as two examples of more complex, serve-it-yourself blogging CMSs. For more on Drupal, visit www.drupal.org where you'll find extensive documentation and a large online community of Drupal developers and enthusiasts.*

How Are Comments and Trackbacks Supported?

Different blogging tools offer slightly different support for comments (and, sometimes, no support for trackbacks), so you'll want to consider that when you're shopping for a system. In the past, for instance, Blogger has been limited in the way it handled comments, often relegating them to a pop-up window; these days, it has more flexibility. Still, it limits you to either offering "open" comments to any visitors or forcing them to sign up with Blogger in order to comment; there's no middle ground that enables a visitor to simply register for commenting on your site. (Kudos to Blogger for offering CAPTCHAs, however, so there's less spam on Blogger sites than there had been in the past. Remember, if you have a choice of using a CAPTCHA system, consider its accessibility to the sight-impaired before enabling it.)

In general, you'll want to consider whether your want the flexibility to enable comments for individual posts or individual blogs (if you have more than one), and whether or not people need to register or not. On the high end, you'll want to decide whether you want to customize the templates for entering comments (for instance, to add a comment box that offers graphical editing tools like a word processor does), whether the software supports smileys (also called *emoticons*), and so on.

Another interesting issue to consider is how you will moderate users, and whether the software offers *blacklisting* capabilities for particular user accounts or IP addresses. This doesn't always work—someone can use a relatively anonymous IP address by signing onto a dial-up service such as Earthlink or America Online—but being able to block certain IP addresses may be an important advantage if you're being harassed by someone or if you've got trolls that are affecting the productivity discussions on your site.

As for trackbacks, your blogging software will either support them or not. As I mentioned in Chapter 1, I don't see trackbacks used as often as you might think, but you might want the option of using them in your own blog entries (when you're writing about someone else's blog entry) or offering them to your readers so that they can note when they're written about your blog entry on their blog. (Blogger, for instance, doesn't have them in the current version.)

Again, I'll point this stuff out as we evaluate tools later in the chapter. Every tool I'm covering offers Blogger's level of support or better for comments, but if you're shopping outside these recommendations, you'll know what to ask.

How Powerful Are the Add-ons for the System?

This can be a big question if you're looking to grow your blog. At the Blogger end of the spectrum, you're able to get your ideas up and online, and you can share them with friends, visitors, and the world. With the latest Blogger extras, you can add interesting things like RSS feeds from other sites, link to your Flickr account for images, and so on. It's pretty cool stuff. But as with many other blogging tools (particularly those that are completely hosted by a blog publishing company), there are limits to what you can integrate into that Blogger blog in terms of Web 2.0 community features.

I've personally settled on ExpressionEngine as an example of a middle-of-the-road, commercial blogging application that offers support for modules. ExpressionEngine costs a little money for a commercial site, but the EllisLab folks themselves have written modules that support an add-on forum, a wiki tool, e-commerce tools for an online shopping cart, and other modules. Third parties have added to that list, with add-ons that give EE the ability to offer voting on entries, tag clouds based on entry tags, user polls, and other fun stuff.

These modules literally work within the ExpressionEngine interface, making it possible to work with them as if they were originally shipped with the software (see Figure 2-5). That's really one of the key advantages of a modular blogging system—you can extend the functionality of the tool so that you are able to offer additional features to your visitors all under the same user-management system. The user enters her password once (assuming you ask users to register and "log in") and then has access to all of your great content and user features. Likewise, you log in once to the administrative interface and can generate various types of content.

WordPress also offers tons of plug-ins that can add to the functionality of the software with items that make it easier to edit blog entries, plug-ins that hook into

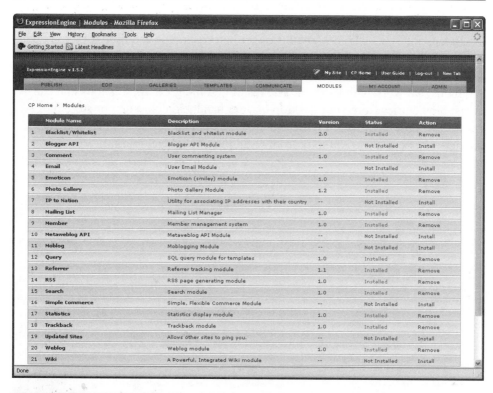

FIGURE 2-5   ExpressionEngine enables you to work with third-party modules from within the EE administrative interface.

Web 2.0 services (like photo sharing, social bookmarking, and video blogging), plug-ins for data backup and management, even plug-ins that help you manage advertisements and "monetize" your content. Of the four major tools discussed in this book, WordPress probably offers the largest range of plug-ins and add-ons that you can use to customize your blogging experience.

How Well Supported Is the Blogging Software by Its Community?

It's not a hard and fast rule, but the more users your blogging software has, the more support you may have when you run into trouble and the more options you'll have for templates, plug-ins, modules, and even "hacks." Blogger is one of the most popular blogging tools available, so that means there are tons of free and paid templates available for you to use if you'd like a fun design for your site.

And it also means there are tutorials, tips, techniques, tricks, and third-party application that make it fun to work with Blogger.

In fact, the folks who designed Blogger before Google acquired it thought that another important component of their success was having an open Blogger *API* (application programming interface), so that third-party programmers can write programs that work with Blogger. The result is some great applications that can create blog entries from your desktop or your handheld computer, or store blog entries and post them later. Figure 2-6 shows a popular application for Mac OS X that lets you post entries directly from within your personal journal.

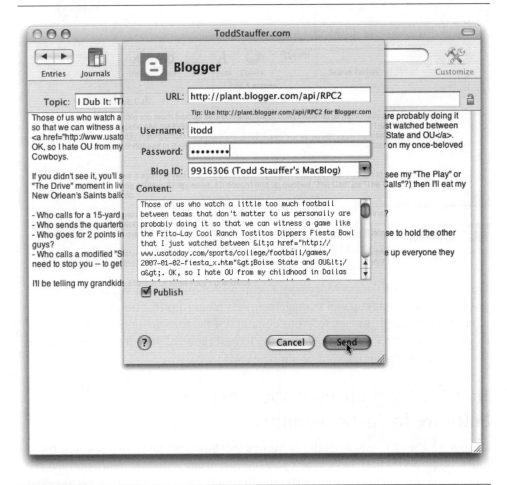

FIGURE 2-6 The application MacJournal offers a feature that lets you publish directly to Blogger.

Other blogging applications can also be judged by their supporters and how much stuff they've worked on to improve the tool, whether with free add-ons or commercial options. ExpressionEngine has a small but fierce group of supporters, which means fewer ready-to-wear templates and add-ons, but a lot of good help in their forums. WordPress has hundreds of developers creating add-ons, writing about solutions to problems and generally plugging away at their own WordPress blogs (see Figure 2-7). And most of these plug-ins and other add-ons are written by enthusiasts and released as open source software—meaning they won't cost you a dime to add to your own blog.

When you're looking into a new blogging tool, I recommend both searching other blogs and sites for discussions or reviews of the tool, and looking into the public forums or other support areas on the site of the blogging application itself.

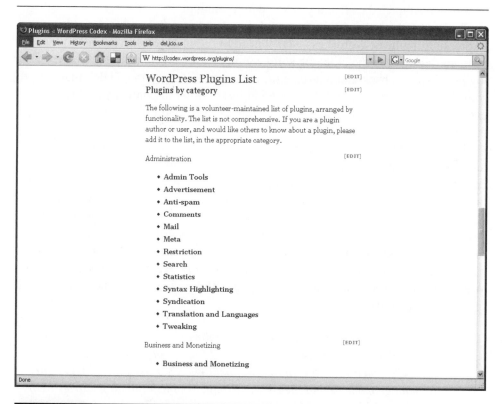

FIGURE 2-7   You'll find a list of plug-ins on WordPress's "Codex" website (the online WordPress site for answers to questions and technical issues—codex .wordpress.org/plugins).

If you find an open community of people who are using, experimenting with, and extending the blogging application, then that might be another factor that helps to suggest it as a good choice. After all, if you get serious about your Web 2.0 blog, then it's likely that at some point you'll want a little help.

Hosted or Serve It Yourself?

One of the major decisions you'll need to consider when you're choosing a blogging tool is whether you want to go with a hosted solution or one that you install on your own web server or web hosting account (which I'm calling a "self-hosted" blogging application). With a hosted solution, like Blogger or TypePad, there's no software to install or configure; you simply log into the service and begin blogging. Often you'll get a URL for your site like *yourname*.blogspot.com or *yourname*.typepad.com and you're up and running.

With a self-hosted solution, by which I mean blogging applications such as ExpressionEngine or WordPress, you'll need to set up a web server account or computer, download the blogging software, install it, and configure it. You then log into a special back-end interface for the software (accessing a URL that's something like www.mycoolblog.com/admin/) in order to publish your blog entries, alter the templates, and so on. Figure 2-8 shows the administrative log-in for ExpressionEngine.

In general, blogging applications that you install and manage yourself offer more flexibility in terms of the features they provide and the extensibility that they can offer. Or, you might choose a self-hosted solution in combination with a web hosting account because you want more control over your data, your backups, and so on. Of course, using such software for your blog has drawbacks, too, in that you'll be responsible for installing any updates and security releases, you'll need to institute a backup plan, and if you decide to change hosting providers, you'll need to do the "migration" to another server yourself. (We'll cover installation of WordPress and ExpressionEngine in Chapter 3 and some of those more advanced topics in Chapter 10.)

TIP　*Actually, you can use some hosted solutions in conjunction a web hosting account, too, so that you can post your blog to your own server. For instance, when I ran the site www.macblog.com, I used the Blogger site to manage my blog, but then I had Blogger publish the blog entries to my own host that was set up to serve files on the macblog.com domain. That way I was able to store images and multimedia on the site for use in my blog, and I was able receive e-mail at the macblog.com domain as well.*

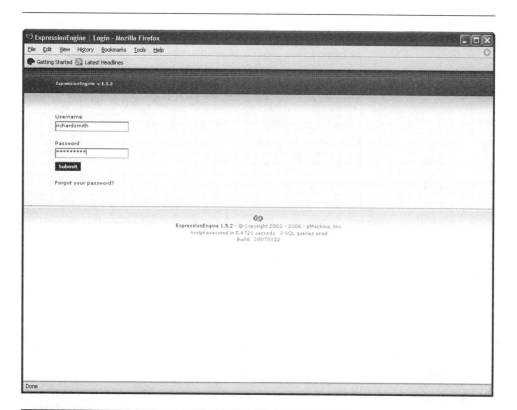

FIGURE 2-8   With a serve-it-yourself blog application, you'll start your blogging sessions by signing in directly via an administrative interface instead of signing in by visiting a blog service's home page.

Choosing a Host

In order to use a self-hosted solution, you'll need to have a web hosting account with an Internet Service Provider or you'll need your own server on the Internet. If you're going the ISP route, you'll also need to make sure that your web hosting account supports the correct technologies for your blogging software. Often that means that the web hosting account needs to support a particular scripting language, like PHP, and that it needs to offer database hosting for MySQL, SQL, or a similar online database technology. (The specific server-side tools I'm discussing, in fact, both use PHP and MySQL.) As you're shopping for a web host, you'll want to make sure that it offers such items that may be required by your blogging software. And with databases such as MySQL, you may want to make sure your web host offers more than one database, as you might find that your blogging software requires one database and something you might add on, such as forums software or some other fun tool, could require its own database.

(With most hosts you can set up multiple MySQL databases; with some low-price hosting accounts, though, there may be limits to the number of databases allowed.)

In addition, you might want to consider some other statistics and typical offerings from hosting companies when you're shopping for a web host:

- **Storage Space**   How much disk space on the server are you allotted and will it cover your needs, particularly if you decide you want to upload photos or other multimedia to your site? Storage measured in the gigabytes instead of megabytes is ideal for a growing blog.

- **Bandwidth Allowed**   How much data are you allowed to send to your visitors before your ISP shuts you down? In some cases it's a few gigabytes of data, in other cases it might reach into the terabytes (thousands of gigabytes) of data. You'll want to know, especially if you expect to offer multimedia files and you suspect you may eventually have a lot of visitors.

- **CPU Usage Limits**   Another thing that's good to ask about, particularly for low-priced accounts, is if there are certain CPU usage limits that can cause your site to appear intermittently even if you've paid your bill and aren't over your bandwidth allowance. It can be annoying to see your site go down in the middle of the day because you have too many people accessing it, thus causing the host's server to reach an artificially set CPU limit.

- **Mailing Lists and Other Scripts**   Some hosts offer a ton of add-on scripts such as blogging and forums scripts, but I'm going to suggest that you look on those as relatively minor additions—after all, there are a ton of free and open source scripts that you can install yourself in your hosting account for little or no trouble. What can be nice is a server that's specifically set up for multiple mailing lists, or *listservs*, particularly if you expect you'll be sending out e-mail newsletters to your visitors. One warning: Some hosts will say they offer you "unlimited" or otherwise very special sounding mailing lists, but then limit you to 50 or 100 outgoing e-mail messages per hour. So, one thing worth asking the hosting salespeople is whether they truly support high-volume newsletters if you think you might want one at some point.

Generally speaking, you get what you pay for when it comes to a web host. Often, the $7-per-month hosts offer impressive looking statistics, but you'll run into some of the limitations I've outlined in the bullet points. With a local ISP, you may spend more but have access to local support people who can help you work out problems (or at least who have to listen to you when you're yelling at them).

With higher-end, performance-oriented accounts, you may get better customer service and more hands-on help with your server even if they're half-way across the country, simply because you're paying for the privilege.

TIP *Actually, the "get what you pay for" advice is a general rule, with some notable exceptions. There are certainly good hosting providers that offer low-cost hosted accounts that will work perfectly well for personal or small business blogs that receive relatively little traffic. One way to decide for yourself is to surf blogs that you respect and see who is hosting them; you'll find that many of them include that information by linking to their host company or putting information about their hosting at the bottom of their blog pages.*

Getting Your Own Domain

Do you have a special address that you'd like for your blog? Addresses such as toddstauffer.com or jacksonfreepress.com are called *domain names,* and they're pretty easy to sign up for. In fact, you don't have to have your own hosting server or server computer in order to have a domain name. You don't have to have a website at all to reserve your name, so you might want to look into it quickly to make sure the name you want hasn't been snatched up.

To reserve a domain name, you'll want to access a domain name provider. My favorite is GoDaddy.com, because it's cheap and offers a number of tools for managing domains, although you'll want to beware that it's a bit, well, "pitchy." Other popular domain name providers include Yahoo! Domains (domains .yahoo.com), Register.com (www.register.com), and Network Solutions (www .networksolutions.com). Any of these services will enable you to search for domain names and register, for a fee, to reserve a name if you find one you like.

You can then do one of a few things with that name. Via the domain name provider's website, you should be able to *forward* a domain name to your blog, whether it's a hosted blog or a server-side solution, so that people who type in www.toddstauffer.com end up redirected to toddstauffer.typepad.com or whatever the URL is for the hosted service. Another option is similar. Sometimes called *masking,* this process allows people to type www.toddstauffer.com into their browser and get routed to the pages from toddstauffer.typepad.com (or whatever URL you're forwarding to), even though they still *see* www.toddstauffer.com in their browser. This effectively hides the fact that you're using a hosted service, but it has its limits, including the fact that masking may make it more difficult for users to bookmark individual blog entries on your site.

(continued)

The third possibility is to point your domain at your web hosting company's *name servers* so that the URL is actually used as the address for your website and/or blog. The name servers will have a URL, such as ns1 .yourhostingcompany.net, which you'll enter at GoDaddy, Register.com, or whichever service you use to reserve the domain name. After that change in address is updated in name servers around the world (it takes 24-48 hours in some cases), then others will be able to access your web hosting account (and, hence, your website and blog) by entering your new URL. This is the traditional approach, but it means you'll need to have web hosting service. (Actually, if you pay for the TypePad premium service, you can point your domain name at TypePad's name servers and your domain will be used to reach your TypePad blog with full URLs for "permalinking" and bookmarking.) If you don't yet have a hosting account or premium TypePad service, you should still be able to register your desired domain name and *park* it at the registrar, usually for no additional fee.

Other Serve-it-Yourself Considerations

If you do opt for a serve-it-yourself blogging tool, then you'll also need to think about some of the other things to have on hand. More than likely you'll be using FTP (File Transport Protocol) to move files from your Mac or PC to your web hosting account, so you'll need an FTP application of some kind. You'll also probably be editing more configuration files and, in some cases, templates and other key files on your own computer instead of via a Web interface, so a good text editor or a program designed to help you edit HTML documents might be a nice addition.

> **TIP**
>
> *When you edit HTML documents, you generally want to avoid using word processors such as Microsoft Word, because those programs tend to store files in their own file formats. (You can use them, but you have to specifically save files as "plain text" and all of the auto-correction features in Word can make editing HTML a pain.) Instead, I recommend you get a text editor designed for Web editing if you're going that route. TextWrangler (www.barebones.com) is a popular free option for Mac users; TextPad (www.textpad.com) is a popular low-cost solution for Windows.*

And you'll want to come up with a plan for using either your hosting service's backup tool (if they offer any) or your FTP program and a reminder system so that you make sure that you frequently back up your database and any pages that you've created since you don't have someone like Blogger to rely on to do it for you! In Chapter 10, I'll cover MySQL more closely, including a look at some of the steps you can take to back up your database on a regular basis.

Should You Go Free or Paid?

The blogging applications that I cover in Chapters 3 and 4, with the notable exception of Blogger, require you to pay *something* to use them. With TypePad, for instance, service costs a few dollars per month for a basic account, although the upshot is that you get quite a bit for those dollars, including storage for images and multimedia files, as well as some very impressive features. With Blogger, you get the tool free and you can host it for free on BlogSpot. The reasons for this are

- Google is intent on dominating the world.

- They're making blogging free in order to spread Google Adwords and other services as far and wide as they can.

That said, Google's approach to "free" is nice—as you'll see, you can even get rid of the little BlogSpot toolbar on your site if you'd like to, and Google doesn't mind.

With the self-hosted tools, you may need to pay to register the software itself, but, regardless of whether it is commercial software or open source software that can be used freely, it's still going to cost you something to host the software on a hosting account or on your own personal server computer.

Paying for blogging service generally means that you'll get a better tool, and more storage space online to add audio, photos, and perhaps even video. And, as I've mentioned, Blogger is a bit more limited than some of the other tools that are available, even if it is also elegant and fun to work with. Those hosted services that you pay a little money for tend to offer additional features and frequent updates to go along with the demand for a little money.

As for commercial software versus open source software, it's an interesting question. With commercial software, if you've paid the registration fee you should be assured of a reasonable amount of customer and technical service that goes along with the product. In the case of a tool such as ExpressionEngine, paying for it should mean regular updates, security patches, and add-ons that are designed to work well with the original product. (ExpressionEngine also offers a no-cost "core" version that offers the blogging functionality but few of the add-on modules such as the forums, wikis, or user management modules.)

That said, the open source model tends to work well, particularly on popular projects such as WordPress. With an open source blogging application, you have many, many different programmers who are building add-ons, testing the original, and often even criticizing the way the application is built and updated. Often, that means you get a very good core product that's both secure and effective.

It can also mean that individual plug-ins—as is sometimes the case with plugins designed for WordPress—are never fully finished. Perhaps someone gets tired of updating a module or something similar happens that results in some part of the functionality never materializing if only because the money motivation isn't there. That can be true of commercial solutions as well, but a commercial solution in that sort of predicament might also be on its last legs as a viable product. In my experience, the further you get away from a project such as WordPress, which has many, many users and contributors, the more likely you are to run into dead-ends with open source software. Again, it depends on how active the community is that supports the software.

In a nutshell, the best answer is that you can get some great stuff for free when it comes to blogging applications, but to go really deep with your blog, you'll probably have to pay something, whether it's paying for commercial licenses, hosting fees, third-party add-ons, or other services that you want to use on your blog. Fortunately, you probably won't have to pay *a lot* to accomplish what you want to on your blog until you finally reach the point where you decide it's time to hire a programmer (or become one) and build a better blog than anyone has yet seen!

NOTE *Here's another thought: If you actively read a number of blogs and you happen to admire their design, take a quick inventory of the blogging tools that those blogs are using. I went through my bookmarks quickly and noticed that a lot of the blogs I visit regularly use WordPress, a few use TypePad, a few use ExpressionEngine, and a handful use other solutions such as Scoop (http://scoop.kuro5hin.org/), Vox (www.vox.com), and SquareSpace (www.squarespace.com).*

Meet Blogger

Blogger has been around for a while, both in its pre-Google and Google-owned phases. Easily one of the most popular blogging services, especially for people getting started, Blogger represents a very easy way to get started with a diary-style blog. In some ways it offers much less flexibility than any of the other tools discussed in this chapter, but, at the same time, the fact that it's so popular means that you'll find a lot of support for Blogger, a lot of third-party templates, and some fun plug-ins and widgets that you can use with Blogger to access different services.

Blogger Pros and Cons

One thing that differentiates Blogger from some other tools is that it's designed to help you publish a blog comprised of *static* HTML pages on the Web. Many blogging tools essentially re-create the blog every time a new person arrives at your website by consulting a database and then placing the entries in a template "on the fly." Blogger doesn't do that; instead, each time you add a new entry, Blogger re-writes the HTML documents for your site so that they're updated with the changes. This can cause it to take a little longer for Blogger to update a site when you make a change, particularly if that site has many pages of archives. But it can also mean better loading times for your visitors—your blog pages may arrive in your visitor's browser a bit quicker than with some other tools.

Here are some other strengths that Blogger offers:

■ **Integration with Many Third-Party Tools**   Because Blogger is the most popular option for blogging on the Web, many Windows, Macintosh, and Linux applications exist that allow you to update your blog from within the application. This is even true of other Google tools such as Google Docs and Spreadsheets.

TIP   *Applications that can update a Blogger-based blog run the gamut; on a Mac, for instance you'll find Dashboard widgets written by Google (http://www.google.com/macwidgets/index.html), journaling applications such as MacJournal (www.marinersoftware.com) and blog editing software such as MarsEdit (www.red-sweater.com)—both of which work with other popular platforms, too. For Windows, there's w.Bloggar (www.wbloggar.com) and WinJournal (also from Mariner at www.marinersoftware.com).*

■ **Support for Multiple Authors**   Blogger will support multiple authors for your blog, each of whom must have a Google log-in and be granted access to your log from with the administrative controls. Once you've done that, they're ready to post.

■ **On-screen Editing**   In the "new" Google-developed Blogger, you can edit entries and other elements of your blog simply by clicking small Quick Editing icons that appear when you're logged into Blogger and you're browsing the page. That can be a lot easier (and perhaps more fun) than digging into the behind-the-scenes templates and controls.

- **Integration with Google Adsense** Anyone can add Google text advertising to their blogs, but Blogger has controls for it—including access to statistics and other fun stuff—from within the Blogger interface.

- **Visual Template Editing** The latest version of Blogger enables you to edit your blog's template without digging into special commands or HTML codes. You can simply drag and drop to add new "widgets" to your page. Of course, if you want to you can still dig into the code.

If there's a weakness to Blogger it's that the application itself lacks much modularity in terms of enabling you to add high-end user management features, a forum, wiki, or a great deal of the customization options that other blogging tools offer. Likewise, some of the more sophisticated blogging tools offer support for multiple blogs, or for merging different blogs into "portals" of information and so on. (That's not to say you can't use Blogger with other web tools installed on a hosting account; you certainly can. It's just that some blogging solutions integrate more of those tools into the same package.)

That said, since you can edit the HTML of your template, you can take advantage of all sorts of Web 2.0 options that are discussed in later chapters. And, Blogger can post your blog to your own hosting account, so it can sit side-by-side with any serve-it-yourself tools you decide to add later. And the fact that Blogger generates standard HTML pages can be handy, as it causes less of a load on your hosting account's server computers.

So, if your goal is easy blogging with just you or a few authors, you don't mind having your entire blog entry appear on the main page of your blog and you like the flexibility of posting to BlogSpot or to your own Web hosting account. Blogger is a great way to get started blogging.

Get Started with Blogger

The Blogger sign-up process consists of heading to the Blogger site, entering your Google account information (or, if you don't already have a Google account, you'll create one), and then making some choices about the name of your blog and where you'd like the blog to be posted. You can either publish it on the BlogSpot service (which is part of Blogger/Google) with a unique URL such as *yoursite* .blogspot.com, or you can set up Blogger so that it can access and publish your blog to your web hosting service via FTP.

Here are the basic steps:

1. To get started with Blogger, point your browser at www.blogger.com. Once there, you'll see the welcome screen for the Blogger tool (see Figure 2-9).

FIGURE 2-9   Visit www.blogger.com to get registered and start using the tool.

2. What you do next depends on whether or not you already have a Google account:

■ If you already have an account with Google (perhaps for Gmail, Google Documents, or some other service), then enter it in the Sign In section at the top of the screen. That will bypass the registration screen, enabling you to move on to accepting the Terms of Service, and then to creating your blog on the Name Your Blog screen (see Figure 2-10).

■ If you don't have a Google account, click the Create Your Blog Now link. That will take you to a registration page, where you'll be asked to create a Google account. With the account created (you may have to verify your e-mail address first), you're ready to create a blog.

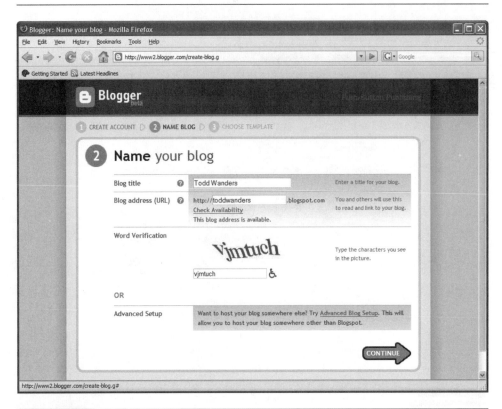

The Name Your Blog screen is where you'll set up your first Blogger blog.

TIP

If you've had a Blogger account in the past and haven't checked it out in a while, you may be able to "reclaim" it by clicking the "Claim your old Blogger account" link at the top of the page. Blogger has gone through some changes, including now requiring a standard Google account for you to use it. So, you'll walk through some steps to associate that old account with Google so you can get blogging again.

3. On the Name Your Blog screen, you'll do one of two things, depending on how you want your blog published:

   ■ If you want to do things the easy way and use the BlogSpot service to host your blog, then simply enter a name for your blog, enter a one-word title that will complete the blogspot.com URL, and click the Continue button. If that URL is available, you'll see that it's been assigned to you; if it isn't, you'll be asked to choose another one.

(Notice that you can click the Check Availability link if you're testing names and Blogger will let you know if the name is available.)

■ If you'd prefer to use Blogger to publish your blog to your web host or your personal server, then you can click the Advanced Blog Setup link. That takes you to the Advanced Blog Setup screen (see Figure 2-11), where you enter a name for your blog, and the FTP information associated with your web hosting service or the web server that you have access to. That includes the FTP address, a path to the location on the server where you'd like the Blogger pages to be stored, a name for the main page that should be created by Blogger on that server, the URL to the blog, and then the FTP username and password so that Blogger can log into your server in order to post the log and updates. Enter the Word Verification and click Continue. If all goes well and Blogger is able to access your server,

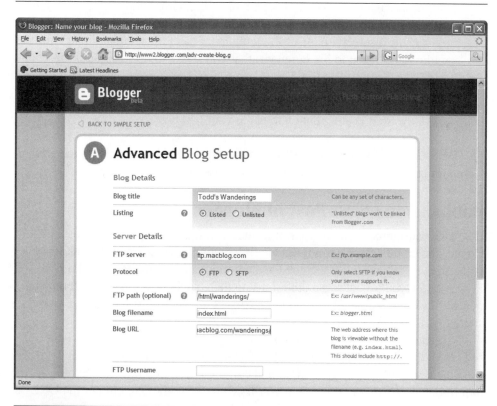

FIGURE 2-11   On the Advanced Blog Setup screen you can enter information necessary to have Blogger post your blog to your third-party web host or web server computer.

then you'll move on to the next screen; otherwise, you'll need to change any information that's wrong so that Blogger can access the server. (Or, alternatively, you can switch back to the simple setup and use BlogSpot.)

TIP   *If you haven't yet successfully used FTP to connect to your hosting account, getting Blogger connected could be frustrating. Make sure you have all of the FTP account information and path settings handy from your hosting service before attempting this. Also, you can get back to the Advanced options via the Publishing option under the Settings tab in the Blogger admin control panel at a later time if you decide you want to use Blogger to post to your hosting account. You should also know that publishing via FTP means you cannot use some of Blogger's advanced "drag-and-drop" templates.*

4. Once your blog is set up, you'll see the Choose a Template page. You can scroll through the screen to take a look at the basic templates that Blogger offers; note the Preview Template link beneath each, which you can click to see a full-screen image of the template. Select the template image (or the radio button next to the template) that you'd like to use for your blog, then click the Continue button.

5. You'll see a screen telling you that your blog has been created. To get started, click the Start Posting button to begin your first post.

Once you've clicked the Start Posting button, you're taken directly to the editing screen for creating a new post, which we'll discuss in the next section.

Publish Your First Post in Blogger

If you've configured your Blogger blog successfully, you should have reached the Create screen; this is the main interface for creating new blog entries. Take a look at the screen and you'll see that the Create option is under the Posting tab (see Figure 2-12); you've got some other tabs up there such as Settings and Templates that we'll examine more closely in the next sections. For now, though, let's get started with your first post.

To create a new post, you begin by entering a title for the post in the Title box. Note that this is used for the URL of your post, so it's a good idea to get it right the first time; if you go back in and edit the post's title later (something I, unfortunately, do all the time), then you'll be changing the title but not the URL to the full posting. Just FYI.

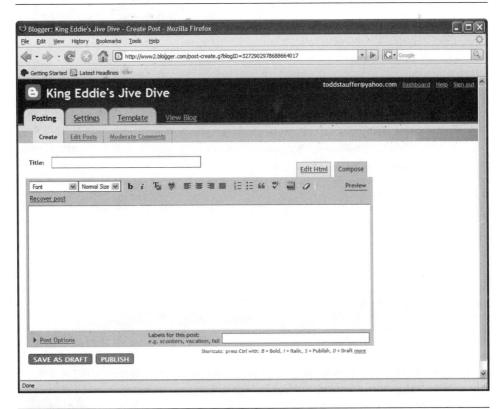

FIGURE 2-12   The Create screen is where you may well spend a lot of your blogging time in Blogger.

Press the TAB key or click your mouse in the main text area and begin typing. You'll notice that you have a few tools at your disposal, similar to those you'll find in a word processing program. Simply type paragraphs of text, then press RETURN or ENTER to create a new paragraph. (Note, also, that as with any computerized text, you don't need to enter two spaces between sentences. That's old typewriter stuff.) To change text to bold or italic, for instance, you can highlight the text and click the "B" icon for bold text or the "i" icon for italic text. (You can also click one of those buttons to turn on that style for the text that you're typing, then click it again to return to the normal style.)

Need to link to another page on the Internet? Highlight the text that you want to use for your link text, then click the small Globe icon in the content field's toolbar.

A dialog box appears so that you can enter
the URL to the page to which you're linking;
enter the URL, then click OK.

You can align the text of your
paragraphs, if desired, using the four
alignment buttons in the content field.
Just click to place your cursor in the paragraph that you want to align and click one
of those buttons; in order, they are: left, center, right, and justified.

For a bulleted or numbered list, you can begin by typing a series of paragraphs,
with a return between each. Then, highlight them and click the button for the type
of list you want to create.

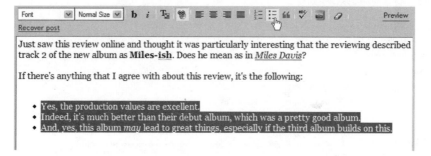

One interesting command that you'll use much more in blogging than in any
sort of word processing (except, perhaps, academic writing with a lot of citations)
is *blockquote* formatting. This is the formatting you can use when you're quoting
text from someone's website or blog, which is, after all, a pretty common thing
to do. To turn a paragraph (or more) of text into a blockquote, simply select it
and click the Blockquote button. That will cause the text to be inset and set apart,
making it visually clear that you're quoting someone else.

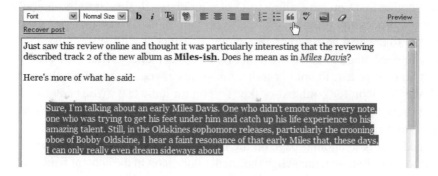

Using the Blockquote feature also, depending on your template, might cause
the quoted text to be boxed, appear in a different font or font weight, and so on.

TIP *Done some formatting that you wish you hadn't? Highlight the formatted text and then click the Eraser icon that appears in the content field's toolbar. That will remove any formatting and return the selected portion to plain old text.*

Also found on the content area's toolbar is the image button (it looks like a little picture of something). Click it and you'll see a new window, as shown in Figure 2-13. This window enables you to choose photos or other computer images that you want to display as a part of your blog entry.

You've got two basic choices for how you're going to get an image to appear as part of a blog entry. First, you can choose an image on your hard disk that you want to upload to BlogSpot (or to your personal server, if you've set up Blogger to post to your own web host). To do that, click the Browse button on the Add an Image From Your Computer section of the window. That causes the Open dialog box to appear, so that you can locate the file on your hard disk. Once you've found it, click Open in the dialog box, and that will return you to the Add an Image window, where you'll see the name of the file you've chosen in the entry box next to the Browse button. (If you'd like to upload more than one image at time, you can do that by clicking the Add Another Image link and going through the process again.)

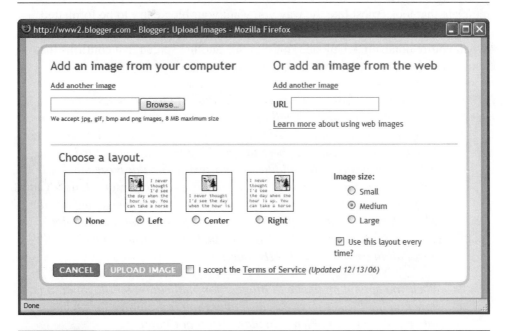

FIGURE 2-13 The Add an Image window enables you to add images to your blog entries.

The other way to get an image into your blog entry is to point to an image that's already on the Internet. For instance, if you have an image stored at an image-hosting service or on your own personal web hosting space, you can enter a URL to that image so that it is displayed in your blog entry as well. To do that, simply enter a URL to that image in the Or Add An Image From the Web section of the window. (For instance, if I had an image stored in the root directory of the web host that serves my personal website, I might have an image URL that looked like this: http://www.toddstauffer.com/image.gif.)

> **NOTE**
>
> *When you link to an image (as opposed to uploading an image or photo of your own from your hard disk), Blogger doesn't copy that image to BlogSpot or to your hosting account; it loads that image from the remote server. In some situations, this can be considered "stealing bandwidth" because you're causing someone else's web server to display the image on your page. You should always (a) display images to which you have the intellectual property rights, and (b) copy and host those images yourself, when possible. I'll discuss blogging and images more in Chapter 6.*

Once you've chosen the image that you're going to add to your blog entry, the next step you take is to decide how it will be aligned relative to the text in your blog entry (left, right, or center). In the Choose a Layout section, select the template that looks most like the way you want your blog entry to be formatted. Finally, you can choose the size of the image as it will appear in the blog entry. When you're done, click Upload. You may see another screen that confirms that your image has been uploaded; click Done to return to your post.

> **NOTE**
>
> *In the version of Blogger current at the time of this writing, the code for any image you upload will appear at the top of the entry box, not in the spot where you had placed your cursor. So, you may need to select the image and drag it elsewhere in your blog entry if you wanted it to appear somewhere in the middle of your text. To do this more quickly, you can select the image and then cut it using your browser's Edit > Cut command, then place your cursor where you want the image and use the Edit > Paste command to put the image where you want it in the blog entry. That might prove a little quicker, and in my testing, that correctly moves all the underlying HTML code.)*

> **TIP**
>
> *When you upload an image to Blogger for publication on BlogSpot, it is stored on the Picasa service, which offers you free storage for an image gallery. We'll discuss Picasa in more detail in Chapter 6.*

Now, edit your post, add any additional text, and you're ready to publish that entry after considering one other command—Check Spelling. Click the Check Spelling button and Blogger will highlight and underline words that it doesn't have in its dictionary; click the word to choose a replacement from the drop-down menu that appears (see Figure 2-14). Notice that you can't type in the Check Spelling mode, so if Blogger doesn't offer the correct replacement, you'll need to make a mental note to change the word manually when you return to editing mode. When you're done using the Check Spelling feature, click Done Spellchecking to finish editing the entry.

Finally, if you're done with all your typing, image uploading, and spell checking, you can get ready to publish your entry. First, you may want to preview it. Click the Preview link in the top-right corner of the editing interface and you'll

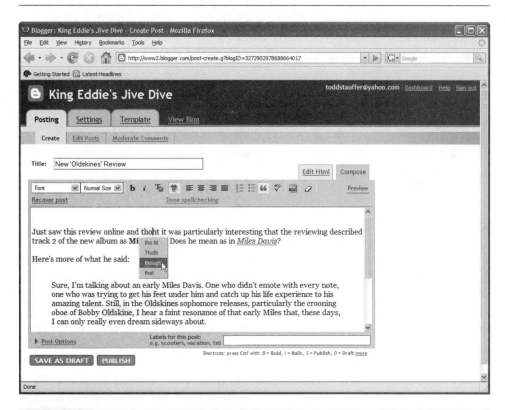

FIGURE 2-14   In Check Spelling mode you can select replacement words for those not recognized by the Blogger dictionary.

see Blogger switch to an approximation of how your post will look once it's published. (It may differ from the final blog entry because the Preview window doesn't take into account any custom templates or changes to your blog's style sheet that you may have made.) If you don't like what you see, click the Hide Preview link to keep working on your entry.

NOTE *Blogger also offers an Edit HTML tab that you can use to access the raw HTML that is used to build your entry, if you're familiar with HTML. If you aren't familiar with HTML, you might want to consult Chapter 4 to see how some of these codes work.*

Next, you may want to make choices about whether or not you want comments on this entry. And you can opt to set a different date and time for the entry if you'd like to. (Unlike some other blog software, changing the time or date won't cause the post to appear automatically at a later date because, as mentioned, Blogger doesn't build its interface dynamically when visitors come to your site—the pages must be published first before they will appear online.) To make any of those choices, click the Post Options link.

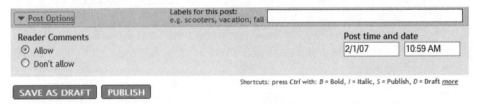

Make your decision about whether or not to allow comments on this entry, then change the date and time for the blog entry if desired.

If you like the preview and everything else looks good, you're ready to click the Publish button. When you do, you'll see Blogger respond with an animation that shows that Blogger is publishing the new entry; Blogger may also need to make changes to your archives and other pages, so it can take a moment or two. (It also takes time if Blogger has to log into your personal web hosting account in order to upload files.) When it's done you'll see a success screen that enables you to view your blog (or open your blog in a new window) so that you can see your handiwork in all its glory (see Figure 2-15).

TIP *Right next to the Publish button is a Save Draft button, which you can use to save an entry that's in progress but not ready to be published yet. You can return to it at a later time to finish the entry and publish it.*

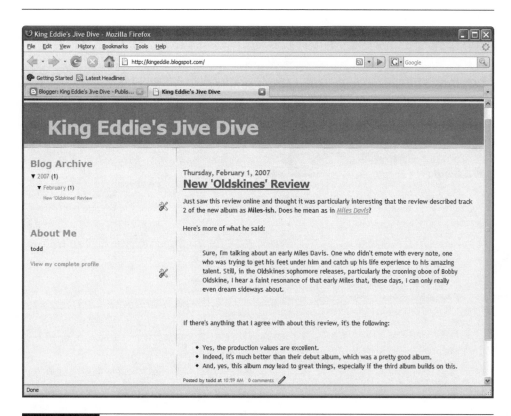

FIGURE 2-15   After clicking Publish, the entry is added to my blog and uploaded to the Web.

Edit and Manage Posts in Blogger

Once you've created a post, Blogger offers you two different ways to edit it. The more traditional way (and the one that works every time) is to click the Posting tab, then click the Edit Posts link. When you do, you'll see a list of posts such as those shown in Figure 2-16.

To edit a post (to make changes, check spelling, add images, and so on) simply click the Edit link next to its title. That launches the Publish interface where you can work with the post just as you did when it was first created. Once you've made your changes, click the Publish button again to publish your blog with those new changes.

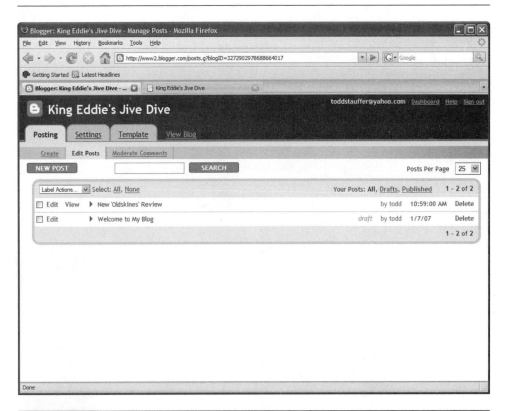

FIGURE 2-16   When you click Edit Posts, you'll see a list of your posts starting with the
most recent.

You can also delete a post from this interface by clicking the Delete link in
that post's row. You'll be asked to confirm your decision, and then the post will be
deleted from the Blogger system.

If you've enabled comments for your posts, then you may sometimes find
that you need to delete the comments; even though Blogger can be set up to
require someone to have a Google ID before they can post, you'll still sometimes
find comments touting other blogs or similar "spam" posts that don't have any
relevance to what you're saying. (Or you may otherwise find someone's comment
offensive or inappropriate.)

2

TIP *On the Comment Settings page (under the Settings tab, choose Comments), you can configure Blogger so that anyone can comment, only registered Blogger users can comment, or only members of your actual blog can comment. That latter option can be handy if you want a private blog for business or organizational purposes. The Comment Settings page is also where you can turn on comment moderation, discussed later in this section.*

Here's how to delete a comment:

1. On the Edit Posts screen, click the Comments link that appears on the Edit Posts screen next to each entry. (The actual link shows the number of comments as in 1 Comment or 4 Comments; if a post doesn't have comments, it won't show a link.)

2. What you see next will be the actual Blogger entry where those comments appear. Click the small trashcan icon that appears next to the comment that you want to get rid of.

3. You'll see a confirmation screen; click the Delete Comment button to remove it from your blog. (Note that it actually stays in the system so that you can reinstate the comment, if desired, unless you click the Remove Forever option before choosing Delete Comment.)

Blogger offers another way to delete comments via the Moderate Comments option. This option is available to you if you opt to moderate comments (so that they have to be approved before they appear on your blog). From the Posting tab you can choose the Moderate Comment link to see those choices. (If you haven't yet turned on comment moderating, you'll be directed to do that on the Comment Settings page.) What you'll see is a list of comments; if you want to allow a particular comment to appear, click to place a checkmark next to the comments that you want to publish, then click the Publish. Alternatively, you can click Reject to keep a comment from appearing on your blog (see Figure 2-17).

Alter Your Blog's Template in Blogger

Blogger gives you two different approaches to customizing the "look and feel" of your blog: you can edit the raw HTML of your pages or you can use Blogger's drag-and-drop tools to make some decisions about the layout of your blog, to edit the sidebar information, and even to change the overall look of your blog pages. In this section we'll look at Blogger's automated tools and you'll see how to dig into the HTML as well.

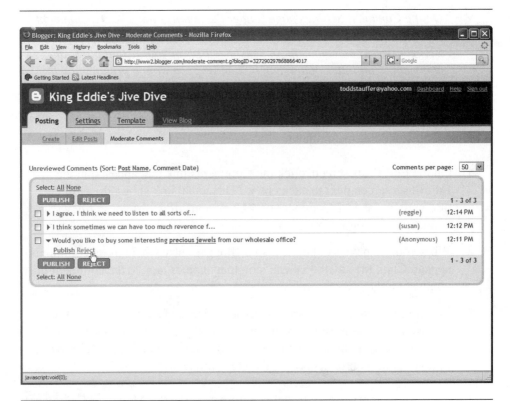

FIGURE 2-17 The Moderate Comments option enables you to decide which reader comments appear on your blog and which don't.

To edit your template, click the Template tab in the main Blogger interface. There, you'll see the Page Elements page, which enables you to add and drag elements around to determine the layout of your page (see Figure 2-18).

For starters, you may find that you only have a few elements to drag around; if you want to create more, click the Add Another Element link on the page, either in the sidebar or in the footer of the template. When you do, you'll see a new screen that offers a number of choices for new Page Elements, as shown in Figure 2-19.

Some of these elements are pretty basic—they enable you, for instance, to create "blogroll" lists of your favorite blogs or personal information that you want to share with your readers. Others can be a bit more sophisticated, such as an element that enables you to add headlines from an RSS feed elsewhere on the Web. (More on RSS in Chapter 5.)

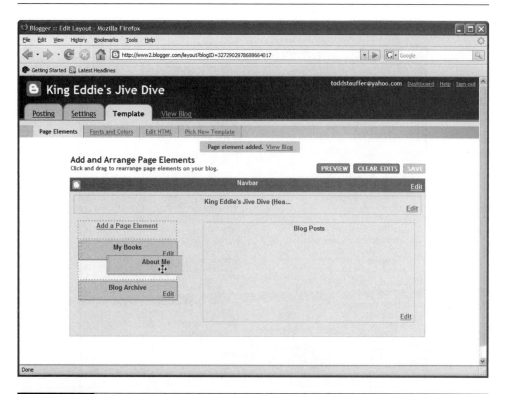

FIGURE 2-18   With Blogger, you can drag the Page Elements around on the representation of your blog to change the way you template is arranged.

To add an element, simply click the Add to Blog button under that element in the Choose a New Page Element window. Depending on the element, you may then see some setup options, such as a URL for the headline feed or image that you're placing. You'll then be returned to the layout window, where you can drag that element around to place it where you want it as part of the blog's template.

Once an element has been placed on the page, you can drag it around to choose where it will appear in the template or click the Edit link in that element to call its properties window back up and edit it again. To save the template changes and republish your blog, click the Save button on the template page and then click the View Blog link to see your changes in action.

Of course the Template tab in Blogger has a lot of other features, including the ability to edit the HTML directly, which we'll talk about in more depth in Chapter 4. In the meantime, these drag-and-drop capabilities are pretty powerful.

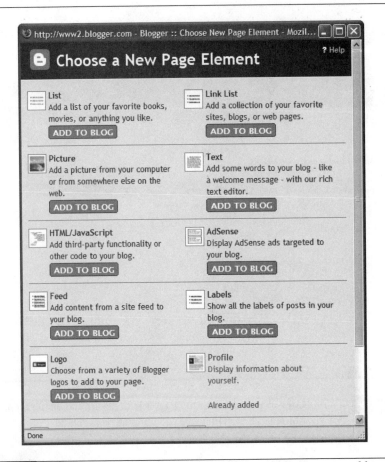

FIGURE 2-19 Here's a look at the different Page Elements that you can add to your blog design.

Log In and Out of Blogger

One last thing to discuss quickly is the logout process; when you're done working with your blog in Blogger, you should click the small Logout link that appears at the top-right of the Blogger window. That closes out your session with Blogger. To log back in, you can return to the www.blogger.com interface and log in again using your Google account and password. That gets you to your "dashboard" where you can choose the blog you want to update (that's right—Blogger enables you to have more than one, if desired).

Explore TypePad

TypePad bills itself as a blogging solution for businesses and professionals—and that may be, in part, because SixApart, the company that published TypePad (as well as Vox.com, LiveJournal, and the self-hosting tool MoveableType), wants to justify charging users to blog via the service. (It's also the "pro" solution compared to its Vox and LiveJournal offerings.) TypePad, in truth, does offer some very nice features, including some options that Blogger is just catching up to like visual editing of the template and a number of professional-looking templates for your layout.

There's no doubt that TypePad is slick, offering good integration with many Web 2.0 services and plenty of customization options. In fact, putting together a great-looking blog in a matter of moments is possible and easy with TypePad. Making that great-looking blog unique and totally yours takes a lot longer; in my opinion, Blogger and many of the server-side solutions are much more customizable at the template level than TypePad. (TypePad relies a bit more heavily on the "themes and blocks" approach instead of the "template and tags" approach that Blogger, ExpressionEngine, and many others take. That said, you can dig into the templates; it's just a bit more effort.)

The cost for the service is generally only a few dollars a month, depending on the plan that you opt for and the number of authors and blogs that you want to have participate. If you don't want to pay anything for a hosted blog, however, then Blogger or WordPress (covered later) might be better choices. If you don't mind paying, though, then I think you'll find that TypePad is the sort of service that works hard to *justify* the fact that they're asking you to pay, meaning they're constantly offering new features and widgets to improve your blog and try to get some traffic to it.

TypePad Pros and Cons

Here's a quick look at some of the strengths of TypePad and perhaps a drawback or two as compared to other options:

■ **Quick Setup and Easy Template Switches**   Within certain limits, it's easy to set up a blog and try the different templates that are offered by the service. This can make for a fun experience if you're interested in simply getting up and running quickly with an attractive blog. In fact, you can save different designs and change them out as desired, perhaps to show the passing changes or to offer a weekend theme vs. a weekday theme for your "going out" blog, etc.

- **Tons of Widgets** A hallmark of the TypePad services is that SixApart is constantly adding new "widgets" to the service. A widget is a small sidebar item that you can add to your blog that either integrates with another Web 2.0 service or offers some feature. For instance, you can add widgets that play your favorite music, allow your users to chat online in a "live" window, send text messages, access a Google calendar or view news headlines, funny quips, cartoons, and so on. Part of why people pay for TypePad is the fact that they aggregate all of this stuff in one place so you don't have to scour the individual sites to see how you can integrate widgets into your blog design.

- **Photo Galleries and TypeLists** TypePad makes it easy to add some fun features that you see on a lot of blogs, such as blogrolls (links to other blogs you like); "what I'm listening to now" lists of the media, books, and music that you're enjoying; and lists such as that. Likewise, TypePad makes it easy to create a photo gallery (if you have the more advanced versions of the service), so that you can upload digital images that you've taken and make them available online.

- **Visual Content Management** Along with support for these widgets and galleries comes the ability to quickly and easily move those items around on your page. With the themes-and-blocks approach that TypePad takes, it becomes easier for them to allow you to move those blocks around in your design. With drag-and-drop ease, you can move things around on your blog's design so that, say, you can put a random gallery image at the top of the left sidebar, an Amazon wishlist under it, a blogroll under that, Google ads in the right sidebar, an About page link below that ... and so on.

- **Support for Multiple Blogs** With the advanced (and more expensive) accounts, you can have multiple blogs under the same general username and URL, so that toddstauffer.typepad.com can be used for blogs such as toddstauffer.typepad.com/macstuff/ and toddstauffer.typepad.com/bloggin/ or whatever. Then, using headline feeds and other tricks you could actually roll all those blogs into one "super" blog of sorts.

- **Hosting Services** With the account that currently costs about $15 per month, you get a full gigabyte of storage for pages, photos, and multimedia files that you upload. You can also take advantage of the domain mapping service, so that you could register a domain like http://www.toddstauffer.com/ and use it instead of http://toddstauffer.typepad.com/. So, unlike Blogger, for instance, which encourages you to use the service to publish your blog to a web hosting account if you want additional storage and so on, TypePad *is* acting as a web hosting account and offering some of those sorts of services.

As for weaknesses, I've found it cumbersome to try and dig into the TypePad templating system in order to truly change the design of the pages. You can customize a little bit without too much pain, such as changing the top image for your blog and editing the style sheet, but really digging in and changing the look and feel is a little more difficult than I prefer. Of course, they do that on purpose— if it's too easy to dig into the templates then you're likely to break TypePad's visual editing and module widget options.

Another little gripe: Considering TypePad is billed as being designed for business users, I'm a little surprised that there aren't more collaborative options. In particular, TypePad doesn't allow more than one person to manage the blog (although you can invite "guest" and "junior" bloggers who can add posts to your blog) and, perhaps more significantly, it doesn't offer any sort of integration for e-mail newsletters, wikis, forums, online data-entry forms, e-commerce or any other such "extras" that might be handy for business users who want to blog partly for the purpose of capturing data from their visitors so that they can e-mail reminders, follow-ups, or offers from them. Of course, there are other services you can use for all that, but it'd be nice if the "business"-focused blogging tool had some of those things integrated. (As we'll see, some of the serve-it-yourself options such as ExpressionEngine do offer those sorts of services.)

All in all, TypePad is a great blogging service for a "one-to-many" type blog for building a readership, and you'll find that many high-powered bloggers (particularly some pundits and business-guru author types) use it in exactly that way. It also happens that it's well-designed, and a pleasure for typing, posting, and basic site configuration, as everything seems to work with little effort. Because of that, you might be more willing to update the site and keep it active so that visitors see a vital blog and therefore feel like they have a reason to return. Plus, the widgets and other features such as photo galleries and TypeLists offer just enough flexibility and fun to be worth the price of admission.

Set Up TypePad

To get started with TypePad, visit the TypePad website and click the Free Trial or Signup links or buttons on the site. You'll then be walked through a process of creating an account and registering for the service. One important note is to consider the level of service that you want; with the lower-end services, you may not get as many features as I'm discussing in this section. (For instance, the most basic service offers only one blog and no access to photo albums as of the time of this writing; the highest level of service boasts increased control over the HTML of your site.)

As part of that process, after you've chosen a URL for your blog(s) and the level of service, entered your billing information, and so on, you'll get to the Design Your Weblog page, where you are asked to create your first blog. At the top of that page, you can give the blog a name, which will be used as the title of the blog pages and will appear in the header section of the initial blog design.

Next, choose a layout (see Figure 2-20) from the options presented. All of the initial choices are popular options for blogs; which you choose really depends on how much ancillary information you intend to show to your readers. For instance, if you know you'll want your site to have links to a photo album or Flickr photo widget, plus statistics about the site, recent comments, perhaps a podcast link, and so on, then you'll want to choose one of the layouts that includes one or two sidebars for that non-blog-entry info. It's up to you.

NOTE   *With the higher levels of paid service from TypePad, you'll find that you can alter this layout later and even choose from some others that focus on integrating images or other multimedia into your layout. So, if you're looking to create a "photo" blog or a blog that's very multimedia-focused, you'll find more options after you've created this initial blog.*

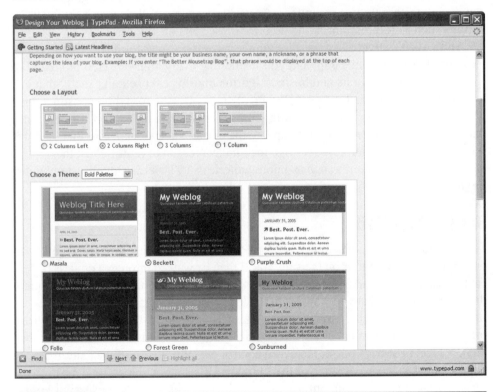

FIGURE 2-20   Choose a basic layout when you create your first blog for TypePad.

The next step is to choose the theme for your blog from those options provided. Note that the interface lets you see different theme groupings—for instance, you can choose among subtle and bold color schemes, themes with a fairly specific audience or purpose (weddings, births, holidays) or you can choose to view all of the themes and just click the one that you like the most. When you select a theme, you'll see its radio button become active, as shown in Figure 2-21, which tells you it's the one that TypePad will be using for your blog. (Again, you can change this theme later if you decide you want a different look.)

Finally, on that same page you can choose the privacy level for your blog. A Publicized blog is one that anyone can visit on the Web. It's included in the TypePad update lists and new entries will be distributed to services that help people search blogs. The Not Publicized option means that the blog can be accessed publicly over the Internet, but TypePad won't put your new entries on special lists or search engines. And the Password Protected option means that visitors will need to have a password in order to visit and read your site.

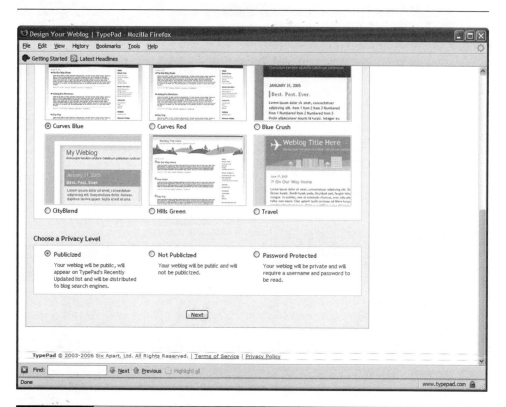

FIGURE 2-21   Selecting a theme for the blog's design in TypePad

(When you select the password-protected option, you're immediately asked to enter a username and password that you'll need to distribute to your users so they can visit the blog.) Make a privacy choice and then click the Next button.

On the next page you'll confirm your account creation, and then you'll be congratulated if the sign-up process goes well. Next, you're on to the TypePad dashboard screen (see Figure 2-22), where you'll see tabs across the top of the page to enable you to access the different features of your blog; you'll also see a small control area that enables you to quickly begin a blog entry, work with your photo galleries, and so on.

Publish Your First Post in TypePad

Once you're on the TypePad dashboard screen, you're ready to begin publishing. To enter your first post, click the Begin a New Post button that appears on the screen.

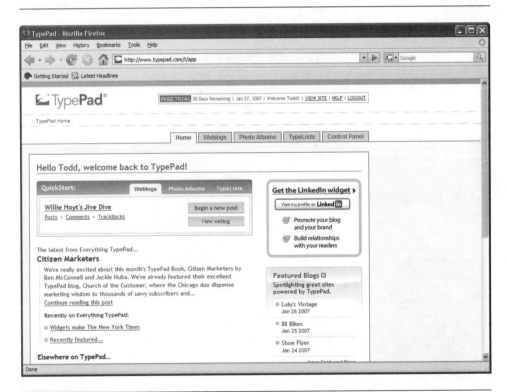

FIGURE 2-22 The TypePad dashboard is where you'll land whenever you log into the service.

(You can also get at these controls by clicking the Weblogs tab at the top of the window and finding the Create a Post command from there.) When you've done that, you'll see the Compose a New Post interface, which should look familiar if you've used any other blogging tools, or, for that matter, a word processor (see Figure 2-23).

If there's anything confusing about this interface, it's the way that TypePad seems designed to keep you one click or so away from all of its different features. You'll notice that you're on the Post tab, and New Post is selected under that tab; if you need to manage existing posts or look at recent comments and trackbacks on your site, then you can click those other controls.

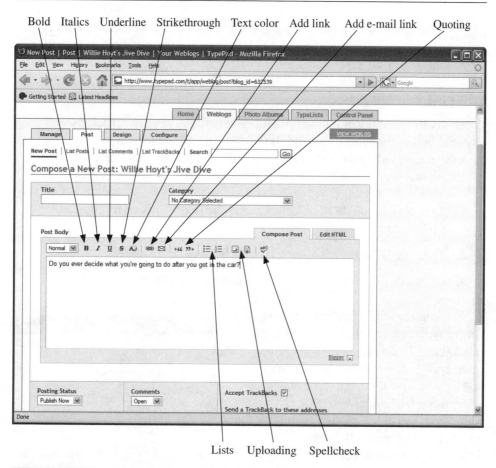

Bold Italics Underline Strikethrough Text color Add link Add e-mail link Quoting

Lists   Uploading   Spellcheck

FIGURE 2-23   The TypePad Create a Post interface

Format Your Blog Text

For now, though, you're entering a new post. I won't walk you through every tool—again, they work much like the Blogger tools discussed earlier in the chapter, if you'd like to cross-reference there. Start by entering a Title for your post and, if desired, select a category for the post form those defaults that appear in the Category menu.

Now, click in the main Compose Post area and start typing or pasting text in. For bold, italic, underline, strikethrough or to change the text color, you can type something in the entry box, then highlight the text and click one of those buttons. You can also click the button first and then type in that style; click it again to turn the style off.

> **TIP** *If you want to see more of the Compose Post text area at once, click the Bigger link at the bottom of that text area; the area will expand to show more of your post.*

Add Links

TypePad offers a shortcut button for adding hyperlinks to your entries, as well as a special button for adding a mailto: link for e-mail addresses. (When your visitors click the mailto link, your e-mail address will pop up in their e-mail program.)

Here's one way to add hyperlinks and mailto: links:

1. Type text, highlight it, and click either the Insert Link or Insert Mail Link button.

2. Then, in the box that appears, type a URL or e-mail address.

3. Click OK in the dialog box and the text turns into a clickable link.

You can also add a hyperlink before you've typed the text that you want to be "clickable." To do that, simply click the Insert Link button without having any text highlighted. You'll see the same dialog box asking for a URL; after you click OK in that dialog box, you'll see another asking for the text that will be made clickable.

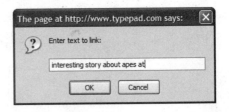

Enter that text and click OK again. You'll see the new link in your post window.

<table>
<tr><td>NOTE</td><td>You can add a mailto: link in the same way, but the address itself is automatically added as the text in the entry; you aren't given the option of typing different text for it.</td></tr>
<tr><td>CAUTION</td><td>Placing your e-mail address or even a mailto: link to your e-mail address on your blog may not be a great idea; automated programs roam the Internet looking for e-mail addresses to "harvest" for use in spam applications. If you can, I'd recommend making your e-mail address available via a contact form or through the author profile tool that your blogging software makes available.</td></tr>
</table>

Add Quotes and Lists

Other shortcut buttons allow you to style certain text as "quoted" text, which can be handy when you're blogging about what other people have written and you need to quote them, perhaps with a link. Most of the time (by which I mean all over the blogosphere, not just with TypePad) a typical blog will show quoted text as indented in some way so that it stands out from the text that the blogger has written.

JANUARY 27, 2007

New Stuff Posted at LoungeList

I couldn't believe what <u>this guy</u> had to say about my friend Darren:

> Darren has to be one of the greatest guitar players ever to take a stage -- particularly a 5-by-7 plywood stage that was outside on a sidewalk in Jackson, Mississippi, in the pouring rain with a flapping tent over his head. He still plugged his guitar in, which is something I would have thought twice about. But, then, once he started playing, I figured he must know there's something up there watching over him closely.

Darren is good, and I've always felt kind of honored to be able to see so many of his shows and to be asked by him to help with the artwork and sometimes with other types of publicity, or even to help run an event when it's a local charity thing and so on. He's a great guy, and I'll be pretty surprised if he doesn't make it big sometime pretty soon.

In TypePad, you can mark the text as a quote (you're actually assigning it the "blockquote" tag in HTML) so that your theme can style it in whatever way it wants, whether it simply indents it or does something more interesting like put it in a box, give it a background, and so on. Just place the cursor in a paragraph of text and click the leftmost quote button, which is called Begin Quote. If you decide to return that paragraph to normal, you can click the quote button on the right side, the End Quote button.

NOTE   *In Chapter 4 we'll discuss Cascading Style Sheets, which offer special codes that you can use to customize the appearance of HTML elements like a blockquote. In fact, as you'll see later in this section, TypePad offers special tools that specifically enable you to add CSS descriptions to enhance your TypePad blog.*

Next to the quote buttons are the bullet and numbered list buttons. If you'd like to create a list, simply press RETURN or ENTER between each paragraph that should be a list item. Then, select them all and click the Unordered List button to turn your paragraphs into a bulleted list or the Ordered List button to turn those highlighted paragraphs into a numbered list.

Insert an Image

To add an image to your blog entry, place the cursor at the place in your post you'd like the image to appear and click the Insert Image button. (If you will be using the text wrap feature, you should place your cursor above the text that you'd like to have wrap around the image.)

This brings up a window that enables you to browse for the image that you want to add on your hard disk (click the Browse button). Once you've found it, you can then opt to add the image using the Default image options that TypePad offers or you can customize those options. Click the Use Custom Settings radio button to customize those settings (before you change anything you're looking at the defaults, so clicking this button can be handy just for learning what the default settings are).

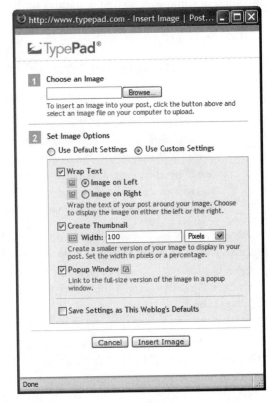

The custom settings enable you to do a number of interesting things to the image:

- **Wrap Text**   If this option is turned on, TypePad will wrap text adjacent to or following the image tag around the image you upload. Choose Image on Left to have the text wrap around it to the right of the image; choose Image on Right for the opposite effect. If you turn Wrap Text off then the image will appear *inline* with the text, which usually means a paragraph above and below the image, with no text appearing to the image's left or right.

- **Create Thumbnail**   If this option is turned on, then TypePad will create a second version of the image you've uploaded at the width, in pixels, that you specify. (It will automatically set the height so that the thumbnail image is in the same proportions as the original.) That thumbnail image will be inserted into the blog post instead of the original. (So, turn this off if you know the original will be an OK fit without alterations.)

- **Popup Window**   If this option is selected, then the image that is placed in the blog post will be clickable. When clicked, the original image will appear in a pop-up window.

- **Save Settings as This Weblog's Default**   If you make some choices that you decide you want to use for most of your image uploads, then turn on this option and when you click Insert Image, you'll also be storing any changes as the new defaults.

Click Insert Image and the image will be uploaded to your storage space on the TypePad servers and it'll be added to your post.

NOTE   *Again, see Chapter 6 for more discussion regarding copying and displaying images (or other multimedia files) that you didn't create.*

Upload a File

Uploading a file is similar to uploading an image except that TypePad will create a link to the file (so that it can be clicked and downloaded by the user) instead of inserting an image for viewing. When you click Insert, the file is uploaded and a link is created to that file.

Check out his latest tune: Download Rico.mp3

Check Spelling

The last little button on the TypePad posting interface is the checkmark, which means checking your spelling. Click it if you'd like to give you entry a little "once over." When you do, a new window appears, with the spellchecking interface. If a misspelling is found, it's highlighted and underlined in the window and suggestions are offered so that you can select an alternative.

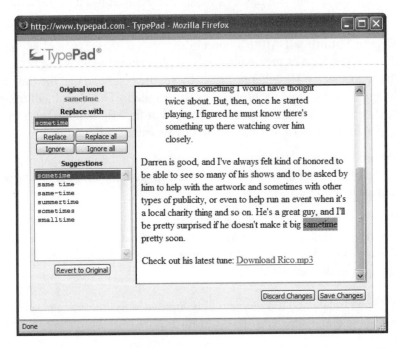

If a good alternative doesn't show up, then you can type a new word in the Replace With entry box. Click Replace, if appropriate, or use the Replace All, Ignore, or Ignore All buttons just as you would in a typical word processor on your PC.

View HTML Mode

By default, you edit posts in TypePad using a visual editing mode for the editing. It's nice, but if you know HTML coding fairly well, you might prefer to be able to dig in and simply type the codes yourself for type styling and so on. Plus, TypePad doesn't offer a way to, for instance, display an image in your post that comes from elsewhere on the Web instead of uploading it, unless you manually add an HTML image tag.

2

To see the HTML code, click the Edit HTML tab at the top-right of the editing window. That changes the interface so that you can see the raw HTML for your post. Go in and alter anything that you need to change, and then you can click the Compose Post tab to switch back and see a visual rendering of your changes.

Publish Settings

Once you're done typing, uploading, and spellchecking, you're ready to make some publishing decisions. TypePad does this slightly differently from some other blogging tools; the upshot is the same, but some of the terminology is a little different. Below the Compose Post window is an area that has the Posting Status menu in it. This is where you can choose to publish the post immediately upon saving it, save it as a draft (so that it's in the system but not yet published on your blog) or set it to publish at some point in the future. If you want to do the latter, choose Publish On from that menu and a window appears. In that window, you can choose a time and date for the post to be published to your blog.

In the Comment section, you can choose whether or not you want people to be able to comment on this blog entry. If you don't want people to be able to comment, choose None. If you do want to allow comments, choose open. Later, after the blog entry has been published and people have commented, it might make sense to re-edit this entry and choose Closed, which means the post and comments remain online, but the conversation can't be added to. You can do that whenever you get tired of a particular thread or you simply want to archive it but don't want anyone else adding to it.

In the Trackbacks section, there are two different things you can do here. First, you can opt to allow trackbacks to this entry. When turned on, readers will see a trackback URL they can use in their blogging software when they blog about your entry. When they publish their response, a link back to their blog will appear on your original entry. If you don't want to accept trackbacks, then click to clear the checkmark from the Accept Trackbacks button.

The second thing you can do here is actually send a trackback yourself if this blog entry is a reference to someone else's blog post or postings. To do that, type or paste the trackback URL into the Send a Trackback To These Addresses text area. When you publish the entry, the trackback will be sent and your entry may then be referenced on that other blog.

With those decisions made, you can click Preview, if you like, to see exactly what the final blog entry will look like when rendered. In the Preview window you'll have the option to click Re-Edit this Post if you want to go back to the editing screen or Save this Post, which will save it to the system and, if it's set to publish immediately, it'll appear on your blog.

If you don't choose to preview, you can save the entry from the main Compose screen. Click Save at the bottom of the window to save the post and publish it if you're set to Publish Now.

Edit and Manage Posts in TypePad

Once you've got a post or two in the system, you can manage those posts—including editing, deleting, or taking a look at the comments and trackbacks—by clicking either the Post tab or the Manage tab in the main interface for your blog and then clicking the List Posts command that appears just beneath that tab. That gives you a screen that looks like Figure 2-24.

To re-edit an existing post, simply click its link in the List Posts listing. That will bring up the Compose screen again so that you can manage changes.

That Compose screen will be a little different than it was when you initially created the post. At the bottom of the screen you'll find two new sections called Manage Comments and Manage Trackbacks. Under Manage Comments you'll see a list of the comments that have been added by visitors to your blog. Click a comment and you can edit it, if desired. Or, place a checkmark next to a comment (or next to multiple comments) and you can click the Delete Checked button to delete those selected comments. Likewise, you can edit or delete trackbacks in the Manage Trackbacks section.

To Delete a post, you can place a checkmark next to that post on the List Posts screen, and click the Delete button. Likewise, you can perform some other actions on checked posts by choosing from the More Actions menu. That includes turning

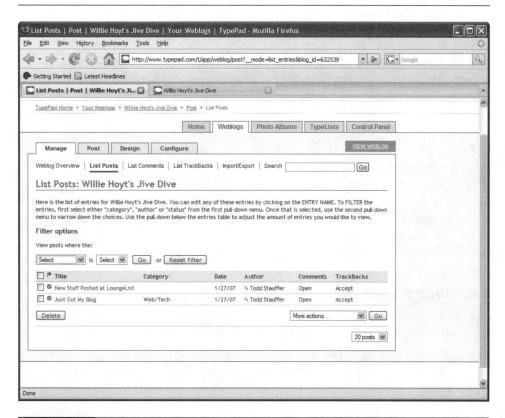

FIGURE 2-24   The List Post screen is a jumping off point for managing posts you've already created.

on (opening) and off (closing) comments, listing comments, turning on and off trackbacks, and making the selected post(s) Featured, which means the post is displayed at the top of the blog and others scroll beneath it, even if those entries are newer. (Some blogs call this making an entry "sticky," because it sticks to the top of the blog regardless of its published date and time.) Featured entries show up in your list with a star next to their name; you can only have one featured entry at once.

If you want to deal directly with all of the comments on your various posts, you can click the Post or Manage tab and then click List Comments (this works for trackbacks as well with the List Trackbacks link). That loads the List Comments (or List Trackbacks) screen where you'll see a list of the recent comments or trackbacks that have been added to your site by visitors. Click a comment in the list to edit it, or click the checkbox next to the comment (or trackback) to select it, and then click Delete.

By default, comments are not moderated, meaning they are posted to your blog immediately after they are adding to the system by your visitors. If you've turned on moderation (you'll see how in the upcoming section "Configure Your TypePad Blog"), then you'll also have the option of selecting comments on the List Comments screen and clicking the Approve button to approve a comment for publication. When you do, that comment will appear under the blog entry for which it was intended.

> **TIP** *Click the main Weblogs tab in the TypePad interface and you'll see an interesting option called Set Up a QuickPost Bookmarklet. What this does is enable you to create a bookmark in your Web browser that leads directly to a post entry screen for your blog—it's perfect for when you're surfing around and suddenly have an inspiration to blog something. Follow the on-screen instructions in order to choose the type of posting interface you'll see and then to create the bookmark in your browser.*

Configure Your TypePad Blog

TypePad offers a variety of configuration options that you can get at by clicking the Configure tab in the main interface. There you'll see options ranging from Categories to Publicity to Authors and Feedback. Let's quickly look at what's going on in this section; with some of these options, I'll elaborate in later chapters of the book.

Weblog Basics

Click this link (actually, it opens automatically when you click the Configure tab) and you can change the name of your blog and enter a description or catchphrase that will automatically appear under the title of your blog in many of the default TypePad themes. More advanced is the option to change the name of the folder for your blog. This is the folder where your published blog files are stored, and it's part of what makes up the URL for your blog, so there's a chance you won't like the folder name that's automatically created. (In my example, with a blog named "Willie Hoyt's Jive Dive," the folder is named willie_hoyts_jive_dive. That's a little cumbersome for a URL.)

Changing the name of the folder is a simple matter of typing in the new name and clicking Save Changes. However, when you change the name of your blog's folder, TypePad does not automatically move any images or files that you've uploaded to your site, so those images won't appear and links to files will be broken.

2

You'll need to go back into all entries you've created with images or files and re-upload them. Likewise, if your blog has been around long enough for people to link to any of your entries (or even to your home page) those external links will break because you're changing the location of the files. So, with that caveat, you can go ahead and change the name of your blog's folder to something more memorable and click Save Changes. When you do, you'll see a message that tells you that the changes have been made but not yet published; click Publish My Site to put those changes into effect.

Archiving

Under the Configure tab you'll see the option for Archiving; click it and you'll see the various options that TypePad offers for archiving your old posts, including suggestions about which method works best for a given type of blog.

Categories

Click into this screen in order to turn on and off the default categories that you can assign to your posts. If you never use a particular category, you might opt to turn it off. And, at the bottom of this screen, you can enter additional categories that might work better with what you're blog is all about.

Publicity

On this screen you can decide whether or not you want some of the popular blog-tracking sites to be alerted when you've created a new entry on your blog. If you choose to Publicize your site, click the Yes button and then choose the services that you would like to have updated.

Feeds

On this screen you can customize the RSS feeds that are offered to your visitors. RSS feeds enable a visitor to "subscribe" to your blog (all they have to do is click the feed's link on your home page) so that they can see new entries in their feedreader without actually visiting your site. On this page, you can turn on an RSS feed for your blog and you can choose whether or not the feed will show your entire blog post or just a small excerpt. When you've made your changes, click Save Changes.

The screen can also be used to configure Feedburner, which I'll discuss in more detail in Chapter 5.

Authors

On the Authors page you can invite others to become authors on your blog. TypePad recognizes two types of authors: Guest Authors and Junior Authors. A Guest Author is authorized to post entries directly to your blog; Junior Authors can post entries, but they are closed by default, and don't show up on your blog until you approve the entries, which you can do from the List Posts link under the Post and Manage tabs.

To invite someone to become an author at your site, simply type their name and address into the Invite Additional Authors list, and then choose the type of author you're inviting them to be (Guest or Junior) from the Access Level menu. Next, you can write a personal message to the person or people you're inviting to let them know why they're getting the e-mail; in that e-mail, they'll also get instructions for adding themselves to the blog.

When you've made you choices and entered some text, click the Send Invitation(s) button. You can then return to the Authors page to see your Open invitations and to figure out if your invited authors have signed up.

Feedback

The Feedback page is where you can set some preferences for how comments work on your blog. If you want to authenticate your readers, so that they have to be registered before they can post to your site, then you can opt to use the TypeKey system that's offered by TypePad. Your options are

- **Required** If selected, this means that your users must be TypeKey members or they cannot post comments.

- **Optional** In this case, a TypeKey member can post comments easily, but someone who does not have a TypeKey account just has to jump through a few more hoops (offering an e-mail address, etc.).

- **None** In this case, all visitors on your site who want to comment can be unregistered.

Next, you have other options for unauthenticated commenters, if you've chosen either Optional or None in the TypeKey section. You can turn on Require Email Address and/or Require CAPTCHA from your unauthenticated commenters.

In the Moderation section, you can turn on the Hold Comments for Approval option if you'd like to approve comments before they're posted to your site. You'll need to check your Comments List periodically to see if someone has commented and whether you want to approve the comment(s) for publication.

In the Comment Formatting section, you can opt to allow your commenters to use some HTML in their comments, or not. Likewise, you can turn on Auto-link URLs if you want TypePad to automatically turn any URLs that the commenter types into hyperlinks.

The other options are self-explanatory. If you feel like you're getting a lot of e-mail from your blog, you might consider turning off the Email Notification option, which is on by default. And if you generally write blog entries where you disallow comments, you can turn off the Default for New Posts option so that you have to specifically turn *on* commenting when you're creating a new post if and when you create a post on which you want to invite comments.

Finally, the rest of that page is devoted to two similar options for Trackbacks— you can turn off e-mail notification for trackbacks and you can opt to change the default for new posts if you generally disallow trackbacks and don't want to be forced to change that option on your posts all the time.

Preferences

The Preferences page focuses on some basic options concerning the way posts are ordered and displayed, as well as some settings that govern which of your posts appear on your front page and so on. Here's a quick rundown:

- **Posts to Display**   Use the menus to choose the number of posts that should display on your blog's front page. Note that you can also choose to have a certain number of *days* display, so if you're a prolific poster or you tend to post very short entries, you can have say, five days worth of entries appear.

- **Order of Posts**   Choose whether the most recent post appears at the top or the oldest post appears at the top of your page. Note that this is only ordering the limited number of posts that you've set to display on the front page. Your "oldest" post won't forever be the first one you ever wrote, just the oldest within the five days or ten posts or so that you choose to display.

- **Limit Posts by Category**   If you only want certain of your blog's categories to appear on the front page you can use this menu to select a single category, or select the option Assign Multiple Categories if you'd like posts from more than one category to appear.

- **Display Language**   Choose the language to use for headers, links to your posts, and dates.

- **Date Format**   Choose a format for dates on your blog.

- **Time Format**   Choose a format for displaying the time in your blog.

- **Posting Status**   Choose the default setting for posting status; if you tend to write long posts and need multiple sessions with TypePad before one is done, then choosing Draft as the default might make sense.

- **Text Formatting**   Choose whether or not line breaks in your post writing will automatically be preserved. You'll generally turn this off if you prefer to edit the raw HTML of your entries.

- **Excerpt Length**   If your RSS feed has excerpts of your posts (instead of the full text), then you can choose how long those excerpts will be with this menu.

Create a Photo Album in TypePad

One of the features that make TypePad worth paying a little money for are the Photo Albums, which are designed to enable you to quickly and painlessly post digital photos or other image files to your blog. If you've got some digital images that you'd like to share with your audience, then you'll probably enjoy the photo albums—they're a bit limited compared to some external options like Flickr, but they're fun to work with for creating a basic gallery or two of our images.

Create and Populate Your Album

To create a photo album in TypePad, head up to the top of your dashboard page and click the Photo Albums tab. That takes you to the Your Photo Albums page, where you can create a new photo album following the step-by-step instructions. You'll start by giving the album a name and then giving the folder for that album a name (which should be a bit simpler, all one word and no special characters.) Then click Create.

Add Photos   After creating an album, you'll see the List Photos page; in the future, you can get to this by clicking the Photo Albums tab in the main interface. To add photos to your album, click the Add Photos To This Album link.

Now you'll see the Add New Photos page. Here you can enter the location for photos in GIF, JPG, or PNG formats. (More on those formats in Chapter 6.) In the Select the Number of Photos You Wish to Upload in This Batch menu, choose the number of photos you'll be sending to TypePad; when you do, you'll see the number of text boxes on the screen change. Then, for each line that represents an image, click the Browse button and use the Open dialog box to locate the image you want to send.

> **2** **Browse your computer for the photos you wish to upload**
>
> Click the Browse button to locate photos on your computer. Each individual photo should be selected by a different Browse button. Once you've selected your photos, add them to this photo album by clicking UPLOAD.
>
> Photo formats that TypePad Photo Albums support: GIF, JPG, PNG
>
> | C:\Documents and Settings\All Users\Documents\My Pi | Browse... |
>
> | C:\Documents and Settings\All Users\Documents\My Pi | Browse... |
>
> | C:\Documents and Settings\All Users\Documents\My Pi | Browse... |
>
> | | Browse... |
>
>   [**UPLOAD**]

TIP

There's another interesting option in the Select the Number menu: I'm Uploading a Zipped Folder. This enables you to send an entire batch of images to your photo album without going through the process of browsing and locating each one in the interface. So, if you've got a ton of photos you want to post, do that by creating a zip archive of the folder of images in your hard disk, then choose that option and Browse to locate that zipped file. Plus, TypePad has a Windows application you can download to your computer so that you can upload batches of images more easily.

Once you've located the images you want to upload, click the Upload button. You'll see a pop-up window appear that lets you know what the progress of your upload is.

Once uploaded, the List Photos screen will show each of the photos that you've uploaded, including a thumbnail of the image. You can click the thumbnail or the name of the photo to edit information about it, including a change to the name or a caption for the image.

In the top corner of the List Photos page, you'll see a link to View Album; you can click that to see what your album will look like to visitors to your site. That's all it takes to upload images.

 *Need to add more images later? Click the Photo Albums tag, then click Add New Photos in that photo album's section, or click the album's name and you'll see another Add New Photos link.*

Design Your Album

The default look of the photo album is pretty bland, but you can do a little something about that. With the Photo Albums tab active, click the Design tab that appears. On the Select Your Photo Album's Design page, you can do a number of things:

- Click the Layout link to view different layouts and select a different photo album "cover page" and your main viewer "photo" pages. Click Save Changes when you've made those choices.

- Click the Content link to decide which content elements will appear on your cover page and which will appear on your photo pages. That includes items like the photo album's name, photo title, photo caption, and EXIF data that may have been stored with the image when it was taken by a digital camera. Make choices and click Save Changes.

- Click the Style link and you'll get an opportunity to change the theme for your photo album. From the menu, select the different built-in styles and you'll see the sample screenshots change. When you find one you like the look of, click Save Changes.

Configure the Album

Click the Configure tab and you can make some basic choices about the name of the album and how images are uploaded. In the Photo Album Basics, enter a new name, if desired, and a description. (The description is used in a certain photo album layout—the Photo and Introduction cover—that begins with a single image on an opening page.) You can also turn on the option Use a Cover Image/Photo and then browse for that image if you're using the Photo and Introduction cover.

In the Advanced Configuration section, you can make choices about the number of columns of images that should be used on your photo album's cover page (for those layouts that show more than one image) and how the images should be cropped. You can also choose to change the default size of the thumbnail image that is presented on cover pages.

Beyond that, you can choose a different date format for the photo album pages to display, and you can change the order in which images are displayed, so that they're showed in ascending or descending order based on the photo's date taken (what the camera assigned to it) or based on the photo's title in alphabetical order.

2

In the Your Photo Pages section, there's a pretty important setting, the Photo Size menu. When you upload images to TypePad, it not only creates a thumbnail image of the photo, but it also shrinks the photo to a certain width. That way the images don't take up too much storage space and they display nicely on the typical computer screen. Choose a size you're comfortable with; if you love your own photography and have great shots you want to share with your visitors, you might want this set to the highest setting.

NOTE

One thing to watch out for—if you find yourself uploading both landscape- and portrait-oriented images, you'll need to make sure that in both cases the originals are at least as wide as the pixel setting that is chosen here. Otherwise, images that are narrower than you've selected will be blown up a bit, which could make them appear pixilated when viewed by your visitors.

TIP

What do you do if you want to offer your visitors higher-resolution versions of the images shown in your photo album? TypePad's defaults are too low for images that will be printed on a color inkjet or laser printer, for example. The best way is to upload those images to a hosting service and then link to the high-resolution image from the description that you give each photo in your album. (You could conceivably upload them to TypePad as a file in a blog entry instead of as an image, and then link to that blog entry's permalink or to the image file itself, but remember that you have limited space, about 1GB, with the Pro account as of this writing.) The user can then click the link to download the high-resolution image.

When you're done tweaking the photo album settings, click Save Changes and those changes will be implemented.

Link to Your Album

So now that you have the album created, how do you link to it from your blog's front page? The easiest way is to dig into the design of your blog and then add a photo album widget. Choose the Weblogs tab, then the Design tab and click the Select Content link. On the Select Content page, find the Photo Albums section; you should see your new photo album listed there. Click to place a checkmark next to the photo album (or albums, if you've created more than one) that you'd like to add to your blog, then scroll down and click Save Changes. Now, you can view your blog to see the new photo album widget that appears, or head over to Order Content if you'd like the album viewer to show up in a different part of the sidebar.

NOTE   *You'll learn more about changing and ordering content in the section "Tweak Your TypePad Design," later in this chapter.*

Add Lists to Your TypePad Blog

TypePad offers its special TypeLists feature for bloggers who want to add content to the sidebars of their blog design. Unlike some blogging tools, TypePad makes it very difficult to dig in and change the HTML on your blog's front page. That's how I've typically altered the front page templates of my blogs to, say, show off the books I've written or to tell people the songs I'm listening to. With TypePad, you're encouraged to use the TypeLists for that, instead, and then add the TypeLists as if they were any of the other built-in or third-party widgets that TypePad handles so well in its design tools.

To create a TypeList, click the TypeList tab at the top of any TypePad admin page. Then follow the two-step process on the Your TypeLists page that appears: choose a list type and give the list a name.

Now you should see the Recent Items list, which won't have anything in it. Click the Add a New Item link and a pop-up window appears where you can give the item a name and enter some the details of what you want to post online. Note that you can use HTML, if desired, so it's possible to type in anchor tags for hyperlinks, image tags for images, or basic type styling tags for italics, bold, and so on.

TIP   *If you want to upload an image to your site without going through a blog entry or a photo album interface, you can choose the Control Panel tab and click Files to upload files directly to your TypePad server space. You can then enter an image URL (`<img src="http://yourname.typepad.com/nameofimage.jpg">`) to the title of a TypeList item, thus making it an image instead of text. Likewise, if you opt to create a TypeList of links, you can add the image link to the title and then enter a URL in the Link URL entry box that links that image to a new website or page.*

Once your list is created, you can click the Add This List To our Weblog(s) or About Page link in the Recent Items window, or you can select Weblogs | Design | Select Content to add the list to your weblog's design as described in the next section.

I encourage you to play with the different types of lists to see which ones work best for what you're trying to do—generally speaking, if you're trying to add some sort of images or text to the sidebar and one of the widgets won't work for you, a TypeList can be configured to do the job.

Tweak Your TypePad Design

We'll get a little more detailed with general blog design principles and CSS commands in Chapter 4, but for starters, TypePad offers some very friendly design tools for altering the look and organization of your blog. And, as mentioned, TypePad offers a number of widgets that can be added to your blog to customize its offers and, perhaps, have a little fun.

To get to all of these options, you can click the Design tab in the main TypePad interface for your blog or, from the top-level Weblogs tab, click Edit Design for the blog that you want to edit. That brings up the Design page shown in Figure 2-25.

We'll examine each of the design options in turn. Before you get started tweaking, though, it's worth noting that the Design tab offers a link called New Design, which you can use to create a different design from the one that you currently have and save it separately. That way you can switch between stored designs without being forced to make manual changes every time you want to

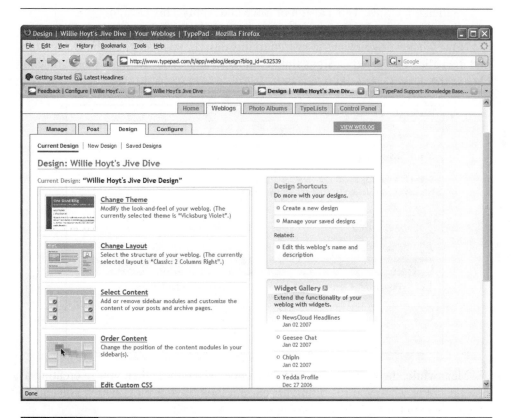

FIGURE 2-25   The Design page in TypePad gives you a number of options for changing the look of your blog.

switch the look of your site. Here's how (note that most of these choices are discussed in more depth in the sections that follow this one):

1. Click New Design under the Design tab.

2. Choose a Layout on the Design Builder: Layout page and click Step 2: Select the Content for Your Weblog.

3. Make content selections on the Design Builder: Content Selections page and click Step 3: Order Your Weblog Content.

4. Choose the order of your content items on the Design Builder: Content Ordering page and click Step 4: Customize Your Weblog's Style.

5. Alter the theme for your blog and then click Step 5: Save Your Template.

6. On the Design Builder: Save Template Set page, give your template a name in the Name field and type a description if desired in the Description field, then click Save This Design or Save and Apply This Design.

Now, whenever you want to switch to this design, you can click the Design tab and then click the Saved Designs link. On the Manage Your Designs page you can choose the design you want to use.

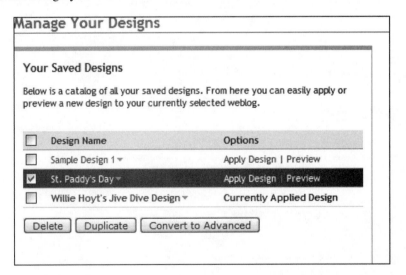

Meanwhile, the rest of these options can be used either when you're creating a new design or when you're editing the current look of your blog, which you can do by clicking the Current Design link under the Design tab.

Change Theme

Click the Change Theme option and you'll see a page that resembles the one you used to choose the original theme for your blog when you signed up for TypePad service.

At the top of the page you have two main choices: Pre-defined Theme and Custom Theme. If you choose Pre-defined Theme, you can then choose from one of the themes provided by TypePad. Simply choose the type of themes you want to view from the Show menu, then select the theme you want to use for your blog. At the bottom of the page you can choose Preview to see what your theme will look like, or choose Save Changes to put the new theme into effect.

Select Custom Theme and things get a little more complicated. You'll notice that the options change, giving you the ability to alter items such as the Background color, the top banner on the page (you can change the colors and text style or upload an image for the top banner), the way Weblog Posts appear and the appearance of Sidebar items. Here's what happens when you click the Edit This Element button under each of the options:

General Page Settings   In the pop-up window that appears, you can make choices about the main body of your blog page, as well as the sidebars that appear on the front page.

- **General Settings**   Choose colors for the background of the page, whether or not the entire front page should have a border, what style that border should be, and what color. Use the pre-set color buttons or choose a Web-friendly "hex" color as discussed in Chapter 4.

- **Main Content Column**   Here you can choose the size for the main content column, a background color, a border, and a border color. The typical size for the main content column is 400 pixels, which, when added to two 200-pixel sidebars (in a three-column layout) adds up to a fairly standard 800 pixels. If you've opted for a different layout (which you can change on the Change Layout page discussed later in this section), then you might want a different size for your main content section; perhaps 600 pixels if you only have a left or right sidebar.

- **Right Column and Left Column**   In these two sections of the pop-up window you can make similar choices: column width, background color, border style, and border color.

- **Link Style** Here you can make choices for the color of links on your page, depending on what's going on with that link. The Normal Link color is the link before it's been clicked. The Active Link color is the color of the link *while* it's being clicked. The Visited Link color is the color of a link once you've returned to your page after the link has been visited. The Hover Link color is the color that the link changes to when the mouse pointer "hovers" over it. You can also choose a link style from either Underline or Bold, depending on how you want all the links on your page to appear visually.

NOTE *Chapter 4 will discuss link design for blogs, and you can use that discussion to help you make choices here in TypePad.*

When you've made your choices, click Save Changes to put those changes into effect.

Page Banner In the Page Banner pop-up you make decisions about the top banner that appears for your site. Choose a background color, a border, a border color, the color for your text heading, how that text is aligned, the style for the text and the text's font and size.

As an option, you can use an image for the top banner of your site. TypePad recommends that you create an image that is about 770 pixels wide for a three-column layout. (The typical width of a three-column layout is 800 pixels—400 pixels for the main content area and 200 pixels for each sidebar, and the banner image will have 15 pixels of "padding" on each side by default.) For two-column layouts, then, you might want to create an image that's 570 pixels.

TIP *On the Customize Your Theme page, TypePad tells you the current widths of your columns in the General Page Settings box. Add those together to get the width of your blog's design.*

The image that you create should be in JPG, GIF, or PNG format. To upload it, put a check in the Use This Banner Image Instead of a Text Title option and then click the Browse button to find the image you want to upload.

When you're done with the Page Banner settings, click Save Changes.

Weblog Posts In the Weblog Posts pop-up window, you can make choices about the font, font color, text alignment, text style, border, and border color for the blog entry's Date Header, Post Title, the body of the post, and the Post Footer. TypePad shows you a live sample of each element as you're adding it, so you can just experiment if you like. Click Save Changes when you're done.

Sidebar Items   In the Sidebar Items section you can make choices about the titles of sidebar items, the font styles for text in the sidebar, the border and alignment of images that appear in the sidebar, and the way that links appear in the sidebars. Note also the option Use the General Page Settings Link Style for the Sidebar, which you can use if you'd like to use the same link styles that you set up in the General Settings pop-up. Click Save Changes when you're done.

Change Layout

In the Change Layout tools, you can choose from one of the Classic Layouts (2 columns, 3 columns, or 1 column) or you can make a selection from the Mixed Media Layouts, which are better for sites that rely heavily on the Photo Galleries feature that's available to users of advanced versions of TypePad. Make your choice and click Preview to see what your selection will look like or Save Changes to put the changes into effect.

NOTE   *Some of the Mixed Media layouts are less effective for displaying all of the widget modules that TypePad makes available for your blog. If you're a photographer or an avid snapshot blogger, though, those layouts can be great for a photo-centric blog.*

Select Content

In the Select Content tools, you can scroll through the options and place checkmarks next to the elements that you want to have appear on your blog. At the top are the basic Weblog elements (the Date Header, Post Title, and Post Footer are all options) as well as archiving options.

Below that are the Sidebar Modules. The Built-In Modules are those that TypePad makes available to you for use exclusively on your TypePad blog, including items such as Text Ads, a Tip Jar (for accepting donations from visitors), an Amazon wish list, and items related to the categories on your site. (See Chapter 7 for a discussion of categories, tag clouds, and social bookmarking.)

Also in that section are controls for adding Widgets, Photo Galleries, TypeLists, and Feeds to your blog's design. If you've already a gallery or a TypeList or two, you'll see them in this section. Place a checkmark next to those that you'd like to add to your blog design.

Widgets are small sidebar items that TypePad has created in partnership with other Internet companies. These widgets offer a variety of functions and features that link out to other services on the Internet. To add a new Widget, click the Widget Gallery link. That brings up TypePad's list of different widgets that you can add to your blog. Now, just find the widget that you want to add, click the

Get This Widget Now button, and configure it (it may take some registration and other configuration). Once you've gotten the widget up and running, you'll see it appear in the list of Widgets on the Select Content tool; make sure it has a checkmark next to it so that you can use it in your design.

By default TypePad creates a feed of your blog's entries so that visitors can subscribe to the content on your site. On the Content Selections page, you can add feeds to your blog design from *other* blogs, so as to publicize the latest headlines from your favorite blogs (or other sites that provide feeds) on the Internet. To do that, click the Add a New Feed button. In the pop-up window that appears, enter the URL to an RSS feed for another blog, and then click Continue. If you've chosen a valid RSS feed, then you'll see the dialog box reconfigure so that you can enter a title for the feed and choose how many headlines you want to display.

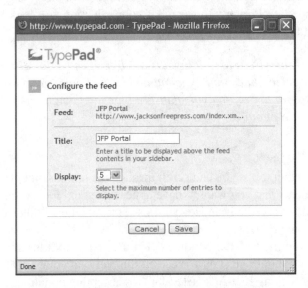

Click Save when you've made those choices. The feed will now appear on the Content Selections page where you can check or uncheck it for display on your blog.

When you're done selecting content items for your blog, click Save Changes at the bottom of the page. You're ready to arrange that content in your design.

Order Content

The Order Content tool couldn't be easier to use. What you'll see is a visual representation of your blog design. Using drag-and-drop, simply move the little blocks around on the screen to choose where you would like each module or widget to appear on the page (see Figure 2-26).

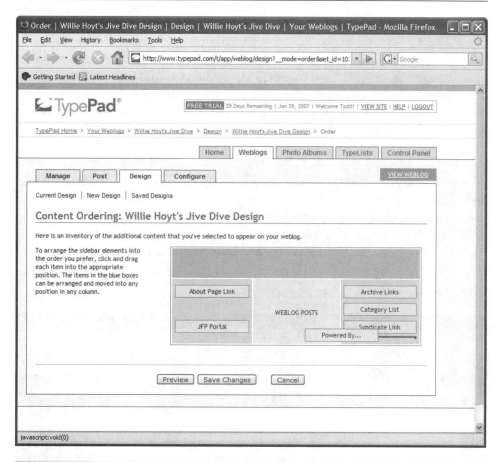

FIGURE 2-26 Drag and drop the boxes around in the representation of your blog design to re-order the content.

When you've made you choices, click the Save Changes button to put those choices into effect.

Edit Custom CSS

We won't go deep into this, as there's extensive coverage of CSS in Chapter 4, but for now you should know that this is where you can add CSS templates markup for your TypePad blog. What this can enable you to do is create styles for the tags used in your blog in order to change their appearance in most modern Web browsers.

For instance, earlier in the editing of TypePad posts you learned that you can quote text from other blogs (or other sources) using the Begin Quote and End Quote buttons. If you view the HTML of a post that includes the quoting feature, you'll see that the quoting is accomplished by placing the quoted text between `<blockquote>` and `</blockquote>` HTML tags. Using CSS in the Edit Custom CSS tool, you could attach style commands to the blockquote tag so that it, for instance, always has a border drawn around it and a background color that sets it apart from the rest of your blog. In the Custom CSS tool, you would add something like this:

```
blockquote {border: 1px dotted; background: #FFB; padding: 5px}
```

That might look a little complex, but it's simply telling the visitor's browser that items inside a `<blockquote>` tag should have a border with a one-pixel dotted line, a background that is light yellow, and that the text within that border should be padded on all sides by five pixels of space. The result looks like Figure 2-27.

Make your CSS changes and click Save Changes to have them applied to your blog design.

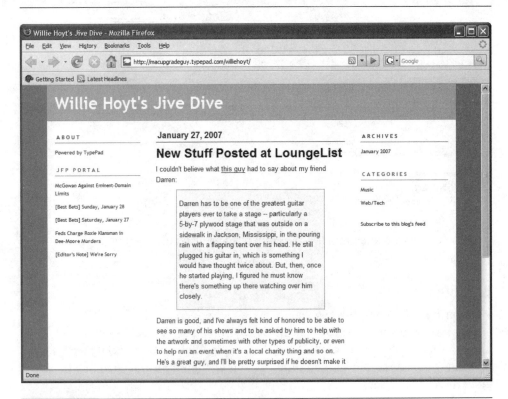

FIGURE 2-27   Here I've altered the style of the blockquote tag in my blog layout.

Republish

Once you've made all of these changes to your blog's design, it's time to republish
the site. TypePad will generally make automatic changes to the main page of your
site, but it doesn't always make changes to the archives and other elements. To
make sure everything is styled according to your changes and preferences, click
the Republish Weblog button at the bottom of the Design page. You'll see a pop-up
box that asks you which pages you want to republish. Make your choices and click
Publish. After a moment, your blog will be republished and you'll be given the
option of clicking a link to view it in all its newly refreshed glory.

2

Chapter 3

Explore More Blogging Options

How to…

■ Get started with WordPress blogging software

■ Get started with ExpressionEngine blogging software

In Chapter 2, I mentioned that I have been mulling whether to use Blogger, TypePad, or WordPress for my personal blog. For the site that I spend most of my time with—www.jacksonfreepress.com—choosing the ideal tool has been a more arduous process, in part because that site offers a number of different blogs rolled into one destination, and getting all of those blogs to work together can be tough. When you take a piece of software and really reach for its limits—particularly when you aren't a serious programmer capable of hacking your way through problems—then it helps if that software is designed to grow with you. Some programs are, some aren't.

During the course of writing this book I've been migrating the Jackson Free Press site from a blogging program called pMachine Pro to ExpressionEngine (software written by the same company, but so completely re-written that the upgrade isn't exactly a cakewalk) and I'm still in a testing phase to determine whether that was really the right call. I've also considered the other tool I'll be talking about in this chapter, WordPress, although it's more up to the task of handling sophisticated personal blogs and blogs for businesspeople. The truth is, both of these self-hosted tools have their strengths and they're both very exciting platforms if you see your blogging going to the "next" level of creating online communities.

In this chapter, I'd like to explore WordPress and ExpressionEngine in depth so we can take a look at the strengths and weaknesses of each.

WordPress

WordPress has become an extremely popular platform for blogging in the past few years, offering a host-it-yourself tool that focuses on the essentials of blogging—themes, user registration, comments, trackbacks, and so on—while attempting to build a tool that is fast, well-written and that conforms to Web standards, making it work well in as many different web browsers and on as many different computing platforms as possible. It's an open source project and it has a strong community of users, including many who write plug-ins and themes to help you extend your WordPress blog and make it do tons of Web 2.0-style stuff.

In fact, WordPress is both a hosted and a self-hosted tool; at WordPress.com, you can sign up for a hosted WordPress account and be walked through some simplified steps to create a blog using WordPress technology, but on the WordPress.com servers.

At WordPress.org, you can download the open-source, self-hosted version of WordPress, which requires that you have your own hosting space that supports PHP scripting and a MySQL database. If you've got that, then you can download the latest version from WordPress.org and install it yourself. That's what we'll focus on in this section of the chapter, although be aware that many of the things you can do with the self-hosted version of WordPress can also be done with the hosted version at WordPress.com if you don't already have a web hosting account or if you simply don't want to fool around with the installation.

> **NOTE** *What's the difference? With self-hosted WordPress, you'll have more flexibility to install your own themes or alter the templates for your site. You'll also be able to install more third-party plug-ins to extend your blog. And, if you end up getting a lot of traffic and/or wanting to post a lot of images and multimedia, then a self-hosted installation is probably the best bet. Of course, it's pretty easy to export from and import to different WordPress installations, so you could conceivably start with the hosted solution and upgrade to a self-hosted blog later, if desired.*

WordPress Pros and Cons

WordPress is really good blogging software. Written from the ground up in 2003, it's not based on as much legacy code as both Blogger and TypePad, and it's designed to be efficient and standards conforming. It's also designed to power blogs that have a Web 2.0 sensibility, in the sense that less is more and an under-designed site is at least somewhat encouraged. Here's a look at the standout features:

- **Easy Installation and Interface**   WordPress is very easy to get up and running considering that it's a self-hosted solution, so that you'll have a blog going in a few minutes as long as you have a hosting account and access to login information about your MySQL database. Once it's installed, the interface is very friendly, with a one-thing-at-a-time attitude about posting, editing, and managing your blog.

- **Support for Registration and Multiple Authors**   WordPress can work as a one-to-many, few-to-many, or even a community blog if you desire. The registration and login process is straightforward and registered users can be upgraded to full author or even administrator status.

■ **Page Tool**   Somewhat unique among blogging solutions is WordPress' Page editor, which enables you to create and edit simple "static" web pages for your site. From within the interface you can edit About pages, product pages, and other pages that you might want on your blog, even going so far as to include comments and other WordPress features on those pages. And using third-party templates and WordPress Plug-ins, you can create different types of static pages quickly, using WordPress not just for blogging, but as a user-friendly content management system for putting information about your business, your career, or other fun (or lucrative) stuff about yourself online without forcing all of that content into the time-based chronology of your blog.

■ **Plug-ins and Widgets**   WordPress offers support for third-party WordPress plug-ins that you can access via the administrative tools. Plug-ins have been written by a community of users to do all sorts of things, from automatically posting your entries to social bookmarking services to adding an events calendar, music, video players, and so on. Likewise, widgets are available for particular WordPress templates that can make adding items to your blog sidebars very easy.

One drawback to WordPress is that it doesn't support multiple blogs in a single installation, which can be handy for more complex sites such as magazine-style blogs. (That said, there is a multi-user WordPress that is available separately, allowing many different individual users to create their own blogs. They still don't integrate in the same way that blogs do in ExpressionEngine, for instance, which allows you to create much more complex "portal" sites.)

WordPress also has an HTML-based templating system which can be a plus for Web programmers, but doesn't offer the same level of drag-and-drop customization as do some of the hosted solutions. And sticking to pre-configured themes is encouraged, because a good deal of the templating is done in PHP and can be complex for non-programmers to change. That said, WordPress is so popular that there are tons of pre-configured themes out there, both free and commercial options, so you're likely to find one you like if you search long enough.

Get and Install WordPress

To get the self-hosted version of WordPress, point your web browser to http://www.wordpress.org and find the download link or button. When you get to the download page, you'll be directed to a .zip file that you can download to your PC's hard disk. Follow the online instructions to get the most recent stable build of WordPress.

When the download is completed, take these steps:

1. Launch the WordPress.zip document in order to extract its contents. When the extraction process is done, you'll have a new WordPress folder on your hard disk.

2. Open up that folder and you'll find a file called README.html, which you can double-click and view in a Web browser. It'll walk you through the installation instructions, which are pretty simple: You open the configuration file called wp-config-sample.php in a text editor (WordPad in Windows or TextEdit in Mac OS X), and input the information that it needs to connect to your web host's database server and the database that you've created for WordPress (or the database that's available for it, if you didn't create it yourself).

3. Then you save that file as wp-config.php, making sure to save it as a *plain text* file, not a *rich text* one, and make sure it has the .php filename extension.

NOTE   *Where do you get this database information? If your web hosting account offers a control panel interface, you can probably find out about (or create) a MySQL database from within that control panel. That's where you'll find the database name, username for the database, and password. You may also need a special hostname; it's usually "localhost," but not always. (One of the hosting companies I use requires specific names for the MySQL hostname.) If you can't get at this data from within your hosting account's control panel, you'll probably need to contact your ISP's customer or technical support people.*

4. With that out of the way, you can then upload the entire WordPress installation to your web hosting account via FTP. It doesn't have to go into a particular folder on the remote server—in fact, if you want people to access the blog as your main index page on the site, then you should upload the *contents* of your expanded wordpress folder to the root-level of the remote host. That might be right inside a folder called web or www or content or wherever your ISP directs you to place your HTML files.

TIP   *See the sidebar "Installing WordPress in a Sub-Folder" for another option for installing WordPress.*

5. Once you've uploaded the files, head back to your web browser and load the page /wp-admin/install.php on your site. (For instance, on my site I'd load http://www.toddstauffer.com/wp-admin/install.php, since I FTP'd everything to the root level of my hosting account, which has been assigned the domain name www.toddstauffer.com.) When you do (and if you're successful) you'll see the installation wizard, which will walk you through the process of getting your blog started and creating the database tables that WordPress needs to function.

6. When the installation wizard is done, you'll be told your username and password for logging into the administration page; click the link to that admin page and log in. If you're successful, the result will be a screen that looks like Figure 3-1. From there, you can get started with your first post.

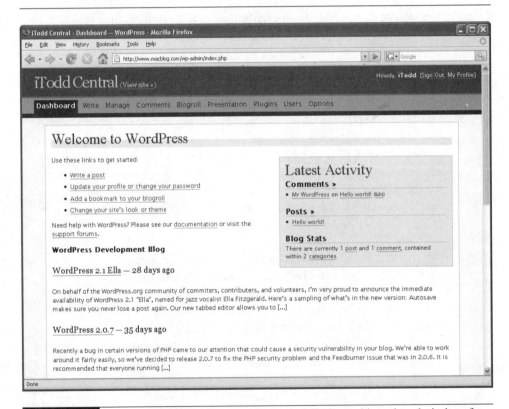

FIGURE 3-1   I've installed WordPress and successfully logged into the admin interface, where I can get started publishing or I can read the latest news from the WordPress people.

NOTE *The Logout option in the admin interface is in the top-right corner by default; the link to WordPress' online documentation is found at the bottom of every admin screen.*

Installing WordPress in a Sub-folder

By default, if you want your WordPress blog to be the index page of your website, then you copy all the WordPress files and folders to the root level of your hosting account. But you may, instead, wish to place those files in a *sub-folder* of that root folder, perhaps called something such as "blog" or "wordpress." There are two reasons to do this. On one hand, you may not want your WordPress blog to be the index of your site, but rather a section of your site—maybe your blog is important to you, but you want it to be linked from your main page. On the other hand, you may indeed want your WordPress blog to be the index of your site, but you want your WordPress files separated in their own sub-folder for easy access on your web hosting account.

The procedure for both setups begins the same way. Using your FTP application, create a sub-folder inside the root of your web folder on the host account. Call it whatever you'd like to use as part of the URL to reach your blog, such as "blog" or "wordpress" or "news," and so on. For this example, let's call it "blog." Now, upload all of your WordPress files and folders to that sub-folder. If your goal was simply to have a separate blog on your site, you can access it at http://www.yoursiteURL.com/blog/ or link to it using that same URL. You're done.

If you do still want your WordPress blog to be the index page of your website (so that your visitors will see the blog's index page when they type in **http://www.yoursiteURL.com/** in a browser), then you'll need to do a little extra surgery.

Here's how it works. On the root level of your web folder (the same place where you would generally install the WordPress files), create a new file called index.php. With the file created, edit it and enter just this:

```
<?php
header( 'Location: http://www.yoursiteURL.com/blog/' ) ;
?>
```

That URL should point to the location of your sub-folder that you created for WordPress. Now, save that file. Whenever people access your site's URL, they'll be redirected to the sub-folder that you've created where the WordPress files are stored.

Publish Your First Post with WordPress

To begin your first post, click the Write tab in the main WordPress admin interface. That takes you to the Write interface, with the Write Post secondary tab highlighted. Enter a title for your post in the Title entry box, and then begin typing in the main text area. As shown in Figure 3-2, WordPress has shortcut buttons for formatting in the interface, as we've seen in the other blogging solutions in this chapter.

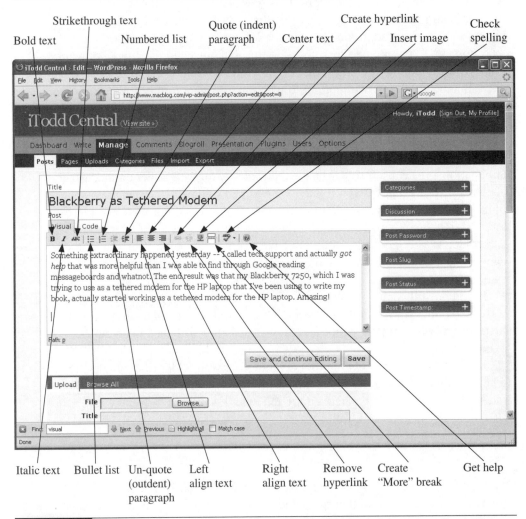

Strikethrough text

Bold text

Numbered list

Quote (indent) paragraph

Center text

Create hyperlink

Insert image

Check spelling

Italic text   Bullet list   Un-quote (outdent) paragraph   Left align text   Right align text   Remove hyperlink   Create "More" break   Get help

FIGURE 3-2   The WordPress interface includes command buttons for common formatting options. Just highlight a word or paragraph and then press the button you want to use for formatting.

Highlight a word and click the bold, italic, or strikethrough buttons to format the selection with those highlights.

WordPress automatically saves your entry every minute as you're editing, but if you like to save even more often than that, you can click the Save and Continue Editing button at any time to save your work without publishing the entry.

You can also highlight a number of paragraphs and turn them into a bullet list or a numbered list using the appropriate command buttons. Or, for quoting, select a paragraph or two and click the Indent button to create the quoted text. (You can also use that button to indent a list, if desired.) Once a paragraph is indented, you can click the Outdent button to remove the indenting. And, again with paragraphs, you can choose to left-align, center, or right-align the text.

Create a Hyperlink

To create a hyperlink, highlight the text that will become a link and click the Insert/Edit Link button. A pop-up window appears, where you can enter the URL for the link, choose a Target (whether it should open in the same window or a new one), and give the link a title. (The title doesn't change the link text, but it does appear when you mouse over the link in many browsers.)

Click Insert and you'll see the highlighted text change into blue, underlined text, indicating that it's a link. If you need to remove a link that you've created, highlight the linked text and click the Unlink button.

In some browsers that don't support the WordPress Visual Editor (or, if you've got the WordPress Visual Editor turned off in your account preferences), you'll see a slightly different, and more simplified, version of the Link window.

Enter the URL and then click OK. The highlighted text will now be surrounded by the HTML anchor (`<a href="http://www.somelink.com/">` and `</a>`) tags. To remove the link, simply delete those tags (and everything contained in them) from around the text.

Upload an Image

Uploading an image to add to your entry is a multi-step process:

1. First you need to upload the image, which you can do in the Upload section of the page. Click the Browse button and then use the window that appears to locate the file that you want to upload from your PC's hard disk.

2. Enter a Title for the image and a description, if desired.

3. Click the Upload button.

4. The result will be a view of the image in the Browse mode. You can now choose whether the full image, a thumbnail of the image, or the title of the image will be shown in your blog entry, and you can decide if the image in your entry will link to the file, a page that shows the image, or if there will be no link.

5. Click the Send to Editor button to send the image to the main text area.

6. Highlight the image in the text area and click the Insert/Edit Image button. That gives you additional options, including Alignment. If you would like your blog text to wrap around the image, choose Left or Right alignment.

7. Click Update in the window when you're done making changes.

If you don't need to upload the image, but rather you're going to link to an image that's already on the Internet, that's a bit easier. Simply place your cursor in the entry where you'd like the image to appear and click the Insert Image button. The Insert/Edit Image window appears. In that window, enter the URL to the image that you'd like to include in your post, then make any other choices, including Alignment for the image. Click Insert and the image will be added to your blog.

> **TIP** *The Insert/Edit Image window offers some other interesting options such as the Vertical Space and Horizontal Space options, which you can use to give your image a few pixels of white space, particularly if you're using the align left or align right options to wrap text around the image.*

Create a More Link

WordPress has an interesting approach to the whole "more" link idea in blogging. As I've mentioned in earlier chapters, some blogs show the entire entry on the front page of the blog; some show a snippet of the entry, and then a More or Continue link so that you can click to read the entire post. With WordPress, you have the option of doing either. If your post is short enough, you can simply type it in the text area and then save or publish the post as normal. If you're writing a longer post, though, you might want to create a More section. To do that, place the cursor where the More section will start and then click Split Post with More Tag button. That draw a line in the post to show where the more section will begin once the post is published.

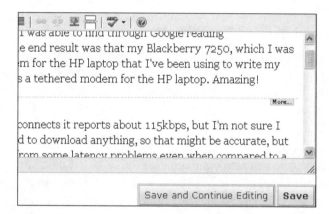

Edit HTML Code

In the Visual Editor interface you'll see two tabs: Visual and Code. The Visual tab is used when you want a WYSIWYG rendering of your post. Click the Code tab, and you'll see the raw HTML that's used to format your post. If you know a little something about HTML, you can change the codes (or add some more) as desired. When you're done, click the Visual tab again to see your handiwork.

NOTE   *If your browser doesn't support the Visual Editor or if you have the option to view the Visual Editor turned off in your user profile (accessible from the top-right corner of the admin interface), then you'll only see the HTML mode.*

Check Spelling

The last little command shortcut before the Help button is the Check Spelling button, which you can click at any time while you're editing your post. When you do, the Check Spelling interface takes over and guides you through the process.

Check Spelling isn't available in the HTML editing mode or when you have the Visual Editor turned off.

Add Categories

WordPress has a great interface for categories; off on the right side of the post is the Categories interface. You can select from the existing categories to assign them to this post or, if the right category doesn't exist yet, type it in and click the Add button. Now, the category exists and you can assign this entry to it.

Disable Comments and Trackbacks

By default, both Comments and Trackbacks are enabled for WordPress posts. If you'd prefer not to enable one or the other for this particular post, then click the plus sign in the Discussion bar and you'll see checkboxes for Comments and Trackbacks. Uncheck whichever you would like to disable.

Publish

Before publishing, you can also opt to change the timestamp on your post so that it goes live on your blog at some later date. In the Post Timestamp section of the window, turn on the Edit Timestamp function, and then change the date to a later time and/or date. The entry will be published when you click the Publish button, but it will not appear on your blog until the timestamp time and date have arrived.

You'll see some other options on the Post screen, including the Option Excerpt entry field, which you can use to give a short description of this entry that will be used for RSS feeds and for search results. Otherwise, you're ready to post your first entry. To do so, simply click the Publish button that appears under the editing text area. That will make the post go live on your site. If you'd prefer to save the post for editing later, click the Save button and it will be saved as a draft, meaning it doesn't yet appear on your site.

You can also set the time or date to an early hour or day that has already passed, if, for example, you want to order this entry before another you've already published.

Now you're ready to preview your blog. Click the View Site link next to your blog's title in the admin interface, or right-click View Site (CONTROL-click on a Mac) and choose to open the link in a new window so that you don't replace your admin interface with the blog. How does it look? Pretty plain (see Figure 3-3). I'll discuss changing that later in this chapter.

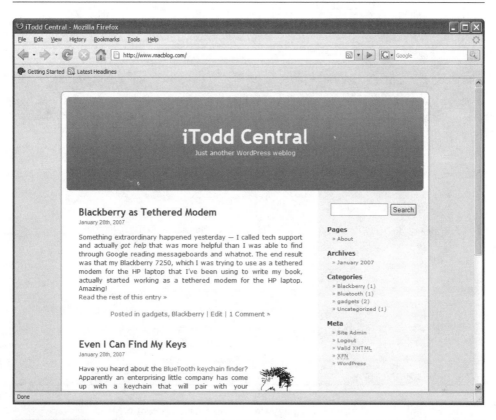

FIGURE 3-3 Here are a few posts added to my WordPress blog, which is using the default "Kubrick" theme.

Manage and Edit Posts with WordPress

Once you've got some posts entered, you may want to start editing and managing them. To do that, you begin in the Admin interface by clicking the Manage button in the admin interface. Next, make sure that Posts is selected in the secondary list of tabs. Now, you should see a list of your most recent posts to the blog, as shown in Figure 3-4.

TIP *You can also edit individual posts when you're viewing your blog in a web browser and you're logged into WordPress. Look for the Edit link; when you click it, it will launch that entry in the admin interface for you to make changes.*

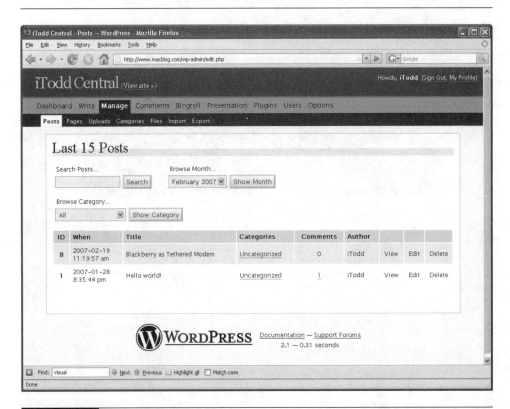

FIGURE 3-4   The Manage Posts page shows you a list of recent posts.

To delete a post, simply click Delete next to that post.

To Edit a post, click the Edit link that appears in that post's column. That brings back up the post writing interface, with a few differences. The interface now shows a full preview at the bottom of the screen (actually, it's sort of a snapshot of the page as it was before you began editing it again) and you'll see an existing timestamp for the entry in the Timestamp section. Make your changes and click Save to have them go live immediately.

If you'd like to remove the post from your blog but keep it in the system for editing, open the Post Status item and switch it to Draft. Then click Save and the post will no longer appear on your blog pages.

Configure Your WordPress Blog

On the Options tab in WordPress, you can tackle all sorts of configuration issues that affect your blog. Here's a quick look at each of the tabs:

- **General Options**   Here you can enter a Title and Tagline for your blog, which will be used in the header for your blog pages. On this tab you can also make choices about whether or not your blog offers open registration (as opposed to only allowing the users that you register from within the admin controls to access certain features) and if users must be registered and logged in to comment. Along with those, the Date and Time options are here for formatting the date and time formats that are used in your blog entries.

- **Writing Options**   On this tab you'll find options that govern the size of the posting text area, the default post category, and the default category for items entered using the bookmarklet. You can also set up a POP account on your hosting server that accepts an e-mail that can be posted directly to your blog for posting-by-email. And you can enter the URLs for services that you want to "ping" whenever you publish a new blog entry.

- **Reading Options**   You can set a page other than your latest blog posts as your front page, using the static page capability of WordPress (discussed later in this chapter). You can also select the number of posts to show on the front page and the number of posts to send in your RSS feed.

- **Discussion Options**   Here you'll set the defaults for a number of behaviors such as updating trackbacks, whether you allow comments on posts, and whether you receive comment notifications by e-mail. You can also decide if (and set up *how*) you want to implement comment moderation, where a comment must be approved by you (or another blog administrator) before it will appear on the blog.

NOTE   *WordPress offers a very interesting system for catching certain words and/or IP addresses and placing the comments that match those items into moderation so that you can check the comment before allowing it to post. You can also cause certain types of comments or comments from certain posters to be "blacklisted," meaning they're deleted immediately as spam.*

- **Privacy Options**   Here you can choose whether your site is available to search engines or if it blocks spiders and crawlers.

■ **Permalink Options**   Here you can decide how permalinks will be formatted (whether the URLs look like queries, or if they look like the year, month, date, and name of the post).

NOTE
In order to use some of these "pretty" URL formats you'll need to do some setup work. They require a host that runs Apache as the server, and you'll need to create a new file, called a .htaccess file, and place it on your server. For instructions on how to do all that, see http://codex .wordpress.org/Using_Permalinks.

■ **Miscellaneous**   Here you can choose the folder for uploaded files to be stored in and you can make a few other choices that are important in special circumstances.

Add to Your Blogroll

For heavy customization of your blog, WordPress relies on you to dig into the themes and templates that are used for the blog's presentation, which is discussed later in this section. One easily customized section of your blog is the *blogroll*, which is simply a list of the blogs or other sites that you enjoy visiting and that you'd like to show to others who access your blog.

To edit your blogroll, click the Blogroll tab in the WordPress admin interface. There you'll see the Blogroll Management screen. Click the Add Links link in order to add your favorite blogs or sites to the blogroll. That brings up the Add Links page, shown in Figure 3-5.

To add a link to your blogroll, enter a name for the link in the Name entry box and then enter the blog's (or site's) URL in the Address entry box. You can also add a description for the site if desired; often the description will appear when users hovers their mouse pointer over the link on your site.

Before you click Add Link, however, you may want to make a few more choices. The Add Links page actually has a few options that add some complexity. (To view some of these options, you'll need to click the "X" on the right side of their titlebars). Those options include

■ **Categories**   You can categorize your links so that they can be displayed in different ways on your blog, if desired. Create a category by typing it into the Categories entry box and clicking Add. Then, place a checkmark next to that category if you want it associated with the link that you're creating. (Some templates recognize the categories and split your blogroll out to

FIGURE 3-5   The Add Link page enables you to add other sites to your blogroll.

show them separately; others don't. The WordPress Default template does, so if that's what you're using you'll find categories handy for organizing links to other sites.)

■ **Link Relationship**   The Link Relationship builder uses the XHTML Friends Network (XFN) protocol to represent the relationships you may have with the person who owns that site. Various social networking sites can use that information to learn more about the blogs to which you link.

■ **Target**   Choose "_blank" if you'd like this link to open in a new browser window; choose "_top" if you'd like to appear in the same browser window. (The top command is also useful because it will clear out any HTML frames that are in the current window, just in case your template design includes them.)

■ **Advanced**   Here you can enter a link to an image of the blogger or site owner (or some other representative image) and that site's RSS feed. You can also give the blog a rating (from 0-9), which can be used to sort the links on your blogroll. (If you give a link a 0 then it will be sorted randomly, which is cool if you don't want to "rank" blogs and have them appear in the same order all the time.)

TIP   *If you add images to your blogroll, you'll want them to be very small in resolution—something along the lines of 80 pixels by 80 pixels or so. In some templates, these images actually appear in your sidebar, so if they're larger, they may break the flow of your blog's pages.*

■ **Visible**   You can turn the link off here if you'd like it not to be visible on your site but you're not yet ready to delete it from the system.

Once you've entered information and made your choices of the various options, you can click Add Link to add the link to your blogroll. Once added, the link will appear on your blog's pages wherever blogroll links are placed by your template (usually in the sidebar).

To see your list of links and/or to edit or delete them, you can click the Manage Blogroll tab. There you can sort the links (especially if you have a lot of them) and select more than one of them to delete if necessary.

Create and Manage Pages

Another powerful feature in WordPress is the ability to manage special pages that have static content—content that doesn't make sense as part of the chronological organization of your blog posts—from within the interface itself. This can be handy for any number of purposes, such as an About page that gives information about you, a résumé page, pages that support your work (I, for instance, might have a page that linked to all my books, or pages for each book that list errata and further discussion), or pages that offer more complex lists of links, discussion points, articles, or poetry—stuff that the built-in Blogroll feature doesn't handle very elegantly. The other cool part is that in many WordPress templates, those pages are added automatically as links or tabs in the main interface, making it easy for your readers to get to them.

NOTE   *By default, WordPress already has an About page created. You can edit that page by clicking the Manage button and then clicking the Pages tab, as we'll see later in this section.*

To create a new page, click the Write button in the WordPress admin interface, and then click Write Page. You'll see a slightly different interface from the Write Post screen, as shown in Figure 3-6.

You edit the page using the same basic interface that is used for posts: Use the Visual tab to create the page in a WYSIWYG environment, or switch to the Code tab if you'd like to input HTML codes directly. At any point you can click Save and Continue editing just to make sure your changes are committed to a draft version (so you avoid losing changes if something happens to your Internet connection) or Save to save the page as a draft and not yet publish it.

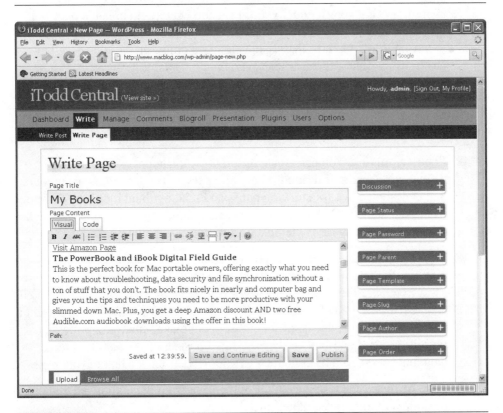

FIGURE 3-6   From within WordPress you can create a static page that shows content other than your blog entries.

Down the side of the interface you'll see a number of different options bars that have a "+" symbol for opening them. They include

■ **Discussion**   You can turn on and off comments, so that readers can comment on this page if you'd like them to.

■ **Page Status**   Once the page has been published, you can change its status here, or you can make a page Private so that only authorized users can see it.

■ **Page Password**   How do people view a private page? Via the password, which you can enter here.

■ **Page Parent**   Here you can determine whether or not this page has a "parent" within your hierarchy. For instance, you might create a page that lists a number of longer articles that you've written that you prefer not to have as blog posts. In that case, you might create an Articles page that has links to each of those articles, and then you could create individual article pages that have the Articles page as their parent. In many templates, links to those subpages will appear in the Sidebar underneath the parent page.

> **Pages**
> » About
> » My Books
>   » Blog On: Errata

■ **Page Template**   You can create different template pages that are used to display your pages, if desired. Many bloggers create a single new template that is designed just for showing pages and making them look a bit different from your standard blog entries. To select a template you've created, click this option and choose the template from the drop-down menu.

■ **Page Slug**   This is a special name given to the page that can be used with plug-ins. For instance, the Static Front Page plug-in can be used to give your site a front page that is one of the pages you create (the one with the slug "home") instead of a blog interface. That makes it possible for you to present a brochure-like front page (something that might make sense for a professional practice or a bed-and-breakfast or any small business that wants to offer a blog, but not *only* a blog), and then let your readers click a link to your blog.

■ **Page Author**   Choose the author of the page from the authorized authors who are part of this WordPress installation.

■ **Page Order**   Choose a numbered order for this page if there are subpages on its same level. For instance, on the main hierarchy, your About page might be 1, your Products page 2, your Contact page 3, and so on. This is used by templates that automatically order the page links that appear in your blog interface.

When you've made all of your selections and entered content for the page, click the Publish page. That will cause the page to go "live" on your site.

When you need to edit a page later, you can do so in one of two ways. If you're currently logged into your WordPress account, you will find an Edit link on any of the pages you've created as you view your own site. Clicking that link takes you immediately to the admin interface so that you can make edits to the page.

If you'd like to see all the pages you've created at once, click the Manage button in the WordPress admin interface and then click Pages. You'll see the Page Management screen, where you can choose to edit a particular page, or where you can delete a page quickly. You can also create a new page from that interface.

> **TIP** *You can make a WordPress page the home page of your site, if you'd like to present a non-blog page (instead of your blog index) when people first visit your site. In WordPress 2.1 and higher, go to Options | Reading and in the Front Page section, you can set the front page of your site to be a static page that you've created instead of the index page for your blog. Now, that's the page visitors will see when they enter http://www.yoursiteURL .com/ or http://www.yoursiteURL.com/index.php in a browser in order to reach your site.*

Tweak Your WordPress Theme

Your WordPress theme can either be changed wholesale or it can be tweaked using the WordPress Theme Editor. If you like the general look to your site, tweaking may do you some good; if you're looking to completely change the look and feel, then you'll need to go with a new theme. You do either of those things by first clicking the Presentation button in the WordPress admin interface. That puts you on the Themes tab, where you can choose different themes for your site (see Figure 3-7).

By default, WordPress gives you two themes to play with, the WordPress Kubrick theme (shown back in Figure 3-3) and the WordPress Classic theme, which is even duller. (OK, it's a fine template. And it's worth noting that the included themes tend to be very simple, fast-loading, standards-compliant, and work well with advanced WordPress features such as Sidebar Widgets, discussed later in the chapter.)

To add a new theme, you can surf the Internet to find an available WordPress theme; there are tons available, some for free and some requiring a payment. From the Themes tab, you can click over to the WordPress Theme Directory (scroll down to the Get More Themes section) to see what you can drum up directly from WordPress. Others are available for Themes.WordPress.net, or you can look for WordPress themes using a Google search or other search engine on the Web.

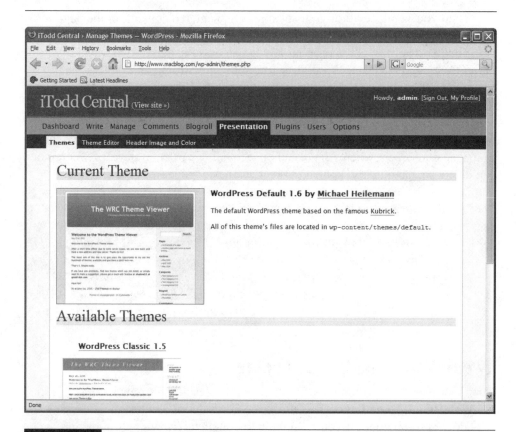

FIGURE 3-7   The Themes tab enables you to select a different theme for your blog.

NOTE   *You should make sure that the themes you download are expressly designed for the version of WordPress that you have installed. As of this writing, that's version 2.2; themes designed for earlier versions of WordPress may not work correctly.*

Generally a theme will be available for download in the form of a zip archive. To install that theme, you'll follow these general guidelines to install and select the theme:

1. Uncompress the archive, preserving the directory or folder structure that is stored in that archive. (Usually you can do this by double-clicking the archive on both Mac and PC systems.)

3

2. Using an FTP client, upload the theme to a new folder in the wp-content/ themes directory. If the archive decompressed with a single main folder holding all of the subfolders (for instance, it created a folder called cooltheme with a bunch of subfolders in it), you should be able to upload that folder cooltheme directly to the themes directory.

3. Open the Presentation screen. (If the Themes page is already open, just refresh it in your browser.) You should see the new theme appear under Available Themes, ready to select (see Figure 3-8).

4. Click the theme and the page will reload. You should then see the newly selected theme appear at the top of the page as the Current Theme. You'll also see a link at the top of the window that you can click to View your newly themed site.

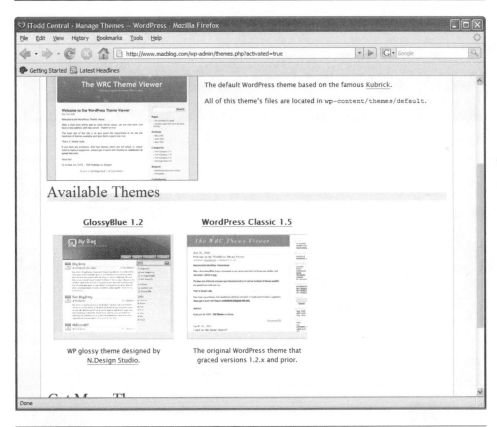

FIGURE 3-8   I've uploaded the GlossyBlue 1.2 theme and it's now available for me to use.

 *Check the theme's download files for an INSTALL or README file. Some themes have more complex requirements for installation. For instance, some require additional plug-ins to work correctly.*

Aside from simply switching between themes, WordPress also gives you the ability to dig in and edit the code that makes up any given theme. That gives you the freedom to change things that your HTML and CSS coding skills can give you. (If you don't have any skills, you can read Chapter 4 and develop some.) The Theme Editor is accessed on the Presentation tab by clicking Theme Viewer. On that page, you'll see a pull-down menu that enables you to choose the theme you want to edit. Along the right side, you'll see the different template files that can be edited; in the middle of the window, you'll see a text area that shows you to the raw template files and enables you to make changes (see Figure 3-9).

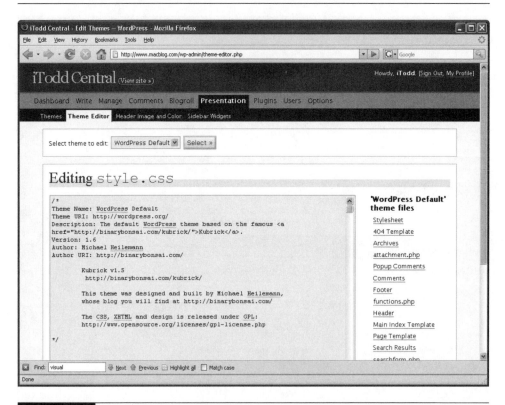

FIGURE 3-9 The Theme Editor enables you to make changes directly to your theme's template files.

As you can imagine, having access to the files at this level means you can do quite a bit of customization. One thing that's worth noting is the list of files down the side; WordPress uses some standard names for templates, including Header, Footer, Index, and Sidebar. These templates are designed to hold information that you might expect—the Header includes the top-bar image or title for your blog, and the Sidebar holds items that appear in the sidebar of your blog, such as the categories, archives, and links in your blogroll. So, if you'd like to re-order the items in your sidebar, or add static text to your sidebar, then editing the Sidebar template is the way to do that.

> **NOTE**   *If the template supports WordPress widgets, you can use those instead of editing your template directly. Widgets in WordPress work like they do in other popular blogging tools such as TypePad, enabling you to add sidebar content and link to popular Web 2.0 services from your blog.*

For example, a section of the sidebar for my site using the WordPress Default theme looks something like this in the Theme Editor:

```
<!-- Author information is disabled per default. Uncomment
and fill in your details if you want to use it.
                    <li><h2>Author</h2>
                    <p>A little something about you, the author.
Nothing lengthy, just an overview.</p>
                    </li>
-->
```

That paragraph of text between the `<p>` and `</p>` tags is something that I can edit and save to the sidebar so that my site is personalized and the "Author" section says something about me. I would then delete the HTML comment tags (`<!--` and `-->`, including the "comment" text), so that the entry looked like this:

```
                    <li><h2>The iTodd</h2>
                    <p>Todd Stauffer is the author or co-author
of over three dozen books on computing and technology. He's also
the publisher of the Jackson Free Press, Jackson, Mississippi's
free news and culture weekly.</p>
                    </li>
```

Click Update File and, the next time a blog page is loaded that includes that sidebar, the new "About" information will appear.

Of course, you can dig much deeper into the templates, although you'll notice that they are a combination of HTML markup and more complex PHP logic. That's because they're designed to be used over and over again for a variety of different types of pages, and alter themselves accordingly. In Chapter 4 you'll learn some basic information that can help you manipulate these themes.

> **NOTE** *If you can't edit your templates, you'll see a message in the Theme Editor that says:* If this file were writeable you could edit it. *The reason you see that message is because you don't have the correct permissions set for the files on your web server. Using your FTP application, you should be able to set the preferences for either the template's folder and all its contents, or for each individual template file you want to edit. To do so, log into your hosting account via FTP, then locate the template files (they should be in wp-content/themes/). Select the folder or files and look at the Information or Properties on those files, depending on the FTP application you're using. Do you see permissions settings? Yours should be 666 (read, write for all users). In some cases, you may need to set these permissions to 777 (all access for all groups), depending on your host.*

Add Plug-ins

WordPress has such an active following that when version 1.2 came out, the WordPress developers decided it was time to support plug-ins that could be contributed by developers in the WordPress fan base. A WordPress plug-in is simply a bit of code that extends the capabilities of WordPress. The basic underpinnings of WordPress are designed to take up as few resources as possible and to generate the site quickly for visitors—remember, unlike Blogger or TypePad, WordPress creates each page "on the fly" by accessing data in a MySQL database and placing it in the appropriate place based on the themes and templates it's supposed to work with. That's what makes it easy to switch themes, when necessary, but that approach can also make it take up more resources on your server computer.

So, a lot of whiz-bang functionality is left to plug-ins, which you're free to use or ignore on your blog. Getting to know the plug-ins can be a hobby all its own—there are hundreds of them, contributed by many different developers, and they're found in a variety of repositories or by entering "WordPress plug-in" in a search engine such as Google. You can also get the repository of plug-ins that WordPress itself is tracking by visiting http://wordpress.org/extend/plugins/ in your browser.

Once you've found a plug-in that you'd like to work with, the first thing to make sure of is that it's compatible with your version of WordPress. You should be able to learn that from the plug-in's documentation. (For this example, I'll install the ImageManager 2.0 plug-in by Per Søderlind at http://www.soderlind.no, a plug-in that adds functionality for uploading images to your blog entries and manipulating them.) Here are the steps:

1. Download the plug-in file. In most cases it will be a .zip archive.

2. Extract the plug-in's files (usually by double-clicking the .zip archive in Windows or in the Mac Finder). This should create a folder named for the plug-in.

> **TIP** *Before moving on to the next step, it's a good idea to look in that folder for a README file, just in case the plug-in has special instructions or requires another plug-in for full functionality. Some do.*

3. Using your FTP application, copy the folder from your hard disk to the wp-content/plugins/ folder on your web server.

4. Once the plug-in is uploaded, you can refresh the Plug-ins page in the WordPress admin interface. You should see the new plug-in appear.

5. Click the Activate link next to the plug-in's description to make it active and available for use on your blog (see Figure 3-10).

What happens next depends on how the plug-in is designed. In some cases, the plug-in may add a tab in your admin interface; in others, functionality is simply added to the Post or Page screen, or elsewhere in the admin interface. In some other cases, you'll add the plug-in code directly to your templates, according to the directions given by the plug-in's documentation. For instance, in the case of ImageManager, a tab is added under the Options screen in the WordPress admin interface, where you set some options for the tool (the defaults for formatting images) and make some choices regarding the way the plug-in works. Then, in the Write and Page interfaces, an ImageManager button is added to access the tool.

> **NOTE** *There's another tab on the Plugins page called Plugin Editor. If you're a programmer type, you can look at the source code of a plug-in and alter it, if necessary. You may also find that some plug-ins have key documentation as part of their code that might give you a clue as to how to use it if you're having trouble.*

> **TIP** *It's important to back up your WordPress database and installation since you're working from your own server computer. To do that, visit http://codex.wordpress.org/WordPress_Backups to learn step by step the recommended procedure. There's also a backup plug-in available for WordPress 2.1 and above at http://www.ilfilosofo.com/blog/wp-db-backup. Chapter 10 discusses backing up WordPress in more detail.*

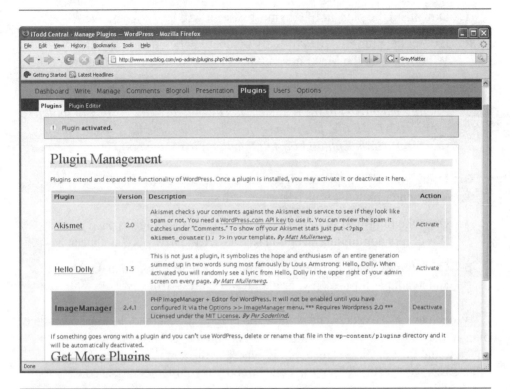

FIGURE 3-10 After uploading the plug-in's folder to my web hosting account, I see the new plug-in appear within the WordPress admin interface, where I can activate it.

Add Widgets

Growing in popularity among WordPress users are widgets, which are similar to plug-ins, but focused on adding functionality and connections to other Web 2.0 services. As of version 2.2 of WordPress, the ability to work with widgets is built into the installation and included templates; if you don't yet have version 2.2, you should upgrade in order to work with widgets.

NOTE *If you're not using one of the default templates, then you'll simply need to make sure that you're using a widget-ready template. As you surf for templates, you'll find that most of them let you know if they're widget-ready or not.*

> **TIP** *The WordPress Sidebar Widgets FAQ (http://wordpress.org/extend/plugins/ widgets/faq/) contains instructions (for power users and programmers) to modify non-compliant themes to work with widgets.*

Next, open the Plugins page in the WordPress admin interface, and then activate the Sidebar Widgets plug-in. The result will be a new link on the Presentations tab called Sidebar Widgets (see Figure 3-11).

By default you'll see some basic sidebar items on the Sidebar Widgets page, including items that you've already dealt with in the main WordPress interface, such as Categories, Pages, and Links. Drag them around to arrange your sidebar.

Widgets that can be configured from within the Sidebar Widgets interface have a small icon floating on the right-hand side of the widget's box. Click that icon and you'll see the options that you have for configuring the item.

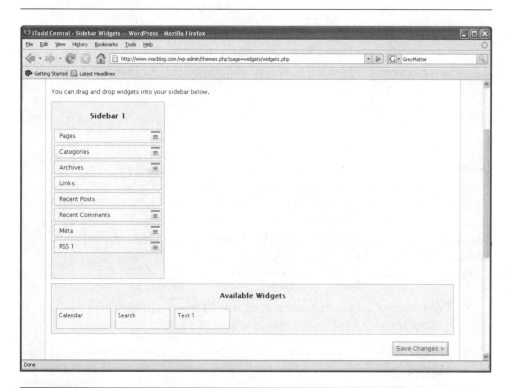

FIGURE 3-11   The SideBar Widgets page enables you to drag and drop widgets onto your sidebar (I've already dragged in a couple for this image).

Notice also on that page that, when you scroll down past the widgets, you're given the option to select multiple text and/or RSS widgets. You can then configure those items accordingly. For instance, a Text widget can accept text, links (in HTML format), or even image tags, if desired. The result is a simple box for text or markup that can be used for pretty much whatever you want. Shown here is a text box that I marked up as an "About" on my blog.

About the iTodd

Todd Stauffer is the author or co-author of more than three dozen books on technology, blogging, Web design and the Macintosh. He's also a freelance writer, a radio host and the publisher of the Jackson Free Press, the alternative newsweekly for Jackson, Miss.

To add new and exciting widgets to your blog, you'll need to download those and add them to your Widgets folder. (You can actually store them anywhere in the Plugins folder but, unless the widget's instructions tell you otherwise, the Widgets folder is a handy place to put them.) You'll then find them in the Plugin Management interface, where you can activate them. Once activated, they'll be active on the Sidebar Management page, where you'll be able to arrange them and configure them just as you do other widgets.

NOTE   *As we talk about other Web 2.0 features in subsequent chapters, I'll try to point out when there's a known WordPress widget for that service. Most of the popular image sharing, bookmarking, and other social sites have at least one widget for integrating with WordPress.*

Manage Users

One last thing to discuss regarding WordPress is its user management features. WordPress enables you to define different roles for people who are registered to log into your blog. If you require registration for commenting, then, by default, those users are Subscribers. (You can change that on the Options | General page.) Subscribers can post comments to your blog (if you require registration) and can read items (if you've marked your blog as private).

Other levels of users include the following:

■ **Contributor**   A Contributor can upload files and edit existing posts as well as comment and read a blog if it's private.

■ **Author**   An Author can upload files, edit posts, create new posts, and read a private blog.

- ■ **Editor**   An Editor can moderate comments, manage categories, manage blogroll links, upload files, post in HTML, edit posts, create posts, edit other author's posts, create and publish Pages, and edit Pages.
- ■ **Administrator**   An Administrator can do anything an Editor can do, plus switch and edit themes, activate plug-ins, edit plug-ins, edit users, manage options, and import files.

3

NOTE   *The Owner account you created when you installed WordPress is a super-user account that has access to all Administrator functions. You might consider creating a second account for yourself in some cases, so that you're not always logged into the Owner account.*

To manage existing users or create new users, click the Users button in the WordPress admin interface. On the Authors and Users tab, you can click Edit on a user's line to see their detail and change their role, if desired.

To create a new user, scroll down to Add New User and enter at least the required information. Then, choose a role for that user and click the Add User button. That person can now log in with the username and password that you assigned them and, depending on the role, they can perform tasks on your blog.

NOTE   *Do you see a Register link on the front page of your blog? (By default, it shows up in the Meta sidebar item.) If you don't, then you may have the option Anyone Can Register turned off on the Options | General page. When that option is disabled, then no one new to your blog can register. That can be a problem if you happen to have Users Must Be Registered and Logged In To Comment turned on, as it means no one new will be able to comment!*

ExpressionEngine

ExpressionEngine is almost the antithesis of a blogging tool such as WordPress. With a relatively smaller base of users, ExpressionEngine is proprietary, developed by EllisLab, Inc., with the feature-rich versions offered for somewhat pricey commercial licenses. (Personal and non-profit sites can get away with cheaper licenses.) Although ExpressionEngine has an architecture that allows for plug-ins and even full-blown modules for adding features and functionality, the developer base is rather small, so there are fewer add-ons than with WordPress.

NOTE *While they aren't covered in this book, Wheatblog (wheatblog.sourceforge .net) and TextPattern (www.textpattern.org) are both simple-yet-powerful blogging platforms, and there are tons of others, such as "portals" that make user forums front-and-center (PHP Nuke at www.phpnuke.org and GeekLog at www.geeklog.net). Drupal (www.drupal.org) stands out as a blogging tool that also works in many different ways as a community platform for all sorts of sites, from basic blogs to newspapers and social networking sites. (And even ExpressionEngine's older sibling, pMachine Pro—http://www.pmachinepro.com/—is still a strong value for blogging and community building, although it's no longer actively developed.) In fact, there are hundreds of blogging tools and content management systems. Visit www.cmsmatrix.org for a sampling.*

What ExpressionEngine is, however, is a blogging tool that's focused squarely on the needs of Web designers. With its emphasis on utterly malleable templates, someone with knowledge of HTML can design a blog that looks completely unlike any other. Not limited to "sidebars" and standardized two-or-three-column layouts, ExpressionEngine is used for sites as diverse as personal blogs, photoblogs, business sites, charitable organizations, newspaper sites (like mine), and community portals. And because it's developed for commercial purposes, it has a small team of developers that march out new features for ExpressionEngine on a fairly regular basis.

And, having said all that about the commercial nature of ExpressionEngine, it's worth noting that there's actually a free version, too. ExpressionEngine Core offers fewer of the bells-and-whistles of the commercial version, but it can be used for a basic personal blog and website. If you have any experience with HTML and Web design, you might at least consider giving ExpressionEngine a spin for your blog.

Like WordPress, ExpressionEngine uses PHP for its scripting language and MySQL as its database, so you can install it on the vast majority of web hosting accounts. The home site for ExpressionEngine is www.expressionengine.com.

NOTE   *While there isn't quite a "hosted edition" of ExpressionEngine the same way there is of WordPress, EllisLab does have a related hosting service called EngineHosting (www.enginehosting.com), where you can have ExpressionEngine pre-installed.*

ExpressionEngine Pros and Cons

ExpressionEngine builds on EllisLab's experience with its original blogging platform, pMachine Pro. The original was great software, too, built for something a little beyond blogging—call it a community management site. With support for multiple blogs, newsletters, forums, and other features, pMachine Pro is a very full-featured application that, for instance, made www.jacksonfreepress.com run for nearly five years.

ExpressionEngine offers many of the same advantages, but it was re-written as a completely new product in 2004 apparently because of dissatisfaction that pMachine Pro's creator, Rick Ellis, had with the way that pMachine Pro had been coded. ExpressionEngine is designed to be considerably more modular in its approach, supporting entire functionality in modules that can be installed or uninstalled individually. As an example, EllisLab sells a separate module for ExpressionEngine, the Forums module, that is similar to full-fledged forums applications such as phpBB (www.phpBB.org) or the popular VBulletin (www.vbulletin.com) software.

Here's a look at some of the strengths ExpressionEngine offers:

- **Modular Approach**   ExpressionEngine supports add-on modules that offer a suite of features (a wiki module, forums module, a photo gallery module, a simple commerce module) as well as plug-ins that offer basic functionality and improvements.

- **Support for Multiple Blogs**   Unlike WordPress, you can create many different blogs within the same ExpressionEngine installation. You can have blogs on different topics, blogs run by different authors or even a mix of community blogs to which anyone can add a post and private blogs in which only you or your trusted editors can post. For community sites, online newspapers and magazines, and similar sites, that means you can have a news blog, a music blog, an events blog, a community blog, a sports blog, and so on.

- **Flexible Templating System**   With ExpressionEngine you build your own templates using tags that access blog content and HTML for the design and markup of your pages. So, for instance, if you'd like a single page to show headlines from three different blogs, you simply design the columns and rows of the page and use a special ExpressionEngine tag in each section to display the headlines from each blog. Likewise, the templating system can be used to integrate "static" content with blog content in such a way that you can build an entire site—About pages, product pages, even a shopping cart using the Simple Commerce module—from within the ExpressionEngine admin interface.

- **RSS Builder**   Using a combination of blogs and categories, you can build your own RSS feeds, enabling you to serve more than simply your blog's front page contents to subscribers.

- ■ **Image Manipulation**   ExpressionEngine enables you to resize images and create thumbnails as you upload them; the commercial version also includes a photo gallery module that allows you to build online photo galleries complete with descriptions, user comments, and even an image toolbox for cropping and editing images as you upload them.

- ■ **Advanced Membership Features**   The commercial version of ExpressionEngine includes the ability to send an e-mail to your members (or sub-groups of members), and it includes features for enabling members to communicate with one another. Members have their own profile pages, can subscribe to certain blog entries (receiving an e-mail when a new comment is added), and even have a small notepad for jotting down notes.

- ■ **Mailing List**   The commercial version of ExpressionEngine includes a Mailing List Manager that enables you to offer a double opt-in mailing list to people who visit your site.

- ■ **Stats Features**   With ExpressionEngine you can learn stats about your blog such as how many visitors and registered users are on at one time, what pages are being viewed most often, and what the most popular posts are. Again, for designing your own magazine-style or community-focused site, those features can come in very handy.

If you don't have much web design experience, you should be aware that there are fewer themes and templates pre-built for ExpressionEngine than for any of the other tools that we've discussed. (And those that come with ExpressionEngine are, in my mind, a little wanting.) While you can find a few sites via search engines that offer ExpressionEngine templates for downloading, there's a sort of built-in assumption that you want to customize your site if you're using ExpressionEngine.

Also, as mentioned, for all the features that ExpressionEngine offers, you'll need to pay for a license. That also means that a fair bit of the ExpressionEngine community is "commerce-minded" so, where you'll often find plug-ins or extensions in the WordPress community available as open source, in the ExpressionEngine community, I've often found that solutions are sold for a few dollars. That may not be bad—people who make money from their efforts tend to keep at them. But, popular open source projects often seem to draw many more contributors. With ExpressionEngine, there is only a small community of developers working on modules and plug-ins, and while some of their solutions are good (and, yes, some of them are free, too), other requested options and solutions for ExpressionEngine often have to wait for an update from the "mothership."

TIP   *It's always a good idea to visit the forums or other resources for a tool before committing to it, particularly if you're going to pay something. EllisLab offers forums that discuss ExpressionEngine at http://www. expressionengine.com/forums/ that include an area for "pre-sales" questions if you wonder whether or not ExpressionEngine can handle a particular site you're interested in building.*

Get and Install ExpressionEngine

You can always start with the Core version of ExpressionEngine—it's a free download and it'll give you a taste of how ExpressionEngine works. To download Core, visit http://www.expressionengine.com/ and click the Download link. You'll see a free downloads area; choose the Download link next to ExpressionEngine Core. After reading the License Agreement, click the Accept License and Download button. That should cause the ExpressionEngine .Zip file to be downloaded to your machine. Expand that .Zip file to create the ExpressionEngine directory.

To set up ExpressionEngine, you'll need to know the name of your MySQL database, the server address for the database (often, but not always "localhost"), as well as the username and password for the MySQL database. You should then visit http://expressionengine.com/docs/installation/installation.html to view the installation instructions for ExpressionEngine, as they can be a bit complicated and there are some specific recommendations. Here are the basic steps:

1. Gather your database data.

2. By default, ExpressionEngine has a folder called system, which is where ExpressionEngine stores most of the application scripts and where the administrative control panel is accessed. (Once you've installed ExpressionEngine on your Web host, you would access the control panel at http://www.yoursiteURL.com/system/ in a Web browser.) For security reasons, it's recommended that you rename that system folder. (If you call it something else, it's more difficult for someone on the Internet to guess.)

3. Upload the ExpressionEngine files to your hosting account. Note that some key update files don't need to be uploaded if this is your first time installing ExpressionEngine. (See the instructions for details.)

4. Set permissions. You'll need to set different permissions levels for a variety of the folders within the ExpressionEngine installation; this is so that various folders can be uploaded and a few different files can be altered as necessary.

5. Next, if you've opted to download an ExpressionEngine theme from the Template Library or elsewhere, you can copy that theme into the themes/ site_themes folder on your server.

6. Now, open a web browser and point it to the install.php file on your site (e.g., http://www.yoursiteURL.com/install.php). You'll see the installation wizard, as shown in Figure 3-12.

7. Once you get started with the wizard, you'll approve the License Agreement, then you'll enter the name you gave your system folder, if you opted to change it, then click Submit.

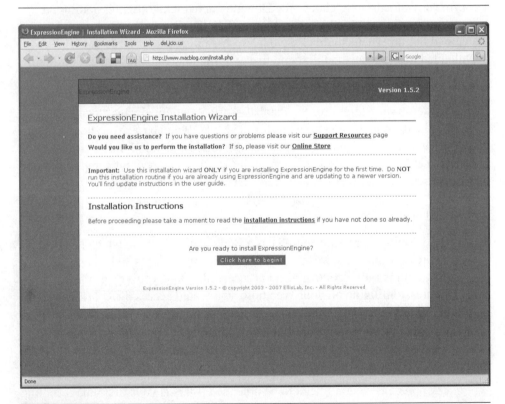

FIGURE 3-12　The ExpressionEngine installation wizard walks you through the installation process.

8. Next, you'll enter your database details, create a new account for yourself, and choose the template that you'd like to use for your site. When you've got all that information entered, the next step is the installation. If all goes well, you'll see a confirmation message from the installation wizard and links to both your control panel and your main site. Click the control panel link and you can log into your site's admin interface; click the main site link and you'll see your new site, as shown in Figure 3-13.

Publish Your First Post with ExpressionEngine

To create your first post, you'll first need to log into the admin interface. (Recall that ExpressionEngine encourages you to change the name of your system folder, so substitute whatever name you used when I mention the system folder.) To log into

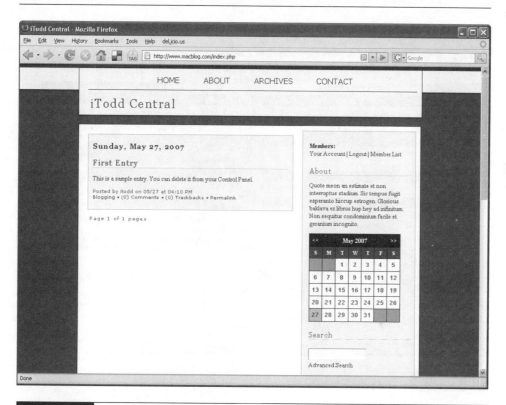

FIGURE 3-13   Here's the beginning of the site I've created, using the default template.

the admin interface, point your browser to http://www.yoururl.com/system/ and, when the login screen appears, enter the administrative user name and password you created during installation. That should get you to the administrative interface (ExpressionEngine calls it the Control Panel), which is shown in Figure 3-14.

The Control Panel includes tabs across the top that you use for managing your blog; you'll also see a News Feed section (these are headlines from the EllisLab blog), a Most Recent Weblog Entries section, Most Recent Comments section, and some other statistics about your blog.

To create a new blog post, click the Publish tab. You'll see the interface change to the Publish Form screen (see Figure 3-15).

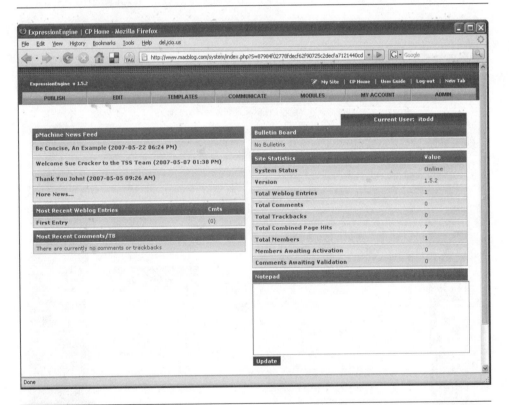

FIGURE 3-14 The Control Panel interface for ExpressionEngine

Entry option tabs

File upload button

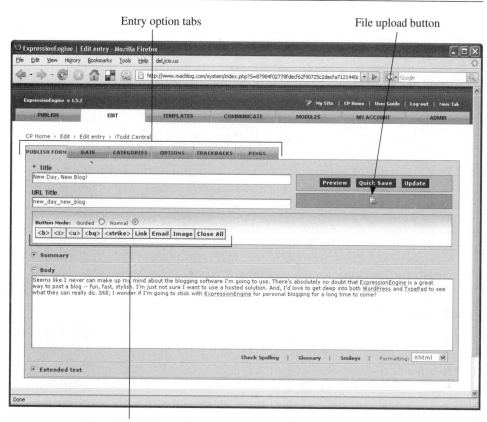

Formatting buttons

FIGURE 3-15 The Publish Form interface is where you'll create new entries.

Here's the process you can go through to create your entry:

1. Enter a Title for your post in the Title text area. You'll notice that the URL Title entry box is filled in as well.

2. In the URL Title entry box, you can edit the URL that will be used for this entry. (By default, ExpressionEngine uses URLs in the format of http://www.yoursite.com/index.php/template/title_of_the_entry/ in order to create permalinks for your blog entries.

3. In the Body area of your post, you can enter the beginning of your post. If you would like the entire entry to appear on the main page of your blog, then enter the entire entry in this area.

4. As with other blog entry interfaces, you can highlight text and then choose the <b> button to make that text bold, <i> for italics, <u> for underlined, <bq> for a block quote, and <strike> for strikeout text. ExpressionEngine will automatically add both the opening and closing HTML tags for each of those formatting options around the text that you highlight.

> TIP
>
> *If you'd like this blog entry to "jump" to a full page, so that some text appears on the main blog screen and some appears when readers click a Read More link, then click the small "+" icon next to Extended Text and type the rest of your entry in the Extended Text box. That way, text in the Body portion will appear on the main page of your blog while text in the Extended Text area will only appear when they click Read More, Comments, or a permalink URL to that blog entry.*

Create a Hyperlink

To create a link, highlight text and then click the Link button. A dialog box appears that allows you to enter a URL; enter that URL for the link and click OK, then enter (or alter, if desired) the text for the link. You can also enter an optional title for the link, which is used (in some browsers) when readers mouse over the link when reading your blog. (It's used in others for special access browsers, such as those that read links to the visually impaired.) When you're finished, click OK and the link is added to your entry.

Add an Image

To add an image to the entry, you have two choices. If you already know the URL to the image, simply click to place the cursor in the entry where you want the image to appear, and then click the Image button. You'll see a dialog box that enables you to enter the URL for that image. Do so and click OK. The image tag is added to your blog entry.

To upload an image from your PC's hard disk, click the File Upload button. When you do, you'll see a new window that enables you to locate the image you want to upload by clicking the Browse button. Once you've located an image, choose the destination directory for the image and then click the Upload button.

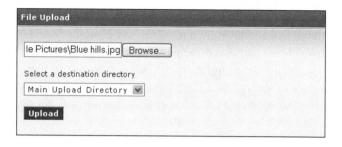

You can also browse your website's existing files by clicking the View button in the File Browser section. That enables you to select a file that you've already uploaded to your web hosting account, instead of choosing one from your hard disk.

You'll then see the Image Upload screen, where you can choose to resize the image, if desired and you can choose how and where the image should be placed in your entry in the Select Your Placement Options section:

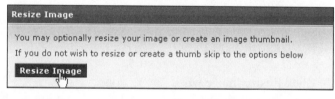

To resize the image, click the Resize Image button. That brings up another window, where you can choose the size that you would like the uploaded image to be. Enter the pixel dimensions for the image, noting that if Constrain Proportions is selected, you can only change the width or the height of the image; the other setting will change so that it remains proportionate to the original.

Resize Image

You may optionally resize your image or create an image thumbnail. Close this window to cancel.

Image Settings

Width 218 | Pixels
Height 59 | Pixels

☑ Constrain Proportions

⦿ Create a separate copy
◯ Resize the original image

Resize Image

Next, choose Create a Separate Copy of the image (in other words, you're creating a thumbnail image that can be used in your blog entry and, when clicked, will show the image in its original dimensions) or choose Resize the Original Image if you'd like ExpressionEngine to upload only an image that is the size of the new dimension you've chosen. (That way the new, small image can be used as the main image in your blog entry, but ExpressionEngine will not upload a second, larger image to your web hosting account.)

> NOTE
>
> *Unfortunately, the wording used in this dialog box isn't terribly clear. Just remember that if you choose to Create a Separate Copy, then ExpressionEngine will upload two images—one that is the original dimensions of the image that you're uploading and one that is the resized dimensions that you've chosen. In other words, the resized image is a* thumbnail *version of the original. If you choose to Resize the Original Image, then only one image will be uploaded. Also remember that you will usually only get good results by making an image* smaller *than its original dimensions when you resize it; if you choose large dimensions for the image, it may become* pixelated *(which means it's blocky looking instead of crisp and focused) when it's resized.*

Click Resize Image when you're done.

Now you can choose how the image is placed in your blog entry. If the image is not a thumbnail image, choose Embedded in Entry (which means the image will appear in the entry itself) or URL Only (which means a link to the image will appear in your blog entry.)

If the image you create *is* a thumbnail (meaning you chose Create a Separate Copy in the Resize Image window), then you can choose Pop-up Image Link.

That will make the image in the blog entry a hyperlink; when clicked, the original image will appear in its own window.

Finally, choose where you'd like the image to appear in your blog post from the Image Location menu. Generally, you'll choose the Body or Extended Text portion of the entry. With that choice made, click the Place Image and Close Window button to place the image's HTML coding (`<img src="..." />`) in your blog entry.

3

☐ Body

Seems like I never can make up my mind about the blogging software I'm going to use. There's absolutely no doubt that ExpressionEngine is a great way to post a blog -- fun, fast, stylish. I'm just not sure I want to use a hosted solution. And, I'd love to get deep into both WordPress and TypePad to see what they can really do. Still, I wonder if I'm going to stick with ExpressionEngine for personal blogging for a long time to come? `<img src="{filedir_1}macbreak_thumb.png" style="border: 0;" alt="image" width="200" height="123" />`

When the link is added to your blog entry, it is always added at the bottom of any text that appears in the entry box. You may need to cut and paste that `<img src="..." />` tag to place the image at the beginning of your entry or elsewhere within the post.

TIP   *You can add the attribute `align="left"` or `align="right"` to an image tag in order to cause the image to align to the left of the text or to the right of the text, thus having the text flow around the image. For instance, `<img src="{filedir_1}Blue_hills.jpg" style="border: 0;" alt="image" width="300" height="225" align="left" />` will cause the uploaded image to align to the left side of the blog entry, with text flowing around the right side of that entry. See Chapter 4 for more details on image tag attributes.*

Check Spelling

To check the spelling in your entry, click the Check Spelling link at the bottom of the entry box. After a moment, a new Spell Check text area will appear beneath the entry box where words are underlined in red that ExpressionEngine believes are misspelled. To change to a suggested spelling, click the underlined word and select a new word from the menu that appears; you can also choose Edit Word from that menu to edit the misspelled word. When you've made changes, click the Save Changes link to close the Spell Check text area. (If you don't make any changes, you can click Revert to Original to close the Spell Check text area.)

Glossary

Click the Glossary link to see a quick listing of basic HTML commands that you can add to your entry. The Glossary also includes a list of special characters such as "curly" quotation marks and an ampersand (&) or Trademark symbol (^{TM}) to your entry. To use one of the HTML commands or special characters, just click it in the glossary and its code is added to the entry box. Click the Glossary link again to close it.

Smileys

To add a "smiley" (also sometimes called an *emoticon*) to your entry, click the Smileys link. You'll see a window of possible smileys that you can add to your entry to add a little fun or express an emotion graphically. Click the smiley you want to add and a code for that smiley will appear in your entry. (In this example, the code `:coolsmile:` adds a little smiley face that wears cool sunshades to the final entry.)

```
☐ Body
<img src="{filedir_1}macbreak_thumb.png" style="border: 0;" alt="image" width="200" height="123" align="right"
/> Seems like I never can make up my mind about the blogging software I'm going to use. There's absolutely
no doubt that ExpressionEngine is a great way to post a blog -- fun, fast, stylish. I'm just not sure I want to use a
hosted solution. And, I'd love to get deep into both WordPress and TypePad to see what they can really do. Still, I
wonder if I'm going to stick with ExpressionEngine for personal blogging for a long time to come? :coolsmile:
```

NOTE   *Adding smileys to your text can sometimes mess up the "flow" of the entry, adding extra space to the line of text that includes the smiley. You may have to alter your template somewhat to make smileys work well— see Chapter 4 for more details on formatting images and style sheets.*

TIP   *Not a fan of smileys? You can turn the smileys off, if desired, so that only the punctuation shows up when you or a user types something like :-).
To do that in the Control Panel, choose the Admin tab, then select System Preferences | Emoticon Preferences. On the Emoticon Preferences screen, turn off the Display Smileys option and click Update.*

Choose the Date

Next to the Publish Form tab is the Date tab, where you can choose the date for your entry. By default, the current date and time are entered based on when you choose to publish the entry. You can change the date in the Entry Date section to a past date if you'd like to "back date" the entry for some reason; you can also change it to a future date if you'd like the entry to appear on your blog site on that future date. By default, the entry will be invisible until that date and time come to pass.

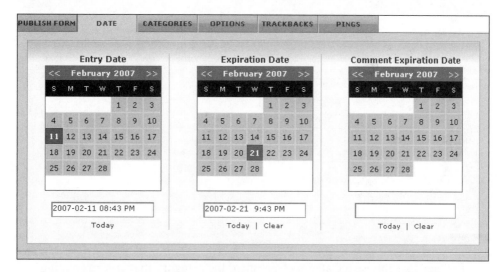

You can also choose an Expiration Date for the entry, if you'd like it to automatically disappear from your blog at a certain date and time. And, you can choose a Comment Expiration Date if you'd like the comments to disappear from an entry after a certain date and time. (If you choose a Comment Expiration Date but not an Expiration Date for the post, then the post will remain in your archives even after the comments are removed from the entry.)

Choose Categories

Your ExpressionEngine blog entries can be placed in multiple categories for organization on your site. To choose categories for the entry, click the Categories tab. You'll see the Categories list; click to add a category for the entry. For multiple categories, hold down the CTRL key in Windows or the CMD key on a Mac while clicking the additional categories you'd like to have this entry assigned to.

If you don't see a category that fits, you can add one by clicking the Edit Categories link. That brings up the Default Category Group window. To create a new Category, click the Create a New Category button. In the Create a New Category window that appears, enter a name for the category in the Category Name entry box (which is required) and then, if you'd like, enter a description for that category. (In many web browsers, this description will appear when your reader mouses over the category on your blog page.) You can also add a Category Image URL if you'd like this category to be associated with an image.

You can also choose a Category Parent for the category that you're creating. This enables you to create a hierarchy. For instance, if you have a category called Technology, you might use it as the parent for a few different categories, such as Apple, Gadgets, Windows, and so on. That way, your readers can either view all of your entries that are related to technology generally, or they can choose to see only the entries on a given subcategory within the Technology category.

When you've made your choices for the new category, click the Submit button. That returns you to the Default Category Group page. You can then elect to create more categories (click Create a New Category again) or click Close Windows and Update Categories in Publish Page to return to the Publish page interface with access to the new categories.

Back in the Publish page, on the Categories tab, you can finish making selections for the categories with which this post will be associated.

Choose Options

Click the Options tab and you can choose the author for the entry, the blog (remember, ExpressionEngine can support multiple blogs once those new blogs are created), and the status of the entry (whether it's Open, meaning it appears online to readers, or Closed, meaning it's saved to your database but does not appear to readers). Other options include

■ **Make Entry Sticky**   This causes the entry to appear at the top of the list of blog entries on your main page, even if newer entries are added. (The regular behavior is for this entry to scroll down the list according to its date and time.)

■ **Allow Comments**   This is turned on by default, but you can turn it off if you don't want readers to be able to comment on the entry.

■ **Allow Trackbacks**   Again, this is turned on by default, but you can turn it off if you don't want trackbacks to appear below the entry's text on its permalink page.

■ **DST Active on Date of Entry**   ExpressionEngine generally turns this on automatically if the post date that you've chosen falls during a time when your local time zone would be recognizing Daylight Savings Time. You should only need to change this entry if you change the date of the entry to a different part of the year. For instance, if you create the post during the summer (when Daylight Savings Time might be observed in your locale) and then change its Entry Date to the late fall or winter, then you might need to turn this option off.

Enter a TrackBack

If the blog entry that you're creating should send a trackback ping to another site (because you're commenting on someone else's blog entry using your own blog and you want them to know about it using their trackback feature) then click the Trackback tab and enter the other blog entry's trackback URL in the Trackback URLs to Ping entry box. (For instance, if you wanted to comment from your ExpressionEngine blog on the blog entry called "I Love Cheese" at my blog at http://www.toddstauffer.com/, then you'd enter the Trackback URL **http://www .toddstauffer.com/2007/02/05/i-love-cheese/trackback/** in this box. That would cause a link to your entry to appear on *my* blog entry, letting people know that you'd commented on the story using your own blog.)

Pings

Click the Pings tab if you'd like to turn on ExpressionEngine's ability to let some of the Internet's blog notification sites know that you've made a new entry. By default, they're turned off. Click to place a checkmark next to the sites that you'd like to notify of your new entry. (See Chapter 7 for more discussion on ping servers.)

Preview and Quick Save

Want to get a sense of what your entry will look like? Click the Preview button in the main portion of the Publish window. That shows you the entry, including formatting, images, and anything else you've added to the markup.

The Quick Save button is just like the Preview button, except your changes are saved to the database at the same time that the preview of your entry is generated. This can be a good idea if you've been working on an entry for a while, as ExpressionEngine doesn't otherwise autosave documents. If something happens to your Internet connection while you're editing an entry, you could lose changes if you don't Quick Save frequently.

Submit

When you've made all the choices available to you and you're ready to publish your entry, click the Submit button. That makes your entry live (if you've selected Open in the Status menu on the Options tab) and available on your blog.

TIP   *Want to view your blog after you've published an entry? In the Control Panel, you'll find a link called My Site. Click that link to view your blog or right-click the link (in Windows or Mac OS X with a two-button mouse; if you have a one-button mouse in Mac OS X, you can* CONTROL-*click) and choose Open in a New Window in your browser.*

Manage and Edit Posts in ExpressionEngine

Once you've created a post or multiple posts in ExpressionEngine, you can manage them and edit them using the Edit tab in the Control Panel. Click Edit and you'll see a list of the posts that you've entered in ExpressionEngine, as shown in Figure 13-16.

Here are some of the things you can do on the Edit tab:

- *Filter the list.* Using the pop-up menus that appear under Edit Weblog Entries, you can filter your list of entries by a number of criteria, including the weblog for the entries, the category, the status of the entry, and/or a range of dates. You can also choose the order of the listing and how many entries should appear in the list. Some of this won't matter until you have many new entries; a combination of these options can be used to quickly find an entry that you want to look at.

- *Edit an entry.* Click the entry's title to edit that entry. You'll have the same tools available to you as when you first posted the entry. When you're done editing, click the Update button to update the entry with any changes you've made.

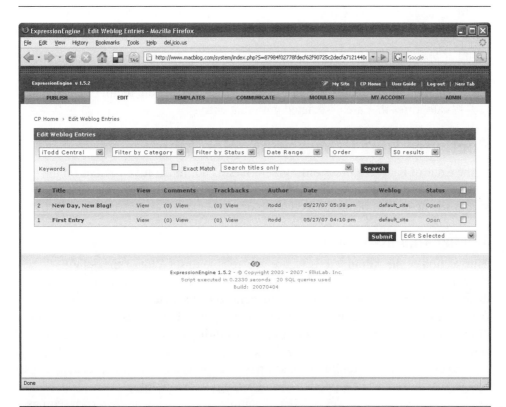

FIGURE 3-16 The Edit tab is used to edit and manage existing entries.

◼ *View an entry.* To see a particular entry, click the View link in its listing.

◼ *View comments or trackbacks for an entry.* Click the View link under Comments or Trackbacks for an entry and you can not only see all the comments on an entry, but you can click a comment to read and/or edit it, or you can place a checkmark next to the comment (or multiple comments) and then choose to close or delete the comment(s) by choosing that command from the Action menu and clicking the Submit button.

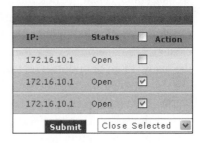

- *Email the author.* Click the link to the Authors name in the comment section and you can e-mail that author.

- *Change the status of the post.* Again, you can click to place a checkmark next to an entry on the Edit tab, and then use the pop-up action menu at the bottom of the list to edit the selected entries, delete them, or change the categories that are associated with that entry.

Configure Your ExpressionEngine Blog

In the Control Panel, ExpressionEngine offers its administrative options on the Admin tab. Click that tab and you'll see a number of different options that enable you to set the default behavior for your blog.

Weblog Administration

This section of the Admin tab is where you're able to set a lot of the default behaviors for your blog. Topics covered include the settings for each blog that you create (if you have more than one), management of the categories that you create for your blog entries, creating custom fields for your blog entries, preferences for uploaded files, custom HTML buttons for the editing interface, and some global settings you can make for your blogging experience.

As you see from the multitude of settings and options, ExpressionEngine is designed with the idea of supported complex blogs with multiple authors. And, when you begin to realize the power of having multiple blogs, each with their own settings, you can see how it's possible, for instance, to create a "community blog" on your site where certain authors (or maybe all registered users) are able to add posts or otherwise participate. ExpressionEngine, in this sense, is good for the different types of blogs I've mentioned: one-to-many, few-to-many, and even many-to-many blogs.

Here's a quick look at some of the options.

Weblog Management   Click this link and you'll see a list of the blogs you've created. (At the point, you'll likely only have one.) You can create another blog by clicking the Create a New Weblog button and then walking through the steps discussed. To edit an existing blog's settings, click the Edit Preferences link. Now you'll see another list of the many different options you can set for this particular weblog, including:

- **General Weblog Preferences**   Here you can edit the name of the weblog, the short name that you'll find in the Publish interface, a description for the blog, the language used and the character encoding preference.

- **Path Settings**   These are the URLs for the various pages associated with this blog.

■ **Administrative Preferences**   You can set the default status for posts that are created in this blog, the default category, and the default settings for options in the Publish interface such as whether or not comments and trackbacks are turned on by default when a new entry is created.

■ **Weblog Posting Preferences**   These are some basic settings about the actual weblog entries in this weblog—do you allow HTML in entries, are image URLs allowed, and are links automatically made clickable?

■ **Versioning Preferences**   If you turn on versioning for this weblog, then a certain number of versions of each post will be saved, so that you can see what changes are made and revert to an older version of a post if necessary.

■ **Notification Preferences**   Here you can turn on notification e-mails that you or others receive whenever a new post is added to a particular blog (this is handy if you have multiple authors and want to know when additions are made) and whether or not you or others receive e-mails when there are new comments or trackbacks posted to this blog.

■ **Comment Posting Preferences**   Here you can determine whether comments are allowed on any post in this blog, whether someone must be a member in order to post a comment, whether CAPTCHAs should be used for comment posts, whether e-mails are required (which is only necessary if you don't require membership for posting comments), whether you want to moderate comments, the maximum number of characters that are allowed in a comment, and a number of other options and limits that you can impose on comments, including whether users must wait a certain interval (in seconds) between posting comments (which can be used to discourage spam) and what sort of HTML and formatting are allowed in comments.

■ **Trackback Preferences**   Here you can set the default preferences for trackbacks for this particular weblog.

■ **Publish Page Customization**   Using these options, you can turn on and off the different options that are available to your blog authors for this particular weblog.

Category Management   ExpressionEngine organizes categories into category groups, which can then be used by one or more weblogs. When you first get started, there's one group, the Default Category Group, which you can add to by clicking the Add/Edit Categories link for that group from within the Category Management screen. On the Add/Edit Categories screen you can manage your categories much as you saw when setting categories in the section "Choose

Categories" earlier in this chapter. You can also use the Category Management screen to re-order the categories to make them easier to choose when you're creating new blog entries.

Custom Weblog Fields   ExpressionEngine gives you the ability to create new weblog fields that can be edited during the Publish process. These fields can then be used in templates to filter your weblog entries or to present different types of information in different types of blogs. (For instance, you could create a Venue field for a blog that's dedicated to entries that are about upcoming events in your area; you would then craft a template that would show that venue information as part of the blog's entry output.)

Custom Entry Statuses   Again, this option is handy for complex blog workflows. If you have multiple authors for your blog, you might create a status other than Open and Closed—perhaps one called Submitted for Editing, so that an editor could come along and copyedit the post or make changes before the post goes "live" on the site.

Custom statuses, by design, do not show up immediately on the blog; they have to be set to Open before they will appear on the site. But you can specify that a certain user with authoring privileges can only submit an entry in a certain status (such as the Submitted for Editing suggestion above) so that they can't ever send a blog post straight through to the public without it being seen by you or another "higher level" editor or administrator.

Custom statuses can also be assigned a color so that they show up better on the Edit tab.

File Upload Preferences   Here you can create new upload destinations, or edit those that you have. For the Main Upload Directory, you can click Edit Preferences to see all of the different preferences that you can set for the directory, including a description; the exact server path for the directory; the URL for the directory; the allowed file types; and a number of formatting options for images and files that are uploaded, including changing the default attributes for image tags. (More on those in Chapter 4.)

In this section you can also determine which member groups (covered in the section "Manage Members" later in this chapter) are allowed to upload images and files.

Default Ping Servers   Here you can specify the ping servers that you want to make available for new blog postings and decide if any of them are active by default. Chapter 7 discusses ping servers in more detail.

Default HTML Buttons   In this section you can add or delete HTML buttons from the Publish interface; if there's an HTML command that you'd like to have handy from with the Publish interface, you can specify what the name of the button will be (in the Tag Name column) and then the opening and closing tag for that command. You can also re-order the commands that appear in the Publish interface if desired.

Global Weblog Preferences   These preferences affect every weblog in your ExpressionEngine installation. Many of these preferences are advanced options for the way ExpressionEngine behaves when it creates URLs, assigned categories, and certain types of database queries.

Members and Groups

ExpressionEngine is designed so that you can have many different members of your site and those members can have different capabilities. From within these preferences you can view the members of your site, create and activate members, set the permissions levels for different types of members, and banner certain types of users. We'll cover these options in the section "Manage Members" later in this chapter.

Specialty Templates

Using these options you can customize the templates that are used to send messages to users who are registered with your site as well as creating a message for when your site is offline. (You set offline status in the System Preferences.)

System Preferences

Here you can set tons of different options that effect how your site operates. Here's a brief overview:

- **General Configuration**   On this screen you can turn your site on and off, enter a license number, name the site, name the index page, and enter important default addresses and behaviors.

- **Control Panel Settings**   Here you can make choices about the theme used for the Control Panel (additional themes are available from the ExpressionEngine website and from users who have published their own themes) and how the Publish tab works when you have multiple blogs.

- **Security and Session Preferences**   These options are global security options that help you make choices about how users are tracked and what sort of data is allowed from users who post comments or blog entries to your site. You can also require certain minimums for the passwords that are chosen by your users.

- **Throttling Configurations** These are advanced settings that allow you to limit the number of pages and submissions that your users can make.

- **Localization Settings** These options enable you to make choices that affect the way your blog processes your local time and date.

- **Database Settings** Here you can choose the type of database setting and whether or not SQL queries can be cached for better performance.

- **E-mail Configuration** These are defaults for the method of sending e-mails from the Communicate tab in the Control Panel. (See "Communicate with Members" later in this chapter.)

- **Mailing List Preferences** These options enable you to determine whether the built-in mailing list is enabled and whether or not new additions to the mailing list generate a notification e-mail to you or other administrators of your site.

- **Image Resizing Preferences** Here you can set defaults for the way images are resized and named when thumbnails are created on your site.

- **Referrer Tracking** Determines whether and how the URLs of sites that refer people to your blog are tracked.

- **Cookie Settings** Here you can set advanced preferences for the cookies that ExpressionEngine uses to track users.

- **CAPTCHA Preferences** Set preferences on this screen for how CAPTCHAs work when you require them for comments and entries.

- **Search Term Log Configuration** Decide whether and how search terms will be logged. (This can be useful for seeing what items you readers search for when they visit your site.)

- **Word Censoring** Determine what words will be censored when they're submitted in posts and/or comments and what will replace those words.

- **Emoticon Preferences** Here you can choose whether or not smileys are displayed in entries and comments and you can point to the directory on your site where those smileys are stored. (If you don't like the default smileys, you can replace them with other images you obtain elsewhere.)

- **Output and Debugging Preferences** Here you can make some advanced choices about the performance and error reporting of ExpressionEngine.

Utilities

The Utilities section includes a number of advanced options that enable you to manage your database, access PHP information, and deal with plug-ins and extensions. You can also view a number of logs from this screen and import entries from pMachine Pro or Moveable Type blogs.

Manage Members

ExpressionEngine Core does not come with member management features that allow readers to register themselves as members of your site; you only have the ability to manually add members by choosing Register a New Member. The idea with the Core version is that you can enable authors and editors for your own blog, but any readers will not be able to become members of the site for commenting or tracking their own stats. If you have a registered personal or commercial copy of ExpressionEngine, then the Members module is installed and activated, making it possible for your visitors to register themselves for your site. When users can register themselves, it becomes more practical to require registration for features such as leaving comments on blog entries.

In either case, you can create new members—for instance, to add authors to your blog or to invite a small number of people to a private blog—via the Admin tab in the admin interface of ExpressionEngine. Choose Members and Groups and you'll see the Members and Groups screen, which enables you to create and manage your member accounts (see Figure 3-17).

Register a Member

To register a new member for your site, click the Register New Member link. You'll then see an entry form that enables you to create a new user account, complete with a username, password, screen name (which is what appears when this user creates a post or enters a comment), and an e-mail address. You can also assign that user to a group in the Member Group Assignment menu, which will determine the privileges that this user has when accessing your blog. When you're done entering information for this user account, click the Submit button.

View and Find Members

Once you have a few members you can use some of the other features found on the Members and Groups screen including View Members, Member Search (to find a member from among a large list), and IP Address Search (which lets you search for members based on the IP addresses that they use to connect to your blog.)

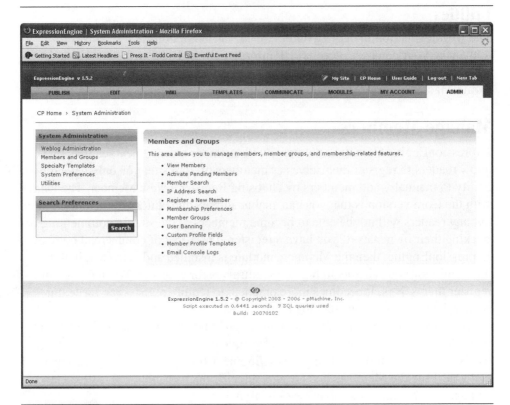

The Members and Groups page enables you to manage users who are registered for special privileges on your blog.

Set Member Preferences

You can click the Membership Preferences link to set certain options regarding how membership is handled on your blog, which is particularly important if you have public registration. Options include

- **Allow New Member Registrations?** Turn it on if you're accepting members. If you have a blog that allows for open commenting and you don't have a desire to allow registered members to send private messages to one another or register to receive a newsletter or e-mail from you, then you can turn this option off.

- **Require Member Account Activation?** One way to at least ensure that you're getting a valid e-mail address from your members is to require them to respond to an e-mail from ExpressionEngine before their membership is activated. You can also opt to only activate members manually—they can sign up, but they don't have membership privileges until you move them from the Pending category to an active category.

■ **Require Terms of Service**   You can have ExpressionEngine automatically present new users with your Terms of Service, which they must acknowledge reading before they can gain access.

■ **Allow Members to Set Their Own Localization Preferences**   This often makes sense to leave turned on, unless, for instance, your blog is designed for a workgroup that needs to center around a particular time zone, or for some other reasons that you don't want users to see the time translated to their own locale.

■ **Enable Membership CAPTCHA**   This option determines whether a new user must use CAPTCHAs to register.

■ **Default Member Profile Theme**   If you have more than one theme installed, you can select it here as the default; members will then be able to choose their own themes when viewing their own profiles.

■ **Profile Triggering Word**   This is a special reserved word (it can't be used in a template name) that, when placed in a URL, will trigger the member profile area. If you wanted to change this to "participants" or "vip" you could, as long as you don't use that same word in a template.

Click Update when you're done making changes.

Manage Groups

When installed, ExpressionEngine includes a handful of Member Group types, which you can use to assign different privileges to different users on your blog. The basics are Super User (your main account), Members, Guests, Pending, and Banned. A Guest, for instance, can view public profiles and comment on blog entries, but cannot send private messages to others, access the Control Panel, or post to a blog.

The trick with ExpressionEngine groups is that you can create a group and offer members of that group any sort of access you want to give them. Create an Editors category, for instance, and you can allow them to edit and delete others' posts, send messages through the e-mail interface and send comments through the blog without moderation, even when other users' comments are moderated; or create a Writers category that has privileges similar to the Members category, except that a writer can post to one or more blogs, and so on.

To view your member groups, from the Members and Groups page click the Member Group links. Now you'll see all of the currently assigned groups.

Group Title	Edit Group	Security Lock	Group ID	Members	Delete
Banned	Edit Group	Locked	2	(0) View	--
Guests	Edit Group	Locked	3	(0) View	--
Members	Edit Group	Locked	5	(1) View	Delete
Pending	Edit Group	Locked	4	(0) View	--
* Super Admins	Edit Group	Locked	1	(1) View	--

* can access the control panel

Create a new group based on an existing one [Super Admins ▾] [Submit]

To create a new group, click the Create a New Member Group tab. Now you'll see an interface that enables you to give the group a name and description and then page through all of the different privilege settings and determine what the members of this group will and will not be able to do. Just click a link to one of those sets of privileges—Comment Posting Privileges, Control Panel Access, Weblog Assignment, and so on—and then make changes of each of the privileges screens to determine what members of this particular member group will be allowed to do. When you've made all of your choices, click Submit to save changes or Submit and Finished to return to the Member Groups listing.

Once you've created a new group, you'll see that group when you're viewing, editing, or registering members for your site. When you find a person who fits the profile for a given member group, you can assign it to them through their profile page.

User Banning

There are two ways you can revoke a user's privileges as a member. One way is to open that user's profile through the Member List (accessible from the Members and Groups page) and set the user's Member Group to Banned.

ExpressionEngine offers even more sophisticated banning for when you're having trouble with a member, visitor, or *trolls*, which is the term used for people who visit blogs and forums and "troll" for fights in the comment sections. From the Members and Groups screen, click User Banning.

NOTE   *These options will only be relevant if you have a licensed version of ExpressionEngine, since ExpressionEngine Core does not support registration by users.*

On the User Banning screen, you can ban users in a few different ways. The first way is to ban them by their IP address. When a user using a banned IP address attempts to access the site, you can allow them only to view the site, you can show them a message (for instance, a message that pretends that the site is unavailable), or you can redirect them to a different website. You have to be a little careful when banning users by IP address, because some services share a pool of IP addresses among different users (such that a user can be assigned a relatively random IP address via a service such as America Online or your local cable provider). But, if you've been tracking a problem user's IP address in their member profile page and noticing that it tends to be static, you can ban that IP.

You can also ban users via their e-mail addresses, in the Banned Email Address entry box. Simply enter any e-mail addresses for users that you wish to ban, placing each on a separate line. Notice that you can ban e-mail addresses from a particular domain, using the wildcard *@domain.com, such as *@toddstauffer.com, just in case you don't want me (or anyone who has an e-mail address on my domain) to be able to become a member of your site.

In the Restricted Username and Restricted Screen Names entry boxes, you can enter usernames and/or screen names that you want to reserve for your own use or which you simply don't want others to use on your blog. This can be handy for restricting the use of your own full name or those of others associated with your organization, for example, to keep others from signing up and masquerading as you.

Once you've decided whom you're going to ban using one of those methods, you can then decide what will happen if a banned user attempts to visit your site. In the When a Banned IP Tries to Access the Site section, you can choose to Restrict Them to Viewing Only, you can select Show This Message and then enter a short text message for them to see, or you can choose Send Them to This Site and then enter a specified URL.

When you've made your choices, click Update.

Customize Your ExpressionEngine Templates

The templating system in ExpressionEngine is one of its signature features. It's very powerful, although it can also take a little bit of a learning curve to truly appreciate it.

Probably the most important thing to remember about templates in ExpressionEngine is that each template is roughly analogous to a different *page* that users can access on your site. You manage all of those pages through the ExpressionEngine interface, and each of those pages can show dynamic blog-based content in them, if desired—blog entries, comments, titles, or anything else that you can create under the Publish tab. You can also create "static" pages by creating a template and then editing the HTML within that template; as an example, many themes come with an About template that you can edit from within the ExpressionEngine admin interface; you can change the text so that it talks about you, your blog, your interests, and so on.

NOTE *Of course, some templates, such as the Comments template can be used over and over to create different dynamic "pages" that are served to your visitors. In a default ExpressionEngine installation, the Comments template is used to display any of your blog entries in its entirety, including any comments that have been added by your readers.*

Likewise, you can create new templates that are designed specifically to display other information you want to convey, such as the products or services you offer, the plays you've written, the stamps you collect, and so on. In addition, new templates can be created that show the contents of additional blogs that you create in ExpressionEngine; for www.jacksonfreepress.com, for instance, we have a news blog, a music blog, a features blog, an opinion blog, and so on. Using templates and special ExpressionEngine tags, I can show the contents of each of those blogs on their own template pages, or I can mix and match the blog entries, headlines, and comments from a number of different blogs on a single template page.

I mentioned that templates are like HTML pages, and it's true that you access them a little like you access HTML pages on a "static" website, with a difference or two. For instance, if I created a page called about.html and uploaded it to the main web directory for my site http://www.macblog.com/, then I would access that page at http://www.macblog.com/about.html in a browser.

With ExpressionEngine, that URL is slightly different. If I have a template named About, and the website is called www.macblog.com, then (assuming I'm using default settings) the URL to that page would be http://www.macblog.com/index .php/site/about/ when entered in a browser. Note that the URL is a little different (almost as if About was its own folder on the website) but that construct is required in order for ExpressionEngine to dynamically create the page that is displayed to users and keep the URL relatively "pretty." The index.php is called the "main site file" in ExpressionEngine, and it's crucial to making the site work correctly.

TIP *Actually, you can change the name of the main site file from index.php to something else more customized, if desired, but only if your web host is running Apache web server with the* AllowOverride *option turned on. You'll have to consult your web host to make sure that's true. The instructions for changing the name of your main site file are found at http://expressionengine.com/docs/installation/renaming_index.html.*

ExpressionEngine throws another wrinkle into the whole template-URL system, too, in that it allows you to create special template groups, which are sort of like folders on a web host. If I created the folder mysite on my web host and uploaded the file about.html to that folder, then the URL would be http://www .macblog.com/about/about.html when accessed in a browser. If I create a new template group in ExpressionEngine called mysite and then create a template called about within that group, the URL to it would be http://www.macblog.com/ index.php/mysite/about/ when entered in a browser. If your blog is relatively small, you may not have a need to create different template groups, but they are handy for organizing a much larger site from within ExpressionEngine.

View the Templates

At its most basic level, the ExpressionEngine template system isn't much different from the WordPress system shown earlier in this chapter. From within the ExpressionEngine admin interface, you can access a number of different templates that are used to show the contents of your blog—you do that by clicking the Templates tab in the admin interface. That brings up the Template Management page. Those templates, as shown in Figure 3-18, include pages such as an Index template for showing the main content of your site, a Comments template for showing the full article content of your blog entries along with any comments, and other templates for displaying other types of output, such as archives and headline feeds.

So, to make edits to the look and feel of your blog, you can begin by clicking the name of a template and viewing its HTML source. ExpressionEngine deals exclusively in "code"—HTML and CSS, primarily—for its web design, so you won't find much in the way of drag-and-drop editing for changing your templates around. But, if you're willing to dig in and make changes, you can do that by clicking the Index template or Comment template, for example, and then viewing and editing the code.

For CSS changes—style sheet changes to fonts, certain defined "divisions" of your page's layout, and so on—you can make changes in the main CSS style sheet for your blog. You'll find that generally listed as an entry called site_css or something similar; that's where you can make CSS changes that often affect the look of your entire site.

Understand Template Tags

While you'll get a better sense of how to do the actual HTML and CSS editing in Chapter 4, one thing worth discussing in this section is the unique nature of ExpressionEngine *tags*. Tags are the special codes used to access ExpressionEngine so that you can show different blog information that is stored

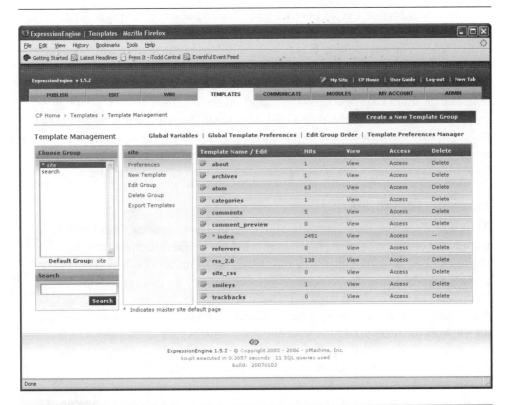

FIGURE 3-18   The Templates tab in the admin interface enables you to edit the look and feel of your blog.

in your site's database—blog entries, comments, headlines, user information, and so on. ExpressionEngine tags are a bit complex (once again), particularly when compared to, say, Blogger tags. But the ExpressionEngine tags are very powerful and customizable.

Here's an example of the standard ExpressionEngine tag that's used to show multiple blog entries on the index page of your site:

```
{exp:weblog:entries weblog="todds_blog" orderby="date"
sort="desc" limit="15"}

{date_heading}
<h2 class="date-header">{entry_date format=' %l, %F %d, %Y'}</h2>
{/date_heading}
```

```
<div class="post">
<h3 class="post-header">{title}</h3>
<div class="post-summary">
{summary}
{body}
{extended}
</div>
<div class="post-details">
Posted by <a href="{profile_path=member/index}">{author}</a> in
{categories}
&#8226; <a href="{path=site_index}">{category_name}</a>
{/categories}
<br />
{if allow_comments}
({comment_total})
<a href="{url_title_path="{my_template_group}/comments"}">
Comments</a> |
{/if}
{if allow_trackbacks}
({trackback_total})
<a href="{trackback_path="{my_template_group}/trackbacks"}">
Trackbacks</a> |
{/if}
<a href="{title_permalink={my_template_group}/comments}">
Permalink</a>
</div>
{paginate}
<div class="paginate">
<span class="pagecount">Page {current_page} of
{total_pages} pages</span>  {pagination_links}
</div>
{/paginate}

</div>
{/exp:weblog:entries}
```

This will probably look a little complicated at first, but all that it's really doing is enabling you to tell the template that you want to show entries from a particular weblog, and then it tells the template how to format those entries when they're shown on this page. The key element is the ExpressionEngine tag that starts the entry:

```
{exp:weblog:entries weblog="todds_blog" orderby="date"
sort="desc" limit="15"}
```

This is the "opening tag" that tells the template that, in this portion of the page, it's going to load entries from the database that are stored in the weblog specified (in this example it's `todds_blog`) and place them on the page in descending order by date (like a typical weblog does). The limit to the number of entries on this page will be 15 entries.

Then, all the way at the end of the example is this tag:

```
{/exp:weblog:entries}
```

That's the "closing tag"—it tells ExpressionEngine that everything between the opening tag and this closing tag is the formatting for each individual blog entry. For instance, you'll see buried in the formatting codes the following:

```
<div class="post">
<h3 class="post-header">{title}</h3>
<div class="post-summary">
{summary}
{body}
{extended}
</div>
```

Some of this is HTML and CSS stuff that we'll cover in Chapter 4. But notice the {title}, {summary}, {body}, and {extended} tags—all of those are commands that, when found inside the {exp:weblog:entries} and {/exp:weblog:entries} tags, tell ExpressionEngine what parts of each blog entry we want to display using this template. In this case, you see that we're telling ExpressionEngine to format the title of the blog entry using the <h3> HTML tag (it has a particular "class" that, according to CSS, will tell it what fonts and other style items to use) and then we're going to display the entire entry on this page—we'll show the summary, body, and extended text that were entered in the Publish section when you create a blog entry. (In this example, it's kind of like the way Blogger shows entries—you get the whole thing on the index page of your blog.)

If, instead, we wanted to show just the body of the entry, with a "more" link to the comments page (so that people can decide if they want to read the entire entry or not) then the code would look like this:

```
<h3>{title}</h3>
<div class="post-summary">
{body}
{if extended != ""}
<p>
<a href="{title_permalink={template_group_name}/comments}">
```

```
Continued...</a>
</p>
{/if}
</div>
```

In this example, the body of the entry is shown on this page and then, if there is text in the extended portion of the entry (the command {if extended != ""} means *if the Extended entry field in the blog database for this entry isn't blank*), a hyperlink labeled "Continued..." is displayed. That link points to the Comment template, so that if the reader clicks the link, they'll see the entire entry, along with any comments that have been made on that entry.

[Desk] Thursday Legislative Update

by Adam Lynch

House floor action consisted largely of highway designations and personality commendations on Jan. 25. The House did pass HB 963, which increases the time within which the state should demand payment of sales tax revenues from individuals, as well as HB1028, which prohibits certain acts used to duck paying sales tax (such as telling the retailer that the purchased items are for resale).

HB 1027 is another revenue enforcer, allowing the State Tax Commission to deny the application for a license plate permit or revoke the permit of any person failing to pay any state taxes, fees, penalties and/or interests owed to the state.

The House also passed—strangely, without real debate--HB 1321, which creates a commission bearing the proud name of America's first and last Confederate President. The bill containing the building blocks for the Jefferson Davis Bicentennial Commission now heads to the Senate.

Continued...

Posted by admin at 03:12 PM on 012607. Discuss (9)

So, as you can see, the ExpressionEngine template and tag system can be very powerful; because you can specify what blogs to show and how much of each entry to display, you can come up with complicated pages that show entries from multiple blogs, allowing your user to click into all sorts of different blogs of information.

> **NOTE**
>
> *For more information on the many different tags that can be used in ExpressionEngine, I suggest consulting the online documentation. You can get there by clicking the User Guide link at the top right of the admin interface or directly on the Web at http://expressionengine.com/docs/.*

Create New Templates

ExpressionEngine also gives you the ability to create new templates; these can be used for "static" pages on your site (a Contact page or information about your products, services, etc.) or they can be pages for additional blogs, pages designed to show certain information about your blog(s) in different ways (such as a "recent comments" page), and so on. You can also create a new template as a new CSS file (for additional—or different—custom style sheet information) or as a new RSS feed.

To create a new template from the Templates tag in the admin interface for your blog, click the New Template link that appears in the middle column of the Template Management screen, underneath the name of the current template group. (By default, you'll probably only have two groups: site and search. For your blog's main pages, the site template group is used. If site is selected, you'll see "site" in the header of the middle column.) When you click New Template, you'll see a New Template Form page where you can create the new template.

New Template Form		
Template Name		
The name must be a single word with no spaces		
(underscores and dashes are allowed)		
Template Type	Web Page ▾	
Default Template Data		
⊙	**None - create an empty template**	
○	**Use a template from your library**	
○	**Duplicate an existing template**	site/about ▾
Submit		

Here's how to create the new template:

1. Enter a name for the template in the Template Name entry box. Note the rules: it should be a single word, no spaces, underscores, or dashes are allowed. (The template name will ultimately be part of the URL to access the page it creates.)

2. Choose a type from the Template Type menu. If you're creating a static page or another template for viewing data from your blog(s), you will want to choose Web Page; if you're specifically creating a CSS style sheet or RSS feed, you can choose those options. The JavaScript and Static pages are special cases that you'll only use if you're digging deep into coding your site. (JavaScript is used for storing scripts that are called from within other templates on your site; Static is most often used for creating portions of your site that are HTML only and that don't require *any* ExpressionEngine tags, which is rare.)

3. In the Default Template Data area, you can choose None if you'd like a blank template, or Use a Template From Your Library if you have a library of templates. You can also choose Duplicate an Existing Template if you want to use that as the starting point for this new template.

> **TIP** *What's the template library? These are sample templates stored in the system/templates/ folder with a .tpl filename extension. By default you won't have any, but you can save a sample template there if you find you often create templates and want a starting point.)*

4. Click the Submit button. Your new template is created and will be shown in the Templates list.

Now, you can edit this template as you can any others in your template list, so that you can create a full HTML document that, if desired, includes ExpressionEngine tags and commands.

To access the new template on your site, you simply add it as part of the URL, following the format http://www.mysite.com/index.php/template_group/new_template/ (as in http://www.toddstauffer.com/index.php/site/books/ for a template I've created called Books). You can use that URL directly in a Web browser or in other links that you create within other templates.

Embedding Templates

One common sight on many blogs is a sidebar—much like the WordPress sidebar discussed earlier in the chapter—that has common contents on multiple pages of your blog. If you'd prefer not to hard-code something like that sidebar into every template page where it should appear, you have another option: you can embed one template inside another. This can be handy for other parts of your blog's design as well, such as the banner area at the top of the site or a copyright/ information section at the bottom of your pages.

> **NOTE** *Many ExpressionEngine themes that you can download and install already include Sidebar, Header, Footer, and other templates that are embedded in the main Index and/or Comment templates. It's a common practice, so look for those if you're already using a professionally designed theme.*

To embed a template, you first create the template as discussed in the previous section. Then, you'll add HTML markup, ExpressionEngine tags, or whatever you desire to have in that template. Note that you *don't* need a full HTML page worth of tags (the HTML, HEAD, BODY tags and so on) because this template will be embedded in another template that should already have those items. In other words, it's more of a "snippet" of code than a full HTML page, as are many of the other templates you'll create.

As an example, here's a template I've created and called Header for one of the blogs I've created:

```
<div id="banner">
<a href="{path=site/index}">
<img src="http://www.statedesk.com/images/StateDesk.gif"
align="left" border="0" /></a>
</div>
<ul>
<li id="nav-1">
<a href="http://www.statedesk.com/index.php/">HOME</a>
</li>
<li id="nav-2">
<a href="http://www.statedesk.com/index.php/events/">EVENTS</a>
</li>
<li id="nav-5">
<a href="http://www.statedesk.com/index.php/gallery/">PHOTOS</a>
</li>
</ul>
```

This template holds the code to display the top image of this particular blog and then the navigation links to the various pages that have been created for the blog. Instead of typing all this into each of the templates created, it's saved as the header template and then embedded into those other templates using a command such as:

```
{embed=site/header}
```

In this example, site is the template group name and header is the name of the template that is being embedded.

Create a New Template Group

If you find that you're creating a lot of new templates, you may want to create a new template group, which can be used as a sort of "virtual folder" for organization and easier management of a larger site.

For instance, if you have many different pages that are devoted to music on your site, you could create a new template group called Music and then create all of those related templates within that template group. Remember that a new template group creates a new "folder" in the URL used to access it, so if you create that new Music template group, the URL to access templates within that group will be something like `http://www.yousite.com/index.php/music/template_name/` in a browser.

To create a new template group, click the Create a New Template Group button at the top-right of the Template tab screen. You'll see the New Template Group page.

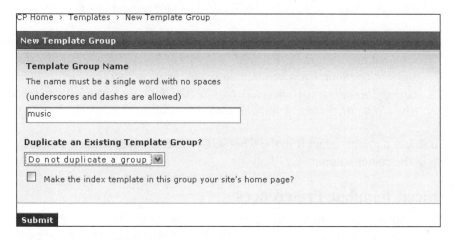

Enter a name for the template group, and then choose whether or not you want to duplicate an existing group's templates from the Duplicate an Existing Template Group menu. Finally, turn on the option Make the Index Template in This Group Your Site's Home Page if you want this page loaded as the home page of your ExpressionEngine site. Click Submit and the new group is created.

NOTE *If you make the Index template of your new group your site's home page, that new Index template will be accessed when the base URL to your ExpressionEngine site is accessed. (So, for instance, if I change the Music template group so that its Index template is the home page for my MacBlog site, then visiting http://www.macblog.com/ will display the Music group's index, not the Site group's index as it used to.) This can significantly alter the way you access pages and templates on your site, so think it through before implementing the change.*

Now, back in on the Template Management page, you'll see the new group appear in the Choose Group column; select it and the template list will change to reflect the templates in the group. You can now start creating new templates for that group.

To edit the group, make sure it's selected in the Choose Group column and then click the Edit Group link in the center column. You can then change the name of the group or opt to make its Index template the home page for your site. Click Update when you've made the change, or click the Templates link at the top of the window (in the "breadcrumbs" links that look like CP Home > Templates > Edit Template) to move back to the Template Management page.

NOTE   *"Breadcrumb" links are a common occurrence in many blog's Web-based admin interfaces. They're usually a series of links with a separator that show the path that you've taken to get to the page you're viewing. (They're called "breadcrumbs" because they're like the breadcrumbs that Hansel and Gretel dropped to know the path they'd taken through the woods.)*

To delete a group, select it in the Choose Group list and then click Delete Group in the center column.

Advanced Template Preferences

On the Template Management page you'll see a link for the Template Preferences Manager; this interface is used to make a number of advanced settings for each of the templates in the selected group, including caching settings (whether or not the contents of the page should be "cached" so that a static page is served to visitors for a fixed amount of time) and template access restrictions. These settings can be somewhat advanced in nature, so I recommend consulting the ExpressionEngine documentation (http://expressionengine.com/docs/templates/index.html) before digging into these.

Communicate with Members

The ExpressionEngine admin interface offers a special Communicate tab (see Figure 3-19), which you can use to send e-mail to members. E-mail messages can be sent to your mailing list (if you have a licensed version of ExpressionEngine) or to one or more groups of members.

Sending a message is simple. Simply fill in the Title and Message of the e-mail, and then choose Formatting, Word Wrapping, and Priority options at the bottom of the page. On the right side of the page, you can decide to whom you're going to

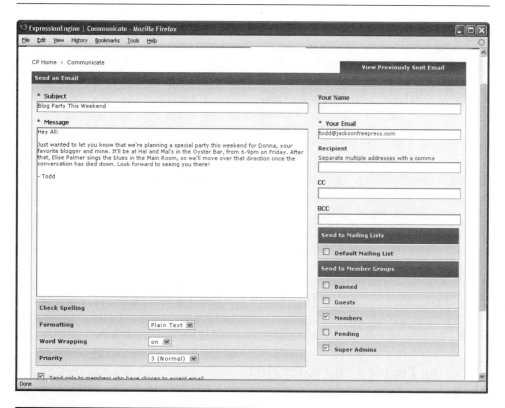

FIGURE 3-19   The Communicate tab is used to send e-mail messages to your members.

send the message. You can enter a Recipient if you're sending to only one user (or multiple users separated by a comma), and you can specific CC and BCC e-mail addresses as well.

If you want to send the message to everyone who has registered for your ExpressionEngine mailing list, you can do that by turning on the Default Mailing List option. If you want to send the message to a particular group of your users, you can turn on that group by clicking the checkbox next to the group's name. (More on the Mailing List options in Chapter 7.)

Down at the bottom of the screen, you can also turn on or off the option Send Only to Members Who Have Chosen to Accept Email. (Obviously, it's probably only a good idea to turn this option off if you're sending out something that everyone on your site *must* see.) Then, click Send It to send the e-mail.

NOTE   *To set up a mailing list, you must have a licensed version of ExpressionEngine and you'll need to enable the Mailing List Module. See the ExpressionEngine documentation at http://expressionengine.com/docs/modules/mailing_list/index.html for details.*

Manage Plug-ins, Extensions, and Modules

Another strength of ExpressionEngine is its support for plug-ins and modules, both those offered by EllisLab and those created by third parties. Plug-ins are generally designed to add special tags that you can use in your templates and themes, making it possible for you to add a special behavior or command that isn't part of the built-in tags.

Extensions are additions that add more than just a new tag; often, they rework or augment features that are already in ExpressionEngine. For instance, a popular extension is the Tiny MCE Extension for ExpressionEngine, which adds WYSIWYG editing to the Publish page when you're adding new entries to your blog.

Modules are more full-featured, enabling you to offer entirely new functionality via your site. For instance, EllisLab offers modules that make a forum, a wiki, or simple e-commerce features available; others offer modules that enable you to add tagging and tag clouds, polls, rating systems, and other fun stuff.

Installing Plug-ins and Extensions

The process is similar for installing plug-ins and extensions. Generally, you'll find plug-ins and extensions via the ExpressionEngine website (http://expressionengine.com/downloads/addons/) or elsewhere on the Web. Most of the time, those plug-ins or extensions are distributed as .zip archives, so once you've downloaded the archive to your computer, you'll want to expand the archive. Then, check the README file or other instructions for specific information. Again, generally, you use your FTP application to upload plug-ins to the /system/plugins/ folder on your web host and extensions to the /system/extensions/ folder on your web host. (Some extensions also require files in the /system/language/ folder.)

Once the files are properly uploaded, you can enable them using the ExpressionEngine admin interface. Click the Admin tab, then the Utilities link. For a plug-in, click the Plugin Manager link and you'll see the Plugin Manager page. Here you can see all of the plug-ins that are installed in ExpressionEngine, as well as a feed of the newest plug-ins from the ExpressionEngine.com site.

CP Home > Admin > Utilities > Plugin Manager

6 Plugins Installed

Character Limiter (v.1.0)
Permits you to limit the number of characters in some text

Magpie RSS Parser (v.1.3.3)
Retrieves and Parses RSS/Atom Feeds

Randomizer (v.1.0)
Allows you to show random text, such as quotes, on your site.

Word Limiter (v.1.0)
Permits you to limit the number of words in some text

XML Encode (v.1.1.1)
XML Encoding plugin.

Wiki Table of Contents (v.1.0)
Adds a Table of Contents to your Wiki articles

Click a plug-in to learn more about it; you'll often get a link to the developer's website and instructions on using the plug-in. (As mentioned, it usually involves a new tag that you can add to your templates.)

For extensions, click the Extensions Manager link on the Admin | Utilities page. You'll see a list of the installed extensions that have been recognized by ExpressionEngine. You can then click the Enable link to enable the extension; once enabled, click the Settings link to change settings for the extension, according to the extension's instructions. You should then see the extension's functionality kick in, whether in the admin interface or elsewhere on your blog.

Manage Modules

To install a module, you may have to jump through extra hoops. Again, you'll likely download a .zip archive, decompress it on your computer, and then upload its files to your web host into the designated folders; at least some portion of the files you upload will be placed in the /system/modules/ folder, although you may place files in other locations as well.

Once the module is uploaded, you can click the Modules tab in the admin interface to see it, along with all other modules that are recognized by ExpressionEngine, including many of the modules that are bundled with the software (see Figure 3-20).

To install a module, click the Install link in the far-right Action column of that module's row. That should refresh the page and you'll see that it's active. Now, click the link on the module to see its settings and preferences, if it has any. For instance, the Mailing List module can be clicked, where you create the mailing list and detail any of the preferences you want to set for it, such as whether or not it has a template for outgoing HTML files. You can also search e-mail addresses and subscribe or unsubscribe users in batches.

	Module Name	Description	Version	Status	Action
1	Blacklist/Whitelist	Blacklist and whitelist module	--	Not Installed	Install
2	Blogger API	Blogger API Module	--	Not Installed	Install
3	Comment	User commenting system	1.0	Installed	Remove
4	Email	User Email Module	--	Not Installed	Install
5	Emoticon	Emoticon (smiley) module	1.0	Installed	Remove
6	Photo Gallery	Photo Gallery Module	--	Not Installed	Install
7	IP to Nation	Utility for associating IP addresses with their country	--	Not Installed	Install
8	Mailing List	Mailing List Manager	2.0	Installed	Remove
9	Member	Member management system	1.0	Installed	Remove
10	Metaweblog API	Metaweblog API Module	--	Not Installed	Install
11	Moblog	Moblogging Module	--	Not Installed	Install
12	Query	SQL query module for templates	1.0	Installed	Remove
13	Referrer	Referrer tracking module	1.1	Installed	Remove
14	RSS	RSS page generating module	1.0	Installed	Remove
15	Search	Search module	1.0	Installed	Remove
16	Simple Commerce	Simple, Flexible Commerce Module	--	Not Installed	Install
17	Statistics	Statistics display module	1.0	Installed	Remove
18	Trackback	Trackback module	1.0	Installed	Remove
19	Updated Sites	Allows other sites to ping you.	--	Not Installed	Install
20	Weblog	Weblog module	1.0	Installed	Remove
21	Wiki	A Powerful, Integrated Wiki module	1.1	Installed	Remove

FIGURE 3-20 Once modules are uploaded, they are "installed" via the Modules page.

TIP *In the ExpressionEngine admin interface you can add a tab for a module as you're viewing it, if you'd like that module to be accessible from the tabs (e.g., Publish, Edit, Templates) that appear. While viewing the module's settings, click the New Tab link at the top-right corner of the page. You'll then see the Add Tab interface that enables you to name the tab and specify (if necessary) the URL to the module that will be accessed from that tab.*

You can also uninstall a module while viewing the Modules page; just click Remove under the Action column for the module's row. You'll likely see a warning that tells you that all data associated with the module will be deleted; consider carefully whether you want that to happen. If you do, click the De-install Module link.

We'll discuss some more of the ExpressionEngine modules in upcoming chapters, as the licensed versions include a photo gallery module (Chapter 6) and a wiki module (Chapter 8), and EllisLab also sells a forums module (Chapter 9).

Chapter 4

Blog Design and Template Editing

How to...

- Understand the Web 2.0 design sensibility

- Learn about XHTML and blog templates

- Edit your blog's templates

- Change the look of your blog with Cascading Style Sheets

Once you've chosen a blogging tool and gotten the framework of your blog up and running, you might want to start tweaking the design a bit. Over the past year or more, many of the major blogging tools have been moving toward a friendly, widget-focused approach to some basic design choices, enabling you to visually move elements of your blog around within the confines of a template. You can put your About block in the sidebar, move your RSS subscription links around, add links to your Flickr image account, and so on.

Digging much deeper than that—or altering the design of your blog in more fundamental ways—can still involve getting "under the hood" and making changes to the underlying XHTML code, the CSS style sheets, or a combination of both. In Chapters 2 and 3 you saw the individual interfaces that the different blogging tools offer for accessing and editing templates and style sheets; in this chapter, I'd like to plunge in and look at some of the standard codes and commands you can use to make those changes a reality.

The Web 2.0 Sensibility

Perhaps the most ambiguous Web 2.0 notion is the one that has to do with design. Generally speaking, Web 2.0 design can boil down to a focus on *simplicity,* where the function of a page, ideally, inspires its design. For a blog, that means that you need relatively few bells and whistles, and that none of the design elements should overshadow the function of the page, which is generally to convey information or entertainment in that way that blogs are supposed to do. The fundamental idea is that if you don't have many distractions on the page then your reader is forced to look at the content. It should be pleasing to the eye and easy to read, but it doesn't need to be overwhelmed with visual elements (see Figure 4-1).

Here are a few thoughts on what Web 2.0 design seems to embody and some of the things you can think about as you're augmenting your blog:

4

FIGURE 4-1   Web 2.0 design is characterized by a simplicity that design firm
Simplebits has captured.

■ *Every pixel counts.* With Web 2.0 design, the purpose is to communicate
information as quickly as possible. There's certainly a clean, attractive
look to many Web 2.0 sites, but it's done in a way that doesn't detract from
what's being said. Instead, the graphical elements are meant to make it
relatively easy to grasp the purpose of the site and to learn the interface or
find what you're looking for. Plus, there's an argument that throwing a little
less content at the reader can make it easier to absorb.

■ *Bold, simple type is better.* Another signature of the Web 2.0 site is larger,
bolder text that grabs the eye and helps you figure out quickly what you're
supposed to read. In the past, many websites were designed specifically to
make sure as much material as possible appear "above the fold" or in the first
screen that appears when the site is loaded. These days, there's an assumption
that people are willing to scroll to see more, and that they'll prefer text that's
easy on the eyes and draws them in to the content (see Figure 4-2).

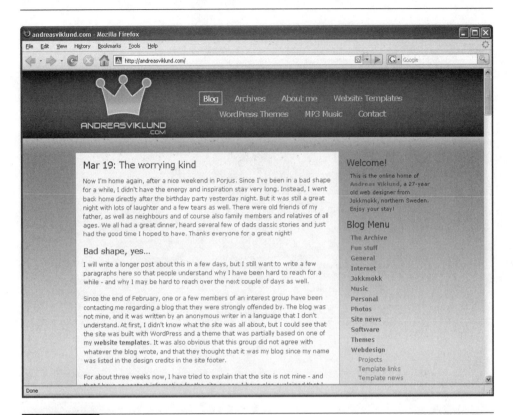

FIGURE 4-2 Andreas Vikland is the designer of many popular WordPress templates; he's also got a blog that's easy on the eyes. He uses type to draw you into the interface.

- *White space is good.* You'll find that a lot of Web 2.0 style designs are offered in chunks, with soft edges and a little bit of white (or off-white, depending on the design) space between the elements. Often the RSS feed icon is floating on its own, or other controls, such as the login or "join our newsletter" buttons, have space around them so that they can be more easily seen. Remembering that white space can free you in your design to cram a little less into your blog's layout, and yet give readers the elements they expect to see (see Figure 4-3).

FIGURE 4-3   The blog at ExpressionEngine's main site offers nice white space, a good clean font, and graphical elements that have a purpose.

■ *Use color and icons instead of relying too much on images.* The trick that a lot of Web 2.0 sites seem to play is substituting large text, bold icons, and rich colors for the image-heavy designs of early websites. There are a few good reasons for this, one of which is that sites that are largely text with a few clever elements can look inviting and yet load quickly in a Web browser. Likewise, sites that rely on color, font choice, and icons can also be designed using "well-formed" XHTML markup code and can be *styled* using Cascading Style Sheets. What that means is that those sites can load and look good on a variety of platforms, including standard web browsers, PDAs, phones, and other devices that can display web pages. The simpler and more universal the design, the more it can be seen.

■ *Use XHTML to build your structure.* With the Web 2.0 approach, web designers are encouraged to use XHTML elements in the simple way they were intended to be used, particularly when it comes to "structural" elements such as lists, headings, and block elements like paragraphs and divisions. When pages are designed well, it gives them the flexibility to render correctly in a variety of Web browsers, from PCs to mobile devices or even assistive devices. One area of the Web where you often see simple, structural designs is with wiki sites, such as Jackpedia.com, a wiki site I've created for collaborative use by residents in my hometown (see Figure 4-4).

You'll find that most of the templates that are made available by major blogging services and/or server-side blog tools have something of a Web 2.0 sensibility.

FIGURE 4-4   Jackpedia is a local wiki site for Jackson, Mississippi, that has a text-heavy design (based on an Expression Engine template by SheCodes.com) that is very functional and attractive, yet loads extremely quickly in a browser window.

Nearly all of them are designed to use well-formed XHTML code, to separate the look of the template (via style sheets) from the text being presented, and to be simple and heavy on white space.

That doesn't mean you can't do some customization to your blog's template, including adding some Web 2.0 flair, such as larger, bolder text, some well-placed icons, and other fun options. We'll take a look at some of the ways you can go about that in the rest of this chapter.

Exploring XHTML and Templates

There's a slight chicken-and-egg problem when it comes to digging into your blog's templates and making changes—more than likely, the first changes you'll want to make will have to do with fonts, text sizes, color choices, and things of that nature. That's the sort of stuff that you'll accomplish by editing your blog's *style sheet,* using CSS (Cascading Style Sheets) markup.

Unfortunately, before you can make informed changes in CSS, you first need to know something about XHTML—even if you don't really plan to make many changes to the underlying XHTML of your blog's templates. So, that's where we'll start in this chapter, with the CSS coverage after that. Of course, it probably can't hurt to know a little something about XHTML anyway, so even if you're just looking to make some visual changes, check out this section and then move on to the section "Edit Your Blog's CSS Style Sheets," later in the chapter.

NOTE   *Wondering where you'll be putting this XHTML and CSS knowledge to use? Each of the tools that we've covered in Chapters 2 and 3 offer some access to the underlying XHTML and/or style sheet templates so that you can make changes. (TypePad is the most restrictive in that you only get access to the underlying templates with the Pro-level license version.) I'll cover how to access the raw templates in the section "Edit Your Blog's Templates," later in this chapter.*

What Is XHTML?

XHTML is what defines a web page; CSS is what determines what the fonts, colors, margins, widths, and even layout of that page will look like once the Web browser is done processing it. To understand CSS, you'll need to know a little something about XHTML, even if you don't necessarily dig deep into the XHTML of your templates in order to make stylistic changes to your blog.

XHTML is the XML (eXtensible Markup Language) implementation of the HyperText Markup Language (HTML), which was the original language for creating

Web documents. (HTML has been recast in XML just to make things all good and modern.) It's called a "markup language" because it's essentially a collection of small codes, called "tags," that are used to mark sections of a plain text document. The tags give that document structure, and when that document is loaded and displayed by a web browser, the tags alert the browser to text that needs to be treated in a special way. Here, for instance, is an extremely basic XHTML document:

```
<html>
<head>
<title>My First Page</title>
</head>
<body>
<h1>Welcome to my Page</h1>
<p>This is the content of my page.</p>
</body>
</html>
```

If you typed all that into an editor like NotePad or TextEdit and then saved it as a plain text file (not a rich text file or something for word processing), then you could name the file with an .html or .htm extension and load it in a Web browser. The result would look like Figure 4-5.

FIGURE 4-5   Here's a basic XHTML page as displayed in a browser.

So, XHTML is basically just a collection of different tags that can be used to mark up plain text and tell a browser how it should organize that text. In the example, notice the two-part markup tags that are used to create a title for the page (`<title>` and `</title>`), to create a paragraph (`<p>` and `</p>`), and to create a "level 1" heading (`<h1>` and `</h1>`). XHTML is comprised of all sorts of these markup commands, from commands that style text to commands that create containers in your document. Of course, there are commands that create links and embed images on the page, as well. Let's take a look at some of those different types of markup tags in turn.

> **NOTE** *There are two general types of tags in XHTML—container tags and empty tags. Containers have a `<>` and `</>` component to them and generally act on the text in between the two. (Notice how the slash character is used to denote the "closing" tag.) Empty tags do just one thing, like draw a horizontal line (`<hr />`). These tags don't need a closing pair, although in XHTML (as opposed to an earlier version of HTML), empty tags do include a trailing slash as part of their code.*

HTML Page Elements

Most of the time when you're tweaking your blog, you'll be editing pages or templates that already exist. Just for the sake of a complete discussion, however, it's worth noting that if you were creating an XHTML document from scratch, you'd need to include a number of elements that are required to make up that page, including a document definition, an `<html>` container, a `<head>` container and a `<body>` container. That might look something like this:

```
<!DOCTYPE html
PUBLIC "-//W3C//DTD XHTML 1.0 Transitional//EN"
"http://www.w3.org/TR/xhtml1/DTD/xhtml1-transitional.dtd">
<html>
<head>
</head>
<body>
</body>
</html>
```

The Doctype Definition

The `<!DOCTYPE>` tag is a special tag that's used to determine the type of XML document that you're creating. (In this case, it's an XHTML document using the "transitional" version of XHTML 1.0.)

The <head> Section

The <head> tag serves as a container for a number of different tags that generally don't show up on the page when it's rendered in a browser, or that show up in special parts of the browser window, such as the text you put in the <title>, </title> container, as in:

```
<head>
<title>My First Page</title>
</head>
```

The <head> section of your XHTML document is often where you'll find style definitions for that page, as in:

```
<head>
<title>My First Page</title>
<style type="type/css">
<!--
body {font-family: arial, helvetica, sans-serif}
h1 {font-size: 24pt }
h2 {font-size: 18pt }
h3 {font size:14pt}
-->
</style>
</head>
```

We'll look at style commands in more depth later in the chapter, but for now, you should know that it's common to place style information in the <head> section of the document. It's also common to link to an external style sheet, particularly when you have lots of style information defined (that's true of most of the blog templates you'll encounter). In that case, the style link may look something like:

```
<head>
<title>My First Page</title>
<LINK REL=stylesheet HREF=http://www.yoursite.com/styles.css
 TYPE="text/css">
</head>
```

That command will cause the browser to locate a separate CSS style document and then apply those external styles to the text that's displayed on this page as it loads.

The \<body\> Section

In contrast to the \<head\> section, the \<body\> section of your XHTML document (or blog template) is where the actual content of the page goes. In a straight XHTML document, you could type in all the content for this page and format it using XHTML tags, such that the \<body\> section of a document might look something like this:

```
<body>
<h1>The Crossroads Film Festival</h1>
<p>March 29 - April 1<br />
4 Days, 60+ Films, Music &amp; Workshops<br />
Parkway Place Theatre, Lakeland Dr.</p>
<p>The Crossroads Film Society presents its <strong>8th
Annual Crossroads Film Festival</strong> from March 29 -
April 1, incorporating 60+ films, local and national recording
artists, pre- and post- parties and a variety of workshops and
panels. Each afternoon kicks off with a Meet & Greet Reception for
filmmakers and passholders, providing multiple opportunities for
fans to visit with filmmakers. Each evening ends with independent
rock at downtown venues.
<p>Screenings begin at 7 p.m. Thursday at <strong>Regal Parkway
Place Theater</strong> (Lakeland Dr @ Airport Rd) and run through
Sunday evening. This year, the festival continues its free
Children's Workshops in animation and filmmaking, beginning at
9 a.m. at <strong>Millsaps College</strong>, followed by a
screening of movies made by kids.</p>
</body>
```

This is a fairly simple example, but this would work just fine in browser window (see Figure 4-6), although it would just look a little boring. (That's what style sheets are for.) Notice that the visible content of the page appears between the \<body\> and \</body\> tags, and that the other markup occurs within containers as well: there's a \<h1\>, \</h1\> container for the "level 1" heading, content between \<p\> and \</p\> tags for the paragraphs, and even a few words here and there inside \<strong\>, \</strong\> tags, which mean "strong emphasis." (Strong emphasis is usually rendered as bold text in browsers that can display bold, but it's flexible enough for other systems such as monochrome displays or displays for Web browsers designed to help the sight-impaired.)

The Crossroads Film Festival

March 29 - April 1
4 Days, 60+ Films, Music & Workshops
Parkway Place Theatre, Lakeland Dr.

The Crossroads Film Society presents its **8th Annual Crossroads Film Festival** from March 29 - April 1, incorporating 60+ films, local and national recording artists, pre- and post- parties and a variety of workshops and panels. Each afternoon kicks off with a Meet & Greet Reception for filmmakers and passholders, providing multiple opportunities for fans to visit with filmmakers. Each evening ends with independent rock at downtown venues.

Screenings begin at 7 p.m. Thursday at **Regal Parkway Place Theater** (Lakeland Dr. @ Airport Rd.) and run through Sunday evening. This year, the festival continues its free Children's Workshops in animation and filmmaking, beginning at 9 a.m. at **Millsaps College**, followed by a screening of movies made by kids.

FIGURE 4-6   Here's the sample <body></body> section viewed in a Web browser.

NOTE *With HTML and XHTML documents, it's important to realize that the line returns that you type into the document are not necessarily recognized by a browser. In order to create a return or "new line" in an XHTML document, you need to either enclose the text in a paragraph or similar container (such as the division -- <div> </div> container), or you can end a line with the <br /> tag, as shown in the example. If you just type a return without the proper XHTML code, the browser will ignore your return. XHTML ignores more than one space between words, too, unless they take place within special containers.*

Here's a quick look at a number of the tags that are used for formatting text within the body section of XHTML documents:

`<p>, </p>`	The paragraph container.
`<div>, </div>`	The division container. Similar to a paragraph, `<div>` is used extensively with style sheets to define the styles (borders, margins, padding, text characteristics, color characteristics) of sections (or divisions) of an XHTML page.
`<span>, </span>`	The span container. This one is used for a small section of text that requires some sort of styling but that shouldn't be set apart from text around it into a new paragraph or division. For example: `Only the span-tagged text is <span style="color: blue">blue in color</span>, while the rest is the default color.`
`<h1>` to `<h6>`	The heading tags, from heading 1 to heading 6.
`<em>, </em>`	Used to emphasize text, usually rendered as italics.
`<strong>, </strong>`	Uses for strong emphasis of text, usually rendered as bold.
`<blockquote>, </blockquote>`	A container used to differentiate "quoted" text from paragraph text, often by indenting the quote vs. the paragraph.
`<cite>, </cite>`	Used for a citation.
`<code>, </code>`	Used to render text differently because it represents computer codes. This is often rendered as a monospace font.
`<ul>, </ul>`	Creates an unordered list, usually rendered as a bullet list.
`<ol>, </ol>`	Creates an ordered (numbered) list.
`<li>, </li>`	Contains a list item, usually within an unordered or ordered list.
`<pre>, </pre>`	Spaces and returns in this text are rendered by the browser exactly as they were typed into the document, and the text is usually displayed in a monospaced font.

Of course, there are other special tags that go into making up XHTML documents, and you've seen some of them already in Chapters 2 and 3, including the `<img>` tag for placing images and the `<a>` (anchor) tag for creating hyperlinks.

Here's an example of the image tag:

```
<img src="http://www.somesite.com/imagename.jpg"
alt="Alternative image description">
```

The `src` attribute is used to tell the browser where it can find the image, while the `alt` attribute is used to give an alternative label to the image in case the browser can't render it or the image is encountered by a browser for sight-impaired users. Other options are possible, including width and height attributes.

The anchor tag generally works like this:

```
Visit <a href="http://www.toddstauffer.com">iTodd Central</a>
to see what I'm blogging about.
```

In the anchor tag, the `href` attribute is used for the URL that the link should point to. A popular optional attribute is the `target` attribute, which can be used to cause the link to appear in a new window, such as in this example:

```
<a href="http://www.toddstauffer.com" target="_blank">iTodd
Central</a>
```

As we'll see later in the chapter, both hyperlinks and images can accept a number of different styles that change the way they appear on the page. And you can usually apply those styles within your blog entries as well as in the templates that create your blog pages, such that you can align images, create clickable images, and so on.

XHTML and Blog Templates

It's mostly in the body section of your blog templates that you'll find the elements that you want to change if you're digging in to spruce up your blog. Generally speaking, you'll find that the templates for your blogs use standard XHTML markup, but often act on special codes that are used by the blogging software to pull items from the database and display them on your page. In ExpressionEngine, for instance, you can dig into the index template for your site and you'll likely see quite a bit between the `<body>` tags that's familiar as XHTML.

Here's the template code for the image that's shown in Figure 4-7, which is an example from an ExpressionEngine blog:

```
<body>
{exp:weblog:category_heading}
<h3>Category: {category_name}</h3>
{/exp:weblog:category_heading}
{exp:weblog:entries weblog="{master_weblog_name}" orderby=
"date" sort="desc" limit="15" cache="yes" refresh="10"}
<h3>
<a href="{title_permalink={template_group_name}/comments}">
{title}</a></h3>
{summary}
{body}
{if extended != ""}
<p>
<a href="{title_permalink={template_group_name}/comments}">
Continued...</a>
</p>
```

```
<p class="posted">Posted by {if url != ""}<a href="{url}">{author}
</a>{/if}{if url == ""}{author}{/if} at
<a href="{title_permalink={template_group_name}/comments}">
{entry_date format='%h:%i %A'}</a> on
{entry_date format='%m/%d/%y'}.
{if allow_comments}
<a href="{title_permalink="{template_group_name}/comments"}
#comments">Discuss</a> ({comment_total})
{/if}
{paginate}
<p class="posted">
<span class="pagecount">Page {current_page} of {total_pages}
pages</span>  {pagination_links}
</p>
{/paginate}
{/exp:weblog:entries}
```

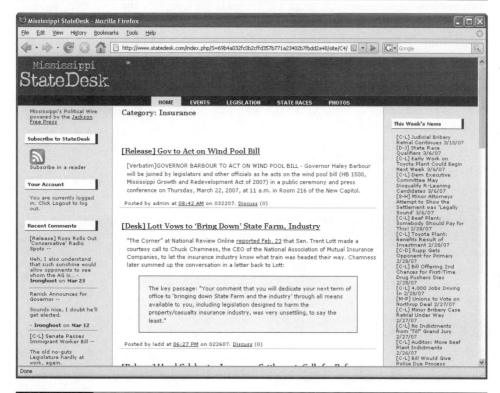

FIGURE 4-7   The template in this section determines the formatting of each blog entry shown here.

In this example, it should be clear that what a template in ExpressionEngine does is use special ExpressionEngine tags (the special curly braces differentiate them from XHTML tags), such as `{exp:weblog:category_heading}`, to tell the PHP processor that some other variables might be used within the XHTML code. So, for instance, in the category section, the tag `{category_name}` appears on this line:

```
<h3>Category: {category_name}</h3>
```

meaning that whatever category is being displayed for this blog, it'll be formatted between `<h3>` tags, which means "level 3 heading." In ExpressionEngine, that heading will only be shown when the blog visitor has clicked a particular category link on the page; if he or she is viewing all of the entries in the category "Gardening," then the heading "Gardening" will appear at the top of the page and it will be formatted as a level 3 heading.

The next long section of the example takes us through the formatting of the individual blog entries. With ExpressionEngine, each entry can be defined and formatted within the template page itself; this is the template for a sample "index" page of the blog, so we're formatting the entries so that they display in typical blog format. What readers of this page will see are up to 15 blog postings, with a headline, content, a "continued" link, and information about the post's author, the time of the post, and the comments, if any, that have been made.

Let's break it down, since what we're looking at is the interaction between the blog's internal codes and the XHTML codes that are used to format the data that's pulled from the database:

```
{exp:weblog:entries weblog="{master_weblog_name}"
orderby="date" sort="desc" limit="15" cache="yes"
refresh="10"}
<h3>
<a href="{title_permalink={template_group_name}/comments}">
{title}</a></h3>
{summary}
{body}
{if extended != ""}
<p>
<a href="{title_permalink={template_group_name}/comments}">
Continued...</a>
</p>
```

In this section, the bulk of the post is actually displayed. First, the ExpressionEngine tag for displaying weblog entries—`{exp:weblog:entries}`—

is invoked with a number of different attributes. None of that is XHTML; it's all internal commands for ExpressionEngine. Part of what that command is saying, however, is that what follows is the formatting for up to 15 posts from the weblog in question.

Each of those posts will be formatted, for starters, with a title that's between level 3 heading tags and is also a hyperlink text.

```
<h3>
<a href="{title_permalink={template_group_name}/comments}">
{title}</a></h3>
```

Next, the {summary} and {body} sections of the blog entry will be placed in the document using whatever formatting has been set for that weblog's preferences in ExpressionEngine. You don't need additional formatting tags for those ExpressionEngine codes because they represent portions of blog entries you formatted when you entered them, to format that in the template because it comes out with XHTML formatting already.

After that, the template to see if the entry has any text in its extended field. If it does, then a "continued" link is displayed. Note that the "continued" link is formed using anchor (`<a href> </a>`) tags that are surrounded by paragraph tags `<p></p>`.

The next chunk of the template is the section beneath the blog entry that shows the author, the date, and, if comments were allowed on the entry, a count of the number of comments for that entry:

```
<p class="posted">
Posted by {if url != ""}<a href="{url}">{author}</a>{/if}
{if url == ""}{author}{/if} at
<a href="{title_permalink={template_group_name}
/comments}">{entry_date format='%h:%i %A'}</a>
on {entry_date format='%m/%d/%y'}.
{if allow_comments}
<a href="{title_permalink="{template_group_name}/comments"}
#comments">Discuss</a> ({comment_total})
{/if}
</p>
```

Notice that paragraph tag around the posted information, which has the attribute `class="posted"`. That's a style sheet attribute that we'll discuss in the next section, but it's interesting to note it here; if you wanted to change the look of any of the text in this section when it renders in a browser, you'd do that by making changes to a style sheet class called "posted" in the style sheet.

A lot of the "logic" in this section is ExpressionEngine's built-in programming code (anything between curly brackets, such as {if url != ""}, which means "if the URL isn't blank"). If you're changing the way something should be accessed from the database in your blog, then that would require using the special built-in tags for that blog software, whether it's ExpressionEngine, WordPress, or something else. If it's the formatting of the *results* of something that blog software pulls from its database, that's done with XHTML codes. Once you've separated out the two, you'll be down the path of knowing how to alter your blog templates.

Edit Your Blog's Templates

Now that we've seen the basics of XHTML and the overall format of the typical web page, the most logical question is to ask how we can dig in and make changes to our blog's template. Here's a quick overview of the access given to us by each of the four blogging systems that were described in Chapters 2 and 3. If you've opted for a different blogging application, more than likely you'll find similar tools in that application.

Blogger Templates

On the Template tab in the admin interface, click the Edit HTML link. That gives you direct access to the HTML version of the template that is used to display your Blogger-based main page and your full-entry pages. (You'll actually find that a good deal of that template is the CSS style sheet code for your blog, which you can change with some help from the next major section in this chapter.)

In the Backup/Restore section of the page, note that you can download a full version of your current template so that you have a backup. You're able to copy it to your PC's hard disk so that you can restore it if you make a mistake or end up unhappy with the changes that you make. You should do that before proceeding.

Once you've made your changes to the template in the Edit Template section of the page, click Preview to see what it will look like or Save Changes to put your changes into effect for the blog.

TIP   *Blogger offers another option discussed in Chapter 2—you can switch to the "Classic Template" approach, which gives you more control over the layout of your Blogger blog using XHTML and CSS. What you lose when you switch to the Classic Template is the drag-and-drop functionality of the Page Elements feature. If you'd rather dig in and seriously customize your blog, you can click the option Revert to Classic Template, which gives you a fully editable Blogger template complete with XHTML tags and the special Blogger tags discussed a bit later in this chapter.*

TypePad Advanced Templates

The basic plans for TypePad don't really give you easy access to the XHTML in your template, but they do make adding custom style sheet markup easy. In the TypePad admin interface, click the Design tab and you'll see the option Edit Custom CSS. It's on that screen that you can add custom CSS elements to your site's design.

TypePad makes XHTML editing a Pro-level feature. First you'll choose a design for your site from the basic designs that can be managed visually. (Chapter 2 covered a lot of that.) Then you'll convert one of those designs to an Advanced design, which can be edited. TypePad encourages you to do it this way (instead of building the design from scratch) so that you begin your customization with a basic, working template.

If you have a Pro account, you can create a new, editable design by following these steps:

1. Click the Design tab.

2. Locate and click the Saved Designs link. That launches the Manage Your Designs page.

3. In the list that appears, place a checkmark next to the basic design that you want to be able to edit.

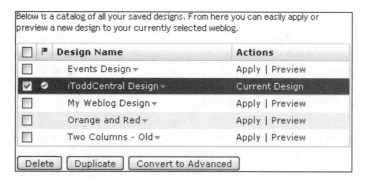

4. Click the Convert to Advanced button. A pop-up window appears asking you to confirm your decision; click Yes.

5. Now, in the list, you'll see a new, cloned version of the template that includes Advanced in the name. Click that design's name and you'll see the

option Edit Templates pop up. Click Edit Templates and you'll be shown a list of the templates that you can edit.

Current Design: "iToddCentral Design [Advanced]"

Advanced Templates

Below is a table containing a list of templates that are used to construct the design and layout of your site.

Create new index template

	Index Templates	Output File	Publish
☐	Archive Index Template	archives.html	Yes
☐	Atom Template	atom.xml	Yes
☐	Main Index Template	index.html	Yes
☐	RSS 2.0 Template	rss.xml	Yes
☐	RSS Template	index.rdf	Yes
☐	Stylesheet	styles.css	Yes
☐	sidebar	sidebar.inc	Yes

[Delete]

6. Click the name of one of those templates and you'll see the Edit Template window appear (see Figure 4-8), where you can dig into the XHTML code and make changes to the layout of your pages or add "hard-coded" elements to the pages such as Google Analytics or advertising codes that you need to add.

After you've made your edits, you can click Save in the Edit Template window, and then you can use the Select a Template to Edit menu to choose a different template to which you would like to make changes. When you're all done, click the Saved Designs link under the Design tab once again, and you'll see the advanced template set; click the Apply button next to that set's name and it will be applied to the blog as your current design, complete with your changes.

NOTE   *Like any other blogging tool, TypePad has an entire language of its own template tags for accessing content stored by the blogging tool. To fully understand your templates, you'll need to dive into that code at least a little. See* http://help.typepad.com/tags/ *on the Web for a detailed discussion of the advanced templates and the TypePad template tags you can use in those templates.*

WordPress Templates

You can edit WordPress templates from within the WordPress admin interface. In the admin interface, click the Presentation tab, and then click the Theme Editor link.

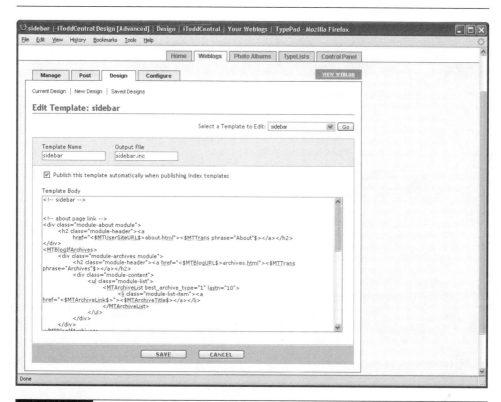

FIGURE 4-8   Editing an advanced template in TypePad

There you'll see a menu that enables you to choose the theme you want to edit at the top of the window, and you'll see a list of the template pages in your theme and you'll be able to view the code itself in the window (see Figure 4-9).

If you see the word "Browsing" at the top of the window, it means the page is not set with *writeable* permissions on your web host's server. In order to edit the pages, you'll need to log into your host account with an FTP program and change the permissions on the template files (found in the /wp-admin/templates/ directory and then in the sub-directory for the templates that you want to alter) so that they can be edited. The proper setting is read and writes permissions for all groups, which, on Unix-based servers, is generally coded as 666.

When you're done making changes to the file, click Update File and you'll be able to move on to another template, if desired. Note that you can edit not just your site's HTML templates, but also the main CSS style sheet for your site.

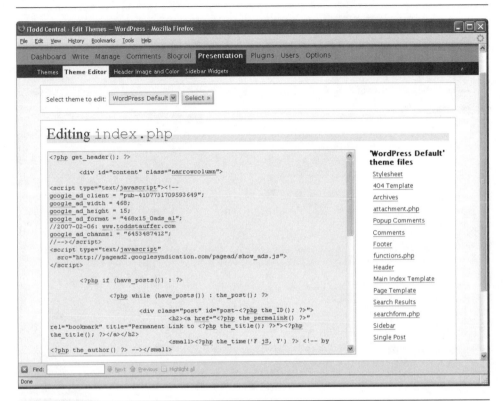

FIGURE 4-9   Editing template code in WordPress

TIP   *You can get started learning about WordPress template tags at http://codex.wordpress.org/Stepping_Into_Template_Tags in the documentation Codex at the main WordPress site.*

ExpressionEngine Templates

ExpressionEngine is designed from the ground-up to give you direct access to your templates for editing. See Chapter 3 for an explanation of how to get into the Templates tab of the admin interface and make changes.

Edit Your Blog's CSS Style Sheets

You've seen that XHTML is a language of commands that can be used to format text that is then displayed in a Web browser. Cascading Style Sheets (CSS) is a special set of commands that can be used to *style* XHTML elements to the extent that the browser can alter their appearance. CSS lets you describe the appearance of a particular XHTML element. For instance, you can decide that all `<h1>` elements will appear in a particular font face, or that all `<hr />` (horizontal rule, or line) elements will appear in a particular color, thickness, or at 50 percent of the width of the rest of the page.

Style Sheets Explained

Style sheets are powerful because they enable you to change the appearance of a Web page without changing the underlying XHTML formatting and structure on the page. That's important for two reasons. First, it allows pages to be *well-formed,* and to use XHTML elements such as the headings (`<h1>`, `<h2>`, `<h3>`, etc.) for formatting reasons, not just for aesthetic reasons. (Some Web designers will wrap text in `<h5>`, `</h5>`, for instance, because it created small, bold text—not because the text was truly a "level 5" heading. That's the sort of formatting decision that CSS is designed to avoid.) The second reason is that using style sheets means that a browser can opt *not* to render some stylistic choice of yours if it will affect the ability of the browser's user to understand or work with your content. So, browsers designed to be accessible to the physically challenged or browsers designed for devices that are limited graphically (like some mobile phones, PDAs, or special-needs web browsers) can still present the formatted XHTML information even if they can't display the fancy CSS codes.

A style sheet is a plain text file, written to the Cascading Style Sheet standard. Generally, it's stored on your host computer in the same directory as your other template files such as index.php or comments.php, and the style sheet file ends with the filename extension .css. The file (which is technically an *external* style sheet, because style sheet definitions can also be embedded in HTML documents) serves as a central repository for all the style definitions for your site.

NOTE *Style sheet support can vary somewhat among browsers, with Internet Explorer notorious for hit-and-miss support of the standards, particularly in versions prior to Internet Explorer 7. The best plan when working with CSS styles is to preview your design in a variety of browsers and platforms (Windows, Mac, Unix-based) whenever possible.*

If you've worked with Microsoft Word's styles (Normal, Heading 1, Heading 2, and so on), you're familiar with the idea—a style sheet definition is simply a preset, named set of characteristics. For instance, using a style sheet, you could define the `<h1>` element so that it appears in a particular font, at a particular size, with a particular font weight, and even in a different color and on a background, as shown here ("DIY Jackson" is an `<h1>` element):

What happens is simple: When a reader's web browser downloads an XHTML document, such as your blog's template, it will notice that the document includes a style definition and a link to the style sheet. So, the browser will request and download the style sheet. It will then use the definitions in that style sheet to determine how the individual elements will look—if the `<h1>` element is defined in the style sheet, it will be rendered according to that definition.

If an element isn't in the style sheet, it will be rendered according to the browser's default settings or any preferences that the user has set in the browser for that element. In fact, some browsers will allow you, as a user, to add your own style sheet to use as the default, thus specially formatting any page that doesn't have its own style sheet. For instance, Internet Explorer enables you, as a user, to create a default style sheet and assign it via IE's preferences settings. So, if you're viewing a page that doesn't have a style sheet, it will use your appearance preferences—fonts, font sizes, and so on.

Adding Styles to Your Templates

As a Web designer, you have two ways to add style definitions to a page. The first way involves typing them directly into the HTML document, using the `<style>`, `</style>` container. (Most of the time, this is done in the `<head>` section of the document, as was discussed earlier in this chapter in the section "HTML Page Elements.") For instance, that's how Classic Blogger templates pages work. Here's an example; notice that this is the beginning of a long style sheet definition that's in the `<head>` section of the Blogger template (that's why we're starting with the `<title>` tag, which is also in the `<head>` section):

```
<title><$BlogPageTitle$></title>
  <style type="text/css">
body {
  background:#ccc;
  margin:0;
  padding:20px 10px;
  text-align:center;
```

```
font:x-small/1.5em "Trebuchet MS",Verdana,Arial,Sans-serif;
color:#333;
}
```

In this example, CSS is used to set styles for the `<body>` of the document that will work as defaults when other XHTML elements aren't specifically defined. (Don't worry about how the styles actually work; we'll get to that in a moment.) Later within that same section (and still between the `<style>` and `</style>` tags) is more markup that determines how links will look and behave within the template:

```
/* Links
————————————————————- */
a:link {
  color:#b30;
}
a:visited {
  color:#666;
}
a:hover {
  color:#c63;
}
a img {
  border-width:0;
}
```

The other way to add style elements—and the way that's pretty much standard for all of the blogging tools discussed in this book aside from Blogger—is to link to an *external* style sheet document. This has the advantage of enabling you to use the same style definitions with different HTML documents without retyping or copying and pasting the style definitions into each page. It also means that a single change to the style sheet can be seen on multiple pages all over your website. This linking approach is the way that TypePad, WordPress, and ExpressionEngine all work. It's done using a special link in *each* XHTML document that is to be associated with that style, as in this example:

```
<link rel="stylesheet"
href="http://www.mybigsite.com/blog/styles-site.css"
type="text/css" />
```

This link element appears in the `<head>` container of the document (usually just after the `<title>` element, although it can be placed anywhere in the `<head>` section) and generally points directly to the style sheet document using an absolute URL.

So, if you opt to change to a different style sheet document for this template, you can do so by altering this link on that XHTML document's page. (Similarly, you can add the `<link>` element to a static page you're posting outside of your blog's interface and give it the same style sheet markup as your blog's pages.)

Style Sheet Definitions

You've seen how style sheets are embedded or linked, but what you need to know is how the actual style definitions work. You'll work with two basic types of style definitions—an actual element and a *class*. When you define an element's style, you're making choices for how that element will look every time you use it. If you create a class definition, you then have more flexibility throughout your template to assign that style class to only the instances of the element where you want those styles to take hold (for instance, `<h1 class="timestamp">`), leaving other instances of that element to be assigned a different class (for instance, `<h1 class="title">`) or no class at all.

In order to create a style for every instance of a particular element (this is called an *element-level definition*), you edit the style sheet and add the element's name, followed by an opening bracket and then a series of style definitions, with each definition followed by a semicolon. Here's an example:

```
H1 {font-family: verdana, sans-serif; font-size: 20px;
color: #33333; font-weight: bold;}
```

You can also, for the sake of readability, stack each of the attributes you're changing. The web browser doesn't care because it doesn't interpret the new lines (when you press RETURN or ENTER):

```
H1 {
  font-family: verdana, sans-serif;
  font-size:   14px;
  color:       #333333;
  font-weight: bold;
}
```

To define a class, all you need is a well-placed period. You can define classes for a particular element, as shown here:

```
H1.red {

  color:       #ff0000;

}
```

Now, in your blog templates, you can use the defined class to change the way some of your headings look by using something like this:

```
<h1 class="red">{title}</h1>
```

In a blog template that uses the `<h1 class="red">` tag for entry titles, this change will cause the title of the entry (or multiple titles on the page, in the case of a template designed for multiple-entry pages, such as a blog's index page) to appear in red when viewed in a web browser. At some later point in the template you could use just a plain `<h1>` element, and it would be styled according to whatever is defined for `<h1>`, such as the typical gray or black text. If no style is defined for `<h1>`, the browser will display it according to the browser's user preferences or the default for `<h1>`.

Notice, too that in the example above, I didn't repeat all of the elements from the element-level (`H1`) definition in class (`H1.red`) definition, because class definitions override their associated element-level definition. That's why they're called *cascading* style sheets; when you use the `<h1 class="red">` tag in your markup, then any style definitions that are already set for the `H1` element will "cascade" down to that class level and be used for styling the text unless they are specifically overridden in the class definition. (Which is how we changed the color of the text in the `H1.red` definition.) Plus, if you *add* anything else to the class definition that isn't in the element-level definition, then that new style will be used in addition to those that are defined at the element level.

Note that you can also create a class that isn't associated with a particular element—that way, you can use this class with any element you desire. All you have to do is omit the element from the definition and simply define a class by starting it with a period, as shown here:

```
.red {
 color:        #ff0000;
}
```

Now, this class can be used with any element that makes sense, such as the paragraph element (`<p class="red">`) or a heading element (`<h2 class="red">`). It could even work for a list item (`<li class="red">Item One</li>`).

Change Styles

When you're first getting started, you probably won't actually add many entries to your style sheet, because most of the elements that are in your templates, by default, are already defined in the style sheet that came with your blog's theme.

So, you'll likely begin by just tweaking styles that already exist in your weblog's style sheet. Before you can do that, though, you'll need to know a little about how the CSS standard works, because that's what defines the actual attributes and values you'll use within a style sheet.

The CSS standard focuses on the visual portions of the web pages you create, with three major types of properties that are relevant to what we're discussing here—font-, text-, and block-level attributes. Let's take a look at some examples of each.

The home of CSS online is http://www.w3.org/TR/REC-CSS2/ at the W3C's website. This particular document is pretty formal and convoluted, so you might want to look for a better CSS reference, such as the StyleGala CSS Reference (http://www.stylegala.com/features/css-reference/).

Font-level attributes include the `font-family`, `font-style`, `font-weight`, `font-size`, `font-variant`, and `color` properties. Using them, you can determine a fairly exact look for the fonts used in your document. You can also experiment with the look of the elements that are already in your blog's style sheet. For instance, here's a snippet of code that could be used to create a new class (called `content`) for blog entries:

```
.content {
    padding: 0px 15px 10px 15px;
    background-color: #fff;
    color: #666;
    font-size:14px;
    font-family:georgia, verdana, arial, sans-serif;
    font-weight:normal;
}
```

Here's what that looks like in a browser when we take some blog codes and enclose them between `<div class="content">` and `</div>` tags:

[Rally] Step up For Children Rally and Press Conference

Things are really heating up at the Capitol, and pro-education legislators are looking to The Parents' Campaign network members (you!) to win full funding for our children! All eyes are now focused on next week's rally, and legislators have said that your attendance there will be the key to a full-funding victory.

Continued...

Posted by admin at 02:53 PM on 01/11/07. Discuss (0)

This class definition, as you can see, has entries for a number of the font-related properties. If you'd like to tweak them, you're free to do so—just jump in and start making changes—but with a few caveats:

■ The `font-family` property can accept a single font's name, but it's usually a good idea to include a series of font names, separated by commas, so that a browser can choose a secondary font if the first one listed isn't available on that computer. (For instance, some computers don't have the fonts Verdana and Helvetica installed, but might have Arial installed.) You should also include `serif`, `sans-serif`, or `monospace` as the last entry so that the browser has a choice just in case none of your listed fonts is available.

TIP   *You should specify the font that you most want to use first in your list and then follow it up with potentially more common fonts (such as Arial and san-serif) later in the list.*

■ The `color` property refers to the color of text when the class being defined is applied to a text container element. It's technically the foreground color. You specify it with a three-digit hexadecimal number that represents the Red, Green, and Blue values for the color.

TIP   *Hexadecimal (which means base 16, so letters are used to represent numerals over 9) color values are either three-digit hex numbers (for example, 878 or FDF) or three two-digit hex numbers (887788 or FFDDFF) representing the amount of red, green, and blue that make up the color. (For example, 000 is black, FFF is white, F00 is bright red, 090 is a medium green.) HTMLHelp.com has a very handy color chart you can use to determine what colors are right for a particular property setting (http://htmlhelp.com/cgi-bin/color.cgi).*

■ The `font-size` property should include a number and the unit of measurement for that size, such as `px` for pixels, `pt` for point size, `in` for inches, or `cm` for centimeters.

NOTE   *Even if you specify the font-size, this is only a baseline—in most visual Web browsers, users can still increase or decrease the size of all fonts shown in their browser window, if desired.*

■ Bold and italic are defined using different CSS properties. The `font-weight` property can be `bold`, `bolder`, `lighter`, or `normal`; the `font-style` property can be `normal` or `italic`.

■ The `font-variant` property is a special case that can be used to make a small-caps font.

So, knowing all this, you can change the style sheet entry shown earlier rather dramatically, perhaps to something like the following:

```
.content {
     background:#ddd;
     color:#090;
     font-size:18px;
     font-family:times, times new roman, serif;
     font-weight:lighter;
     line-height:16px;
   }
```

Here's what those alterations look like in a browser (you'll have to trust me that the text is green and the background is now a dark gray):

[Rally] Step up For Children Rally and Press Conference

Things are really heating up at the Capitol, and pro-education legislators are looking to The Parents' Campaign network members (you!) to win full funding for our children! All eyes are now focused on next week's rally, and legislators have said that your attendance there will be the key to a full-funding victory.

Continued...

Posted by admin at 02:53 PM on 01/11/07. Discuss (0)

Along with all these individual properties, you can also use a single `font` property to define many of these choices, which can accept all the preceding values in a row (separated by spaces, if desired). Here's an example:

```
.lightext {font: arial, Helvetica, sans-serif 12px lighter}
```

Another element that can be used this way (and is used this way very frequently) is the `background` property. Although specific background properties are available for use (such as `background-image` and `background-position`), a lot of designers seem to stick with the background property and often for a simple color choice, as in this example:

```
{background: #00FF00}
```

In fact, one tidbit that's interesting about the `background` element is that it can be used with more than just the `body` element of a page; you can use it with many different XHTML elements, such as the `<p>` element, to change the background color for a specific paragraph of text, for instance. It can also be used with the CSS *box* properties to change the look of a particular element. The box properties include `top-margin`, `right-margin`, `left-padding`, `bottom-padding`, `border-style`, `border-width`, and so on. You can use the more general `margin`, `padding`, and `border` properties, too. All this makes it possible to take our sample entry:

```
.content {
    background:#ddd;
    color:#090;
    font-size:18px;
    font-family:times, times new roman, serif;
    font-weight:lighter;
    line-height:16px;
}
```

and change it to something like this:

```
.content {
    background:#ddd;
    color:#444;
    font-size:18px;
    font-family:times, times new roman, serif;
    font-weight:lighter;
    line-height:16px;
    padding: 10px;
    margin: 10px;
    border: 1px dotted;
}
```

The result is that the entries have a light gray background and some padding around the text so that there's a border of color between the text, the dotted-line border, and the white of the page's background. Without the padding, the text would appear right up against the edge of the border, which probably wouldn't look as good (see Figure 4-10). Notice that padding adds space between the border and the text; the margin adds space between the border and the next entry.

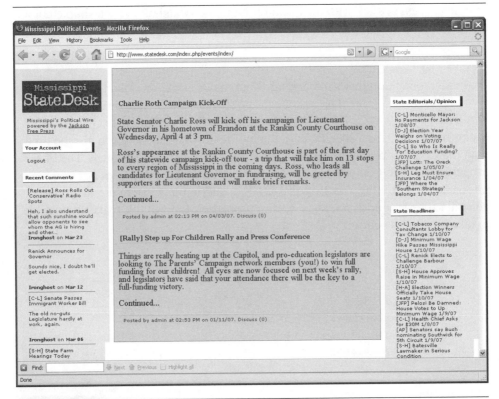

FIGURE 4-10 Here are the re-styled blog entries.

TIP *If you're using Firefox as your web browser you can download a special plug-in called FireBug (www.getfirebug.com). This plug-in enables you to view different elements on a web page to see the style markup that was used to create them, including such things as the padding, margins, and all other sorts of markup. It's great for testing your designs or learning more about other people's CSS.*

You might also wish to play with the text properties, which include word-spacing, letter-spacing, text-decoration, vertical-alignment, text-alignment, and line-height, among others. (See http://www.w3.org/TR/REC-CSS2/text.html for a good explanation of each text property.) These properties enable you to alter the way text appears and behaves on the page, right down to characteristics such as spacing between letters and words.

The `text-decoration` property is of interest, as well, because it enables you to add underlined text (`text-decoration: underline`) or strikethrough-style text (`text-decoration: line`).

The last type of style sheet property I want to discuss is called a *pseudo-class*—a special series of properties that are used with the anchor (`<a>`) element. If you'd like your blog's pages to react to mouse movements, such as "mouseovers" (hovering the mouse over a hyperlink), you can use these special classes. Here's an example from ExpressionEngine's main style sheet:

```
a:link     { color: #000033; font-size: 11px;
font-weight: bold; text-decoration: underline; }
a:visited { color: #000033; font-size: 11px;
font-weight: bold; text-decoration: underline; }
a:active   { color: #333333; font-size: 11px;
font-weight: bold; text-decoration: underline; }
a:hover    { color: #999999; font-size: 11px;
font-weight: bold; text-decoration: none; }
```

These define the look of all the anchor elements on the page in their various states:

- **`:link`**   The state of the anchor text before the hyperlink has been clicked

- **`:visited`**   The state of the anchor text after the click

- **`:active`**   The state of the anchor text during the click

- **`:hover`**   The state when the mouse is over the link

You can change the colors and sizes (although size changes aren't recommended because it can mess up the design of a page) and even add a background property:

```
a:hover          { color: #FFCC66; background: #660066 }
```

This can make for a neat little visual effect when the user points to a link with the mouse, as shown here:

Mark Up with Styles

There's a lot more to the CSS standard, and I suggest you head out on the Web to the sites mentioned previously to get a sense of the breadth of options. (They include some pretty interesting properties, including properties that can govern how text-to-speech browsers for the visually impaired should *speak* the text contained in certain elements.)

Before we move on from this section, however, it's worth discussing two important elements that are particularly useful in XHTML for designing and altering your pages to work with style sheets: the `<div>` (division) element and the `<span>` element.

It's easiest to think of the `<div>` element as sort of a super paragraph element that you can use to define sections of your document. In fact, entire pages can be parceled up and designed using the `<div>` element and some clever style sheet markup.

> **TIP**   *It's a little outside the scope of this book, but the `<div>` element can be used with a special style sheet specification called CSS Positioning for some very advanced web page layout tasks. See http://www.w3.org/TR/WD-positioning for the specification or http://www.brainjar.com/css/positioning/ for a tutorial. You'll find that most of the blog templates use CSS for positioning, generally by creating sidebars that float to the left or right of the main content area.*

Use `<div>`

At the most basic level, the `<div>` element can simply be used to organize and format large chunks of your page at one time:

```
<div class="centered">
...a bunch of elements and text
</div>
```

The `<div>` element is also used heavily to apply certain style classes to groups of elements, as in this example from ExpressionEngine's template code for displaying multiple entries on an index page:

```
<div class="content">
{exp:weblog:entries weblog="{master_weblog_name}"
orderby="date" sort="desc" limit="15" cache="yes"
refresh="10"}
<h3>
<a href="{title_permalink={template_group_name}/comments}">
{title}</a></h3>
{summary}
{body}
{if extended != ""}
```

4

```
<p>
<a href="{title_permalink={template_group_name}/comments}">
Continued...</a>
</p>
{/if}
<p class="posted">Posted by {author} at
<a href="{title_permalink={template_group_name}/comments}">
{entry_date format='%h:%i %A'}</a> on
{entry_date format='%m/%d/%y'}.
<a href="{title_permalink="{template_group_name}
/comments"}#comments">Discuss</a> ({comment_total})
</p>
{/exp:weblog:entries}
</div>
```

Note how the entire entry is enclosed in a `<div>` element that is used to assign the style class `weblog` to the entire entry—in fact, that `<div>` is applying the `content` class that we edited in the previous section. All of the text that appears in the `<div>` section that isn't overridden by another style definition will be displayed according to that `content` class. That's how just a few new CSS tags were able to make such a dramatic difference to the entries shown back in Figure 4-10.

Of course, some of those elements enclosed in the `<div>` tags *do* have overriding style definitions—the `<h3>` element used for the headline has a special style sheet entry, for instance, and the variables that represent information about the entry (the author, date, and so forth) are surrounded by a `<p>` element that assigns the class `posted` to the enclosed markup.

You might, however, notice something different about those two examples; the `<h3>` element doesn't have a class definition in the markup itself, while the `<p>` element does. Here's the `<h3>` element again:

```
<h3>
<a href="{title_permalink={template_group_name}/comments}">
{title}</a></h3>
```

However, the `<p>` element does have a class associated with it:

```
<p class="posted">Posted by {author} at
<a href="{title_permalink={template_group_name}/comments}">
{entry_date format='%h:%i %A'}</a> on
{entry_date format='%m/%d/%y'}.
<a href="{title_permalink="{template_group_name}/comments"}
#comments">Discuss</a> ({comment_total})
</p>
```

The reason for that is that it's possible, within a class definition, to offer alternative definitions for elements that appear within that class. So, in the style sheet for this blog, you'll find the following definition:

```
.content h3 {
    font:bold 14px Georgia, arial,sans-serif;
    margin:2px 12px 2px 2px;
    padding:2px;
    color: #009;
    border-bottom:1px solid #CCCCCC;
    text-align: left;
}
```

This tells the browser that any `<h3>` elements that appear within the content class should be styled in that way. But this style would have no bearing on any `<h3>` items that appear outside of the `<div class="content">` tag pair, unless the `<h3>` tag itself is styled as `<h3 class="content">`.

NOTE   *If you dig deeper into CSS definitions available in references such as http://www.stylegala.com/features/css-reference/, you'll find that some style elements can accept a series of definitions divided by spaces, such as* `border-bottom:1px solid #CCCCCC;` *as an example. What that definition means is "use all of these items to create the style" as opposed to lists separated by commas, such as* `font-face: Georgia, arial,sans-serif;`, *which mean "whichever of these works best." Note that you can mix them, too, as in* `font:bold 14px Georgia, arial,sans-serif;` *such that the font will appear bold, in 14-pixel type using Georgia, if it's available, and Arial or a standard sans-serif font if not.*

The `<p>` is different, however, because, in the example above, it does have a specific style class applied. Here's that definition from the style sheet:

```
.content p.posted {
    color: #333;
    font-family: Verdana, Arial, sans-serif;
    font-size: x-small;
    border-top: 1px solid #ccc;
    text-align: left;
    margin-bottom: 25px;
    line-height: normal;
    padding: 3px;
    padding-left: 10px;
}
```

Why do it this way? So that only the container `<p class="posted">` is styled with the `posted` class while other `<p>` elements within the `<div class="content">` tag pair are not affected.

> **NOTE**
> *You can use the special `style` attribute to the `<div>` element to add a style that isn't defined in the style sheet—for example, `<div style="font-size: 16pt">` could be used to assign all fonts inside the `<div>` element to 16 points (unless overridden by another style definition). Note, though, that "well-formed coding" in XHTML and CSS suggests that it's better to place all of your style definitions in one place (either in the HEAD of your document or in a separate style sheet file). So, it's best to create a new class with style definitions and then assign that class to the `<div>`.*

Use <span>

The other style element, `<span>`, is used when you don't want to create a block-level element using the `<div>` container (`<div>`, after all, creates white space—a

Check Hot Spots with CrazyEgg

Ever wondered what your blog readers click on? CrazyEgg (http://www.crazyegg .com/) enables you to look at how people are using your blog. This web-based tool can track what they're clicking on your site and how frequently; it can even offer graphical overlays to show you the "hot spots" on your site where people are clicking often (see Figure 4-11).

In order to use CrazyEgg, you have to sign up for the service and then place some special code on the pages that you want to track. You do that by cutting and pasting the code into the template pages that you want to learn more about; since you're interested in learning how people are using your blog's index page, you'll probably want to paste the code there. CrazyEgg, in fact, recommends that you paste it into your main templates just above the `</body>` tag toward the bottom of the page.

CrazyEgg is a commercial service; you can track 5,000 page views per month and up to four different pages without paying anything. To get more analysis than that, you'll need to sign up for one of the paid accounts.

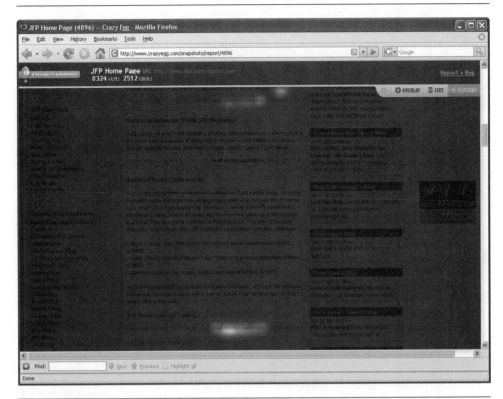

FIGURE 4-11   CrazyEgg gives you a visual sense of where people are clicking on
your blog.

line break—on either side of it, just as `<p>` does). You can use `<span>` the same
way you might use the `<em>` or `<strong>` emphasis element, as shown here:

```
Posted by: <span class="red">{author}</span> on
{entry_date format='%m/%d/%y'}
```

Of course, you can use the `<span>` element in regular markup (for instance,
on static pages or in the static content on your template pages) as well as in
conjunction with template variables, as shown earlier. After all, the template
variables will simply be substituted with the actual entry's text once the page is
published—that's the whole point of separating your content from your template
design.

Chapter 5

Share Your Blog Headlines and Story Feeds via RSS and Atom

How to...

- Learn about syndicating your blog's headlines
- Understand syndication ("feed") standards
- Subscribe to other blogs' headlines and read them
- Publish feeds from your blog so others can access your headlines
- Use the Feedburner service for advanced feeds and statistics about your subscribers

An important characteristic of the Web 2.0 landscape is the prevalence of *feeds*. Feeds make it possible for people to read headlines and content from your blog without reloading your blog's home page on a regular basis. Instead, they can subscribe to a feed from your blog and then have it checked periodically for updates, often by an application called a feed-reader. The feeds can come in different formats and different levels of detail—for instance, you can opt to send just headlines, or to send entire blog entries or something in between.

In this chapter we'll examine the reasons why you might want to syndicate your blog content and then we'll take a look at the different standards and formats used to do that, particularly Real Simple Syndication (RSS) and Atom. Next, we'll explore each of the major blog tool's built-in options, as well as FeedBurner, a popular third-party option. Finally, we'll discuss some of the design considerations in terms of how you should offer feeds to your users.

Why Syndicate?

A blog feed is a simple document that is published on your website every time you make a significant change to your blog. It's available publicly, so when a visitor to your site "subscribes" to the feed, he or she is telling an application of some kind to periodically check that feed file and see if there have been any updates to the site. The feed-reader application can then display the headlines, blurbs and, depending on the feed, it may be able to display the full text of the story and maybe even some images (see Figure 5-1).

By offering headline and/or story feeds to the people who visit your site, you give them a reason to visit again; if they liked what they saw the first time, then the subscription will enable them to keep up with what you're doing in their feed-reader. When they see a story they want to read, they can click over to your site to check

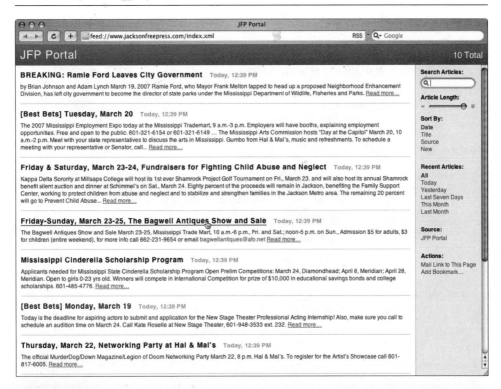

FIGURE 5-1   Apple's Safari browser can display feeds directly in the browser window, giving you an idea of what a single feed looks like.

it out. Figure 5-2 shows an example; using Google Reader, a popular feed-reader, I'm able to quickly sample some of my favorite blog headlines and make decisions about what I want to read. Note that with Google Reader, you can either look at the headlines generated by a particular site or you can group all those headlines together and quickly scan a number of blogs to see what might catch your interest.

Aside from applications that are designed specifically for feed-reading, feeds can be useful in other ways, as well. For instance, feeds can be used to make your headlines appear on other sites such as people's personal Yahoo! or Google home pages. By adding your feed to their home page, they can open this morning with headlines from your site.

If someone *really* likes your blog, they can use your feed to syndicate your headlines into their own website design so they can show their readers what your latest entries are. That's a great way to build some traffic. Depending on the topics you blog about, you might find aggregator sites that will post your headlines if

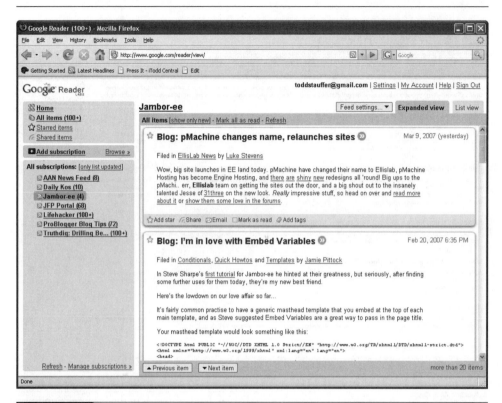

FIGURE 5-2   Google Reader is a browser-based feed-reader for quickly scanning the headlines of your favorite sites.

they judge your content worthy, or that will roll your posts into a larger repository of interesting posts based on your feeds.

TIP   *Need another reason? On large sites, you may find it handy to syndicate headlines from the blog section of the site to another section that isn't a blog. Consider, for instance, that you've got a blog for your company's website, but the primary purpose of the site is to sell a product or service. Using syndication, you may be able to get the site's main content management system to easily display headlines from the company's blog on the home page and/or on related product pages. I do this in some cases with the Jackson Free Press (www.jacksonfreepress.com). In order to get the headlines from some blogs onto the front page, I actually use a blog's feed, which can then show up on the front page (or any other page of the site) as headlines.*

Understand Syndication Standards

There are two different major formats for headline syndication on the Web—RSS and Atom. RSS is a sort of umbrella term that describes a number of different specifications, including RSS 0.9, RSS 1.0, RSS 2.0, and so on. Atom is a separate standard that describes an XML protocol that accomplishes pretty much the same thing as RSS, but that offers some additional flexibility. Which you choose is probably more a function of what your blog application has built-in than anything else, although you may wish to offer an Atom feed if you're looking for the most advanced, standards-compliant option. Just know that syndication is often generally called "RSS" even if it uses Atom protocols.

Atom and RSS

It's worth knowing that many, if not most, feed-readers will accept either type of feed, although some blogging software offers only RSS or Atom, and some blogging "parsers" (commands or widgets that display headlines on your blog pages) may require one or the other.

Here's a little more in-depth look at the various RSS and Atom standards:

- **RSS 0.9**   In this case, RSS actually stands for RDF (Rich Document Format) Site Summary and it was the RSS standard first developed for the My Netscape portal in the mid-1990s.

- **RSS 0.91**   This was a "prototype" specification that simplified the original RSS approach and made it slightly more universal. Oddly, it found wide use, even as a prototype, in part because it was used frequently by sites other than Netscape to offer syndication of articles.

- **RSS 1.0**   This was an open standard developed by the RSS-DEV working group in late 2000. It's similar to RSS 0.91 but builds upon it by offering more features.

- **RSS 2.0**   This standard, also based on RSS 0.91, was spearheaded by Dave Winer (of www.scriptingnews.com and one of the earliest bloggers on the Web) and is now controlled by a group within Harvard University. It's the de facto standard for a lot of syndication these days, including podcasting, as it supports "enclosures" within feeds. (RSS 2.0 is technically the first to be called Real Simple Syndication, although that's generally how the generic term RSS is defined these days.)

■ **Atom 1.0**   While similar to RSS, Atom was built from the ground up to be based on XML and modular. That means it's a little better at syndicating things other than blogs—say, photo galleries and wikis—and it's likely to be extended further in years to come. It's also more flexible in terms of what can be presented in the blog entries and other items it displays, supporting well-formed XHTML, images, multimedia, and so on. In some respects, Atom could be moving toward a standard not just for syndication feeds, but for blogging applications to use for the markup of content in general.

Over the past few years, syndication has been slowly moving from being completely RSS-based to seeing more and more Atom implementations. Most commercial feed-readers will read Atom just as easily as RSS 2.0 and some major blogging tools, such as Google's Blogger, default to creating Atom feeds, although RSS is offered as an option. Because RSS 2.0 is copyrighted and "frozen" in its development by Harvard, it's possible that future blogging tools and feed-readers will continue to migrate toward generating and displaying Atom feeds. (Not that Atom will necessarily "win" this standards war, if that's what it is, but just that more and more tools will likely offer both for the foreseeable future.) For now, whatever your blog tool generates will work and whatever you throw at your feed-reader will probably show up as headlines and blog entries that you can peruse.

NOTE   *Atom vs. RSS is for Web nerds what Mac vs. PC is for some operating system nerds and what beta vs. VHS was for some home video nerds—controversial. For now, though, either will suffice for headline sharing and podcasting, which are the two major uses of feeds at the moment.*

Anatomy of a Feed

All of these feed types tend to convey similar information, although the tags and names used for RSS vs. Atom feeds vary somewhat. In both cases, though, the fundamental idea is to standardize the way people can subscribe to new content on your site, of course, so the formatting is actually pretty simple.

Feed documents can be broken into two basic sections—information about the feed itself and the actual content of the feed. The first section of the document is the *channel* (in RSS) or *feed* (in Atom) section, where information about the feed is found; this is generally information about the blog that has generated the feed.

RSS 2.0 Feeds

In RSS 2.0, the channel section is broken down into the following items:

- **<title>**   The title of the feed. Feeds are often the headlines for a particular blog or set of blogs, but they can also be, for instance, a feed of all the comments for a given blog posting. So, the title can vary and be specific or generic depending on the feed.

- **<link>**   A link to the URL of the weblog's home page or to a particular blog post if the feed is for a post and its comments.

- **<description>**   An optional description of the blog, the feed, or the site where the feed comes from. (The tags should be there, but they can be blank if desired.)

So, the standard opening of an RSS feed will look something like this in a plain text document (that is, when it's not being *parsed* by a browser or feed-reader):

```
<rss version="2.0">
<channel>
<title>Mississippi StateDesk</title>
<link>http://www.statedesk.com/index.php</link>
<description>Political news and opinion from around
the state of Mississippi</description>
```

RSS 2.0 offers a number of optional elements for the channel definition, including:

- **<language>**   The language (English, Spanish, etc.) that the feed is using.

- **<copyright>**   Copyright information for the contents of the feed.

- **<managingEditor>**   An e-mail address for the person who manages the blog or item that is being fed.

- **<docs>**   The URL to the documentation for this feed standard.

- **<webmaster>**   An e-mail for the webmaster of the site that originates the feed.

- **<pubDate>**   The publication date of the contents of the channel.

- **<lastBuildDate>**   The most recent date that the channel was rebuilt with new content or changes to the existing content.

- **<category>**   A category for the content of the channel.

- ■ **<generator>** Information about the application used to create the feed.

- ■ **<ttl>** Time to live. This tells the feed-reader how long it can cache the feed before it should load it again from the source.

> **NOTE** *There are a few others in the RSS 2.0 standard that are very specific to the applications serving the feeds and that generally aren't used by blogs.*

Here's an example that incorporates more of these items:

```
<channel>
<title>Mississippi StateDesk</title>
<link>http://www.statedesk.com/index.php</link>
<description>Political news and opinion from around the
state of Mississippi</description>
<language>en-us</language>
<pubDate>Tue, 20 Mar 2007 04:00:00 GMT</pubDate>
<lastBuildDate>Tue, 20 Mar 2007 09:41:01 GMT</lastBuildDate>
<docs>http://blogs.law.harvard.edu/tech/rss</docs>
<generator>Expression Engine 1.5.2</generator>
<managingEditor>editor@statedesk.com</managingEditor>
<webMaster>admin@statedesk.com</webMaster>
```

After the channel information is entered, you then get to the item information, which is enclosed in `<item>` `</item>` tags. Information between those tags tends to include

- ■ **<title>** The title of the item.

- ■ **<link>** A link to the page where the item is found.

- ■ **<description>** The blurb, introduction, or full text of the item.

So, an example of that portion of the feed would be

```
<item>
<title>Barbour Signs New Film Incentives Into Law</title>
<link>http://www.statedesk.com/barbour_signs_law/</link>
<description>(Jackson, Mississippi)- Governor Haley Barbour
today signed Senate Bill 2997 to provide additional and improved
incentives for the film industry. The bill was unanimously passed
by the Mississippi Legislature during its 122nd Session.
</description>
```

Other optional elements for the `<item>` tag include:

- **`<author>`**   E-mail address of the author of the item.

- **`<category>`**   A category for the item.

- **`<comments>`**   A URL for the comments page of the item.

- **`<enclosure>`**   A URL for any multimedia enclosures for this feed. (This is how podcasts are created, by linking to an MP3 or similar multimedia file.)

- **`<guid>`**   Text that uniquely identifies the item—usually created by the content management system or blogging application.

- **`<pubDate>`**   The publication date of the item.

- **`<source>`**   The RSS channel that the item is a part of.

So, a more complete `<item>` section might look like

```
<item>
<title>Barbour Signs New Film Incentives Into Law</title>
<link>http://www.statedesk.com/barbour_signs_law/</link>
<description>(Jackson, Mississippi)- Governor Haley Barbour
today signed Senate Bill 2997 to provide additional and improved
incentives for the film industry. The bill was unanimously passed
by the Mississippi Legislature during its 122nd Session.
</description>
<author>adam-smith@statedesk.com</author>
<pubDate>Tue, 20 May 2007 08:37:32 GMT</pubDate>
<guid>http://www.statedesk.com/
release_barbour_signs_film_incentives/#When:17:45:01Z
</guid>
</item>
```

So what would a full feed look like? At its most basic, a feed could look like this and be perfectly usable:

```
<?xml version="1.0" encoding="utf-8"?>
<rss version="2.0">
<channel>
<title>Mississippi StateDesk</title>
<link>http://www.statedesk.com/index.php/site/index/</link>
<description>Political news and opinion from around the state of
Mississippi</description>
<language>en-us</language>
```

```
<item>
<title>Barbour Signs New Film Incentives Into Law</title>
<link>http://www.statedesk.com/barbour_signs_law/</link>
<description>(Jackson, Mississippi)- Governor Haley Barbour
today signed Senate Bill 2997 to provide additional and improved
incentives for the film industry. The bill was unanimously passed
by the Mississippi Legislature during its 122nd Session.
</description>
</item>
<item>
<title>Tax Bill Supporters Mull Options</title>
<link>http://www.statedesk.com/supporters_mull_options/</link>
<description>Proponents of the cigarette tax bill are considering
other methods for getting the embattled bill out of the Senate
Finance Committee after Finance Chair Tommy Robertson said he would
kill the bill.</description>
</item>
</channel>
</rss>
```

Notice that the channel tag is closed after a number of item tags have been created and closed; each item is enclosed in its own tag, then the entire thing is wrapped in the channel tags. Of course, you could have any number of items in the feed, although it's typical to publish 10 or 15 items per feed.

With the blogging systems that enable you to edit its RSS template, you'll find that you can often create a template for a feed and then plug in information from the blog database using whatever special tags are made available by the blog engine, whether it's WordPress, ExpressionEngine, or something similar. More on those specific tools later in this chapter.

> **TIP** *You can often few RSS feeds by loading one in your Web browser and then using the View Source command. You can also visit www.toddstauffer.com if you'd like to see additional examples.*

Atom Feeds

Atom feeds are very similar to RSS feeds, but some of the tag names are different and the approach is designed to be slightly more uniform. Here's a sample feed:

```
<?xml version="1.0" encoding="utf-8"?>
<feed xmlns="http://www.w3.org/2005/Atom">
 <title>StateDesk</title>
```

```
<subtitle>Political news and Opinion for Mississippi</subtitle>
<link href="http://www.statedesk.com/" />
<published>2007-03-14T17:45:01Z</published>
<updated>2007-03-15T04:14:21Z</updated>
<author>
  <name>Adam Smith</name>
  <email>adam_smith@statedesk.com</email>
</author>
<id>tag:statedesk.com,2007:03:14</id>

<entry>
  <title>Barbour Signs New Film Incentives Into Law</title>
  <link href="http://www.statedesk.com/barbour_signs_law/"/>
   <id>tag:statedesk.com,2007:index.php/site/index/1.110</id>
    <updated>2007-03-15T04:14:21Z</updated>
    <summary>Governor Haley Barbour today signed Senate Bill
2997 to provide additional and improved incentives for the film
industry. The bill was unanimously passed by the Mississippi
Legislature during its 122nd Session.</summary>
 </entry>
</feed>
```

Atom can be just as simple as RSS 2.0. It can also be a lot more complicated, as there are many additional elements and attributes that can be assigned to a given entry or feed. In a very general sense, however, you'll note that the `<feed>` `</feed>` tags work much like the `<channel>` `</channel>` tags do in RSS 2.0, and the `<entry>` `</entry>` tags are analogous to the `<item>` `</item>` tags in RSS 2.0.

Unlike RSS 2.0, Atom is a standard that will very likely continue to be added to and augmented, not unlike the work that has been done over the years on the HTML and XHTML standards. And Atom is developed with XHTML in mind, so you'll see (if you decide to dig deeper) that Atom feeds can actually serve up XHTML-styled content, offering more flexibility for embedding information into feeds and altering the presentation of your content via the feed. While RSS 2.0 offers attributes and elements that were each added with a specific purpose, Atom is designed to be a framework that can be augmented and built upon as the needs and reasons for feeds change and grow.

NOTE   *The Atom specification can be found at http://tools.ietf.org/html/rfc4287 on the Web, where you can dig very deep into its additional elements, attributes, and more examples.*

Subscribe to and Read Headlines

If you've ever found yourself loading site after site in your Web browser to check in on all your favorite bloggers or news sites, then you might find that feeds can come in handy for your own browsing needs. What a feed does is give you the latest changes on that remote site—all you have to do is choose an aggregator or feed-reader of some sort and then subscribe to those headlines from within the reader.

Choose a Reader

You've got two basic types of reader to choose from: browser-based readers and standalone applications. In your browser, a number of sites can aggregate your subscriptions and give you the opportunity to look at your feeds in different ways, including:

■ **Google Reader (www.google.com/reader/)** As mentioned, Google Reader is a popular way to deal with your headline subscriptions.

■ **Newsgator (www.newsgator.com)** Newsgator is a feed-reader and a home page site in the My Yahoo! service. When you log into the service you can add your own feeds or select from feeds from popular sites and blogs around the Internet.

■ **NewsIsFree (www.newsisfree.com)** Similar to Newsgator, NewsIsFree acts as a home page and an aggregator where you can display popular news headlines and your own favorite feeds from blogs and other sites to which you subscribe.

■ **Bloglines (www.bloglines.com)** One of the more popular aggregators is Bloglines, which focuses on allowing you to manage your own feeds as opposed to getting you started with national feeds, etc. Bloglines has special tools for managing podcasts and even for creating a "clip blog" that you can publish for others to see. And you can publish your feed subscriptions as a blog roll, which can be a fun feature to add to the sidebar of your blog for showing others your favorite blogs.

■ **NetNewsWire and FeedDemon (www.newsgator.com)** Aside from their online reader, Newsgator offers desktop versions in the form of NetNewsWire for Mac, FeedDemon for PC (see Figure 5-3), NewsGator Inbox for Microsoft Outlook, and NewsGator Go for Windows Mobile. Desktop newsreaders have the advantage of allowing you to read downloaded stories when you're not online, and letting you sort through stories quickly without opening a browser window. Plus, it can sit in the background and check your subscriptions frequently.

■ **AmphetaDesk (www.disobey.com/amphetadesk/)**   Another desktop newsreader available for Mac, Windows, Linux, and others. This one is open source and has a popular following, so you can customize it with templates and set a number of options in terms of how it interacts with your Web browser and displays "channels" of headlines and stories.

Subscribe to Feeds

So once you have some sort of reader, how do you subscribe to feeds? In many cases, you can subscribe from within your browser window simply by clicking the URL to the feed. In fact, you'll find that many sites these days have some standard

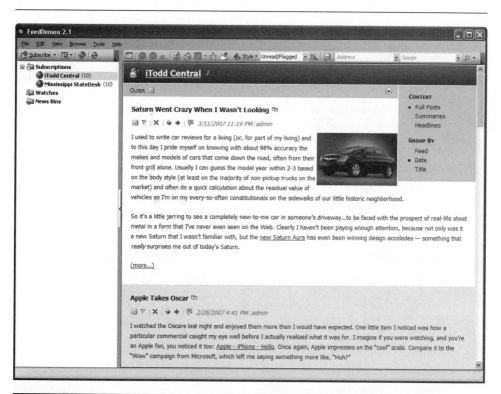

FIGURE 5-3   FeedDemon in Windows gives you a desktop option for reading blog and website headlines.

places where you'll find a link to the feed; in modern browsers, a feed will often appear in the location bar for a site that has an RSS or Atom feed published.

The orange icon with the dot and two lines is something of a universal sign for RSS and Atom feeds. In fact, it was the logo originally created for the My Netscape home page, which Netscape has released into the public domain for free.

If you don't find the subscription link in the location bar, you may still find a "subscribe to our feed," "RSS," or "index.xml" link somewhere on the page. When you do, clicking that link may display the feed's contents in your browser window (in some browsers) or it may display a form to subscribe to that feed in your feed-reader (in some other browsers). For instance, when you click a feed link in the Firefox Web browser, you're shown a built-in interface for subscribing to that feed in a feed-reader (see Figure 5-4).

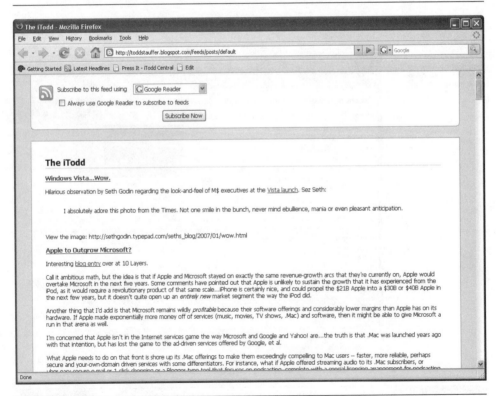

FIGURE 5-4 Click a link to a feed in Firefox and you'll be able to add it to your feed-reader by choosing the feed-reader at the top of the page and clicking Subscribe Now.

In Firefox, pull down the Subscribe To This Feed Using menu and you can choose from some default options or you can click Choose Application to locate a different application (such as a desktop feed-reader) that you want to use for this feed. Firefox also offers the option of storing subscribed feeds as Live Bookmarks, which enable you to see recent headlines from within the Firefox bookmarks interface.

In Internet Explorer 7 and higher, clicking a feed link causes the feed itself to appear in your browser window. You can then click Subscribe To This Feed in order to add the subscription within Internet Explorer itself. (Apple's Safari works much the same way.)

5

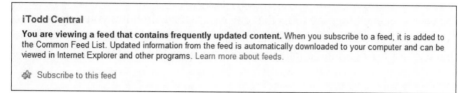

If you're using a third-party or web-based feed-reader and your browser won't automatically subscribe feeds to that service or application, you can always cut and paste. Load the feed's URL in your browser and then copy and paste it into the feed-reader's subscribe tool. Shown is an example in FeedDemon.

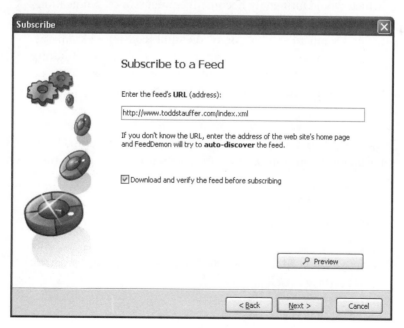

Once the subscription is added, you should be able to track updates to the subscribed blog and read either the headlines or the full stories in your feed-reader, depending on what type of feed the blog is publishing. You should also be able to click a link to the entry that you're reading in order to launch the full item in your browser of choice.

Publish Feeds from Your Blog

As I mentioned, when it comes to RSS vs. Atom, you'll probably use the feed style that is offered by your blogging software. If your software offers both, don't be afraid to use Atom; it's generally as widely adopted by feed-readers as is RSS 2.0. In the case of some blogging tools that can create feeds in both, you may want to offer both. In this section we'll take a look at how you add or manage feeds from within each of the blogging applications discussed in Chapters 2 and 3.

The Feed Icon

Years ago, Netscape introduced a special icon for its MyNetscape service, which would ultimately become the precursor of syndication feeds. As it turns out, the company designed an icon that has continued to be a de facto standard symbol for syndication feeds of all kinds.

You can get that icon for your own use by downloading it at http://feedicons.com/ on the Web. Although often orange, the icon can be customized in applications such as Adobe Photoshop and Adobe Illustrator, as well as resized.

To use the icon on your pages, you'll want to edit your templates so that the icon image is also a link to your feed. So, once you've uploaded the icon to your hosting account somewhere, you would use code such as this to create the link:

```
<a href="http://www.mysite.com/myfeed.xml">
<img src="http://www.mysite.com/images/feedicon.png"
style="border:0"></a>
```

Of course, you'll need to change the URLs to the appropriate names, including the feed icon itself.

Blogger Feeds

It was a big deal when Blogger switched over to offering Atom feeds by default, in part because it helped to legitimize the format for feeds, as Blogger is a pretty big deal in the blogging world. Setting up feeds in Blogger is pretty much automatic—by default, Blogger creates a feed for your blog and offers it in the Atom 1.0 standard. In fact, it offers three feeds by default: a feed of your posts, a feed of the comments on all your posts, and a feed of the comments on a particular post.

To customize the way Blogger handles your feeds, go to the Settings tab for your blog's admin interface and click the Site Feed link. There you'll see preferences for your feed, as shown in Figure 5-5.

Blogger has two modes for feed preferences: Basic and Advanced. In the Basic mode, you can simply choose whether you'd like your blog's feed to show the full content of your posts or a shortened version. Choose Full or Short from the Allow

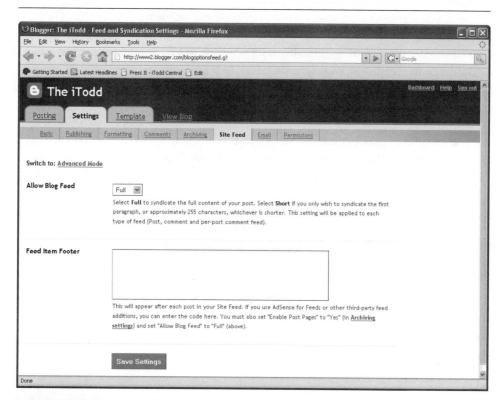

FIGURE 5-5   The feed settings for Blogger

Blog Feed menu. To switch to Advanced mode, click the Advanced Mode link.
Now you can choose how much of each content should be in each type of feed.

You can also add a Feed Item Footer in either mode; the footer is often used for
AdSense advertising within Blogger feeds.

With your feeds configured, you can access them by viewing your site. The
link to the feed for your posts is generally found at the bottom of each page; when
clicked it will either display in the browser window or you'll be prompted to
subscribe to the feed. You can also add a link to your feeds in the sidebar of your
blog, if desired; the Blogger tag for putting your side feed links in the sidebar is:

```
<$BlogFeedsVertical$>
```

The code for per-post-comment feeds (feeds of the comments that are added to a
particular post) should go in your Blogger template inside the `<ItemPage>` tags, in
the same general area as the tags that display comments. That feed tag looks like this:

```
<$BlogItemFeedLinks$>
```

Note that you may want to place some paragraph tags and style calls around
those feed tags to make them look good on the page, as in:

```
<p id="postfeeds"><$BlogItemFeedLinks$></p>
```

If you do that, you'll want to add some style sheet declarations to the style
sheet section of the Blogger template; Blogger's Help file recommends adding
something along the lines of:

```
#blogfeeds {
    [insert formatting here]
    }
#postfeeds {
    [insert formatting here]
    }
```

TIP   *See Chapter 4 for more on CSS and style sheets.*

TypePad Feeds

If you're blogging in TypePad, you'll find that, as with Blogger, your basic feeds are set up automatically. (In fact, TypePad automatically creates RSS 1.0, Atom 1.0, and RSS 2.0 feeds.)

To customize them, click the Configure tab under the main Weblogs tab and then click the Feeds link. On the Feeds page, you can turn your feeds on and off and you can choose what content you want sent in your feed—either the Full Post or Post Excerpts. In terms of options for the built-in feeds, that's pretty much it.

TIP   *TypePad does have one other interesting option for feeds; you can set it up to work directly with FeedBurner for your feeds instead of using the built-in tool. That way you can customize your feeds and track users. See the section "Use FeedBurner" later in this chapter.*

In many of the default TypePad blog designs, the link that enables readers to subscribe to your feed is found in the sidebar as a text link called Subscribe to This Blog's Feed. If you'd like to change the location of that feed link, you can do that by choosing the Design tab and then the Order Content link. Now, you can drag the Syndication Link box to a new location on your blog or in your sidebar to change its location.

WordPress Feeds

WordPress creates two feeds by default, an Entries feed and a Comments feed. In many of the templates, those two feed links appear in the Meta section of the sidebar.

Within the WordPress interface, these feeds can't really be altered much. You can, however dig into the templates and make some more in-depth changes.

Edit WordPress Feed Templates

WordPress offers a few different templates that can be edited to change the way your feeds are formatted. To do this, you'll need to use an FTP program to copy the files from your hosting account to your desktop to edit them. (Some FTP programs offer the ability to edit the file and then save it immediately from within the FTP application's interface. That works, too, in this case.)

The files that you can edit are

- `wp-atom.php`   The template for Atom 1.0 feeds

- `wp-rss.php`   The template for RSS 1.0 feeds

- `wp-rss2.php`   The template for RSS 2.0 feeds

- `wp-commentsrss2.php`   The template for RSS 2.0 feeds of your comments

Open one of those files and you'll see the formatted document with WordPress tags used to substitute information from your blog. In most cases, the default works fine. But, if you're interested in editing them, there's a full explanation and some examples in the WordPress documentation at http://codex.wordpress.org/Customizing_Feeds.

Add Feeds from Other Blogs

You can add feeds from other blogs to your WordPress blog's sidebar, as was discussed in Chapter 3. Here's how:

1. To add an RSS feed from another site to your sidebar, choose Presentation in the WordPress admin interface and then click Sidebar Widgets.

2. At the bottom of the Sidebar Widgets page, you'll see an area where you can choose the number of RSS feeds that you want for your page; choose at least one from the menu and click Save. That will cause a new RSS box to appear in the Available Widgets box.

3. Now, drag the RSS box from the Available Widgets box to your blog's design and drop it (probably somewhere in the sidebar).

4. On the RSS box you should see the small edit control on the right side of the widget box. Click it and a dialog box appears.

5. Put the URL to the feed and an option description in that dialog box. Click the Close control when you're done with it.

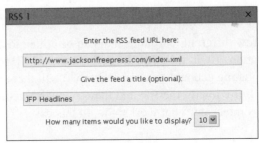

6. Click Save Changes in the Sidebar Widgets screen. Now you can view your blog and see the new headline feed.

Headline feeds are one way that you can use multiple installations of WordPress and still have sort of a relationship among them. With headlines from your different blogs (whether they're by the same author or not) you can feed people back and forth between them. This is great whether you're showing your friend's headlines, your company's, or your boss's.

RSS in ExpressionEngine

ExpressionEngine offers built-in support for RSS 2.0 and Atom feeds for your main blog, as well as the ability to create additional feeds if you have multiple blogs. You can also customize feeds to offer just headlines or full entry output, output from more than one blog, a new comments feed, and so on. Feeds in ExpressionEngine are templates just like blog pages and comment pages. So, creating a new feed is actually pretty easy to do once you know how it works— you create a new template for that feed, and then you specify the information that's supposed to be generated for that feed using the {weblog:entries} tag in much the same way that you can tell an ExpressionEngine blog page how it should display blog entries.

Access and Edit the Default Feeds

Whenever you install ExpressionEngine and create a blog, two default feeds are created for you. Like other ExpressionEngine pages, those feeds are created as templates within the system. So, to access the feeds, you use the typical ExpressionEngine URL-building approach. For instance, for the template named rss_2.0, which is the default RSS 2.0 template, the URL would be

```
http://www.yoursite.com/index.php/site/rss_2.0/
```

Accessing that feed in a browser for my StateDesk.com site, for instance, renders an RSS feed, as shown in Figure 5-6.

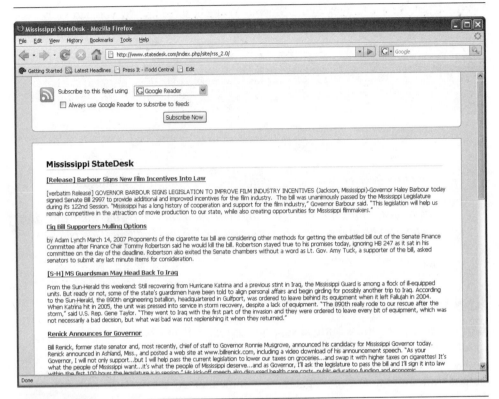

FIGURE 5-6   The built-in RSS 2.0 feed in ExpressionEngine

By default, you'll find at least two templates for RSS feeds that are standard when you install ExpressionEngine—one is an Atom feed and one is an RSS 2.0 feed. You'll get to those by clicking the Templates tab in the main admin interface (see Figure 5-7).

You can edit the templates to change, for instance, whether or not you want the full story to be published via the feed or if you simply want a blurb or a particular section to be published. For instance, in the standard `rss_2.0` feed template, find this section:

```
<item>
  <title>{exp:xml_encode}{title}{/exp:xml_encode}</title>
  <link>{title_permalink=site/index}</link>
  <guid>{title_permalink=site/index}#When:
      {gmt_entry_date format="%H:%i:%sZ"}</guid>
  <description>{exp:xml_encode}{summary}{body}
      {/exp:xml_encode}</description>
```

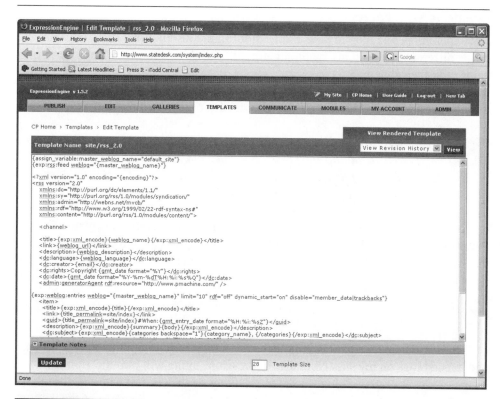

FIGURE 5-7   In ExpressionEngine, feeds are stored as templates.

Notice that you could change the ExpressionEngine tags in the `<description>` portion of the feed so that only the `{summary}` appears, or so that `{summary}`, `{body}`, and `{extended}` all appear in that portion, which would send your full blog posts as part of the feed, as in:

```
<description>{exp:xml_encode}{summary}{body}{extended}
{/exp:xml_encode}</description>
```

Of course, if you don't use the `{summary}` field, as many bloggers don't, you don't have to include it in the feed template. And in some cases when you do use it you might not want to send it in the feed, particularly if it's not the first paragraph of the actual blog post. Save that template and reload the URL for that template in a browser or RSS feed-readers and you'll see that you're now sending full stories with your feeds.

Create a New Feed

Have more than one blog in your ExpressionEngine installation? If so, you can create different feeds simply by duplicating the feed's template (with a different name) and then changing the `master_weblog_name` variable (found at the top of the template) to the short name of the new blog. Now, that newly created template can be accessed by its URL and it will be a feed for the new blog you've specified.

TIP   *To get you started, ExpressionEngine posts basic templates for RSS feeds on its website at http://expressionengine.com/templates/source/category/ feeds/. You can paste these into a new template if you'd prefer to start fresh instead of copying an existing template.*

You can also use ExpressionEngine's built-in "piping" ability to create a feed that includes multiple blogs at once. To do that, you simply add the short names of the individual blogs to the `weblog:entries` tag separated by the pipe character (|) as in:

```
{exp:weblog:entries weblog="news | events | music"
limit="15" rdf="off" dynamic_start="on"}
```

This would create a feed that includes the latest entries from the news, events, and music blogs on my site. Note that ExpressionEngine will pull the 15 most recent entries from those blogs based exclusively on the entries' dates; it doesn't try to balance the number that come from each of the blogs. So, if 14 of the most recent 15 entries from among these blogs were added in the music blog, then all 14 of those entries would show up in the feed.

Also, note the `dynamic_start="on"` attribute. For the `weblog:entries` tag, this attribute only relates to RSS feeds. When turned on, it enables the feed to add just the latest information to a feed-reader when it requests it.

TIP   *The ExpressionEngine wiki offers an in-depth article on creating feeds for multiple weblogs, including information about changing the channel information on the feed to more fully reflect the multiple weblog's titles. See http://expressionengine.com/wiki/RSS_for_multiple_weblogs/ for more information.*

Use FeedBurner

FeedBurner is a service that makes delivering syndication feeds to your blog readers a little more sophisticated, while giving you information about your feed's subscribers in the form of statistics and other tracking information. FeedBurner is a pretty cool service, in that it enables you to ensure that the feed-subscription experience for all of your users is uniform, while giving you a little more to do with your feed and offering you some options for publicizing your blog's content more widely. It does the basics discussed here for free, too, while offering some premium services if you're interested in very seriously tracking your feed subscribers and learning more about what they're reacting to on your blog.

Get Started with FeedBurner

To get started with FeedBurner, head to http://www.feedburner.com/ on the Web and enter either the URL for your RSS or Atom feed, or, in many cases, you can enter the URL for your site directly in FeedBurner. If your site is a podcast site, click the option "I'm a Podcaster." Then, click Next.

> **Start FeedBurning Now. Type your feed or blog URL below. (Why Burn?)**
>
> Learn how to burn your Blogger, TypePad, WordPress, MySpace or podcast/video feed.
>
> http://www.statedesk.com/index.php/   ☐ I am a podcaster! | Next » |
>
> Currently feeding **367,353** publishers who've burned **610,862** feeds (as of 13 Mar 07). More »

FeedBurner will check out your site and let you know if it finds a valid feed. If it finds more than one, you may see a page asking you which feed you'd like to use with FeedBurner. Choose the feed you want to use and click Next again.

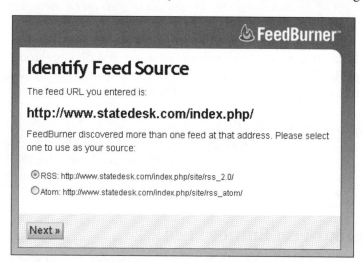

Now, you'll see a Welcome page asking you to enter information about the feed. If you don't already have an account with FeedBurner, you'll also need to enter some registration information. With all that set, you can click Activate Feed to "burn" the feed.

> **TIP** *When you specify the URL for your feed, you can add subfolders if you like, so that http://feeds.feedburner.com/toddstauffer/newfeedname is a valid option. That can be helpful if you keep running into trouble when you're trying to come up with a unique name for your feed.*

If all goes well you'll see a Congratulations screen and you'll be shown the URL to your new feed. The idea is to use this URL for your feed from now on, not the one generated from within your blogging software. So, you'll want to head back to the templates for your site and edit your feed links so that when a user clicks on a link to your feed, they'll access this page instead of the built-in link.

Click the Next button on the Congratulations screen and you can customize the statistics that FeedBurner will report to you. By default, FeedBurner can tell you how many subscribers you have, what feed-readers people are using to read your feed and whether your feed is being used in any uncommon ways (for instance, if it's being republished somewhere). You can turn on an option that tracks clickthroughs, as well, which means clicks back to your site. When you're done making choices, click the Next button.

> **NOTE** *FeedBurner offers a TotalStats paid version that you can sign up for as well. It offers additional statistics tracking and can be used to track the performance of individual items in your feeds.*

With all that done, you'll be shown a page that will walk you through the process of publishing your FeedBurner link on a variety of different blogging platforms, including Blogger, TypePad, and WordPress.

> **TIP** *For a server-side WordPress blog, you can use the FeedBurner plug-in at http://orderedlist.com/wordpress-plugins/feedburner-plugin to redirect all of your feed requests to your FeedBurner feed, ensuring that you capture every attempt to subscribe to your blog's feed. That means your FeedBurner stats will be more accurate and useful.*

Link to Your FeedBurner Feed

FeedBurner offers a number of different ways that you can link to your feed and promote your content. The most basic, of course, is a link to the feed itself, which you can do simply by substituting the FeedBurner URL (for example, http://feeds.feedburner.com/statedesk) for the URL that you currently have in your blog's template, as in this example in my StateDesk blog:

```
<li><a href="http://feeds.feedburner.com/statedesk">RSS 2.0</a>
```

Likewise, you could use the new FeedBurner URL if you're using a feed image link, as in:

```
<a href="http://feeds.feedburner.com/statedesk">
<img src="http://www.statedesk.com/images/feedicon.png"
style="border:0"></a>
```

FeedBurner itself offers many different ways for you to post your feed on your site. To get at them, click the Publicize tab in your FeedBurner dashboard. (If you don't see the dashboard, then start by clicking My Feeds at the top of the page, then click the name of the feed that you want to work with.)

One of the options is to publicize your feed with a "friendly graphic." Click that link and you'll see some options that you've probably seen elsewhere if you often surf blogs. You can choose from the standard feed icon, or you can elect to create a link that automatically adds feeds to a variety of different feed-readers or aggregating tools such as MyYahoo and Add to Google and so on (see Figure 5-8).

Once you've chosen one of the images that you want to use for the link, scroll to the bottom of the page and you'll see a section where you can copy the HTML codes for that link. Now, paste that code into your blog's index template page. That should cause the new image to appear when you reload the page.

As another option, instead of copying and pasting the text, you can create a widget for popular blogging tools. In the Use As a Widget In menu, select the blogging tool that you use and click Go. You'll be taken to your blog, where you'll be shown how to add the widget. Now, you can dig into your blog's design and place the widget where you'd like it on your template pages.

Within the Publicize tool there are many other options you can experiment with, including headline and animated widgets that you can use to show your blog's headlines on other sites, such as your MySpace page or on other websites where you have access to the HTML code. You can even create banner ads of your headlines and content that you can place on other sites.

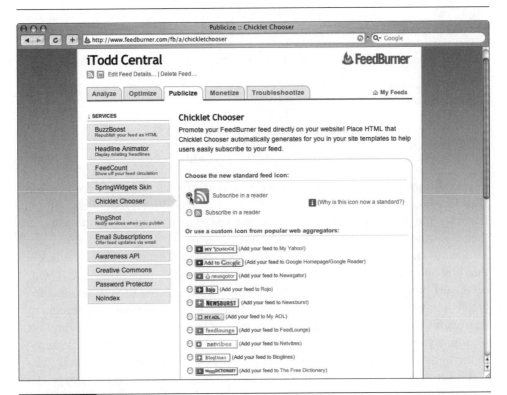

FIGURE 5-8 From this page in FeedBurner, you can choose to create image links that help your readers subscribe to your feed.

TIP *If you're using TypePad, you can connect to FeedBurner and configure your feed from within the TypePad interface. When viewing the admin interface for the blog, choose Configure and then Feeds. At the bottom of the Feeds page you'll see an option to Connect to FeedBurner, which enables you to log into FeedBurner and access a feed you've already created or create a new one if you haven't yet "burned" your TypePad feed.*

Set Your Discoverable Links to FeedBurner

Simply creating the link to your FeedBurner feed in your blog template may not be enough; you may also want to change the "discoverable" links to your feed so that browsers that auto-discover feeds will find the link to FeedBurner, not to your blog's built-in RSS or Atom feed. To do that, you'll need to dig into your templates.

What you're looking for is a tag in the <HEAD> of your template document that looks like this:

```
<link rel="alternate" type="application/rss+xml"
title="RSS" href="http://www.toddstauffer.com/rss.xml" />
```

Now, you'll change that link so that it points to your FeedBurner feed, as in:

```
<link rel="alternate" type="application/rss+xml" title="RSS"
href="http://feeds.feedburner.com/toddstauffer.xml" />
```

5

> **NOTE**   *The "new" Blogger is a special case; you can't edit the `<link>` text directly, even though it's there. For instructions on making the new Blogger use your FeedBurner feed as its auto-detect feed, visit http://forums.feedburner.com/viewtopic.php?t=3377 in the FeedBurner forums.*

Customize the Feed Page

By default, the FeedBurner feed page is very similar to a typical feed page when it's clicked by the user. FeedBurner, as it's configured by default, simply offers you a convenient way to create links to your feed (including all those popular links directly to aggregators and custom home pages like Google, MyYahoo!, MSN, and so on) and some tools for tracking how many subscribers you have and how active they are.

FeedBurner can do some other things, however. For instance, click the Optimize link, and you'll find the BrowserFriendly option, which leads users to a new landing page when they click your subscribe link. To activate BrowserFriendly, click its icon on the Optimize page, then make your selections in the Appearance options. These options enable you to determine which subscription options you're going to make available to your readers as well as how much of the feed you want to show to them on this landing page. When you're done, click Activate.

The result is that whenever someone clicks your FeedBurner link from your blog's home page, they now see the BrowserFriendly page (see Figure 5-9) instead of the raw RSS feed or the browser's own rendering of the feed. The BrowserFriendly page enables the reader to quickly subscribe to your blog using their favorite feed-reader. Or, if they don't have a feed-reader installed, they can choose to see your headlines on their aggregator page or custom home pages such as MyYahoo!.

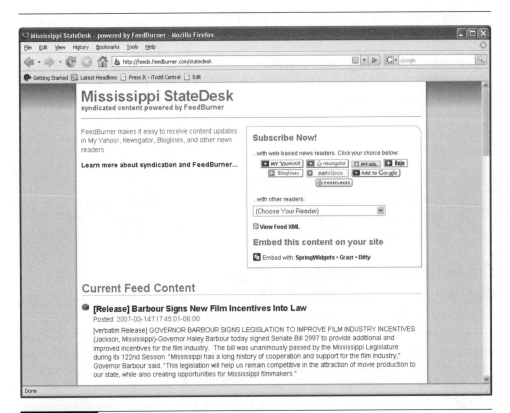

Check Your FeedBurner Stats

Some of what's fun about FeedBurner is checking your stats once you have your feed out there and you've gotten some subscribers. Whenever you log into your FeedBurner account, you'll see a dashboard that shows you some of the feeds that you've created and some basic stats for them. If you've just gotten started, you may not see much in the way of activity. Click a feed and you can dig further into that feed's stats on the Analyze tab.

Again, when you first get started you won't see many subscribers, but once you've got a few, you can click the Subscribers link under Feed Stats to get a sense of how many subscribers you have and learn a little more about them.

The Live Hits link shows you information about people who are accessing your feed, even if they aren't subscribing. It can certainly be an interesting page to watch (see Figure 5-10).

> **TIP** *You can set up FeedBurner to track information about people who visit your site and not just people who access your feed. To do that, click the link under Site Stats and walk through the activation process. You'll need to add special HTML to your pages in order for the tracking to work.*

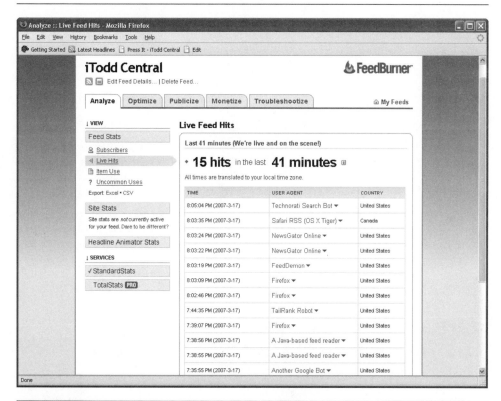

FIGURE 5-10   The Live Links page shows you people who are accessing your site's FeedBurner feed.

Chapter 6

Multimedia and Your Blog

How to…

- Add photos to your blog
- Create a podcast or audio blog
- Post video on your blog (and the Internet)

The popularity of "Web 2.0" services is a direct result of the rise of broadband access to the Internet. As the "pipe" has gotten wider, bandwidth-demanding content such as audio and video is more popular because it's more convenient to deal with. Thus, some of the Web 2.0 service sites that have appeared in recent times make it very easy for you to listen to audio or view video that others are sharing and post that video to your site—or edit and post your own.

And, of course, photos always add an important visual element to your text-heavy blog, whether it's photos in the posts themselves or in a sidebar link to your galleries. Plus, to add tons of interest (and, hopefully, loyal listeners and viewers), you can incorporating audio and video into your blog. In this chapter, we'll look at some of the different ways you can add photos, video, and audio to your blog to make it that much more interactive and interesting for your visitors—and to share with others through Web 2.0 services on the Web.

Add Photos to Your Blog

Are you a little bit of a shutterbug? If so, you might be the type who likes to add photos to your blog, whether it's just to share your snaps with your adoring public, drum up a little interest in your art, or post important images that add to the conversation you're having online. In any case, what we're talking about here is something beyond the simple addition of photos to blog entries, which we discussed for each blog tool in Chapters 2 and 3. If you're interested in posting galleries of photos for your readers to browse, you've come to the right place.

There are a few different directions we can go here. If your blogging tool offers a built-in photo gallery, then we can dig in and use that—of the tools covered in this book, both TypePad and ExpressionEngine (if you have a paid license) offer galleries. For blogging tools that don't offer a built-in gallery, we can turn to hosted photo services such as the extremely popular Flickr service, as well as some of its rivals.

TIP *If you have a self-hosted blog and you don't have a built-in gallery solution (for instance, if you're running WordPress) then you have yet another solution—you can install standalone photo gallery software, such as the popular open source Gallery application (http://gallery.menalto.com/).*

Consider Other People's Photo Rights

Whether you're adding photos to blog entries (a "photoblog" can be a popular way to pass the time, where blog entries are mostly photos along with some descriptive text) or going whole-hog and creating a photo gallery or sharing photos using a Web 2.0 service, you need to carefully consider the source of your photos. If you took the photos yourself, then you should be set—if they're of people, it's always safer to get a written permission or photo release from that person, just so they don't later feel that you've violated their privacy.

If you didn't take the photo or create the artwork, you're in a different realm. The Web makes it very easy to copy, save, upload, download, and link to images on the Web, but intellectual property rights can (and sometimes should) get in the way of all that free linking. Before you go posting someone else's photos or artwork to your blog, you should think about it first. Here are a few guidelines:

- *Don't steal bandwidth*. It can be tempting to link to a photo on someone else's site using an `<imc src="http://www.theirsite.com/theirimage.jpg">` tag to embed the image on your blog. This is bad form, however, because it forces their server to send the image to your visitor's Web browser even though they aren't receiving any benefit from the traffic. And remember, people often have to pay for sending requested files in the form of bandwidth surcharges. If you're using someone else's image, copy it to your hard disk and then upload it via the blogging or photo gallery tool to your own host.

- *Is the image copyrighted*? You also need to think carefully when using someone else's photo or artwork because it's very likely copyrighted and that person's property. It's worth noting that there are different types of copyright licenses; for instance, one type of license that is growing in popularity is the Creative Commons license, where photos may be used by others under certain circumstances without contacting (or paying) the owner. (Some photo sharing services enable users to offer their photos under the Creative Commons license; see http://creativecommons.org/ for more information.) If you're using photos specifically released in the public domain or using a Creative Commons or similar "open" copyright notice, then it may be safe to use. (You should still abide by the terms of the license; some Creative

(continued)

Commons licenses require attribution, for instance.) If an image doesn't specifically have a shareable copyright notice or terms for posting it yourself (such as with some PR photos) then you should consider it copyrighted and avoid using it. If it does offer sharing as an option, then you should also attribute the image to its creator or copyright holder and, ideally, link back to wherever you found the image (or post some similarly beneficial link for the copyright holder).

■ *Is your use of the image "fair use"?* This is the exception to the copyright rule—using a copyrighted image because it's "fair use." Fair use is a legal doctrine in the United States that allows you to incorporate copyrighted material into your work if it passes certain tests, for example, if you're including it for the purpose of academic discussion or parody, if the use is "transformative," if it doesn't hurt the commercial value of the material, and so on. This is a complicated mess and I'm not an attorney, but you can read more about it at http://en.wikipedia.org/wiki/Fair_use. Very generally speaking, you'll find that people will often download and then publish images from elsewhere on the Web, sometimes "transforming" the image (by, say, cropping it closer or taking a screenshot of a video) and sometimes by creating a smaller version of the image and linking to the original source. You'll need to make your own decisions, but keep in mind that there's a fine legalistic line between fair use and copyright infringement. When it doubt, avoid using an image that doesn't belong to you and hasn't been made available specifically for public use. On your blog, you're always safest when you're using your own photos!

Add a Built-in Photo Gallery

If you're using TypePad or ExpressionEngine, you can essentially flip a switch and begin working with a new, slick photo gallery. TypePad's photo gallery feature is extremely easy to get up and running, particularly if you're pleased with one of the built-in templates. (With TypePad, once you add a gallery you also have the option of re-tooling the design of your blog so that the gallery is a key element in the blog's layout.) ExpressionEngine's gallery is powerful, but it also can take a little extra tweaking if you want something beyond a basic design for your gallery.

Here's a quick look at how to work with either of those applications.

Create an Album in TypePad

TypePad calls photo galleries "albums" and enables you to create them as separate entities from your blogs. So, if you've got more than one blog and would like to show images from the same gallery, that's completely doable; likewise, you can create multiple galleries and use those on a single blog. Here's how to get started:

1. From the TypePad dashboard, click the Photo Albums tab at the top of the interface.

2. On the Photo Albums page, click Create a New Photo Album.

3. That alters the screen so that you can enter a name for the photo album and a short name for the albums folder on the service. Do so and then click Create New Photo Album.

4. The next screen is the Add New Photos screen, where you can choose to upload a batch of new photos for your album. Begin by telling TypePad how many photos you want to upload, and the screen will display enough entry boxes for those photos (it's OK if you don't use every entry box).

5. Next, click the Browse button next to each entry box so that you fill it in with photos that will be uploaded.

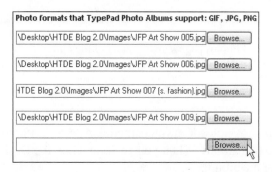

6. When you're done adding photo links, click the Upload button at the bottom of the screen. The result will be the List Photos page shown in Figure 6-1.

7. On the List Photos screen, you can click the Photo Title of any of your photos to see the Edit Photo Record page. On that page, you can make changes to the title of the photo, you can give it a short description and you can enter information such as the location where the photo was shot and the date it was taken. (Some of this information may appear automatically if your camera stored it on the photo's file.) When you're done editing, click Save.

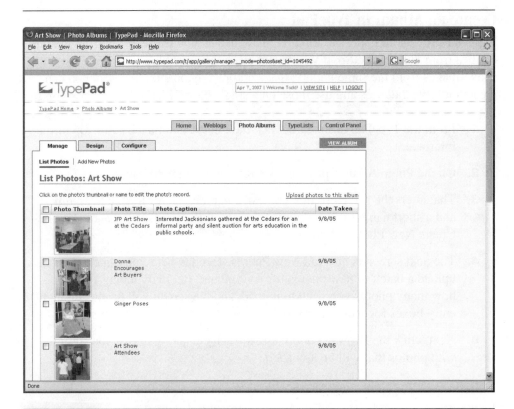

FIGURE 6-1 The List Photos page shows you all of the photos that you have uploaded to your TypePad photo album and enables you to name them and edit captions.

8. With your photos uploaded, you can click Add New Photos if you need to add more to this album. When you're done, click the Design tab to move on to designing the album.

9. On the Design tab you'll see options for changing the way your album looks in a browser; if you like the default look, you can simply click Publish. If you'd like to change something about the design, you've got three different Edit links that you can click: Layout, Content, and Style. (Note that once you're on one of these pages, such as the Photo Album Layout page, links to the other two appear in the top-right corner of those pages.)

■ **Layout**   Click the Layout link and you'll see the Photo Album Layout screen, where you can choose from a variety of different options for the cover page of your photo album and for the photo pages themselves. TypePad offers a number of different options that incorporate thumbnails, full views of images, and combinations of the two. When you're done, click Save Changes.

■ **Content**   On the Photo Album Content page you can choose what content you want to appear on your cover page and on your photo pages. You can opt to include a description of the photo album, the individual captions of the photos and other details. When you've made your choices, click Save Changes.

■ **Style**   On the Photo Album Style page you can choose from a number of built-in style templates for your photo album from the menu that appears. When you've made your choices, click Save Changes.

10. Next, click the Configure tab to set some basics about this photo album— including its name and description, which are used on many of the cover page layouts—as well as some advanced options. In the advanced options, for instance, you can choose what size thumbnail you'd like to use in your album, whether thumbnails should be automatically cropped so that they're uniform in dimension (all square, for instance), and some details such as the date format for your albums. Click Save Changes when you're done.

You may have noticed while setting up your photo album that there's often a View Album link at the top of the page. Click that link and you'll see your photo album appear in a new window. As you check, if you don't see your album's descriptions or photo names shown correctly, dig back into your Design and Configuration tabs and make sure you saved all the changes that you intended to make.

NOTE   *Need to delete a photo album? Click the Photo Albums tab at the top of the TypePad admin interface and you'll see a list of your current photo albums. Click the Delete link in the detail box for the album that you need to get rid of, and then, in the dialog window that appears, click Yes, Delete.*

Once you've got a photo album up and running on TypePad, it's actually a standalone entity; you could link to it, send e-mails with the URL to friends, and so on. Of course, TypePad is designed to integrate the photo album into your blog's design, which you can do using the Design tools for your blog. Here's how:

1. To begin, click the Weblogs tab at the top of the TypePad admin interface, then, for the blog you want to alter, click the Design link. (If you're already viewing the admin interface for a specific blog then click the Design tab.)

2. On the Design page, click the Select Content option.

3. Now, on the Content Selections page, scroll down to the Photo Albums section and place a checkmark next to the photo album that you'd like to include in your blog's sidebar. Scroll to the bottom of the page and click Save Changes.

NOTE   *There's another, alternative option on the Content Selections page, where you can opt, instead, to show links to all of your TypePad photo albums. Under the section Your Photo Albums, place a checkmark if you'd like those links to appear in your sidebar.*

4. Next, back on the Design page, you can click the Order Content link in order to move the photo gallery widget around on the page. When you're done, click Save Changes.

That's it. With the widget on your blog's page, you can view your site to see the new photo gallery in action (see Figure 6-2).

You can have multiple photo galleries on your blog's home page, if desired, and it's worth noting that some of the built-in layouts for TypePad blogs can be very multimedia-centric.

Add a Gallery in ExpressionEngine

The other blogging tool we've been discussing that offers a built-in gallery solution is the licensed version of ExpressionEngine. (The free "core" version of ExpressionEngine doesn't have gallery functionality.) The gallery in ExpressionEngine comes in the form of a module which must be activated, giving you the ability to upload images, title them, create templates, and so forth.

To get started with a photo gallery, you'll need to enable the module and then configure your gallery. Here's how:

1. Click the Modules tag in the ExpressionEngine admin interface and locate the Photo Gallery module.

2. Under the Action column for the Photo Gallery, click Install.

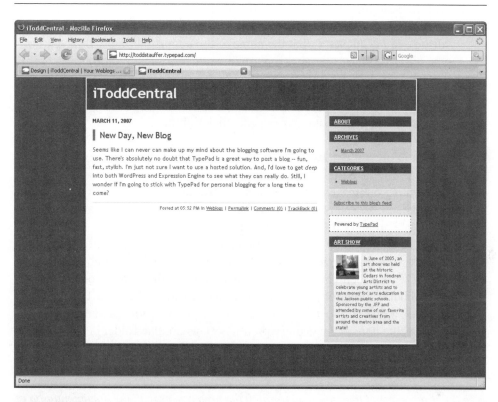

FIGURE 6-2   The photo gallery widget is up and running at the bottom of the sidebar on my TypePad blog's home page.

3. Once it's installed, click the Photo Gallery link (it's the title of the module in the list).

4. You'll see the Image Galleries screen. Click the Create a New Gallery link.

5. You'll be instructed to create a folder on your web server for the files. Using an FTP program, access your account and create a new folder, ideally inside the images folder that was created when you installed ExpressionEngine. Now, make sure that folder has permissions set to 777 via the FTP software.

6. On the Step One page, enter the server path to the image folder you created; note that you can also sort of guess at the path (for instance, if you create the folder galleries inside the main images folder, then entering **images/galleries** will likely allow ExpressionEngine to find the folder.) Click Submit.

7. If ExpressionEngine finds the folder, then you'll see Step Two, where you can create a name for the template group for your galleries. (Remember, as discussed in Chapter 3, that the name of the template group will be part of the URL for your galleries.) Enter that name and click Submit.

8. Now you'll see a screen with a ton of different preferences. Click the Show/Hide All button to show all of the options if they're currently hidden. You can then make your choices and click Submit.

The most important entries to make are the name and short name of your gallery, along with the correct URL to the comment page for your images if you offer commenting on images. (That option is lower on the preferences page; it's filled in by default, so you probably only need to change it if you rename the gallery template group or the comment template itself.)

The next most important consideration is whether or not you want to have a "batch" processing folder; with a batch folder, you can upload a number of images at once via FTP, and then you can process them through the ExpressionEngine interface without waiting for them to upload. In order to do that, you'll need to create a folder on your host account, set it to 777 permissions, and then tell ExpressionEngine here in the Gallery preferences where that folder is and what it's called. Once you've made all those choices and entries, click Submit at the bottom of the Preferences page.

TIP   *I recommend that you read through the preferences with the documentation at http://expressionengine.com/docs/modules/gallery/control_panel/preferences .html, as the preferences can change with different versions and they can be somewhat complex.*

Once you have your photo gallery up and running, you're ready to add images to it. First, though, ExpressionEngine requires at least one category for the image gallery before you can add images. Click the Categories tab and then click the Add a New Category link. In the Add a New Category window, enter a name for the category, a description and, if you like, a special folder where images in this category will be stored. (The folder will be created as a subfolder on the main gallery folder.) When you're done, click submit. (Figure 6-3 shows the Add a New Category screen.)

You can create additional categories if you like, or you can use categories as a way to create "subfolders" within your main galleries folder, essentially building separate photo albums of images around central themes. It's up to you.

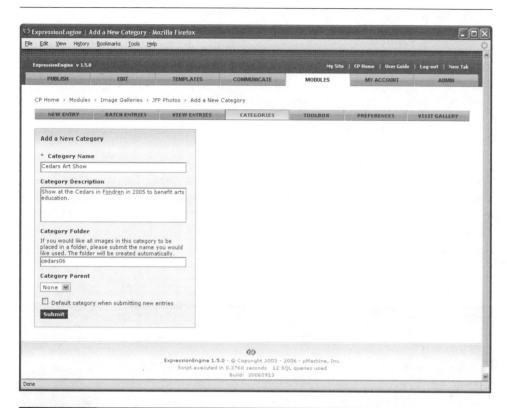

FIGURE 6-3   Creating a category for the ExpressionEngine photo gallery.

Now, to add photos to your gallery, you can begin by clicking the New Entry link in the Gallery module's interface. When you do, you'll see the New Entry screen. Here's what you'll enter:

- **File Name**   Click the Browse button to locate the image file that you want to upload to your photo gallery. When you do, you'll see an Open dialog box; locate the file and click Open and the full path to that file will appear in the File Name text box.

- **Entry Title**   Type a title for this image.

- **Date**   This will be filled in automatically using the date that you're posting the image, but you can change it if you'd prefer to use a different date for the image.

- **Category**   Choose the category for the image from the menu.

- **Status**   Choose whether the image is Open (visible) or Closed (not visible).

- **Allow Comments**   A check in the checkbox means people can comment on this image. (If you don't see the option, then comments have been turned off in the main Preferences section for the entire Gallery module.)

- **Caption**   Enter a caption for the image, if desired.

- **Views**   You can start the views counter at a different number if desired.

When you've made all these choices, click Submit New Entry. That causes your image to be uploaded to your host, created as a thumbnail and as a "medium-sized" image according to the settings in the Gallery preferences; it's then placed in the gallery. To see the image in the gallery, click the Visit Gallery button in the Gallery module interface and you'll see a new window appear with your gallery (see Figure 6-4).

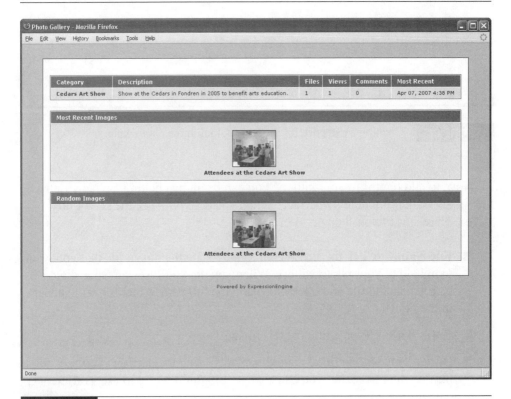

FIGURE 6-4   Here's my new gallery, complete with an image.

The other option for uploading photos is to use the "batch" mode, which is similar to the New Entry except that ExpressionEngine automatically processes the images placed in a special batch folder, as was discussed earlier. So, to use batch mode, first upload images to the Batch folder (via FTP) that you specified in the Gallery preferences. Then, click the Batch Entries button in ExpressionEngine. What you'll see is an interface that shows you each of the images that's been uploaded to the Batch folder, where you'll be able to give the images a name, a title, and a date; choose a category; and so on (see Figure 6-5). When you're done, click Submit this Entry and you'll move on to the next image.

Once you've gotten through the group of uploaded images, you'll find that you reach a "Batch Processing Complete" page and your photo gallery is populated; you can delete the photos from the Batch folder and/or upload more to it, if desired.

6

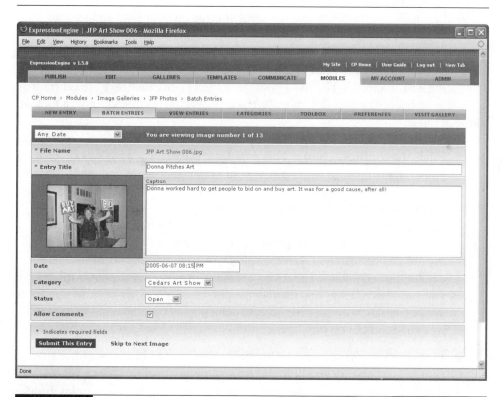

FIGURE 6-5   Here's an example of the Batch Entries interface, where you page through each image to give it a title and caption.

Your gallery has a template just like your blog, comment pages, and others; to change the look and feel of your basic gallery template, you'll need to dig into the Templates tab of the ExpressionEngine interface and make changes to the files.

Use a Web 2.0 Photo Hosting Service

The Web 2.0 mentality means some fun stuff with photos. Instead of simply displaying images online on your blog, using a Web 2.0 service gives you an opportunity to *share* images with others around the world. Indeed, photo sharing is one of those areas where "tagging" really comes into its own on the Web, because you can use photo hosting services to surf photos in loosely defined topics, channels, regions, or whatever else might interest you. So, if you're a photographer or a shutterbug, adding your own photos to one of these services is a fun way to participate on the Web.

And even if your goal is to just get some images on your blog and your blog software doesn't include a built-in gallery solution, that shouldn't be an issue; you can easily add photo galleries using third-party Web 2.0 services. And there are even some advantages such as photo "widgets" that make your galleries more interesting and automatic. The most popular is Flickr.com, but there are others that offer similar benefits and different feature sets as well. Let's quickly take a look at a few of those:

- **Flickr (www.flickr.com)**   This popular service, owned by Yahoo!, enables you to upload groups of photos to your personal account and make them available to your blog visitors via special widgets that you can place in the sidebar of your blog's interface. Flickr doesn't have storage limits, but it does restrict free users to displaying only their 200 most recent images. Flickr is also designed as a photo-sharing community, so, by default, your images can be searched, viewed, and even used by others (images are, by default, posted under a Creative Commons license). By the same token, you can search, view, and display the photos of others, as well, so that from your own blog you can give access to the photos of others that might be related to topics you blog about.

- **Picasa (www.picasa.com)**   Google's alternative to Flickr is a little less about photo sharing and little more about photo hosting. In fact, it's an option for hosting photos that you want to post from Blogger, and it offers some features that make it appealing to bloggers.

■ **Photobucket (www.photobucket.com)**   With an emphasis on supporting social networking tools like MySpace and Friendster, Photobucket is also great for storing photos for blogs. It offers one-click posting to a number of blog tools including Blogger and TypePad. One advantage over Flickr is that Photobucket doesn't restrict the file types of images that you store nor does it care how you link to them; it's totally acceptable, for instance, to store photos on Photobucket that you then embed in your blog using `<img src=>` tags, something that Flickr doesn't encourage.

The way these services work is rather similar, so I'm going to focus on Flickr in terms of step-by-step discussion. If you'd prefer to try one of the other sites, by all means please do—each has its own strengths.

Set Up Flickr

One thing interesting to note about Flickr is the way it handles your images; it's designed to upload your image in full quality (and size) from the desktop version, so that nothing is lost in the translation of the image from the desktop (or from your digital camera) to the Web. That's important for a number of reasons, not the least of which is that many Flickr photos are made available under the Creative Commons license, which means they can be reused by others with varying levels of permission (but generally no financial compensation).

TIP   *Flickr offers additional features for Pro account users that make it possible for a photographer to protect the original high-resolution photographs that you post and share only lower-resolution images, or to share the high-resolution photos only with certain friends. Head to http://www.flickr.com/account/prefs/downloads/ to determine who can access your photos.*

Flickr free accounts also have a size limit for uploaded images (5 MB), which means you may have to do some tweaking before uploading very large images or images taken at a high "megapixel" level on your digital camera. For instance, you may need to open TIFF or RAW images in a photo editing program and save them as JPG images to make them smaller in file size. You may also want to use the software to change the resolution of the image to 72 dpi and, at most, 1024 pixels wide. Using a free account, Flickr will automatically process your images so that they are limited to 1024 pixels wide, so you might as well do that yourself at high quality.

Pro-level accounts can upload images up to 10MB in size and, as mentioned, can make the original high-resolution photos available for downloading. If you're really into photography and sharing, see http://www.flickr.com/upgrade/ for details.

To get started with Flickr, head to http://www.flickr.com/ and click the Sign Up link. Fill in the sign-up form or, if you already have a Yahoo! account, you can use that information to log into Flickr as well. Once you've created a new account, you can upload images from the "Hello" page by clicking the link Upload Your First Photo. You'll then see the Upload Photos to Flickr screen shown in Figure 6-6.

Here's how to use the Upload Photos to Flickr screen:

1. To upload a photo, click the Browse button next to a blank text area.

2. In the Open dialog box that appears, locate the photo you want to upload on your hard disk. When you find a photo, click Open.

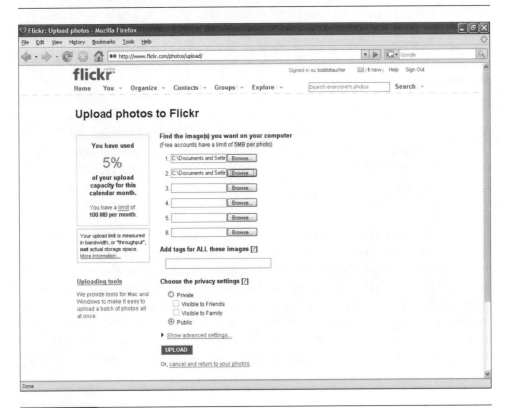

FIGURE 6-6   The Upload Photos to Flickr screen is similar to other photo upload screens.

NOTE

Flickr can work with many different photo formats, translating them into a Web-friendly JPG file format.

3. You can continue to add photos in the available lines. When you're done adding photos, choose whether the photos are Private or Public by clicking the appropriate radio button. If you choose Private, you can then select whether the photos are visible to all of your Friends or only people that you have marked as Family.

TIP

You can click Show Advanced Settings to see more options, including the ability to set a "safety" level for images. (For content that may be objectionable to some, you can mark it as Moderate or Restricted so that it doesn't show up for people browsing at the Safe level.) You can also choose a different type of content type if you're not uploading images.

4. When you're ready to upload the photos to Flickr, click Upload. Flickr will go through the upload process, which make take a few moments.

5. Once the images are processed you'll see the Describe Your Photos screen, where you can enter a title for your image and a description (see Figure 6-7). When you're done labeling your photo, click Save. You'll then see the Describe Your Photos screen for any additional photos. If you're done describing photos, you'll be taken to your photo album.

Once you've uploaded some images you can see them on your personal photo page, which you get to by clicking the You link at the top of the Flickr site. You can then do a number of things to the image using the links that appear below the image. For instance, you can change the image's status (from Public to Private or vice versa) and you can delete the image.

Click the image and you're taken to a detail page that shows a larger view of the image and gives you more options, including editing the tags for the image, changing the copyright level you're assigning to the image (click the Edit link next to the current copyright level), and changing other information about the image. Along the top of the image itself, you'll find some other options, including adding a note, adding the image to a particular Set that you've created (that's one way that Flickr enables you to group images), or sending the images to a particular Flickr group.

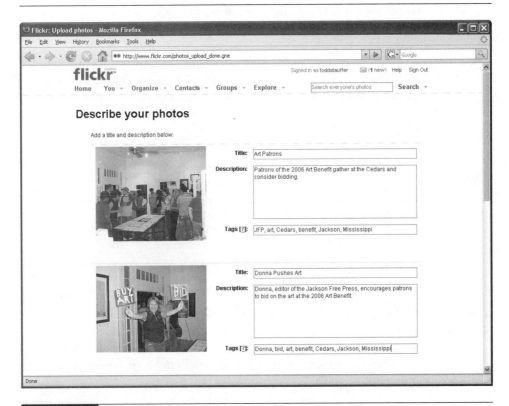

FIGURE 6-7 You can enter a title and description for your uploaded photo on the Describe Your Photos page.

> **TIP**
>
> *There's a lot more to explore when it comes to effectively using and arranging your Flickr account. You can start by clicking the Organize link to get a sense of how you can organize your images into Sets and Groups, as well as options for tagging your images so that they're well categorized. And if you use Flickr a lot, you may want to look into the standalone Flickr tools available at http://www.flickr.com/tools/, which make uploading images to and working with Flickr a drag-and-drop process.*

Get Flickr Images on Your Blog

What we're concerned about in this book, though, is how you can get the images onto your blog. You can take one of two approaches. The first way is to click the Blog This link—this literally enables you to post image-centric entries to your blog from Flickr. You'll configure Flickr to access your blog and upload entries, including links to your images on the Flickr site. Here's how it works:

1. When viewing an image detail page, click the Blog This link. When you do, you'll be instructed that you need to set up the Blog This feature.

2. Walk through the steps for your particular type of blog—Flickr supports Blogger, TypePad, WordPress, or nearly any blog that supports the Metaweblog API, which includes ExpressionEngine.

TIP   *To use the Metaweblog API support built into ExpressionEngine, you need to enable the Metaweblog API module (via the Modules tab in the admin interface) and configure it for connections. See Chapter 3 for details on ExpressionEngine's modules.*

3. Once you've got the Blog This link set up, when you click the Blog This link for a particular image, you'll see a pop-up menu that enables you to choose the blog to which you want to post. Choose the blog and you'll see the Compose Your Blog Entry screen shown in Figure 6-8.

The other way to get images into your blog entries is a bit more hands-on. On the photo detail page, click the All Sizes link. That shows you a new page, called Available Sizes, where you can choose from different sizes of your image. Choose the image size that will make the most sense for your blog entry, and then copy the HTML from the bottom of that page.

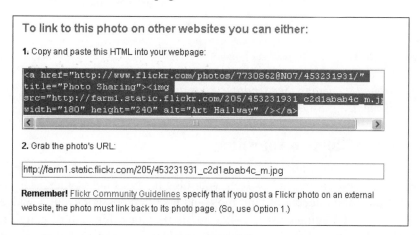

You can then paste that code into your blog entry form and it should cause the image to appear *and* link back to Flickr so that your readers can click it to see it larger.

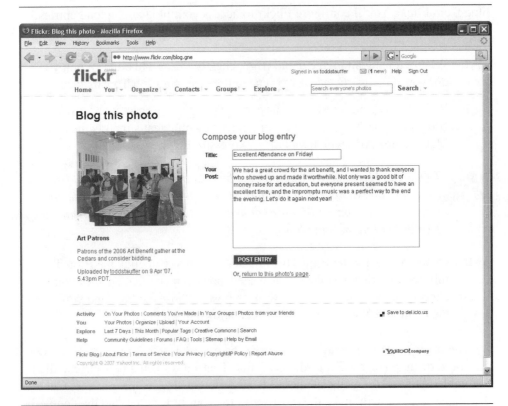

FIGURE 6-8   Using the Blog This feature, you can create image-centric blog entries from within Flickr and post them on your own blog.

TIP   *You might want to add* `align="left"` *or* `align="right"` *to the* `<img>` *tag in Flickr's code if you'd like to have the text of your blog entry wrap around the image. See Chapter 4 for discussion of the XHTML* `<img>` *element.*

Add a Flickr Badge to Your Blog

Actually, there's another approach you can take to getting your Flickr images on your blog—you can post a link from your blog to your Flickr gallery. This is generally done in the sidebar of your blog, and it's often possible using a widget from within your blogging software—ExpressionEngine offers a third-party Flickr plug-in (http://expressionengine.com/downloads/details/flickr_tools/) and a number of plug-ins exist for WordPress to integrate Flickr images into your sidebar.

Of course, Flickr offers its own option, as well, which can display photos from your Flickr account either via HTML and Javascript or using Flash. To do that, create a Flickr Badge, by opening the page http://www.flickr.com/badge.gne while you're logged into your account. That launches the Create a Flickr Badge tool shown in Figure 6-9.

NOTE   *You can use the Flickr Badge tool to display photos from your own photosets or you can use it to display public images that use certain tags. Displaying public images on your blog can be a fun way to incorporate other people's photos into your blog. For instance, for a conference I recently attended, the event's blog offered a Flickr Badge of images tagged "Portland, Oregon" where the conference was being held. The images added some flash and fun to the blog without requiring the blog's administrator to actually get out there and take the pictures!*

6

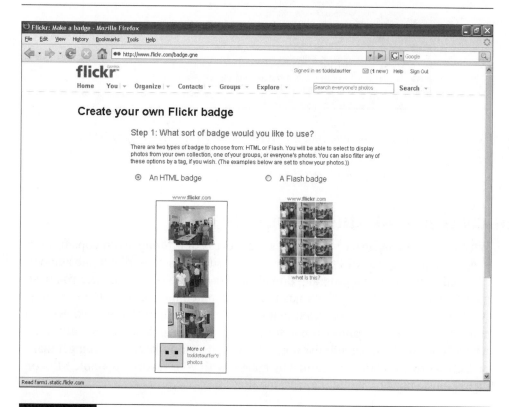

FIGURE 6-9   You can build a Flickr badge for your blog.

Walk through the steps of creating either an HTML or a Flash badge, including choosing the photos or sets that you want to work with. When you're done, you'll be shown the HTML that you need to copy and paste into your blog's sidebar or template so that the badge appears where you want it to on your blog. (See Chapters 2 and 3 for details on editing the sidebars and/or templates of the major blogging tools covered in this book.)

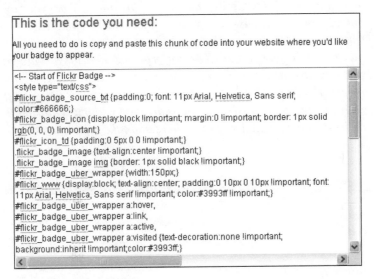

TIP   *In TypePad, you can add this HTML to a Notes-style TypeList in order to have it available for placement in the Content Selection tools. See Chapter 2 for more on TypeLists.*

Podcasting and Audioblogging

What *podcasting* means is simple—it's the process of offering audio clips from your website using an RSS feed, so that your visitors can subscribe to the audio files and, using a special program, download those audio files soon after you post them. Although "podcasting" sounds like it has something specifically to do with Apple's iPod, it doesn't; you can use any sort of *podcatcher* software to download and listen to podcasted audio. (Of course, that includes Apple's iTunes software, which is one of the more popular options.) And, if you'd like to, you can get that podcatcher software to synchronize that audio with your favorite portable MP3 or digital music player—including, yes, the iPod.

From the blogger's point of view, podcasting means doing the following things:

1. Produce some sort of audio (or video) content.

2. Save that audio content as an MP3 file or a similar audio file. (If it's video, you'll generally save it as an MPEG-4 file, although other formats are used.)

3. Upload the digital media file to your blog or a podcasting service.

4. Provide the appropriate type of RSS feed so that a podcatcher can locate the file and download it automatically.

6

More Rights Discussion

So what do you plan to podcast? If your answer is commercial music, then you're headed down an interesting road. Technically, you probably don't have the legal right to create podcasts and host them from your own blog if you're using commercial, copyrighted music as part of your podcast. Instead, if you want to podcast without paying anything, you should consider using only your own musical compositions, music for which you have explicit permission (say, from a local band in your area who wants the exposure on your podcast) or you should stick to a talk-show format that doesn't use music.

If it's important to you that you use commercial music, then you'll need to pay for the web rights to play commercial music via a radio-like licensing agreement. You can do that in a few different ways. First, you can go direct to the music licensing services such as ASCAP at http://www.ascap.com/weblicense/, BMI at http://www.bmi.com/licensing/webcaster/, or SESAC at http://www.sesac.com/.

The other option is to use a service designed for podcasting licensed music. Two such services are LoudCity (www.loudcity.net) and Live365 (www.live365.com). Both enable you to create a "radio station" on their sites that you can link to from your own site; you can also upload shows for podcasting. By paying for the service, you're covered for licensing fees according to the popularity of your show, the quality of the broadcast, and so forth. If you find your show getting popular, it won't be cheap but, then again, maybe you can figure out a way to monetize the show if it's doing well!

TIP *Many different applications are available for recording and editing podcasts, including some software that may be preinstalled on your computer (for instance, GarageBand on the Mac can be used for recording podcasts). One very nice, free and cross-platform solution is Audacity, available for download at http://audacity.sourceforge.net/.*

From Chapter 5 you may recall that RSS and Atom feeds can include an "enclosure" tag. It's that tag that tells a podcatcher where to locate the audio (or similar multimedia) file for downloading automatically. (In podcasting lingo, the overall multimedia blog is the "podcast" and each individual audio or video file is an "episode.")

Podcast Using Your Blog's Feed

So, in order to do some podcasting on your own, you'll need to not only generate the audio or video file, but you'll need to create the RSS feed as well. Depending on the blog software you're using, you can do that from within the tool or using a third-party solution. Here's a quick look at each of the tools discussed in this book:

- **Blogger**   Blogger doesn't support podcasting directly, so you'll need to use the FeedBurner approach discussed in the next section.

- **TypePad**   When you insert a multimedia file into a TypePad blog entry using the Insert File command, TypePad will automatically place that file as an enclosure in its RSS feed. (This also works if you simply link to a compatible audio or video file elsewhere on the Internet.) Note that with TypePad, the name of your blog will be used for the "Podcast Title" and the name of the entry will be used for the "Episode Name" when those items are downloaded by the podcatcher. (If you don't want to have text entries mixed in with podcast entries, it's recommended that you create a new blog specifically for podcasting.) Also, it's recommended that you create an Excerpt in your blog entry to describe the podcast episode, as the podcatcher will use that to describe the podcast file to the user.

TIP *Having trouble? TypePad can be used to create an RSS 1.0 feed that isn't compatible with podcasting, so if your podcast doesn't seem to be working, it's possible that your feed is still "old school." If that's the case, you can simply go to the Design tab, click the Select Content link, and then turn on the Podcast Link option. Now, save the design changes. Your blog will now have a podcast link on its front page that will work with podcatchers.*

- **WordPress**   In WordPress 1.5 and later, multimedia files are automatically supported in RSS and Atom feeds for podcasting. All you need to do is link to a compatible multimedia file in the body of your blog entry and it'll be placed correctly in the RSS feed; when that feed is accessed by a podcatcher, the file will be downloaded.

- **ExpressionEngine**   By default, the solution in ExpressionEngine is to create a custom field for your blog and then add that custom field to the RSS template for that blog. (See Chapter 3 for more on ExpressionEngine templates and Chapter 4 for creating RSS feeds in ExpressionEngine.) That works great if you're using ExpressionEngine for multiple blogs and you want to create one specifically for podcasting. But if you want the simpler solution of having enclosures automatically detected, then you can download the Enclosures plug-in (http://expressionengine.com/downloads/details/feed_enclosures/) and set up your blog template according to the instructions so that it uses the plug-in to detect enclosures and automatically add them to the RSS feed.

FeedBurner for Podcasts

FeedBurner is discussed in some detail in Chapter 5, but it's worth noting here that FeedBurner can work very well with blog feeds that include podcast content. For instance, for Blogger blogs, it's recommended that you use FeedBurner if you'd like to podcast from Blogger. Simply post a blog entry that includes a link to a multimedia file (it can be something stored on the local server or a remote link) and the Blogger feed on its own won't work in a podcatcher. (That's partly because it's Atom-based and partly because Blogger doesn't yet do the automatic stuff that TypePad and WordPress do for podcasts.) If you burn that same feed through FeedBurner, however, it will locate the Blogger entries that include multimedia files and make them available to podcatchers via the FeedBurner feed.

If you already have a FeedBurner account, you can burn new feeds from the My Feeds page. Simply enter a URL for the current Blogger (or other blogging software) feed in the Burn a Feed Right This Instant box and turn on the I Am a Podcaster option:

Burn a feed right this instant. Type your blog or feed address here:

http://toddstauffer.blogspot.com/feeds/posts/ ☑ I am a podcaster! **Next »**

Now you'll be walked through the steps. If the feed is valid and FeedBurner can work with it, you'll be given a FeedBurner URL along the lines of http://feeds.feedburner.com/yourblogsname/ that you can use to link from your blog to encourage your visitors to use within podcatchers.

In some cases, you'll be encouraged to set up SmartCast, a feature within FeedBurner that will automatically locate multimedia files within the feed and make them available as podcast enclosures. (This is handy for ExpressionEngine feeds, for instance, if you don't want to mess around installing a third-party plug-in.) In addition to helping you manage the feed, SmartCast will also enable you to choose some iTunes-friendly preferences so that your feed looks good in Apple's popular iTunes application (see Figure 6-10).

Hipcast.com

Hipcast is a fun way to do your podcasting (whether audio or video) in part because it gives you another way to display audio and video—not only can your users subscribe to multimedia feeds, but the Hipcast.com player window can be

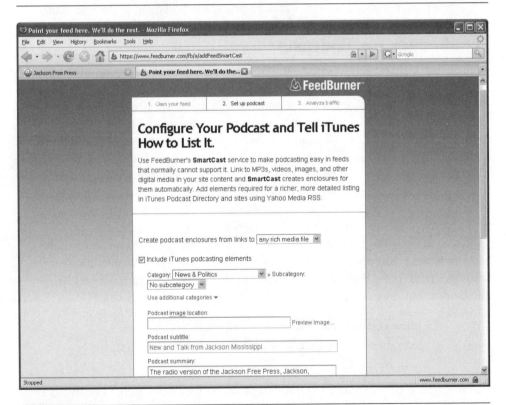

FIGURE 6-10 FeedBurner enables you to set up a podcast feed even if your blogging software doesn't automatically support podcasting.

embedded in your blog entries, giving visitors the opportunity to play one or more of your shows before they decide to subscribe. Hipcast also has a built-in recorder so that you can record audio podcasts on the Web (assuming your computer has a microphone) or it can enable you to podcast over a telephone connection.

Indeed, it's worth noting that you can do both podcasting and *audioblogging* with Hipcast. Here's the difference between the two: Podcasts tend to be thought of as "shows" that have "episodes" and, hence, use RSS so that new episodes can be downloaded by podcatchers and then listened to either on the user's computer or on a device such as an MP3 player or Apple iPod. An audioblog is a little different; in this case, it's simply a blog entry done in audio, with the idea being that the visitor to your site can simply click play on the audio player and listen to whatever it is that you're "blogging." The suggestion, at least, is that audioblogging is a little more freeform with topics and doesn't have the RSS component for subscriptions.

Of course, with a service such as Hipcast, it's possible (and common) to do *both*; you can offer a podcast feed and allow users to listen to individual episodes from within your blog. But, know that you can simply audioblog if you want (or, if you want to get really fancy, you can *videoblog*, or *vlog*) and not worry about creating a podcast with episodes and subscriptions.

In any case, you'll need to sign up before you can do any of this with Hipcast. To sign up for the service, head to http://www.hipcast.com and click the Sign Up link. Hipcast is a commercial service; there's a seven-day trial at the time of writing, but it still requires a credit card sign-up so that you can be billed for a subscription once the trial expires.

Connect Hipcast and Set Preferences

Once you're signed up and logged into Hipcast, the next step is to set it up to work with your blog. The idea with Hipcast is that you'll do your podcast creation and/ or uploading to the Hipcast service, then you'll post that podcast entry to your blog from Hipcast. So, instead of going through your blog's typical interface, you'll need to set up Hipcast so that it knows how to post to your blog.

You'll do that by clicking the Add New Blog link and then walking through the steps of connecting Hipcast to your blog. For many types of blogs, Hipcast uses the Metaweblog API connection so that it can be used as a blog posting application. For WordPress, you should find that URL at http://www.*yourblogsname*.com/ xmlrpc.php; for ExpressionEngine, you'll need to turn on the Metaweblog API module, which will then enable you to learn the URL for any of the blogs that you've created.

Now, with the blog connected, you have a number of different things that you can do. To begin, click Blog Preferences next to the blog that you've configured and you can choose a number of different settings for your podcast, including the style of the player that will be posted whenever you make a podcast entry. You can also set some default headings and categories for your entries, particularly for "moblog" entries that you make by telephone. (When you're posting podcasts by phone to your blog you have less access to the blogging interface, so it posts with some default text and descriptions.)

Create an Audio Blog Entry

If Hipcast is connected to your blog and your service is up and running, you can begin by creating an audioblog entry, if you'd like to. To do so, click the Audio tab at the top of the Hipcast interface. You'll see three options: Record Post, Upload File, or My Moblog. Here's what each does:

- ■ **Record Post**　Click this link and you're taken to the online interface that will attempt to detect your PC's microphone (and video camera, if you have one) so that you can record audio directly over the Web.

- ■ **Upload File**　Select this link and you can browse your hard disk for an MP3 file to be uploaded and posted to your blog.

- ■ **My Moblog**　Select this link and you'll be walked through the process of calling the Hipcast phone number, entering a special PIN number, and then choosing the blog to which you want to send a "moblog" entry by phone.

To me the most unique option that Hipcast offers is the opportunity to actually record a post from within a browser window. If you have a microphone built into your computer or connected (I'd recommend a headset style microphone for best results) you can click the Record Post link. That brings you to an audio recording interface, where you're able to record your audioblog entry (see Figure 6-11).

Click the Configure Microphone button to test and configure your recording device, and then enter a name for your recording and a description. With that entered, click the Record button and begin recording. When you're done, click Stop. You can then click Play to hear it played back; if you like what you hear, click Save. (If you don't like it, you can click Cancel and start over again.)

Once a recording is saved, you're taken to the Jobs screen, where you'll see the audio file. It has to be encoded, so you may have to wait a few moments before it's available to work with. Once it is, you'll see its Status changed to Complete.

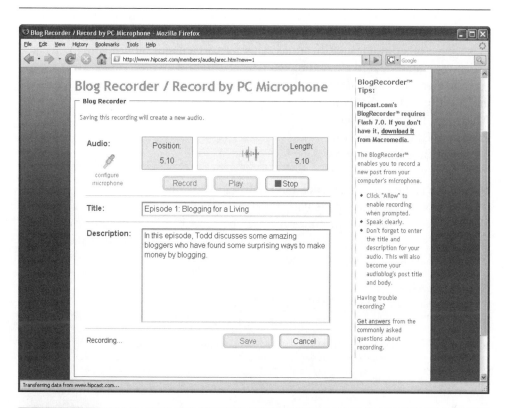

FIGURE 6-11   Recording an audioblog entry in Hipcast

You can then click the Audio tab again to see that your recording has been added to the Audio page.

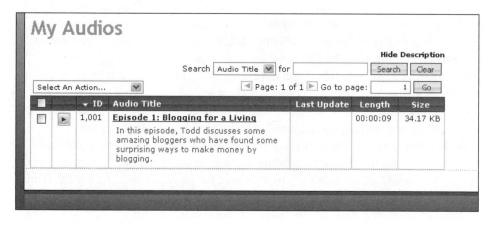

Click the name of the audio recording and you'll see some detailed information about it. Here you'll be able to listen to the recording, change the description, and make some other minor modifications. There's also a major modification you can make; you can re-record the audio.

When you're satisfied with the recording, click the Publish Audio tab. There you'll see the Publish to Blog option; from the Select Blog menu, choose the blog to which you want to publish the audio entry, then click the Publish to Blog button.

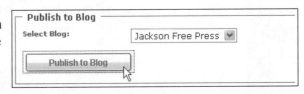

Now you'll see a final page where you can choose a category for the entry. You can preview the style of player that will be posted and you can make changes to the post's title and body. When you're done with that, click the Publish button. Now, check your blog for a new entry.

Create a Podcast

The next step up from recording audioblog entries is to create episodes and arrange them as a podcast. Not only can Hipcast help you create the podcast and make it available for subscriptions and downloading, but it can also make the subscriptions available in a variety of formats, including altering your feed so that it's friendly for iTunes users, for instance. And, Hipcast lets you create more than one podcast for your blog, which can be handy if you have different "shows" that you like to do. (For instance, you may have both a "cooking" podcast and an "on the town" podcast that you want to serve up to your same blog audience without creating two different blogs.)

To get started with a podcast, you begin by clicking the Podcast tab at the top of the Hipcast window, and then click New Podcast. Now you'll need to fill in information about the podcast including a name, description, and, optionally, you can choose some "album artwork" to represent the show. (This is handy for iTunes and others that show an image while the podcast is being played.) When you've made all of your choices, click the Save Changes Now button.

Once you're set up with a podcast, the next step is to create a new post. Click the New Post button and you'll see the New Post screen, where you can add an episode to your podcast. If you're using audio that's already been uploaded or recorded using Hipcast, you can select it in the Media Enclosure section of the New Post screen.

Alternatively, you can specify a different, remotely hosted file in the Remotely Hosted Content entry box. Enter a URL to the media file that you want to podcast.

From there, you can set the Post Settings or use Future Release Date if you'd like to decide to have your podcast episode go live at a certain time. Then, in the New Post section, enter a title and body for the post that will be used to describe this episode of the podcast. When you're done, click Save Changes Now. The next screen you'll see is the View Posts tab, where you can check out your newly created post.

Now, what do you do with the podcast? In this case, it isn't automatically posted to your blog. Instead, you can click the Publish tab to get the HTML that's require to add an RSS feed icon to your blog's sidebar by editing its template (see Chapters 2 and 3 for details). With that, people can subscribe to your podcast using a podcatcher, enabling them to automatically download the episodes that you add to the podcast.

Music for Your Blog

First, a word to the wise: Setting up your blog so that music plays when it loads can be *annoying* to your visitors. I wouldn't recommend that. What you can do, however, is offer up a widget from Last.fm (www.last.fm) the social music service that enables you to build radio stations that play music based on certain styles, similarity to a particular artist, and more.

I'll leave registering and getting involved in the service up to you. But when you're ready to add music to your blog, you can do that via the Widgets page at Last.fm. Visit http://www.last.fm/widgets/ and walk through the process of creating a new Radio Station widget (which chooses songs automatically) or a Playlist widget (which plays the playlist that you've created using the Last.fm service).

Choose the content, color, size, and orientation and avoid turning on Autostart. Then, click the Show Me The Code button and you'll be able to use that HTML code to add your Last.fm widget to the sidebar of your blog.

NOTE   *There are some other options you may want to look into for Hipcast-produced podcasts, including the iTunes Settings tab, where you can activate the feed for iTunes, enter key information that the iTunes Store uses to display podcasts, and set some of the iTunes category information. Once activated for iTunes, your podcast's Publish tab will include instructions for publishing the podcast via the iTunes Music Store.*

Once you've gotten the podcast up and running, you can use the Graphs tab to get a visual sense of how many people are downloading your podcast, or click the Track tab to turn on download tracking for your podcast.

Explore the Hipcast interface to see all of the things you can do, including moblogging (audioblogging or podcasting by calling a special phone number), video blogging, and more.

Offer Video from Your Site

So far we've covered photos and audio, but there's another multimedia enterprise you might consider for your blog—posting video. YouTube is one of the most popular sites on the Web in part because broadband access to the Internet has reached a deep enough penetration point that a lot of people can enjoy at least short snippets of online video. YouTube also makes it easy to share that video with others, by centrally hosting the video, encoding it for playback on the Internet, and making the process of posting video to your blog relatively painless. Of course, YouTube isn't the only game in town—sites such as Yahoo! Video (video.yahoo .com), AOL's UnCut Video (uncutvideo.aol.com), Veoh (www.veoh.com), and Dailymotion (www.dailymotion.com) make it easy for videographers to upload and host videos that can then be shared by others on the Internet.

> **TIP**   *Hipcast, discussed in the previous section, is useful for video blogging as well as audioblogging. It can even enable you to record video directly from a video camera or webcam that's connected to your PC. If you're already using the service for audio, you might want to explore it for videoblogging, too.*

You've got two different things you can do with video on your blog—post someone else's video to your blog entries (hopefully, in the interest of commenting on it and entertaining your viewers) or post your own video via a sharing service and then make it available on your blog. I'll cover both in this section.

Post YouTube Video to Your Blog

Posting video to a blog entry is generally a matter of copying and pasting special XHTML codes from the service to your blog. YouTube and others often make that code obvious when you're viewing the clip in the YouTube interface. Look for code that lets you share or embed the video into your own site.

When you locate that code, copy it and paste it into a blog entry on your site. You'll need to make sure that you post the code *as HTML*, and not as text that will be translated by the blogging software. In TypePad, Blogger, and WordPress, that means switching the HTML editing option in your blog entry window in order to paste the code; in ExpressionEngine, you'll need to make sure that the blog's preferences are set to accept HTML as input. Now, with the code in place, publish the blog entry. The result should look something like Figure 6-12.

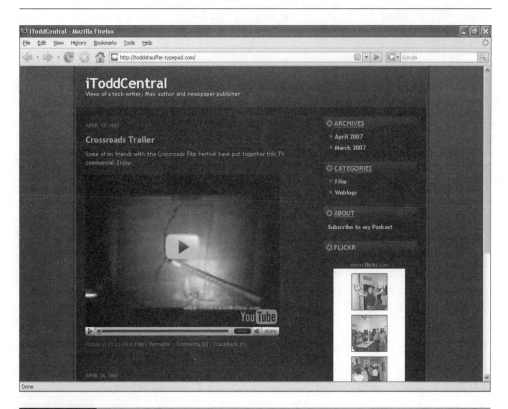

FIGURE 6-12   A YouTube video posted on my blog

NOTE   *If you have trouble with posting video objects in ExpressionEngine, you may need to check your blog preferences. Choose the Admin tab in the ExpressionEngine admin interface, then click Weblog Administration, and then Weblog Management. Now click Edit Preferences and then Weblog Posting Preferences. In the entry Default HTML Formatting for Post Entries, choose Allow All HTML.*

One thing to notice about the codes that are generally offered by video hosting sites is that they'll have sizes for the player built into the code. For instance, here's the YouTube code for the example used in Figure 6-12:

```
<object width="425" height="350">
<param name="movie" value="http://www.youtube.com/v/Mf_hqdAfbX8">
</param>
<param name="wmode" value="transparent"></param>
```

```
<embed src="http://www.youtube.com/v/Mf_hqdAfbX8"
type="application/x-shockwave-flash" wmode="transparent"
width="425" height="350"></embed>
</object>
```

By changing the `width` and `height` parameters of both the `object` tag and the `embed` tag (which are offered for compatibility with a variety of browsers based on Netscape/Mozilla and Internet Explorer code), you can force the player to work at different sizes. One suggestion: Keep the *aspect ratio* the same as the original. If the original is 425 pixels wide and 350 high and you want it to take up less space, then you could alter the settings to something like 300 pixels wide by 247 pixels high, which would be the same ratio of height to width.

Upload Your Own Video to YouTube

In order to display your own video on YouTube, you'll need to register for the service and sign in. Click the Sign Up link at the top of the site and then walk through the registration process.

> **TIP** *Again, the process for other video sharing services is very similar. If there's any difference, it may be in the preferred video format or recommended settings for high-end video. Check the documentation for the service that you opt to use if you're looking at one other than YouTube.*

Once you're signed up and logged in, you can upload video. The default (free) YouTube account limits you to files that are no more than 10 minutes long and/or 100MB in size. YouTube can accept video that's in QuickTime (.mov), Windows Media Video (.wmv), Audio Video Interleave (.avi), or MPEG format (.mpg). If you've already got video created and on your PC in one of those formats, you're ready to go; if you're in the process of creating and editing the video, know that you should output the video in one of those formats with a recommended resolution of 320×240 pixels. Video can be created using any number of popular applications such as iMovie, Windows Movie Maker, Final Cut Pro, Adobe Premiere, and so on.

> **TIP** *According to YouTube, the preferred video format for highest quality is MPEG-4, and the videos that tend to work best are those that are displayed in a standard definition television ratio of 4:3. If you have a wider 6:9 video image (one that was shot on HD equipment or in an 6:9 format) you may want to use your video editing software to letterbox that image at a 4:3 ratio before uploading it to YouTube. See http://www.youtube.com/t/howto_makevideo for more details on formats and other recommendations for best results with YouTube video.*

When you're ready to upload video, click the Upload Videos link that appears toward the top of the screen. You'll see the Video Upload screen (see Figure 6-13). Enter a Name for the file, a short description, tags (to help when people are searching for related videos) and the video category. Then, click Continue Uploading.

TIP

If you have a camcorder or webcam connected to your PC, you can make a different choice here—click Use Quick Capture and you can record a video directly to YouTube using that camera. The camera will need to be discoverable by the YouTube Macromedia Flash application, but if it is, you can record and upload videos directly. This is great for video blogging or for video "responses" to other people's YouTube clips.

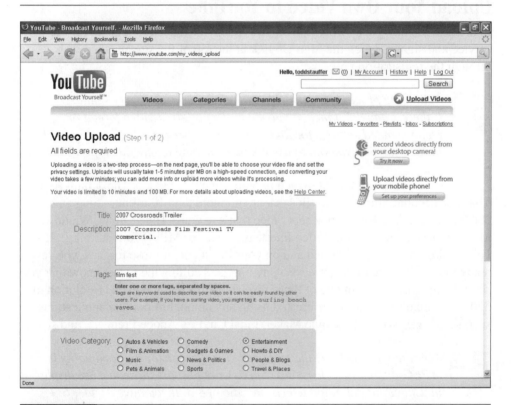

FIGURE 6-13 The Video Upload screen is used to upload video from your PC or to use the Quick Capture function.

On the second Video Upload screen, you'll see a text entry box for the file that you'll be uploading; click the Browse button, then locate the video file on your PC's hard disk. When you've found it, click Open in the dialog box and the file's name will appear in the File entry box. Next, in the Broadcast section, choose whether you want the file to be Public or Private. If you choose Private, you can then opt to e-mail a list of friends and family that are stored in your account settings.

With those choices made, click the Upload Video button. You'll then see the progress as your video file is uploaded to YouTube.

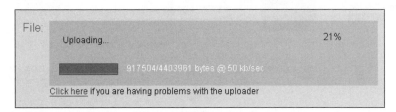

Once that process is finished, you'll see the Video Details screen, where you can edit the name of the video and description, choose categories, add more tags, and then add specifics including the date and location the video was shot, what sort of responses you want to allow (comments, video responses) and whether others should be allowed to embed this video in their own sites and blogs. When you're done making choices, click Update Video Info.

NOTE   *It can take a little while before images appear as part of your video (and, hence, before the video can be played back) because YouTube has to process the video on the back end of its system. Be patient; after your video is uploaded, you should have an image of the video and be able to play it back within a few minutes, although it can take longer depending on the size of the video and how busy the service is.*

Finally, click My Videos and you should see the new video appear as one of your personal videos on the YouTube service (see Figure 6-14) on your personal account page. To edit the video's information again, click the Edit Video Info button. To embed the video in a blog entry on your site, simply follow the instructions outlined earlier in the section Post YouTube Video to Your Blog.

TIP   *Have a video-enabled phone? YouTube and other services can support that format as well, enabling you to make your video on your phone and then upload it to the service, where you can then embed it in a blog entry or link to it on the video host's site.*

FIGURE 6-14   Here's the video I uploaded, shown as one of the videos I have associated with my YouTube account.

Chapter 7

Tag, Bookmark, and Publicize Content

How to...

■ Work with categories and keyword tagging in your blog posts

■ Add tagging features to your blog

■ Link up your blog with Technorati

■ Use social bookmarking tools

■ Create hooks for others to bookmark and share your blog entries

■ Participate in social news sites like Digg.com

Yet another Web 2.0 concept is the notion of *tagging* content, both within your blog and out there on the Internet at large. There's a certain Web 2.0-ish belief that all of this amazing information is at our disposal thanks to the Internet, but it's difficult to get a handle on it without *metadata*—or data *about* data—that can be used to give us a sense of how things fit together. Tags are one way that people have begun to work on offering more information about the information out there on the Web.

Tags can be thought of as free-form categories. If you're working on your own blog and entering a new entry, you might place it in a particular category—say, the "vacation" category—because that's one of the categories that you've set up. But if you had the freedom to assign tags, or keywords, to a blog entry, you might go further than that by tagging your entry as about your "sweetheart" and "Cozumel" and the "beach" and an "engagement." Something like that. Oh, and you got there from the hotel on a "Vespa." What tags do, both within individual blogs and on the Internet in a wider context, is simply give us more information about the posts that are being made, offering readers more entry points into information and entertainment on the Web. Tags give you a way to create free-form associations between your own blog entries, and they can also provide hooks into social networking websites such as Technorati.com. And tags are the heart and soul of some multimedia sharing sites like YouTube and Flickr, where the tags help you locate and share related content with the online community of users.

Beyond tagging, other options such as social bookmarking (creating bookmarks to sites that you share with others) and ratings sites (such as Digg.com) can help build interest and traffic for your blog. The more people link to you, the higher you appear in search engines and the more chances you have that others will discover you. In a similar way, the more active (and interesting) you are when it comes to tagging others and sharing bookmarks, the more likely you're going to get traffic to your blog, too.

So, in this chapter, I'd like to start by discussing the tagging possibilities that may be built in or offered for your blog, as well as discussing some third-party options. From there, we'll look at external Web 2.0 services that can drive traffic to your site including tagging, social bookmarking, and ranking services.

Set Tags and Categories for Blog Entries

Of the four major blog tools we've discussed in this book, all four offer some way that you can get tags associated with your posts. Increasingly, it's a feature that's being built into blogging software, particularly hosted blogging tools, such

Is Tagging Over-Hyped for Blogs?

Some people in the blogging world argue (chief among them in my universe is Jim Bumgardner, the technical editor of this book) that using tags can be overkill for blog entries. Because blog entries are mostly text and, thus, searchable by Google and similar search engine technologies, finding related blog entries is relatively easy. For text-focused blogs, then, it may make more sense to simply place blog entries in a handful of well-defined categories, so that your users can choose to view those different categories if they find them interesting. (Jim points out that categories can also be handy because they enable you, as a blogger, to track the statistics for a particular category of posts and learn what topics people like to read on your blog versus the topics they tend to ignore on your blog.)

Where tags really make sense is for non-textual content, such as images and videos. Because those items can't be searched, it can be extremely handy to have a person tag an image so that a Web 2.0 service such as Flickr knows that the image was taken in "Seattle" in the "Fall" and features a "Giraffe" on a "light rail" train. This is very useful information that the service otherwise couldn't discover using today's searching technologies.

So, why cover tagging at all? First of all, because in some of the blogging tools we're covering, you can use the categories feature in a tag-like way, thus solving the problem without *over*-solving it. Second, tags can still be very important for photo, audio, or video-centric blogs, or if you do, in fact, have a popular blog that covers tons of unrelated topics, such that using categories would be unwieldy. (That'd be tough, but its conceivable.) And, third, tags are important if you're interested in working with Technorati to tag your blog entries and, perhaps, generate more traffic.

as Blogger and TypePad, which tend to offer bells and whistles in an easy way to encourage new users. But tagging can be added as a plug-in for WordPress and ExpressionEngine as well (and both of those already have sophisticated category features built in). This section has a quick look at all of them.

Tags and Labels in Blogger

The "new" Blogger offers tagging in the form of what it calls *labels*. At the bottom of the standard Posting window, you'll see a small entry box where you can enter labels for that post that work just like keyword tags.

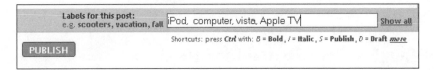

Once the keywords are added to a post, they'll appear at the bottom of the post as links. Those links can then be clicked to see other posts on the blog that have similar labels.

You can also add a list of your labels to the sidebar of your blog using the Template editor in Blogger. Here's how:

1. Click the Template tab in the Blogger admin interface and make sure the Page Elements link is selected.

2. Click the link Add a Page Element in the sidebar of your template.

3. In the window that appears, click the Add to Blog button beneath the Labels option. That brings up the Configure Labels window.

4. In the Configure Labels window, you can choose whether your labels will be sorted alphabetically or by the frequency of the use of the label. Make your choice and click Save Changes.

5. Now, view your blog and you'll see the new Labels element appear in your blog's layout.

```
LABELS

Microsoft (4)
Vista (2)
blackberry (2)
tech (2)
.Mac (1)
Alltel (1)
Apple (1)
Apple TV (1)
EVDO (1)
```

7

TIP *As you'll see in later examples in this chapter, tags are often arranged in "tag clouds," which make the tags a bit easier to see by their "weight" or frequency of use. Blogger doesn't have a tag cloud option built in (as of this writing), but such an option has been "hacked" by some Blogger users. See http://phy3blog.googlepages.com/Beta-Blogger-Label-Cloud .html on the Web for hints.*

Tags and Categories in TypePad

With TypePad, there's an easy way to get tagging-like functionality and a hard way. The easy way is to simply use categories judiciously as you're creating or editing your posts. While on the Post page in TypePad, you can choose a category for your post from the Category menu. The hard way isn't really that hard, as long as you're comfortable with editing templates.

Easy: Set Multiple Categories and a Category Cloud

First, the Category menu offers you the command Add a New Category, which you can use to quickly create a new category that hasn't been created previously. It's not as easy as typing in a quick tag, but it's a start.

Second, the Category menu offers the command Assign Multiple Categories, which you can use to select more than one category for your blog entry. In the Select Categories window that appears, choose the categories you'd like to assign to this entry. Once selected, those multiple categories appear in the menu's entry box.

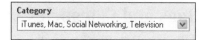

Now, save the entry and you're ready to add your category list or cloud to the blog's layout.

By default, TypePad shows a listing of categories, which can get a little unwieldy if you're adding categories as if they were tags or keywords. So, the solution is to dig into the design of your TypePad blog and set up a category *tag cloud*. Here's how:

1. In the TypePad admin interface, click the Design tab.

2. On the Design tab, choose Select Content.

3. In the Select Content window, turn off the option Categories and turn on the option Category Cloud.

4. Scroll to the bottom of the window and click Save Changes.

Now, if desired, click the Order Content link to dig in and change where the category cloud will appear. Otherwise, you can view your blog to see the new category cloud, which will show a compact list of your categories, with the categories that are used most often appearing larger than categories used less often.

Harder: TypePad Keywords

TypePad offers support for tagging in the portion of its Post window labeled Keywords. Once you've entered a post in TypePad, simply add to the Keywords entry area, separating your keywords with commas.

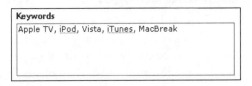

By default, those keywords won't appear in your blog's design, but you can add them by editing an advanced template and adding the tag `<$MTEntryKeywords$>` to your template between the `<$MTEntries$>` tags. See Chapter 5 for more on editing TypePad advanced templates.

> **TIP** *TypePad can also be used directly with Technorati as discussed later in the sections "Technorati" and "Digg and Rating Services."*

Tags and Categories in WordPress

Like TypePad, WordPress allows you to assign multiple categories to a single post (see Chapter 3) and, within reason, you can use the built-in category to set up your blog posts so that they show up whenever a related category is chosen. WordPress doesn't have a category cloud feature built in, but it can be added using a plug-in. Or, if you want to dig deeper into tagging your entries, there's a plug-in for that, too.

Category Cloud in WordPress

If your blog is text-focused (as opposed to a photo blog or an audio blog) then you can create a "category cloud," which uses the built-in WordPress categories to create something very similar to a tag cloud. Here's how:

1. Download the Category Cloud Widget from http://leekelleher.com/ wordpress/plugins/category-cloud-widget/.

2. Once downloaded, you install the widget just as you would a plug-in, by copying the file category-cloud.php to your wp-content/plugins/ folder.

3. Now, in the WordPress admin interface, click the Plugins tab.

4. You should see the Category Cloud Widget; on its row, click the Activate link.

5. Click the Presentation tab, then Widgets.

6. Now, locate the Category Cloud widget and drag it to your sidebar. You can click the small options box to change options for the widget. (For instance, you can set the minimum and maximum font sizes for your category cloud, set the alignment for the cloud, and so on.)

7. When you're done arranging, click Save Changes.

    That's it. View your blog and you should see the new category cloud in your sidebar.

> **Categories**
> **General Stuff** Mac
> Apple Web 2.0 Microsoft
> Blogging JFP Jobs Tech Apple TV
> Journalism Book Vista WordPress
> Video Blackberry Film IPhone
> Festival Google Troubleshooting
> Cars EVDO T-Mobile Sidekick
> Comments Jackson Personal
> Salon Alltel Seth Godin Sports

Tagging in WordPress

As mentioned, WordPress doesn't have true tagging built into it, but you can add it via a plug-in. The popular option is the Ultimate Tag Warrior (http://www .neato.co.nz/ultimate-tag-warrior/), a plug-in that makes it possible to add tags to your posts, turn your categories into tags, and display tags in a list or tag cloud on your blog. To use the plug-in, download it and install it as you would install any WordPress plug-in (see Chapter 3). Once installed, activate it by clicking the Activate button on the Plugin tab.

Once activated, you'll see new items on the Write page in the WordPress admin interface. At the bottom of the entry screen, you'll see a Tags area where you can add tags, separating them with commas.

```
Tags (comma separated list)
apple, apple-tv, itunes, podcast, video, web-2.0, wifi
```

You can also get suggestions for tags by clicking the Get Keyword Suggestions from Yahoo button that appears beneath the Tags entry box. Simply click any of the suggestions to add them to your post as a tag.

Once you've entered all the tags that seem appropriate, click Publish to add the entry to your blog.

Now, you'll want to add a tag cloud to your blog's template. To do that, you'll need to edit the template and add some code. Here's how:

1. Click the Presentation tab in the WordPress admin interface.

2. Click the Theme Editor tab.

3. Now, click the link labeled Sidebar. You should see the message "Editing sidebar.php" on the page; if not, you'll need to set permissions for your index.php page via FTP before you can move on. (See Chapter 4 for details on editing templates in WordPress.)

4. Based on how your sidebar is formatted, you need to add the following to an appropriate section of that sidebar:

   ```
   <?php UTW_ShowWeightedTagSet("sizedtagcloud") ?>
   ```

5. Now, save the Template and check your site to see if it updated correctly. Figure 7-1 shows what it looks like on my blog.

Note that how your template is designed may dictate exactly how you add that item to the sidebar. For instance, in the Sidebar template for the WordPress Default theme, items are surrounded by list item tags, as in:

```
<li>
<h2>Tags</h2>
<div class="sidebartags">
```

7

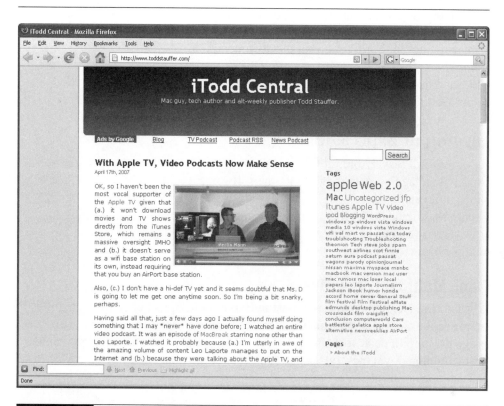

FIGURE 7-1   The Ultimate Tag Warrior tag cloud on my blog

```
<?php UTW_ShowWeightedTagSet("sizedtagcloud") ?>
</div>
</li>
```

You may find that's what you're looking at in your template, or you may not necessarily need to use the `<li>`, `</li>` list item tags.

Note also that there are different options for the UTW tag. For example, you can use a special tag for alphabetical listing of the tags, and set a limit to the number of tags shown, as in this example:

```
<?php UTW_ShowWeightedTagSetAlphabetical("coloredsizedtagcloud","","40") ?>
```

which looks like this in the browser window:

For more details on the options for using and displaying tags in WordPress, visit the documentation at http://www.neato.co.nz/wp-content/plugins/UltimateTagWarrior/ultimate-tag-warrior-help.html on the Web.

Tagging in ExpressionEngine

As with WordPress, ExpressionEngine doesn't come with a tagging feature built into the software, although it can be added using a special plug-in. ExpressionEngine does offer support for multiple categories without a plug-in, however, so you can begin to get some of the benefits of tagging by using the multiple categories feature.

Using Multiple Categories

When you're creating or editing a post in ExpressionEngine, click the Categories tab to see the categories to which you can choose to assign this blog entry. To assign the current entry to a single category, you simply click the category name. Or, by holding down the CTRL key in Windows or the COMMAND key on a Mac, you can click multiple categories.

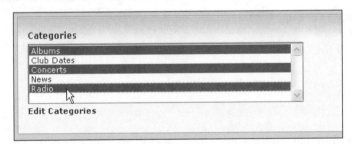

Now, once the entry is saved (or published, if it's new) you'll see the entry's categories in the footer information for the blog entry. (At least, you will in most default templates.)

Posted on Apr 16 2007 at 07:34 PM in Albums, Concerts, Radio | Comments(0) | Trackbacks(0) | Permalink

You can now click any of those categories in the category listings (again, in most templates, you'll find these in the sidebar somewhere) and this entry will appear in that category listing.

> TIP
>
> *A third-party plug-in is available for ExpressionEngine that creates a weighted category listing that is somewhat similar to a tag cloud without requiring you to purchase a commercial module. See http:// expressionengine.com/downloads/details/weighted_categories/ for details.*

Add Tagging Capabilities

Currently, the best way to add true tags to your ExpressionEngine blog is to buy an add-on module from a company called Solspace. To do that, you'll need to access their site at www.solspace.com, then locate the Tag module, register, and purchase it (they accept Paypal and credit cards via Paypal). Then, download the module and install it according to the instructions in the included ReadMe file. (You can reference Chapter 3, as well, for hints on installing modules.)

> CAUTION
>
> *This discussion can get a little confusing because the module is named "Tag," the concept we're discussing is called "tagging," and ExpressionEngine commands that you use in templates are generally referred to as "tags." So, when I'm specifically discussing ExpressionEngine commands, you'll see me say "ExpressionEngine tags" often, even though it may seem a bit clunky, and I'll be a bit more explicit with the standard blogging tags we're talking about in this chapter by calling them "keyword tags."*

7

Once Tag has been uploaded to your web host, you can activate it by selecting the Modules tab in the ExpressionEngine interface and clicking the Install link in its row. Once installed, you can click the module name Tag in the list to see its options.

Once it's installed and active, the Tag module enables you to do a number of things. First, you can capture keyword tags for your blog entries in two different ways—you can either add a form (similar to a comment form) on your blog entries that your users can use for tagging entries, or you can specify a custom field on the blog entry screen within the ExpressionEngine admin interface. That field can be used exclusively for adding keyword tags when you're creating or editing blog entries. Here's how to create it:

1. In the ExpressionEngine admin interface, click the Admin tab.

2. Click Weblog Administration and then click Custom Weblog Fields.

3. Now, click the Add/Edit Custom Fields link.

4. You should see a listing of the current fields in your blog entries. Click the Create a New Custom Field button.

5. Now, you'll create the custom field. Enter a Field Name (such as "MyTags"), enter a Field Label and choose the Field Type. (You can choose a Text Input field, perhaps increasing the number of characters to 256 or so, or you can choose a TextArea if you don't mind it taking up extra space.) The other preferences should be OK, so click Submit.

6. Now, head back to the Tag module (click the Modules tab, and then click the module name Tag).

7. Click Manage Preferences, and then click Create Preference.

8. In the Preference Name field enter a name for this preference (something like My Blog Tags should work). Then choose the Weblog and in the Tag Field menu choose the custom field that you just created. Click Create.

9. Back on the Manage General Preferences screen, choose Comma from the Tag Parsing Preference menu and click Submit.

Now, you can click the Publish tab, choose a blog (if you've created more than one), and you'll see the new field on the Publish page (see Figure 7-2). Make a blog entry as usual, but then add keyword tags in the tag field that can be used to identify or categorize this entry.

The next step is actually getting those keyword tags to appear on your blog. As with most ExpressionEngine template tags, the Tag module offers you some ExpressionEngine template tags that give you a lot of flexibility in the way that you can display the results. One common way is to show the keyword tags at the bottom of each post in the footer area that includes the author, date, and so on. To do that with the Tag module, you'll use a new ExpressionEngine tag, {exp:tag: tags_from_field}.

Take this typical example from the footer of a blog entry in a typical ExpressionEngine weblog template:

```
<div class="summary">
Posted on {entry_date format="%M %d %Y"} at
{entry_date format="%h:%i %A"} in {categories backspace="1"}
<a href="{path=site_index}">{category_name}</a>,
{/categories} |
<a href="{title_permalink={my_template_group}/comments}">
Permalink</a>
</div>
```

This code shows the date that a blog entry was posted, the categories assigned to that entry, and a permalink to the entry. If, instead of categories, you wanted to

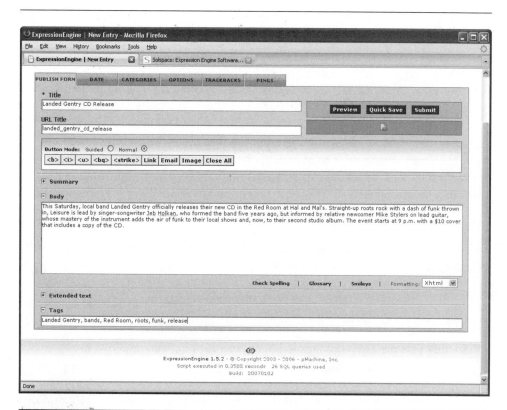

FIGURE 7-2   In this example I've added a custom field for keyword tags at the bottom of the post window.

show the keyword tags for that entry, you could do that using the Tag module's {exp:tag:tags_from_field}, as in:

```
<div class="summary">
Posted on {entry_date format="%M %d %Y"} at
{entry_date format="%h:%i %A"} in
{exp:tag:tags_from_field}{MyTags}{format}{tag}{/format}
{/exp:tag:tags_from_field}|
<a href="{title_permalink={my_template_group}/comments}">
Permalink</a>
</div>
```

Here's a breakdown of what this code is doing:

```
{exp:tag:tags_from_field}
```

calls the special `tags_from_field` ExpressionEngine tag that is part of the Tag module;

`{MyTags}`

tells the `tags_from_field` command what custom field it's looking for in the entry;

`{format}{tag} {/format}`

between the `{format}` tags you can enter the format for the output of each tag, while the `{tag}` attribute is used to actually pull each tag from the field you've created (note that I've added a space so that the keyword tags don't run together when they're displayed);

`{/exp:tag:tags_from_field}`

ends the call to the Tag module and the `tags_from_field` command. The result of adding those codes looks like this in my blog:

> Posted on Apr 21 2007 at 11:41 AM in bands funk Landed Gentry Red Room release roots
> | Comments(0) | Permalink

So, that gets the keyword tags to appear in your blog entries. Now the trick is to make those keyword tags useful; just seeing them probably isn't enough to get you excited about tagging the entries. So, you need to make the keyword tags themselves *hyperlinks* to a page that shows all of the blog entries that include that keyword tag. To do that, you'll tell the Tag module to format the keyword tags to be hyperlinks. Here's an example:

`{format}<a href="tagsresults/{websafe_tag}/">{tag}</a> {/format}`

That changes the list that appears in your blog entries so that you'll now see a series of hyperlinks (the difference is subtle in black and white):

> Posted on Apr 21 2007 at 11:41 AM in bands funk Landed Gentry Red Room release roots
> | Comments(0) | Permalink

When clicked, each keyword tag will now load a special version of the template named `tags`, which you'll now need to create. The new template will take the portion of the URL created by the `{websafe_tag}` element and use it to limit the output of the blog entries to just those that match the specific keyword tag that's been clicked.

> **NOTE** *The special {websafe_tag} element is used so that the URLs created by tags with spaces or other special characters are reformatted properly for URLs. You can also use it in place of the {tag} URL when you're displaying keyword tags, if you like, which will replace spaces in the tag names with plus ("+") signs.*

Here's how to create that new template for displaying entries based on the keyword tag that's clicked:

1. Click the Templates tab in your ExpressionEngine admin interface.

2. On the Template Management page, select the appropriate template group for this blog from the Choose Group menu.

3. In the menu of choices for that template group, click New Template.

4. On the New Template Form give the template a name in the Template Name entry box. (In the example code I just named it `tagresults`.)

5. In the Default Template Data section, choose Duplicate an Existing Template and choose the index template from this blog's template group. Click Submit.

6. Now, back in Template Management, you'll need to click the name of the new template to edit it.

7. In the Template Name window, scroll down and locate the `{exp:weblog:entries}` tag that is used to access the weblog module and display entries. It should look something like this, perhaps with slightly different attributes:

```
{exp:weblog:entries weblog="{my_weblog}" orderby="date"
sort="desc" limit="10"}
```

8. Now, in order to show only items that match the ExpressionEngine tag that you've selected, you'll need to change that code so that it uses the Tag module to display entries. Replace that tag with a tag that looks like this:

```
{exp:tag:entries weblog="{my_weblog}" orderby="entry_date"
sort="asc" limit="10" marker="tagresults"}
```

> **NOTE** *The `marker="tagresults"` attribute is used to tell the module what the name of the template is that you've created for displaying tags. If you don't use that attribute, then it will assume the template is simply called `tag`. If you decided to call the template `tags_detail`, for instance, then you'd need `marker="tags_detail"` in the {exp:tag:entries} opening tag.*

7

9. Next, you'll need to find the closing {/exp:weblog:entries} tag and replace it with {/exp:tag:entries} since we're using the tag module to access the entries instead of the weblog module.

10. Finally, you should make one more change; you'll need the keyword tags that appear on this template to link correctly so that they can be clicked to change the view. So, locate:

```
{exp:tag:tags_from_field} {Tags}
{format}<a href="tagresults/{websafe_tag}/">{tag} </a>{/format}
{/exp:tag:tags_from_field}
```

and change it to:

```
{exp:tag:tags_from_field} {Tags} {format}
<a href="../../tagresults/{websafe_tag}/">{tag} </a>{/format}
{/exp:tag:tags_from_field}
```

11. Click Update to save the template changes.

With the template created, you can now load your blog's index page and click one of the keyword tags that appears in a blog entry. What should happen is you'll see the items shown in the blog change so that only those items using the specified keyword tag are displayed. Click another keyword tag and again the blog will reconfigure so that you're only looking at entries that are associated with that newly clicked keyword tag.

Add a Tag Cloud

As we've seen with other keyword tagging solutions, a popular use of those keyword tags is to display them in a tag cloud, which gives your visitors another way to look at the topics that your blog covers. The Tag module includes a special ExpressionEngine tag for creating a tag cloud. Most likely you'll want to add this to the sidebar of your blog's index page, as well as, perhaps to the template that you create for showing the entries by tag. Here's a sample of the code used for creating a tag cloud:

```
{exp:tag:cloud groups="10" start="8" step="2" limit="20"}
<a href="tagresults/{websafe_tag}"
style="font-size:{step}px; color:white"
"title="{count}" >{tag_name} </a>
{/exp:tag:cloud}
```

Let's break that down a bit. We begin with a new ExpressionEngine tag that references the Tag module and creates the tag cloud:

```
{exp:tag:cloud groups="10" start="8" step="2" limit="20"}
```

This ExpressionEngine tag offers a number of important attributes:

- **groups="x"**   This attribute is used to determine the number of groups that your tag cloud will be divided into so that the terms can be shown in different sizes. If you have ten groups, then there will be up to ten different sizes used to show keyword tags of different frequencies.

- **start="x"**   This attribute determines the starting value that is used to change the font size of the different keyword tags. So, if you want the smallest keyword tag in the cloud to be 8 points (or 8 pixels or 8 picas) then you set start="8".

- **step="x"**   The number you set for the step attribute determines how much each group is incremented between them. So, if you'd like the font from one group to another to be 2 pixels (or points or picas) larger than the previous group, you'd set x to 2.

- **limit=x**   With this attribute you can limit your tag cloud to a certain number of keyword tags.

So that's the opening of the {exp:tag:cloud} tag and its attributes. Next, you actually format the output of the keyword tags the way you'd like them to appear. In my example, you could do something like this:

```
<a href="tagresults/{websafe_tag}"
style="font-size:{step}px; color:white"
"title="{count}" >{tag_name} </a>
```

That makes each tag a hyperlink that leads to the tags template that was created as an example earlier. Notice that the {step} element substitutes a number into the CSS font-style element, and that the actual measurement used is up to you. (I'm using px for pixels, but it could easily be pt for points, or any number of other valid CSS measurement types for font size.) The {tag name} element is used to display the name of the tag, and I've included a space to give it a little more room in the tag cloud. (Note that you could substitute {websafe_tag} for {tag_name} if you prefer to list your multi-word keyword tags as single words with plus signs ("+") between them.

Finally, close the tag cloud with the closing ExpressionEngine tag from the Tag module:

```
{/exp:tag:cloud}
```

Now, save the template and re-load your blog's index page. The result will look something like this:

If you decide to put a tag cloud in the template that you're using for your tag results listings (the template I've called `tagresults` in all of my examples), then you'll need to make sure the path statement works correctly, as in:

```
<a href="../../tagresults/{websafe_tag}"
style="font-size:{step}px; color:white"
"title="{count}" >{tag_name} </a>
```

Alternatively, you could "hard-code" that link (or all of your keyword tag links) so that they load the exact page, as in this example:

```
<a href="http://www.me.com/index.php/site/tagresults/{websafe_tag}"
style="font-size:{step}px; color:white" "title="{count}" >
{tag_name} </a>
```

Just point the anchor tag to your own URL and make sure the complete URL conforms to ExpressionEngine's URL conventions, as discussed in Chapter 3.

NOTE *There's more that you can do with the Tag module; visit http://solspace .com/docs/c/Tag to learn more about what Tag can do.*

Third-Party Tags and Bookmark Sharing

A number of Web 2.0 services exist to help bring some order to the blogosphere. In general, they offer ways for people to look at blogs posts on similar topics or on topics that might appeal to different groups or different interests. They range from Technorati, which uses tags to organize blog entries from around the world (as well as to track links among blogs and rate them for popularity) to Digg and Reddit, which are designed to use the crowds that access them to promote popular blog entries and give them some time in the limelight. Let's take a look at a number of them and see how you can integrate them into your blog so that your readers can help you make a name for yourself.

Technorati

Technorati really riffs on the tagging concept that I've been discussing in the first part of this chapter. While tags are a fun way to access and cross-reference related blog entries on your own site, one component of Technorati is to make that sort of tagging and cross-referencing available across many different blogs at once. The idea is that by feeding the tags that you generate about your blog to Technorati, others can discover your blog entries when they're on the Technorati site and surfing different tags to see what comes up. If you write about investments a lot, for instance, then people who visit Technorati to look at items under the investing tab might be able to see some of your blog entries and, hence, link in and see what you have to say (see Figure 7-3).

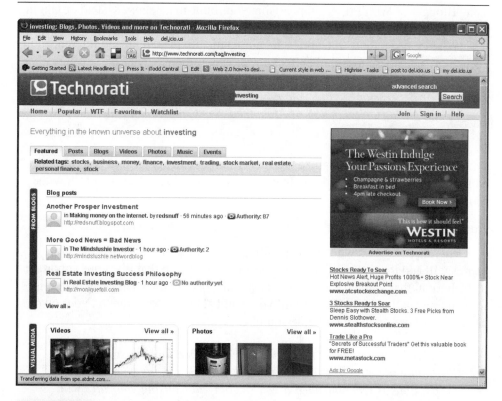

| FIGURE 7-3 | Here's the Technorati tag page for the keyword "investing." Technorati tracks thousands of keywords and shows blog entries and other Web resources that use them. |

Aside from this sort of "social tagging," Technorati offers some other services that we'll touch on, including the ability for you to "claim your blog" on the service and then use some different widgets to track your popularity and, perhaps, drive more traffic to your site.

Technorati Tags

Feeding your blog's categories or tags to Technorati is a two-part process. First, you need to make sure you're using the category or tagging system that's built in (or that you've set up) for your blog. If you don't assign blog entries to categories, then they won't be associated with Technorati tags. Second, you need to ping Technorati to let it know when you've got a new blog entry (discussed in the next section).

For the first part, there are a few different approaches you can take. If you're using Blogger or WordPress, simply using your built-in category system or tagging system should cause your RSS/Atom feeds to include that category information as well. When it does, those categories are automatically picked up and referenced in Technorati's database to a similar Technorati Tag, if there is one.

> **TIP** *For ExpressionEngine, you may have to explicitly add your categories and/or tags to your RSS or Atom feed. See Chapter 5 for details on setting up your feed.*

Technorati will also recognize tags that you manually enter into your blog entries. You can do that by adding hyperlinks to your blog entries that follow the format:

```
<a href="http://technorati.com/tag/[tagname]" rel="tag">[tagname]</a>
```

Generally, bloggers who are manually adding Technorati tags to their blog entries will add them at the bottom of the entry. Note also that it's more important to Technorati that you have the `rel="tag"` attribute in the anchor tag than it is for you to actually link to Technorati; you could also link to a page on your own site or elsewhere on the Internet, if you like.

> **NOTE** *If you're using one of the previously described tagging systems, then adding the `rel=` attribute to the links that determine your tags, if possible, is recommended if you're going to be using your tags with Technorati. If you can add the `rel=` attribute to the tags that are created by your blogging software for categories or tags, you'll find you get better (and somewhat automatic) results if you submit your blog to Technorati.*

TIP   *The page http://www.technorati.com/tools/ links to a number of different tools that can be used to quickly create Technorati tag links, including blog widgets, desktop widgets, and other quick-access services.*

Ping Technorati

If you've got a blog that's using categories, tags, or Technorati tags and you're set up with an RSS feed, then you can make sure that Technorati knows when you've made an update by pinging the service. How you do that depends on your blogging software, but each of them have built into them the ability to send a ping anywhere, including Technorati. The URL for pinging Technorati is http://rpc .technorati.com/rpc/ping, so that's what you'll use when you're setting this up. Here's a look at each of the solutions we've discussed in this book:

- **Blogger**   Actually, Blogger automatically pings Technorati if you set it to place your blog in the Blogger listings. Do that by logging into your Blogger dashboard and clicking the Change Settings option. Locate the Add Your Blog to Our Listings option and set it to Yes, then Save Settings. You entries will now be sent to Technorati.

- **TypePad**   In TypePad, log in and create a new post. At the bottom of the post window is a link called Customize the Display of Your Page. Click that link and in the Post Screen Configuration section that appears, turn on TrackBack URLs to Ping in the Custom section and click Save. Now, in the Send Trackbacks entry box on your post screen, you can enter the URL http://rpc.technorati.com/rpc/ping to send the post to Technorati.

NOTE   *Actually, if you use TypePad, there's an easier way to do this. From the admin interface, click Configure and then Publicity. If Publicize This Weblog is turned on, then Technorati will automatically be pinged with new entries. Technorati will look at your category choices. Or, if you'd like to specifically enter Technorati tags, choose Customize the Display of This Page on the Post page and turn on the option Technorati Tags. That will give you a special entry box for tags that will be associated with Technorati.*

- **WordPress**   When you're entering a post, add the URL http://rpc.technorati .com/rpc/ping to the Update Services entry box. When you send the entry, Technorati will be pinged.

■ **ExpressionEngine** In the ExpressionEngine control panel, click the Admin tab and then click Default Ping Servers. On the Default Ping Servers page, you should see a number of different pings as well as some blank fields. Enter a descriptive name (such as "technorati.com") in the first blank Server Name field and then fill in the URL http://rpc.technorati. com/rpc/ping in the Server Path/URL field. If you'd like to send all of your entries to Technorati, then make sure the Default option is set to Yes. (You can also choose the order where Technorati should appear on the list; enter a number in the Order column.) Now, when you're creating or editing a post, Technorati will appear as an option on the Publish page under the Pings tab and, if you set it as a default, it should be pre-checked.

PUBLISH FORM	DATE	CATEGORIES	OPTIONS	PINGS	

Sites To Ping

- ☐ weblogs.com
- ☐ blo.gs
- ☐ blogrolling.com
- ☐ blogshares.com
- ☑ technorati.com
- ☐ Select/Deselect All

Once you've got pinging set up, it should be automatic; in fact, you can visit a keyword page on Technorati that matches your most recent post and, if you get there soon enough, you should see it on that page soon after you ping Technorati.

TIP *If you'd prefer not to use an automatic solution then you can manually ping Technorati whenever you put up a blog entry that you'd like it to know about. Just visit http://technorati.com/ping/ and enter your blog's URL. You'll also find some third-party options, such as a Technorati Ping dashboard item for Mac OS X (http://www.apple.com/downloads/ dashboard/blogs_forums/technoratiping.html).*

Claim Your Blog

Another important step at Technorati is to "claim your blog." This enables you to let Technorati know that a blog is yours, which enables you to get additional information about the blog and track its progress as people link to it.

Sending Pings

So what's all this about "pinging?" Based loosely on the idea of sonar sending "pings" underwater, pinging in Internet-speak is the act of sending a small bit of data across the Internet to see if another computer is listening; it's also handy for figuring out how long it takes a packet of data to move from one location to another on the Internet—just in case you find that interesting.

For blogging, pinging means something slightly different—it means letting some central server know that you posted something new on your blog. It's sort of a Web 1.0 way of publicizing changes to your website—no tags, user context, or trackbacks—just a little "hey, I posted something new" alert sent to a central server.

How to ping the Technorati servers is discussed in the section "Ping Technorati," but notice that all of the blogging solutions enable you to ping other sites as well, including their home sites (Blogger, TypePad), where new posts are logged and showed to visitors. There are also a few more general services, such as weblogs.com and blogrolling.com. There's no particular harm in pinging these servers if that interests you (unless you don't want publicity), so if it's an interest, go ahead and turn on those features in your blogging software. It may not get you too many new visitors, since those sites tend to be hit with tons of new updates every few seconds, but you never know.

To claim a blog, you first need to register with Technorati. To do, that, click the Sign In link on the Technorati home page. (Actually, it's at the top of most or all of the pages.) There, if you don't have a username and password, you can register and sign in.

Once you're signed in, you'll see an option on the home page of Technorati to Claim Your Blog. Click that link and you'll be taken to a screen where you can enter the URL of the blog that you want to claim and click Begin Claim.

Claim a Blog

Claiming your blog establishes that you are its owner, and allows you to use Technorati services to increase your blog's visibility.

Blog URL   Example: http://myblog.bloghost.com

http://toddstauffer.typepad.com

NOTE   *If you don't see the option, then you can click the Edit link next to your user name in the interface and then click the Blogs tab. Now, at the bottom of that page you should see the Claim Your Blog section.*

Next, you can choose the method that you want to use for claiming your blog. Perhaps the easiest and most secure way is the Post Claim, which enables you to claim your blog by posting a special code in a new entry on your blog. When Technorati sees the blog entry, it knows that the blog you're claiming is one to which you have administrative access. Choose whichever method you'd like to use and then walk through its steps.

Once you've claimed the blog successfully, you'll be asked to describe it and choose some settings. You may also be prompted to install a widget on your blog, if it's compatible with the Technorati widgets or plug-ins. You'll also see code that you can paste into your blog for both Technorati tools and for buttons that you can post on your blog to let people know that you've registered your blog with Technorati. Just copy and paste that code into the appropriate design template for your blog (see Chapters 2 and 3).

When you're done, click Save Blog Info and your blog has been claimed.

TIP   *Other "tools" can be downloaded, placed on your blog and used to interact with Technorati. For instance, you can place a badge on your blog that shows how many other blogs Technorati recognizes as linking to yours. For more on the tools, visit http://www.technorati.com/tools/.*

Add Social Bookmarking Hooks

You're probably familiar with the idea of bookmarking Web pages within your own browser. The idea behind *social bookmarking* is that you can bookmark pages that interest you via a Web service, and then make them available for other people on the Internet to see. The idea is that if your interests happen to coincide with someone else's out there on the World Wide Web, they can start to track the bookmarks that you store on the service, and, eventually, rely on you to help them find interesting stuff on the Internet. They, of course, can reciprocate for you, or perhaps you'll find someone else out there whose bookmarks you find intriguing.

As it so happens, these sites tend to rely on tagging to help you get from one place to another. They're interesting in one particular respect, however—the fact that human beings are doing all of this bookmarking and tagging may lead you to better results than Web spiders on Google and other search engines do. Dive into the world of social bookmarking and you may truly find some websites that interest you.

From your point of view as a blogger, you may want to offer tools on your blog that make it easier for your readers to bookmark your blog entries using social bookmarking sites and tools because, well, you may get more page views that way. And that's the point, right?

NOTE *We'll take a look at del.icio.us in this section, but others that are similar include StumbleUpon (www.stumbleupon.com) and Ma.gnolia (ma.gnolia. com), both of which are social networking/bookmarking hybrids (meaning people put up pictures of themselves and link to other folks as well as share their bookmarks), Spurl (www.spurl.net), BackFlip (www.backflip .com), Netvouz (www.netvouz.com), Furl (www.furl.net), BlogMarks (www.blogmarks.net), BlueDot (www.bluedot.us), and others.*

del.icio.us

7

This is probably the easiest to remember (and hardest to type correctly) URL for a site that remains very popular on the Web, but once you get it, you'll get it. del. icio.us is easily (at least, currently) the top social bookmarking tool, so you'll likely find it handy to add del.icio.us tools to your blog so that others can easily bookmark your entries. And, if you get interested in using the site yourself, you may want an account.

To get started using del.icio.us, just visit its rather unique home page URL (http://del.icio.us) and register as a new user. Once you're registered, you'll be instructed on how to add items to your browser toolbar so that you can bookmark pages that you find interesting while you're surfing. Begin to create a set of interesting bookmarks and you'll, potentially, attract an audience. If so, they might also click into your blog to see what you're all about. (And, of course, you can link to and tag your blog entries on the service, too, particularly the "evergreen" entries that you're proud of.)

To offer del.icio.us tools to your visitors, you don't actually have to be a member of the site—after all, the point is to get them to bookmark your blog on their own del.icio.us page. You can make it easier for them to save your blog entries to their del.icio.us account, however, by visiting http://del.icio.us/help/ savebuttons and copying the code for the del.icio.us button that you can then add to your blog. The code looks something like this (I've cut out a long URL that's part of the code:

```
<a href="http://del.icio.us/post"
onclick="window.open('long URL', 'delicious',
'toolbar=no,width=700,height=400'); return false;">
Save This Page</a>
```

NOTE *This code creates a hyperlink that you can change, if desired, to "Save to del.icio.us" or something similar if desired. Just edit the "Save This Page" text.*

Where should you paste that code? It probably makes the most sense to place it somewhere in the "single post," "comments," or "more" template for your blog, although the sidebar will do in a pinch. Once it's there, your readers can click the button to launch a special window and easily bookmark your blog (or a post within your blog) to their del.icio.us account.

TIP *TypePad offers a number of del.icio.us widgets from within its built-in widget library, and WordPress offers some third-party widgets as well.*

Digg and Rating Services

Need some visitors to your site? If you've got something to say and you can say it in a way that might interest folks, then you're a good candidate for Digg. Digg.com is a site where blog posts and other online stories are submitted and then voted on by the Digg community (each vote is called a "digg"). If a blog entry of yours gets voted up by a number of people and makes it to the first few pages of Digg, then you've got yourself some serious traffic for the next few hours. (More than one Web host has been overloaded by the sudden popularity of a blog entry on the home page of Digg.)

TIP *If you do get involved with Digg, realize that it's a community and it's important to follow some norms. One is that you shouldn't "spam" Digg by putting up every single blog entry you write. While it's occasionally OK to "digg" your own entries, it's frowned upon if you get too crazy about it. If you do digg your own entries, they should be really good and the sort of thing that Digg folks, well, dig. Otherwise, I would try to drive traffic to your site in other ways and then allow your readers to digg you.*

NOTE *Of course, Digg isn't the only such service out there, and if you're truly interested in getting some publicity for your site, it isn't a bad idea to let your users vote you onto some of these different rating services. Other options include the Netscape home page (www.netscape.com), Reddit (www.reddit.com), Tailrank (www.tailrank.com), and Newsvine (www .newsvine.com).*

To add a Digg.com button to your site, you'll head to the Digg site and locate the tools that you want to use. While Digg offers a number of links and buttons to get people from your site to Digg, the most interesting tools for bloggers are those that allow your readers to submit your blog entries directly to the Digg service.

At http://www.digg.com/tools/integrate, you can find a Digg tool that enables you to show the number of diggs that a post has received while enabling Digg users to simply click the button and add their own vote.

NOTE *The Digg Integrate page offers a few different styles for the Digg button, including some that look good in the "meta" line of your blog entries and that are a little less intrusive. (That can be ideal if you don't actually have many diggs on your entries and you don't want to bring too much attention to that fact.)*

The code for the tool is simple:

```
<script src="http://digg.com/tools/diggthis.js"
type="text/javascript"></script>
```

You can paste it in your template anywhere that makes sense to you from a design standpoint. Here's an example where I've also placed a `<div>` tag around the Digg code and used the `float` CSS attribute (as well as the `margin-right` attribute) to work it into the design.

```
<div style="float:left; margin-right:5px">
<script src="http://digg.com/tools/diggthis.js"
type="text/javascript"></script>
</div>
```

VIRB...MySpace Decluttered

April 15th, 2007

0 diggs

digg it

Don't know what good, exactly, another MySpace clone will do for the world as a whole, but it's worth saying that VIRB has some advantages over MySpace. Take it from someone who surfs band pages every week trying to get clips of songs for a radio show...the VIRB feature of turning *off* the customization on people's pages is huge. Huge! That may be the only real feature that VIRB is bringing to the table and yet it's a nice one.

Note that it generally makes more sense to place the link on the full-entry page of a blog entry; otherwise, by default, you'll probably be encouraging Digg readers to digg the main page of your blog instead of actual blog entries using this snippet of code. (This code sends the *current* URL to Digg, even if it's a blog's home page that shows multiple stories.)

Using another snippet of code, you can get around that if you're also familiar with your blog tool's built-in tags for entering the URL of a blog entry. This code looks like this:

```
<script type="text/javascript">
digg_url = 'WEBSITE_URL';
</script>
<script src="http://digg.com/tools/diggthis.js"
type="text/javascript"></script>
```

Depending on your blog tool, you can use a blog-specific tag or command in place of WEBSITE_URL. For instance, in WordPress, the command `<?php the_permalink() ?>` can use used to output the URL to the full-page blog entry, so you can use this code for the Digg button:

```
<script type="text/javascript">
digg_url = '<?php the_permalink() ?>';
</script>
<script src="http://digg.com/tools/diggthis.js"
type="text/javascript"></script>
```

The result will be a link to the permalink of the entry in question, so that your readers can begin immediately to digg a posting of yours, even when they've only seen it on the front page of your blog.

Here's a look at the internal tags for other blogging systems.

Blogger

Edit the HTML of your template (Template tag | Edit HTML) and then turn on the option Expand Widget Templates. Locate this code:

```
<div class='post-body'>
  <p><data:post.body/></p>
  <div style='clear: both;'/> <!— clear for photos floats —>
</div>
```

That's the code snippet that posts the body of your Blogger entry. You'll paste the Digg code in there, like this:

```
<div class='post-body'>
  <p>
  <div style='float:left; margin-right:5px;'>
   <script type='text/javascript'>
```

```
  digg_url = '<data:post.url/>';
  </script>
  <script src='http://digg.com/tools/diggthis.js'
  type='text/javascript'/>
  </div>
<data:post.body/>
</p>
  <div style='clear: both;'/> <!— clear for photos floats —>
</div>
```

Save the template and then view your blog.

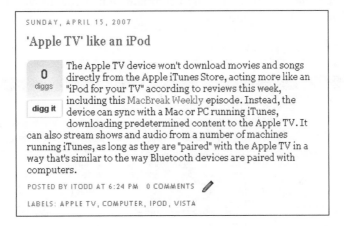

TypePad

If you're using a default, widget-enabled template for TypePad, then you're going to have a hard time editing in a Digg link. If you're using a third-party template or similar, then you'll have an easier time. The key tag that you're worried about is `<$MTEntryPermalink$>`, which is the MoveableType/TypePad code for inserting the URL of a given blog entry. So this code would be useful for an editable template:

```
<div style='float:left; margin-right:5px;'>
 <script type='text/javascript'>
 digg_url = '<$MTEntryPermalink$>'; </script>
 <script src='http://digg.com/tools/diggthis.js'
 type='text/javascript'/>
</div>
```

If you're using one of the built-in, widget-compatible templates, there's another option for adding Digg in TypePad—you can use the integrated FeedBurner tools:

1. First, you'll need to activate FeedBurner from within TypePad, as discussed in Chapter 5.

2. Next, log into your Feedburner account (at http://www.feedburner.com) and activate the FeedFlare option for the feed that is associated with your TypePad blog. You do that by selecting the appropriate feed, clicking the Optimize tab, and then clicking FeedFlare. When you do, you'll see a list of options shown in Figure 7-4.

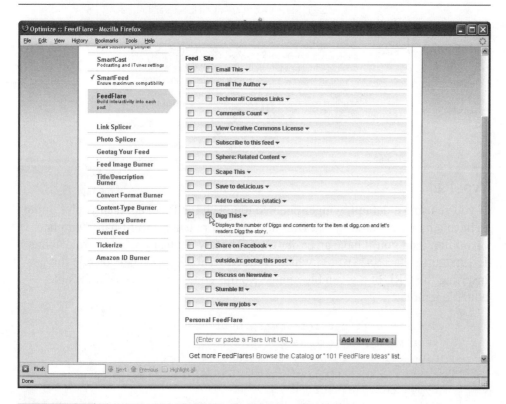

FIGURE 7-4   The options for FeedFlare enable you to turn on links to many different sharing services for both your feed and your blog.

3. Turn on Digg This for both your feed and your blog (or just for your blog) as well as other options you'd like active, and then click Activate at the bottom of the page.

TIP   *Note that FeedFlare can be used for a lot of services including Technorati, del.icio.us, and others.*

4. Now, return to the TypePad admin interface for your blog and click Design.

5. Click the Select Content link, and then locate and turn on the FeedFlare option.

☑ FeedFlare
If selected, FeedBurner FeedFlare will be
enabled for your blog.

That's it. It may take a few minutes for the connections to take hold, and you may have to republish your blog before you'll see them. (On the Design tab, scroll to the bottom of the page to see the Republish Weblog button.)

ExpressionEngine

To add the Digg code to a post in ExpressionEngine, the code for placing the permalink URL is {title_permalink={my_template_group}/comments} in most default templates. So, open your blog's index template and locate the following code or something similar to it:

```
{summary}
{body}
{extended}
```

And add the Digg code right before it:

```
<div style='float:left; margin-right:5px;'>
<script src='http://digg.com/tools/diggthis.js'
type='text/javascript'/>
<script type='text/javascript'>
digg_url = '{title_permalink={my_template_group}/comments} ';
</script>
</div>
{summary}
{body}
{extended}
```

Save the template and reload your blog. You should see the Digg button appear. You can add similar code to the comments template for that blog, as well, so that the Digg button appears on individual entries.

Use a Multi-link Service

So, what if you could add all of these services (or, many of them, at least) with one fell swoop? That's the idea behind services such as AddThis.com, which give you a bookmark widget that you can place at the end of your blog posts so that readers can bookmark the entry on a variety of different social bookmarking and ranking sites.

To work with AddThis, you don't need to register with the service, although you can if you're interested in advanced stats based on who uses your AddThis bookmark. If you're not interested in registering, here's how you go about adding the bookmark widget to your site:

1. Go to http://www.addthis.com and click the Get the Widget button on the home page of the AddThis site.

2. From the Which Kind of Widget menu, choose Bookmarking Widget.

3. Click the radio button next to the type of widget you'd like to use.

4. In the next menu, choose where you'd like the widget to appear. If you choose On a Blog, you'll get code for different blogging systems, including TypePad, Blogger, and WordPress. (Choose Other for ExpressionEngine.)

5. Make a choice from the Want Stats With That? menu. If you choose No, you won't have to register for the widget.

6. Now, if you chose not to have stats, you'll be able to cut and paste the code on the next page and follow the instructions for the blog system that you chose. AddThis gives you explicit instructions for cutting and pasting the code into your blogging template.

If you're working with ExpressionEngine and you chose Other, you can cut and paste the link into your comment template; it won't work in the "footer" of regular blog entries on the home page of your blog, because it looks at the browser window itself to determine the title and URL of the page that it's bookmarking. In a typical Expression Engine template, you can locate the summary information and paste the code for the AddThis icon into that section, as in (again I've cut a long URL that you're better off cutting and pasting from the site:)

```
Posted on {entry_date format="%M %d %Y"} at
{entry_date format="%h:%i %A"} in
{categories backspace="1"}
<a href="{path=site_index}">{category_name}</a>,
{/categories} |
{if allow_comments}
<a href="{url_title_path={my_template_group}/comments}">
Comments({comment_total})</a> |
<a href="{title_permalink={my_template_group}/comments}">
Permalink</a>
<div align="right">
<!— AddThis Bookmark Button BEGIN —>
<a href="http://www.addthis.com/bookmark.php"
onclick="window.open('long URL', 'addthis',
'scrollbars=yes, menubar=no, width=620, height=520,
resizable=yes, toolbar=no, location=no, status=no,
screenX=200, screenY=100, left=200, top=100');
return false;" title="Bookmark using any bookmark manager!"
target="_blank">
<img src="http://s5.addthis.com/button1-bm.gif"
width="125" height="16" border="0"
alt="AddThis Social Bookmark Button" /></a>
<!— AddThis Bookmark Button END —>
</div>
```

With the code added, the link looks like this:

Posted on Apr 21 2007 at 11:41 AM in | Comments(0) | Trackbacks(0) | Permalink
BOOKMARK

Clicking the link invokes the embedded JavaScript commands, which pop up a new window for the user to choose where he or she would like to send bookmarks of this blog entry.

Chapter 8

Collaborate with Users Through Wikis

How to...

- Offer a wiki on your site

- Choose between a hosted or self-served wiki

- Use Backpack

- Use Wikidot

- Use PmWiki

- Use the Wiki Module in ExpressionEngine

What's a Wiki?

Wikis have gained popularity in recent years in part thanks to the success of Wikipedia.org, which has made the idea of a wiki widely understood. A *wiki* (the name is said to be short for the Hawaiian word "wiki wiki," which means "easy") is a website that allows the users themselves to edit pages directly in a web browser. On most wikis, there's a fairly prominent Edit link or button on the page; if you have the correct permissions, you can click that link and then you're able to see that page's content in a web form interface where you can edit the page and submit your changes. The web form used for many wikis tends to be similar to the content areas for a blog posting, although they are often even more simplified (generally wiki pages don't bother with blurb fields and so on). Figure 8-1 shows a wiki page that's being viewing in a web browser, while Figure 8-2 shows that page being edited.

Wiki Syntax and Structure

Most wikis also offer a simplified text formatting syntax of some sort, which enables the person editing it to add bold, italic, bullet points, strikeout text, hyperlinks, and images using formatting that's a little more simple than standard HTML. The formatting can vary depending on the software that's used to create the wiki and the *wiki syntax* employed by that wiki application.

One hallmark of most wiki systems is that the syntax is generally designed to make it possible for the user to create new pages within the website simply by creating a *link* to a page that doesn't yet exist. Once the edited page is published and the new link clicked, the wiki software will automatically create that new page and allow the user to add content to it. In this way, a hierarchy (or "web") of pages can be created on a wiki for whatever reason the wiki's users can envision. And because all of this happens without requiring "administrator" level access to the back-end of the software, wikis are an interesting option for online collaboration—

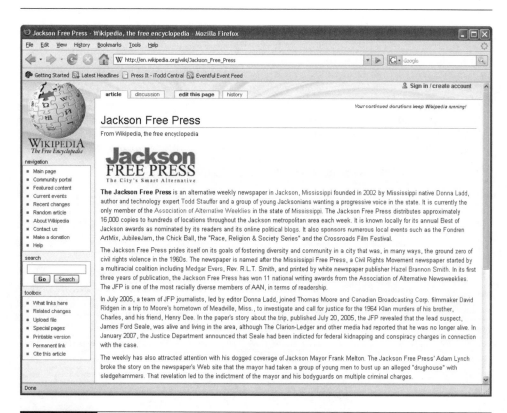

FIGURE 8-1   A typical wiki page viewed in a web browser

you can allow a group of trusted users to edit and create pages or, as in the case of Wikipedia, you can elect to "trust" the entire world of users (with some safeguards, naturally) and allow them to edit and add pages to their heart's desire.

> **NOTE**   *Some wikis use a syntax called "CamelCase" for creating links to pages. With CamelCase, the idea is that, while you're editing a page, whenever you type a word that includes inter-capped letters, it signifies a link. An example might be* `TableOfContents` *or* `UsingWikis`*. Now, when you save that edit, the wiki page will automatically turn those words into a hyperlink; clicking the link will then create the page in the wiki if it doesn't already exist. (If it does exist, then clicking the link takes you to that page.) Other wikis use a different approach, such as brackets for text that should be in hyperlinks, as in* `[[Using Wikis]]`*.*

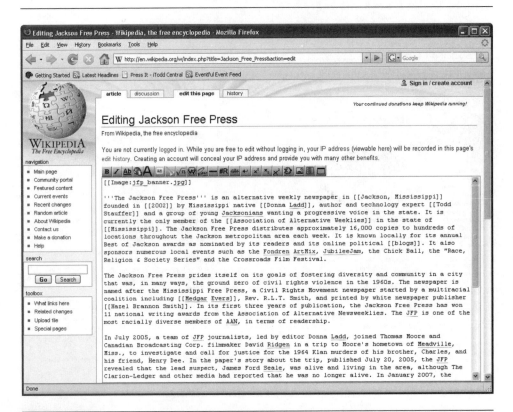

FIGURE 8-2 The same page shown in Figure 8-1, now being edited using the wiki syntax

Because of the simplified syntax and the limits that must generally be imposed on wiki users, wiki pages tend to have a very simple appearance. (Again, if you're familiar with Wikipedia, you're aware of its basic design and text-heavy presentation.) In a sense, wikis are similar to blogs in this respect; once you, as the site owner, set up a template for your wiki, most of the new wiki content will be created and displayed within that template or theme. In general, wiki users won't have access to CSS or other formatting elements. Likewise, it's generally encouraged in wiki documents that users stick to HTML recommended standards for formatting headings and sections of the page in a hierarchical way. For instance, in HTML, you have <h1>, <h2>, and so on through <h6> that you can use to create "headings" in your document. When you're working with wikis, it's recommended that you use those or similar wiki formatting not for appearance (not just to make the text bold and/or bigger) but because the marked up text really is a level 2 or level 3 heading in your document.

Why? One reason is that increased attention to the structure of the document makes it easier for wiki applications to present the information in that document. In fact, some wiki software can do some fun things automatically with a well-formed document, such as making the page more easily searchable or creating an "on-the-fly" table of contents of that page (see Figure 8-3).

Wikis exemplify two different Web 2.0 philosophies at once—user interaction and simple design. Because of these two characterstics, wikis are often used for documentation or for storing "group knowledge" about a variety of topics. Wikis are often used by communities, application developers, or other groups to store the community's knowledge about a particular topic area, region, or interest. As an example, pMachine Inc. offers a wiki that covers the use of ExpressionEngine, including tips, techniques, modules, extensions, and other content that is submitted by their user community and managed by the technical support staff of the company (see Figure 8-4).

FIGURE 8-3   On the "LoungeList" wiki page for the Jackson Free Press, the headings are automatically turned into a table of contents that appears to the right.

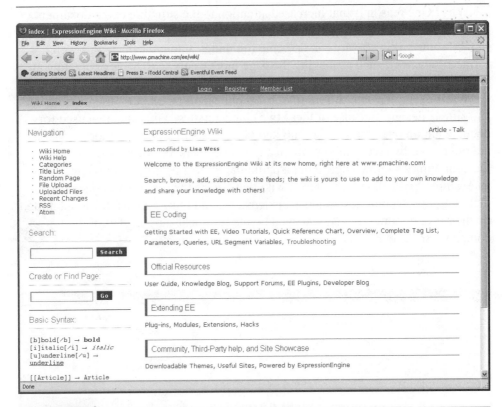

FIGURE 8-4   The pMachine.com wiki offers tips and techniques for using ExpressionEngine that are generated by staff and dedicated users.

What wikis aren't as useful for is time-based information in the same way that blogs are, whether it's a personal diary, news headlines, or ongoing discussions. As is discussed in Chapter 9, you can capture user content that's more suited to blogging by creating a community blog that allows many different people to post to the blog; or, for discussions, you can consider a discussion forum. For relatively "static" information that needs to be shared with a group or with the Web at large, however, wikis can be a great way to make the web publishing process easy for your trusted users or for all of your visitors.

Do You Need a Wiki?

Now that you have some sense of what a wiki is and how the structure works, it might be worth asking the question: Do you need a wiki? Not all blogs do, of course. For one thing, a wiki can require some effort to keep up, and wikis are generally used to fulfill a pretty specific purpose—reference. Where a blog can be used to inform, entertain, or build community, wikis are pretty much one-trick ponies—they're designed for groups to collaborate on building sites that are largely for reference. If you don't have a strong need for quite a few pages of reference material, then you may not need a wiki for your site.

If your blog supports a hobby that's important to you, or if you've built a large community around your blog, then a wiki might make more sense. Wikis are good for holding a great deal of information on topics like software products, comics, travel, movies, fiction, celebrities, politicians, locales, and similar types of data. If you've got a lot of information to create and store about a particular topic (and, ideally, if you're something of an expert on that topic), then a wiki can be very good for that.

By the same token, wikis are generally more successful when they're aimed at a particular topic or purpose, such as, say, documenting the different ways you can use a particular software product or, if you were covering movies, a wiki might be great for documenting the films of Cary Grant, but not as good for simply launching a general purpose "classic" film site. If you have too broad of a topic, a wiki might not be great for organizing that information.

Although it's possible to be the primary person in charge of putting information into a wiki, especially for technical or similar documentation, wikis generally also require a pretty active community in order to be successful. With a small, dedicated group, you can use a wiki for organizational purposes—to document who is doing what for an event, festival, product release, or something similar. For general reference—say a wiki about well-known stuntmen in movies or a wiki about Porsche parts—you may want a larger group adding items to your wiki as it will otherwise seem somewhat barren. If you don't yet have that community built, you might want to work on your blog's traffic before worrying about a wiki.

8

NOTE *For the purposes of building traffic, simply creating a wiki isn't as good as continuing to develop a really good blog. If, however, you or your community can sustain the effort needed to populate a wiki with many pages of interesting content, then a good wiki is great at generating page views, as people tend to surf through wikis looking at different articles and items.*

If you're not yet ready to start a full fledged wiki, you might still want to check out some of the options in this chapter, because even if you want to use a tool like Backpack to simply create a few wiki-style pages that can extend your blog, you may find that handy for lists of photos or Amazon links or for creating other collections and documents that your readers may find interesting. From there, you can build to a wiki if it ultimately seems to make sense.

Hosted vs. Self-Hosted

As with blogging tools, photo galleries, and many other web applications, wiki software comes in both hosted and self-hosted varieties. Which you choose depends on many of the same factors that go into deciding on a hosted vs. self-hosted blogging tool, including whether you have your own hosting account and what technologies the tool supports. Many different wiki solutions are written in PHP scripting language, meaning they're supported on a variety of hosting accounts. Indeed, self-hosted wiki applications can be quite a bit more simple than blogging tools; some of them don't even require access to a database (such as MySQL).

Although I encourage you to consider self-hosted blogging applications, I've found that there are quite a few hosted wiki applications that you can use and integrate quite nicely with your blog, regardless of whether or not your blog is hosted or self-hosted. And there are a number of hosted wiki applications that offer a ton of features that go beyond the (generally speaking) more basic self-hosted scripts that you'll find.

However, what might be ideal for you (as it is for me, particularly for www .jacksonfreepress.com) is a self-hosted wiki solution that integrates with the user management features of your blog. ExpressionEngine, in its licensed versions, offers a built-in Wiki module that can use the same member database that you have for your blog, so that trusted users who have already registered to comment or post on your blog can also be given permissions for editing your wiki. Some plug-ins for WordPress can offer wiki-like functionality as well.

If you're using Blogger, TypePad, or a similar hosted service, then you probably won't have the luxury of offering your users a single login to both your blog and wiki, so you'll either need to allow "open" access to the wiki (which, because it allows absolutely anyone to post, can result in vandalism and spam), edit the wiki on your own without collaborators, use the system to accept wiki input that you moderate, or require your users to create separate accounts to your blog and wiki depending on how much access you want to grant them.

NOTE   *A word on my choices—there are many, many different wiki solutions out there that you can use in a hosted or self-hosted environment and I'm covering very few of them. I've tried to select a handful that are easy to use and that represent a range from offering a minimum of features to offering a fully collaborative environment. You don't have to take my word for it, though—Google "wiki" or check out sites such as WikiMatrix (http://www.wikimatrix.org/), where you can learn the benefits of many different wiki services and applications.*

Other Considerations When Choosing a Wiki

Hundreds of wiki options exist out there if you're willing to download wiki scripts and install them on your server; scores (perhaps hundreds) more exist as hosted services. If you're serious about adding a wiki to your website, here are a few more considerations that may help you narrow things down a bit:

- *Do you like the design?* Most of the wiki application websites you'll encounter will either be using the software that is being offered (whether open source or commercial) or will offer a demo. Wikis tend to be a bit more structured than blogs, at least in terms of how easily they can be themed or "skinned." If you don't like what you see, or if you're not a fan of the syntax that's used by the wiki's site or demo, then you're unlikely to find the installed version to your liking without extensive modifications.

- *Do you like the features offered?* The multitude of wiki options means that some wiki software is designed for specific purposes. A wiki application may be designed with a documentation focus or a community focus, and what you want to do with the software may inform your choice. Some wiki-like applications are actually much more structured than the standard wiki application, but use wiki-like syntax and "easy" editing to enable a group to collaborate toward a particular goal. For instance, BaseCamp (www.basecamphq.com) is a tool offered by the same people who make Backpack (covered later in this chapter), but with a focus on project management. Jot (www.jotspot.com) is a wiki tool with many built-in applications that you can use for contact management, customer relationship management, or even for building a rudimentary blog.

> NOTE   *Having said that about features, realize that wikis are* supposed *to be simple. Having the most features does not necessarily make a wiki application the best product for you. Make sure it has the right features you're seeking. A very simple wiki application is sometimes the best solution, especially if it means that the wiki won't present too much of a learning curve for your users.*

- *Is there an active support community?* The more the wiki software is already in use by avid fans, the more likely it is to have an online community where you can get answers to questions or learn more about integrating the software with your site.

8

■ *Is there an active developer community?* Going hand-in-hand with the idea of getting support from users is the idea of getting plug-ins and other additions from programmers who support the wiki application, particularly if it's an open source effort. The more developers and plug-ins, the more likely you are to be able to quickly and easily customize the tool.

TIP   *If you have strong needs for a big community-based wiki and you're using a blogging solution that doesn't offer a wiki option, you might consider Wikimedia, the open source software that runs Wikipedia and is familiar to many Internet users. The design and functionality of Wikimedia is a bit rigid, but it's also very full-featured and has been tested extensively since it's the foundation of an extremely popular site.*

■ *Do the security settings and user management approach of the wiki software work for you?* If you have a large community of folks that take an interest in your wiki, then you might consider having relatively "loose" security on the site—that is, you should let a lot of people participate. Ideally, your wiki can be "self-policing" in the sense that if some spam does appear or people do something stupid on the site, you or others can clean it up pretty quickly using the Recent Changes or History features of the wiki. If that's the case, you'll want to make sure the wiki supports open access and offers good controls for "rolling back" spam and unwanted content. If the wiki is designed only for you to update—or if it's a private wiki that should only be read, accessed, and changed by a select number of folks—then you'll want to choose a solution that offers that level of security as a feature.

TIP   *Want a fairly exhaustive list of wiki software? Wouldn't you know there's a great list on Wikipedia? Check out http://en.wikipedia.org/wiki/List_of_wiki_software for software written in a variety of different languages and compatible with many different server platforms.*

Using Backpack

Backpack (www.backpackit.com) is a simple, hosted wiki solution that's really geared toward keeping tidbits of your information organized. The software lets you keep your data online either privately or publicly, and it enables you to invite friends, family members, or colleagues to collect information online, manage a project, or take care of To Do lists. However, its "public" feature makes it handy as a simple wiki, as well, that you can use as a static page for your website that's always editable in any browser window. That makes it a great complement to your blog, particularly if your blog is a hosted application that doesn't have a great static pages feature. Backpack pages can be useful for publishing articles, displaying a calendar, or even putting together a basic photo album.

Backpack has some other fun features that I use a lot—it can send reminders to you via e-mail or to a mobile phone, it includes a built-in calendar and its pages offer tools for creating checklists and even for sending content to a page via e-mail. It's also really not a traditional wiki, in the sense that you can't use CamelCase or a similar approach to creating new pages. It does use a simplified syntax for enabling you to edit pages within the browser, so it can be a nice "wiki-like" companion for a blog.

> **NOTE**   *For a similar wiki-like experience, another option is Stikipad.com. Stikipad offers typical wiki features like easy editing and page creation, along with unique features such as a Stikipad-based discussion module. I'll take about that more in Chapter 9.*

To get started with Backpack, head to www.backpackit.com in your browser and register for the service. You'll be walked through the process. Once you're signed in, you'll see a welcome page that looks something like Figure 8-5.

What you're actually viewing is the home page of your Backpack; it has a little primer text at the top that you can get rid of by clicking the Hide This Primer link. The home page is handy for all sorts of things, including links to your favorite sites, To Do lists, reminders, and anything else that seems important to you.

In this section, I want to focus on how you can use Backpack for publishing a *public* page that you can link to from your blog. So, the first step is to create a new page. To do that, click the Make a New Page button. A screen appears where you can enter a new title for the document and then edit the page in the Body Area. Go ahead and type something.

A link toward the bottom of the page called Textile Quick Reference shows you some of the different formatting tricks you can use as you're typing on your page. (Textile is a special markup language that works well for wiki pages.) Surrounding text in asterisks creates bold text (as in, `this is *bold* text`) and you can use the underline character for italic text (as in `this is _italic_ text`). URLs that you enter on the page are automatically turned into links; by formatting the link as `"Visit iTodd Central":http://www.toddstauffer.com` you can create special text that links to the URL after the colon.

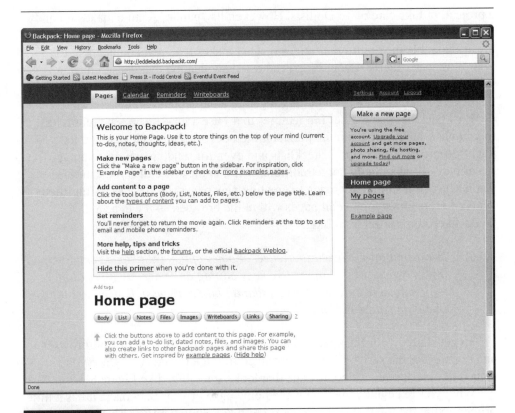

FIGURE 8-5   The Backpack welcome page

Once you've made an entry, click the Create button at that page now includes that content. It's that simple (see Figure 8-6).

To edit a page later, just view that page (you can click it in your sidebar) and then click the Body link. That opens up an entry box (Backpack is very "Web 2.0" in its use of active AJAX scripting) so that you can edit the page. Once you're editing, you'll see a Save Changes button that you can click to make those changes appear as part of the document.

Now, the trick is to make that page available to the public. At the top of the page, click the Sharing button. You'll be moved to a portion of that page where

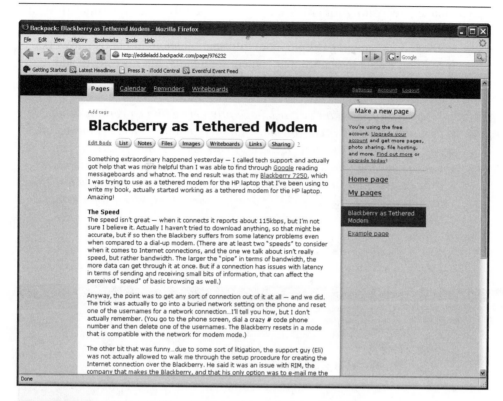

FIGURE 8-6   Here's a new document I created in my Backpack.

you'll see the Sharing information appear. Click the checkmark next to the option Make This Page Public. Note that you're also shown the URL for that page.

That page can now be linked to from your blog (either in the sidebar of the blog design or from a blog entry) so that your visitors can hop over to the Backpack site to see whatever it is that you're using Backpack to display—it can be a permanent repository for articles, images, frequently asked questions (FAQs), or whatever else you'd like to show people. For instance, I've got a Backpack page that I've created for showing people more information about my books; it works great since I don't want to change that content frequently, but it's easy to add images and descriptive text when necessary (see Figure 8-7).

TIP　*You can also share a Backpack page privately with just certain people. In that same Sharing area, you make sure that public sharing is turned off, but then you enter e-mail addresses in the Enter Email Addresses entry box. I sometimes do this when I want to create a page for a particular project—the films we're choosing for our local independent film festival, for instance—so that a group of us can share ideas. When you share a page in this way, your collaborators can both read and edit the page.*

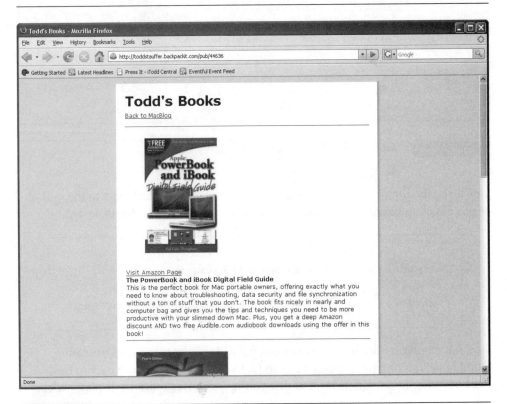

FIGURE 8-7　The Todd's Books page I've created in Backpack is something I link to from my blog.

There's a lot more you can do with Backpack that isn't quite related to blogging, including using the Reminders tab (at the top of the screen) to enter reminders that can be sent to your e-mail or by text message to your phone, or the Calendar, which is available if you pay for the premium service. Writeboards are also interesting, offering free-form documents that can be edited in real-time with collaborators.

Using Wikidot

Wikidot is a hosted wiki application that offers both free and low-costs packages for serving wiki pages. Wikidot is more of a "traditional" wiki than is Backpack, in part because it relies on a wiki-style syntax to create links to pages and to create pages themselves, and in part because it allows you to create a public or private website that is navigable using the links and pages that you create.

As with many hosted services, signing up at Wikidot will result in a site that you can access via a URL such as *yourname*.wikidot.com, which you can link to from your blog. Likewise, Wikidot offers an RSS feed for recent changes that you can display on your blog, for instance, if your blog supports external RSS feeds. (And, if it doesn't, you can use a service such as FeedBurner to add the RSS feed to your blog's sidebar or pages.)

8

NOTE   *I'm covering Wikidot as a hosted service but, at the time of writing, it's been announced that the basic Wikidot functionality will be released as open source software as well, making it possible to install a Wikidot-based wiki on your own server. If that sounds interesting, check http://www .wikidot.org/ for details as the open source project gets underway.*

Get Started with Wikidot

To sign up for Wikidot, open http://www.wikidot.com/ in a Web browser and locate the Create Account link. Click that account and you'll be guided through the process of reading the terms of service, entering account information, verifying your e-mail address, and then signing into the service so that you can access your personal account.

As a registered member, you first visit the profile page, where you can upload an avatar for yourself, edit your profile and make other changes. Wikidot.com is a community network of sorts where you can participate on other people's Wikidot sites, in community forums, and so on. So, even if you don't have your own wiki, you can explore and contribute once you have a username and password.

Also from your profile page, you can create your own wiki by clicking Start Your Own Site. You'll be walked through the steps of creating your new site, which begins by reading and accepting the Terms of Service. You'll then be asked to make a series of preference choices, including:

- **Site Name**   The full name for your wiki.

- **Site "Unix Name"**   The name that will be used to create your wiki's URL, such as toddstauffer.wikidot.com.

- **Subtitle**   A clever or informative subhead for your wiki, if you'd like one.

- **Site Content Language**   The language that will be the predominant language of the content of your site.

- **Access**   Choose whether the wiki will be publicly available to all users or if it is only visible to people who have a password for the site.

> NOTE   *Choosing a public wiki does not mean that everyone on the Internet can necessarily edit content on your wiki; you can set permission for authorized editors later.*

- **Description**   Enter a short description of your wiki.

- **Are You Human?**   Enter the CAPTCHA code shown in order to verify that you aren't an automated online "bot" of some kind.

- **Site Code**   Optional, if you have an offer code.

Click Create Site when you've entered all these choices. If the site is created successfully, you'll be taken to its home page, where you can read some sample text and then, if desired, jump in and start editing (see Figure 8-8).

Edit Pages in Wikidot

To edit a page that already exists, you click the Edit link up at the top-right corner of the page; that causes the page to refresh, displaying a text area where the contents of that page are shown. Now, you can use the mouse and keyboard to edit the page in a way that's similar to editing a blog entry in one of the blogging applications. Indeed, Wikidot includes a graphical editor similar to the editor in ExpressionEngine and the low-resolution version of the WordPress interface, where you can click the buttons for markup.

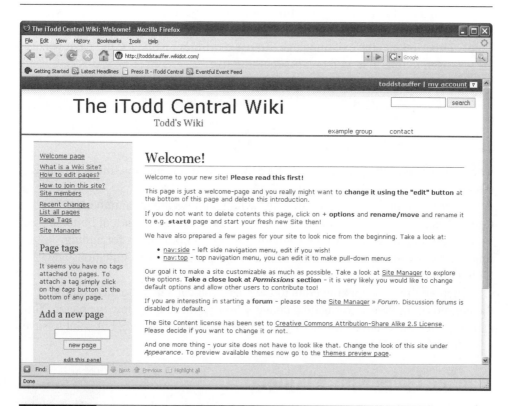

FIGURE 8-8 The home page of my new wiki

There are a few differences, however. With Wikidot, as with many wiki applications, you don't have to type full HTML commands in order to style your text. Instead, there are wiki-style shortcuts for the formatting, such as using asterisks for `**bold**` text, slashes for `//italic//` text, and double lines for `--strikethrough--` text.

NOTE *In wiki formatting you're encouraged to use the different heading levels when you're creating documents and you're encouraged to use them in descending order. In Wikidot, you can use the plus sign ("+") for different levels of headings, as in +heading 1 or +++heading 3.*

Also as is common with wikis, you can type a name for a page within brackets, as in `[[About Us]]` in order to create a link to that page. And, if the page hasn't yet been created, then clicking that link (once the page has been published) will create a new page that you can then edit. If the page does exist, then the new link simply hyperlinks to the existing page. To use a different name for the page versus the text used to link to it, you enter something like:

```
[[About | About Our Company]]
```

or

```
[[Services | More about what we do]]
```

where the name of the page comes before the vertical line and the link text comes after if.

A little uncommon compared to many wiki solutions are the number of different items that you can add to the Wikidot page using its shortcut buttons. You'll find options such as Embed Video, Embed Audio, buttons for adding images, and so on, as well as buttons for adding special text like equations and bibliographical references.

When you're done making edits to the page, you can click the Save button at the bottom of the screen to save the changes you've made and view the page. (You can also click Save and Continue if you'd like to continue editing, but want to save periodically to avoid losing your changes.)

Manage Users with Wikidot

Often, the key to a good wiki is having good people help you update it. That might not always be the case—your wiki might just be a handy way to put together lists of information, documentation, or links to resources that you want to be able to edit easily. But many, many wikis are started for collaborative reasons. If that's why you've got a Wikidot account, then you'll want to add and manage your users.

Assuming that you're signed into your administrator's account on Wikidot, you'll see a link in the sidebar called Site Manager. Click that link to Invite Members and you'll see a page that enables you to enter the e-mail address of a member that you'd like to have as part of your site. If they respond and apply for membership, then you'll see their information appear when you click the Applications link in the Manage Site sidebar.

TIP

The Manage Site sidebar is useful for many things I won't be able to cover in this section, including options to change the appearance of your site, to customize the domain name, to build page templates for your users and many other options. (We will discuss one special option, the Forum & Discussion option, a little later in this chapter.)

Of course, Wikidot will support allowing new members to register when they're viewing your site, as well. To set up online registration, click the Policy link (see Figure 8-9). There you can decide whether you'd like to allow people to apply for membership (turn on the option Enable Membership By Applying if that's your desire) and/or if they can become members simply by knowing a password. (That lets you hand out the password to people that you want to have join and then they don't have to go through an arduous process; they will, however, need a Wikidot membership for this to work.)

If you have applications from new members, you'll see them by clicking the Applications link in the Manage Site sidebar. There you can decide if you'll accept the member. If you do accept that member, you can then see the member by clicking the List Members link, where you can also change that member's status so that he or she can be a moderator or administrator for your site.

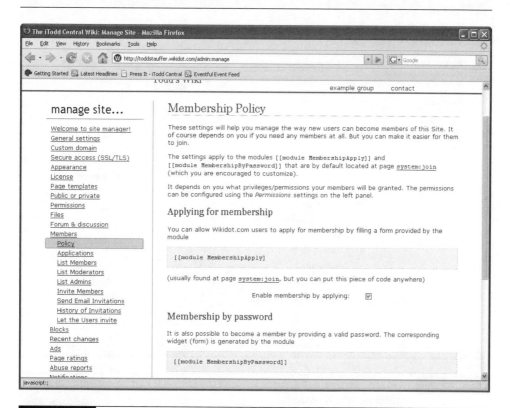

FIGURE 8-9   Use the Policy page to decide whether and how people can apply for membership.

What a member can and cannot *do* on your wiki is important, as well. Click Permissions in the Manage Site sidebar and you'll see the Permissions screen, where you can set the different levels of permission for each different type of user recognized by Wikidot—anonymous visitors, Wikidot users who aren't a member of your site, site members, and creators/owners of a particular page. You can then use the checkboxes to set permissions for that user depending on what you'd like the different membership levels to be able to accomplish (see Figure 8-10).

NOTE *Permissions are only for members and non-members of your wiki; administrators and page moderators have full access to the wiki by default.*

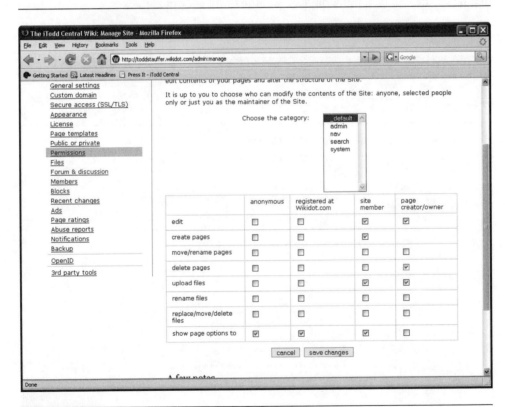

FIGURE 8-10 On the Permissions screen, you can decide what can be accomplished by different levels of users.

Add Wikidot Snippets

As with most wiki services, Wikidot is designed to give you and your users the ability to edit simple pages quickly and easily, which makes collaborating on the web almost fun. (Heck, often it *is* fun!) Beyond those basics, though, Wikidot also offers the ability to add special snippets of code that allow you to do things like embed items, change the layout of your page, and add third-party gadgets or widgets to your page.

The snippets are really just items stored in a special wiki that walks you through the process of adding cool features. While you're editing a page, look for the link to the Code Snippets Collection. (You can get there directly at http://snippets.wikidot.com/.) Now you can browse by clicking any of the links on the page. When you do you'll often see a list of snippets in that category. Clicking a particular solution will show you an explanation and some code you can add to any of your wiki pages.

For example, one popular use of a Wikidot module is the feed-reader, which enables you to place an RSS feed's results within a wiki page. To do that, you cut and paste a code snippet into a wiki page like this:

```
[[module Feed src="http://rss.jacksonfreepress.com/index.xml" limit="10"]]
```

That accesses the module and places the feed headlines on the wiki page where the snippet is saved.

Wikidot offers a number of other snippets and modules that allow you to use your wiki in conjunction with other Web 2.0 applications such as Flickr, del.icio.us, Digg, and many other such sites, enabling you to publish photos, bookmarks, and all sorts of fun stuff. Explore the snippets to see what's added on a regular basis.

Use PmWiki

As with any of the tools and types of applications discussed in this book, there are many options for a self-hosted wikis. I've chosen PmWiki as an example if only because it's appealing as a low-overhead wiki that uses a flat-file approach (meaning it doesn't require a MySQL or similar back-end database), it offers a number of user-created skins, and overall it's pretty easy to get started using. There are literally hundreds of others, including Mediawiki (www.mediawiki.org), the open source application that runs Wikipedia.com; phpWiki (www.phpwiki.org), an extremely popular open source option; and TWiki (www.twiki.org); among many, many others.

To install PmWiki, visit http://www.pmwiki.org/ in your web browser and locate the Download link. There you'll likely see links to both beta and stable releases of PmWiki; choose the version you'd like to install. (I'd recommend choosing the latest stable release, unless you're the curious type that doesn't mind potential problems.) The archives are generally available as Unix-style tarballs or .zip files; for Mac and Windows users, .zip files are generally a little easier to deal with.

NOTE | *PmWiki requires PHP scripting to be enabled on your server or your hosting account.*

Once downloaded to your PC, you can double-click the archive to unpack the files into a hierarchy of files and folders. Once that's completed, you'll need to put the configuration file in its proper place and edit it. Here's how:

1. Create the configuration file for PmWiki. The easiest way to do that is to locate the file called sample-config.php in the docs folder and copy it to the main level of your wiki folder, renaming it to config.php in the process. (See http://www.pmwiki.org/wiki/PmWiki/InitialSetupTasks for details.)

2. Now, in that config.php file, there are some items you may want to edit. These are variables used by the wiki to display pages. To edit the config. php file you've created, open it in a text editing application such as Windows Notepad (see Figure 8-11), Wordpad, or Mac's TextEdit.

3. The items you may want to change include the following (note that in order to activate any of these options, you need to delete the # symbol in front of each entry):

   ■ `$wikiTitle = "PmWiki";` You can change the name in quotes from `PmWiki` to whatever you'd like to call your wiki, such as my wiki site, `Jackpedia`. Note that you also need to delete the # symbol in front of this configuration command to make it active.

   ■ `$EnablePathInfo = 1;` Delete the # symbol in front of this command if you want to see if your server can support "pretty" URLs.

   ■ `$PageLogoUrl = "$PubDirUrl/skins/pmwiki/pmwiki-32.gif";` Change this to a URL that points to the logo file that you'd like to use in your wiki's top banner.

   ■ `$DefaultPasswords['admin'] = crypt('secret');` Change the word `secret` to create an administrative password that is useful for a variety of reasons, some of which we'll discuss in upcoming sections.

```
config - Notepad
File  Edit  Format  View  Help
##  This is a sample config.php file.  To use this file, copy it to
##  local/config.php, then edit it for whatever customizations you want.
##  Also, be sure to take a look at http://www.pmichaud.com/wiki/Cookbook
##  for more details on the types of customizations that can be added
##  to PmWiki.

##  $WikiTitle is the name that appears in the browser's title bar.
$WikiTitle = 'The iTodd Central Wiki';

##  $ScriptUrl is your preferred URL for accessing wiki pages
##  $PubDirUrl is the URL for the pub directory.
#  $ScriptUrl = 'http://www.mydomain.com/path/to/pmwiki.php';
#  $PubDirUrl = 'http://www.mydomain.com/path/to/pub';

##  If you want to use URLs of the form .../pmwiki.php/Group/PageName
##  instead of .../pmwiki.php?p=Group.PageName, try setting
##  $EnablePathInfo below.  Note that this doesn't work in all environments,
##  it depends on your webserver and PHP configuration.  You might also
##  want to check http://www.pmwiki.org/wiki/Cookbook/CleanUrls more
##  details about this setting and other ways to create nicer-looking urls.
#  $EnablePathInfo = 1;

##  $PageLogoUrl is the URL for a logo image -- you can change this
##  to your own logo if you wish.
#  $PageLogoUrl = "$PubDirUrl/skins/pmwiki/pmwiki-32.gif";

##  If you want to have a custom skin, then set $Skin to the name
##  of the directory (in pub/skins/) that contains your skin files.
##  See Pmwiki.Skins and Cookbook.Skins.
#  $Skin = 'pmwiki';

##  You'll probably want to set an administrative password that you
##  can use to get into password-protected pages.  Also, by default
##  the "attr" passwords for the Pmwiki and Main groups are locked, so
##  an admin password is a good way to unlock those.  See Pmwiki.Passwords
##  and Pmwiki.PasswordsAdmin.
#  $DefaultPasswords['admin'] = crypt('secret');

##  Pmwiki comes with graphical user interface buttons for editing;
##  to enable these buttons, set $EnableGUIButtons to 1.
#  $EnableGUIButtons = 1;

##  If you want uploads enabled on your system, set $EnableUpload=1.
##  You'll also need to set a default upload password, or else set
##  passwords on individual groups and pages.  For more information
##  see Pmwiki.UploadsAdmin.
#  $EnableUpload = 1;
#  $DefaultPasswords['upload'] = crypt('secret');

##  Setting $EnableDiag turns on the ?action=diag and ?action=phpinfo
##  actions, which often helps the Pmwiki authors to troubleshoot
##  various configuration and execution problems.
```

FIGURE 8-11   Here's the config.php file being editing in Notepad.

4. Once you've made changes, save the config.php file. (Make sure you save it as a plain text file, not as a Rich Text (RTF) or Microsoft Word document.) Now you're ready to upload.

5. Copy the files to your web server or web hosting account in a publicly accessible directory. You may want to rename the folder (it's something like pmwiki-2.2) to just wiki, and then upload that whole folder to the main level of your hosting account; that way the wiki would be accessed at http://www.*yourURL*.com/wiki/ by your visitors. It's up to you—you can choose any name for the files that you'd like. You can also upload the files to the main level of your hosting account of public server directory so that the wiki is loaded when someone accesses http://www.*yourURL*.com/.

Once you've uploaded the wiki's folder to the server, you've got a few more steps:

1. Using your FTP application, create a subdirectory within the wiki's directory called wiki.d. and set that directory's permissions to 777. You can most likely use your FTP application to create the directory on the remote server and then use the FTP's Properties or similar command to change permissions.

TIP *The PmWiki installation instructions include another slightly more secure option for setting permissions that will work with some servers. Check http://www.pmwiki.org/wiki/PmWiki/Installation if you'd like to try the more secure approach.*

2. Next, launch the document pmwiki.php in your Web browser by accessing it at http://www.*yourURL*.com/wiki/pmwiki.php. (You'll need to change *yourURL* to the URL of your server and use the correct name and/or full path for the wiki directory that you created.) That brings up the PmWiki home page. If you don't see any errors, then the installation should be in good shape.

If your PmWiki installation seems to work, you've still got one last step—you need to create an index.php page for your site. It is *not* recommended that you rename pmwiki.php to index.php. (This is so you can easily update PmWiki with new features or security fixes in the future.) Instead, create a new text file (again you can use Notepad, TextEdit, or a similar program to create the file) called index.php and place the following in that file:

```
<?php include('pmwiki.php');
```

Save the file as a plain text file and upload it to the same directory on your server where the file pmwiki.php is stored. Now, you should be able to access your wiki at http://www.*yourURL*.com/wiki/index.php or, if your server is correctly configured, the index page will display automatically when you access http://www .*yourURL*.com/wiki/ in a Web browser (see Figure 8-12).

The default home page offers some handy links that you might want to bookmark or access and read to learn more about how PmWiki works, what the editing syntax is, and what some of the configuration options are.

TIP *PmWiki.org offers a fairly extensive "cookbook" of "recipes" that are either plug-ins or snippets of code that can be used to do a variety of things, including adding comments to wiki pages, creating a simple forum using the wiki, or even blogging using just PmWiki.*

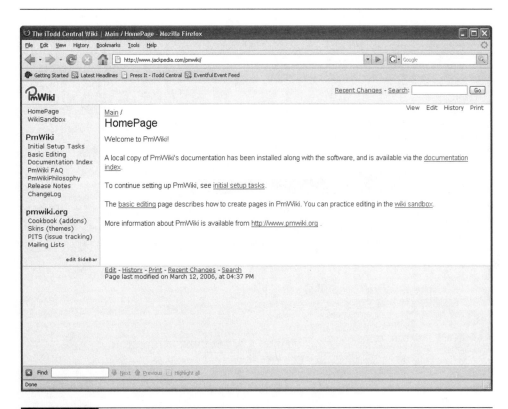

FIGURE 8-12   The default home page of my new PmWiki installation

Edit and Create Pages in PmWiki

Once you're viewing your wiki, you're ready to start editing. You might want to begin on the home page, which, when first installed, offers items that can be helpful, but don't say anything about your personal wiki. To edit that page, simply click the Edit link that appears in the top-right corner of the page. This is how you'll edit any page in PmWiki (see Figure 8-13).

Basic Editing

To enter text, simply type what it is that you want to say, using the RETURN or ENTER key to create paragraphs. While you're typing, you can use a number of different wiki syntax codes to format your text, including:

- Use two single quote marks for italic text, as in `"italic"` text.
- Use three single quote marks for bold text, as in `"'bold'"` text.

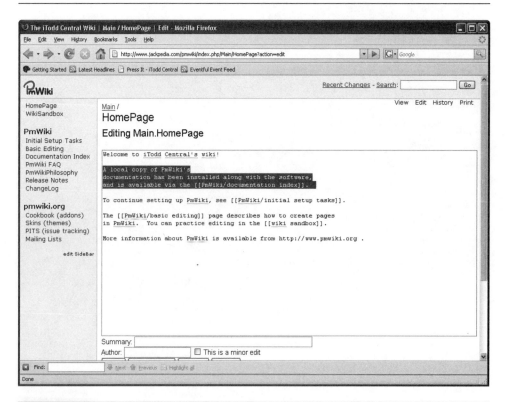

FIGURE 8-13   The editing interface for PmWiki, showing me editing the home page

■ Use four single quote marks for bold and italic text, as in `''''bold italic''''` text.

■ Use @@ for monospaced "typewriter" text as in `@@monospaced text@@`.

■ Use an asterisk for each item of a bullet list, as in:

```
* Item one
* Item two
* Item three
```

■ Use the # symbol for numbered lists, as in:

```
# Item one
# Item two
# Item three
```

■ Use exclamation points for headings, such as `!!Heading Level One!!` and `!!!Heading Level Two!!!`.

■ Use brackets and the plus symbol for larger text (as in `[+bigger text+]`) or brackets and minus signs for smaller text (`[-smaller text-]`).

When you're done editing the page, click the Save button to save the page and view it, or click Save and Edit if you'd like to save your changes and continue editing. Note that before clicking Save, you can enter a name for yourself as the author in the Author entry box, which lets you specify a name for the author of this page. That can be handy for group wikis where you'd like people to know that you were the last person to make changes. Once you've clicked Save, you should see your newly edited page in the browser window.

> **TIP** *The list of options for text editing is fairly extensive, and you can see it by clicking the Basic Editing link that appears at the bottom of the text area when you're editing in PmWiki, or by visiting http://www.pmwiki.com/ index.php/PmWiki/BasicEditing on the Web.*

Build Links

While you're editing a wiki page, you have a few different options for building hypertext links. When you create wiki-style links, you're actually creating new pages in your wiki—as you'll recall, that's part of the fun.

To create a link to a new page for your wiki, enter the name that you'd like for the page between double brackets, as in `[[new page]]`. That will be both the name of the page (PmWiki will automatically turn the text into CamelCase to make the page name work correctly in the PmWiki engine) as well as the hyperlink, so you can enter that link in the course of typing the text, as in:

```
Visit the [[about me]] page to learn more about the iTodd.
Or, visit my other pages:
* [[articles]]
* [[tips and techniques]]
* [[photos]]
```

Here's how that text would render in a browser once the page is saved:

Visit the about me[?] page to learn more about the iTodd. Or, visit my other pages:
- articles[?]
- tips and techniques[?]
- photos[?]

Each link is rendered with a small question mark to note that it doesn't yet link to an existing page. When you click that link, you're taken to the editing interface for the newly created page, where you can enter content, make edits, and click Save (see Figure 8-14).

As you can see in Figure 8-14, there are other ways to create links as well, including:

- `[[page name | link text]]` where you define different text for the link that will appear on the page than the name of the page that will be created (or that is being linked to). For instance, my page called `about` could have the link text `About Todd`, as in `[[about | About Todd]]`.

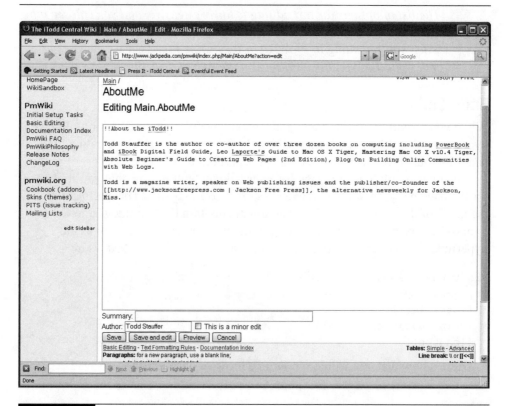

FIGURE 8-14 Editing a page that was created by a link in a previously edited wiki page

- `[[http://www.somelink.com || link text]]` to create an external link with special link text, as in `[[http://www.jacksonfreepress.com || Jackson Free Press]]`.

- You can use the special number sign character to create a link as a reference, as in `[[http://www.seriousacademicjournal.com/article.html | #]]`, which renders as a footnote, as in:

  Most scientists believe that the Earth revolves around the Sun. [1]

- If you simply type a URL, you'll create a link to that URL, as in

  `Visit my site, http://www.toddstauffer.com, to read my latest blogging.`

Links can get even more involved than that, but those are the basic options.

Edit the Sidebar

As your PmWiki starts to come together, you might want to add items to the sidebar in order to make things more convenient for your visitors. To do that, click the Edit SideBar link that appears at the bottom of the sidebar. That enables you to change the text and the links that appear in the sidebar so that they're more meaningful for your site. You might want to create a page of Wiki Rules, for instance, to tell people what they should or shouldn't do when they're editing your wiki, and you might want to edit to particular pages that lead to different sections of your wiki. It's up to you. When you're done editing, click the Save button, just as you would with a normal page, and your sidebar will now appear with the new edits on every PmWiki page.

Add Images

Images are easy to add in PmWiki pages; all you really have to do to place an image on the page is enter a URL to an image. While typing a document, you can add a URL in this way:

```
We're in the new office in Fondren.

http://www.toddstauffer.com/photos/office.jpg

This is the view out our window. Exciting, eh?
```

And the image will be rendered (if the URL is correct) as an inline image in the resulting wiki page.

PmWiki offers a number of different ways that you can render images, including tags that let you float the image to the left or right, add a caption, or do both by creating a frame around the image. Here are some options:

■ **Add a Caption**   You can add a caption by placing a vertical line character after the entry and entering the caption, as in:

```
http://www.toddstauffer.com/photos/office.jpg | The view from my office window
```

■ **Float the Image Left or Right**   Using the `%float%` or `%rfloat%` command before the image, you can cause it to float to the left or right, which means the text wraps around it in the other direction. For example:

```
%rfloat% http://www.toddstauffer.com/photos/office.jpg
```

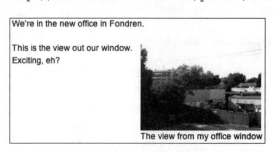

■ **Float the Image with a Caption**   To both float the image and include a caption with it, you use a different command: `%lframe%` or `%rframe%`. For example:

```
%lframe% http://www.toddstauffer.com/photos/office.jpg |
The view from my office window
```

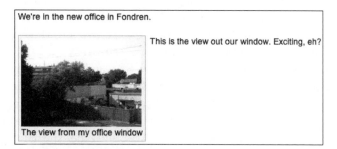

■ **Make an Image a Link**   To make your image clickable, you use the double-bracket approach, as in:

```
[[http://www.toddstauffer.com/photos/office_big.jpg |
http://www.toddstauffer.com/photos/office.jpg]]
```

And there are many more options where those came from, including creating thumbnails, resizing images, and even adding an image that doesn't have the correct filename extension. For more on images, go to http://www.pmwiki.org/wiki/PmWiki/Images on the PmWiki site (you can also get to this page through the locally stored documentation files accessed via your sidebar).

Organize Your PmWiki Pages

Built into PmWiki is the option to create a group-based structure, which allows anyone who can edit the blog to create a new "wikispace" where pages link to one another but are grouped together under a common group name or category. Some wikis call these "namespaces"—this idea is that you can use like groups to pull together pages that are on a particular topic, are "owned" by a particular person or group, or otherwise have a relationship that means they should be subordinate to your wiki as a whole.

Creating a new group couldn't be easier; all you have to do is create a link within an existing wiki page to a new page that includes the group designation as part of the link. Groups are added to links using either a period (.) or a forward slash (/), such that `[[Music.Bands]]` would create a page called Bands in the

Music group. (And, of course, that's how you'd link to the page once it's been created if you need to create another link to it elsewhere.)

You can create a link to the home page of a group by omitting a page name, as in [[Music.]]. If that home page doesn't already exist, it will be created when you view the page and click that link.

And, since you're building standard PmWiki links, you can use the same sort of formatting to create the links, so that [[Music.Bands | view local band pages]] would create a link with the text view local band pages that links to the Bands page within the Music group.

PmWiki has three groups built into it: Main, Site, and PmWiki. The Main group is where all pages are created when they aren't in another group, while the Site group is where special pages such as Site.RecentChanges are stored. (You can consult this page to see all of the recent changes to your wiki.) PmWiki is a group that can't be edited; it holds the installed documentation, FAQs, and other special pages.

> **TIP** *See the page http://www.pmwiki.org/wiki/PmWiki/WikiGroup for more about using groups, including the ability to create special headers and footers.*

Permissions and Administration

One of the original ideas with wikis has been the notion that editing the wiki was actually a wide-open process—anyone can edit Wikipedia, for instance, with only their IP address to identify them. This has carried over into the philosophy behind the design of some open-source wiki applications, and PmWiki is one of those. So, unlike blogging software that is often designed to limit the people who can access your blog for posting articles or commenting, an application like PmWiki makes that a little more difficult. It can, however, be done, by locking particular pages and implementing permissions for particular groups.

Set a Password for a Page

Say you've got a page that you'd like to limit access to—maybe you want to keep others from editing it, but you'll allow them to read it; maybe you want to limit access to both reading and editing it. You do that by setting a page password.

To set a page password, you need to load that page's URL and add the text ?action=attr to the URL. So, for example, if I want to set a password for the page http://www.jackpedia.com/pmwiki/index.php/Music/Music, then I use the following URL:

```
http://www.jackpedia.com/pmwiki/index.php/Music/Music?action=attr
```

The result is a screen that gives me the option of entering a few different passwords for the page:

The options are:

- **Set New Read Password**   Enter a password that any visitor would need to know and enter in order to read the page. You only need to enter this password if you want to limit who can read the page; otherwise, leave it blank so that the page can be seen by anyone who visits, even if they don't have the ability to edit the page.

- **Set New Edit Password**   Enter a password that any visitor would need to know in order to edit the page.

- **Set New Attribute Password**   Enter a password that any visitor would need to know in order to change the attributes (and, hence, the passwords) for this page.

When you've entered a password for those items, click the Save button and the password go into effect. If you ever need to remove a password once it's set, then edit the attributes again and enter **clear** in the password entry box. When you click Save, the password for that page will be cleared.

If you set an administrator's password back in the config.php file, you have another option; instead of entering a password, you can enter the command @lock in one of the fields. That capability will then only be available to the administrator. So, for instance, if you lock the Set New Edit Password entry, then the page can only be edited by someone who has the administrator password.

Setting a Password for a Group

One reason to create groups within PmWiki is that you can set a password for each group. To do that, you edit a special page for the group. If the group is called

Music, and the site is http://www.toddstauffer.com/wiki/, then the URL for editing the attributes for that group would be that URL portion plus the code:

```
pmwiki.php?n=Music.GroupAttributes?action=attr
```

You'll then see a page that's similar to the attributes for individual pages. Enter a Read, Edit, and/or Attributes editing password for the group and click Save. Again, in many cases you may want to set just an Edit and/or Attributes password, if your wiki is largely edited by people whom you know and trust with the password; if you allow open reading and editing, then you might want to set just the attributes password for the group so that others can't lock pages on their own.

By the way, the phenomenon of the group passwords might find you in a situation where you want a page that's within a group that *doesn't* have a password, so that it can be edited by the general public. To make that happen, edit the attributes for that particular page and then enter @nopass in one of that page's password entry boxes and you'll override the group setting so that people can read, edit, or change the attributes of that particular page.

And what if you don't want others to be able to edit your entire site? You can set a password for reading or editing of the entire site, if desired, by editing the config.php file so that it includes the line:

```
$DefaultPassword['read'] = crypt('your_secret_password');
```

or:

```
$DefaultPassword['edit'] = crypt('your_secret_password');
```

If you've got a super-secret wiki that's designed only for a small group, then you can set both of those passwords, effectively making your site a private wiki. (You'll just need to tell your friends the password.)

> **TIP** *PmWiki can offer individual authentication for users on your wiki site, but it's a bit complex. Visit http://www.pmwiki.org/wiki/PmWiki/AuthUser to learn more about the user authentication system.*

Use the Wiki Module in ExpressionEngine

If you have a licensed copy of ExpressionEngine (as opposed to ExpressionEngine Core) then there's a wiki module built into your blogging software. If you're looking for a wiki for collaborative documentation or for easily edited pages to complement your blog, then you can quickly enable the wiki module and be up and running with a wiki.

The wiki module in ExpressionEngine is fairly basic; it offers page editing and creation, wiki-style formatting, and many of the basics that you're familiar with if you've read this whole chapter. Plus, the wiki can be extended in the same way that ExpressionEngine's blog engine can be extended—through plug-ins and extensions—so as it gains popularity, you may see more free and commercial add-ons for it. (As of this writing, there are only a handful.)

If there's a major advantage to the ExpressionEngine wiki module, it's that it works with the same user accounts and passwords that can be used to register users on your ExpressionEngine blog. So, if you're blogging in ExpressionEngine, then using its built-in wiki is particularly handy if you want sophisticated user handling (including blacklisting, different user privileges, and so on) to go along with your blog.

Enable and Configure the Wiki

Before you enable the wiki module, you need to be sure that you've installed a wiki template; by default, the ExpressionEngine installation includes a wiki template, but you can opt not to install it when you're installing ExpressionEngine. In your FTP program, access you server or hosting account and check for the directory wiki_themes inside the main themes directory of your ExpressionEngine installation.

8

TIP   *You can download wiki themes from the pMachine website or elsewhere and install them in this folder if you'd like to use a theme other than the default ExpressionEngine wiki theme. You'll be able to select the theme in the Wiki module's preferences. Simply upload the theme to the* wiki_ themes *directory so that it's available for selection. (You don't have to do this immediately, as the wiki themes are generally designed to be interchangeable even after your wiki is created.)*

To enable the wiki module, log into the ExpressionEngine admin interface and click the Modules tab. There you should see the Wiki module at the bottom of the list. To get started with the wiki, click the Install link in the module's row. Once the module is installed, you'll see that the name Wiki becomes a hyperlink; click it to set up your first wiki.

CP Home > Modules > Wiki > Wiki Homepage		Create Wiki
Wiki		
Full Wiki Name	**Wiki Short Name**	☐ Delete
EE Wiki	default_wiki	☐
		Delete

ExpressionEngine creates a wiki called EE Wiki; click that link to see the Wiki Module Preferences page, where you can rename it and set some other parameters.

TIP   *With the main Wiki Module page open, you can click the New Tab link in the top of the admin interface to add the wiki as a tab, so you can access it quickly when necessary.*

Here are those options:

- **Full Wiki Name**   Enter a name for your wiki—this is what will be used for the title of the wiki in the default header design.

- **Wiki Short Name**   This is the name that's used within ExpressionEngine codes and tags.

- **Text Formatting for Articles**   Choose a style of text formatting for the text that's created by the wiki engine. XHTML is the default and is generally a good choice.

- **HTML Formatting for Articles**   Choose the level of HTML formatting that you want to allow. Safe HTML is the default, but if you trust *all* of your users, then you can choose Allow All HTML.

- **File Upload Directory**   Choose a file upload directory where you'd like files to be uploaded to if your users upload files when they're editing wiki pages.

- **Administrator Groups**   Choose which user groups are allowed to administer the wiki. (If you've created custom groups, you may want to choose from more than one; by default, Super Admins is the best choice.)

- **User Groups**   Choose which users are allowed to edit pages and contribute to the wiki. By default you'll only see Users and Super Admins, unless you've created other groups. ExpressionEngine does not allow anonymous users to contribute to the wiki, so only logged in members will be able to make changes.

- **Number of Revisions to Keep Per Article**   As with many wikis, the ExpressionEngine wiki will save the recent changes to articles and edits, in part so that an earlier article can be reverted to if there's a mistake, spam, or other unwanted edit made to a page. Enter the number here; an excessively large number may make your ExpressionEngine database unwieldy.

- **Number of Edits Allowed Per Author Per Day**   This setting enables you to limit authors that are either prolific, spammers, or generally creating trouble.

- **Email Address for Moderation Notification**   Enter the e-mail address where notifications of wiki changes should be sent.

- **Namespaces**   This is where you create namespaces for your wiki, which are special divisions for wiki content. This is handy if you want divisions in your wiki that go beyond simple categories, for instance if you want portions of your wiki devoted to different languages.

When you've set the options, click Update.

Before you can get started with your wiki, there's one more step—you need to create a template for the wiki so that it can be accessed. Click the Template tab and then create a new template for the wiki. (If you want the wiki to be in a new template group, you may need to create that template group first; see Chapter 3 for details.)

Now, in the template that you've created, you'll need to enter *only* a single ExpressionEngine tag that follows this syntax:

```
{exp:wiki base_path="Template_Group/Template_Name"
wiki="wiki_short_name" theme="default"}
```

So, if you've created a template group called `wiki`, you're going to use the `index` template for that group, and the wiki's name is `default_wiki`, then you'd enter this in the index template:

```
{exp:wiki base_path="wiki/index" wiki="default_wiki"
theme="default"}
```

As another example, take my wiki, which I'm actually going to place in a template called `jackpedia` that's part of the main `site` template group. So, the text that would go in my wiki's index template would be:

```
{exp:wiki base_path="jackpedia/index" wiki="jackpedia"
theme="default"}
```

That's it. Now, access the wiki using the template information to build a URL, as in http://www.jackpedia.com/index.php/jackpedia/ for the last example I just gave. (For the previous example, the URL for accessing the wiki would be similar to http://www.*yourURL*.com/index.php/wiki/ or http://www.*yourURL*.com/index.php/wiki/index/, either of which would work.)

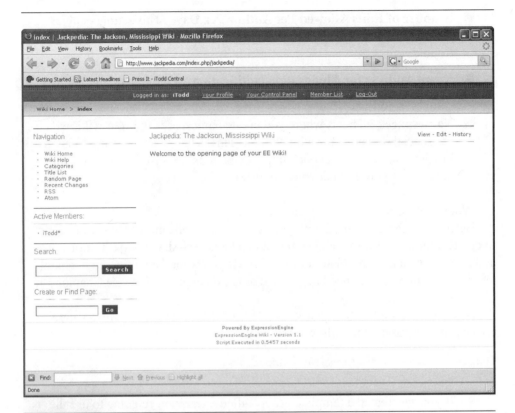

FIGURE 8-15   My new ExpressionEngine wiki, ready for editing

The result will be the home page of your new wiki, which will look something like Figure 8.15.

Edit and Create Pages

Editing and creating pages in the ExpressionEngine wiki is similar to most other wikis, although, as with other wikis, ExpressionEngine has its own style for some markup. To edit a page, you must be logged in; you'll then see the Edit link. Click that link and you're taken to the editing interface, where you can begin editing the page.

The basic editing of ExpressionEngine pages supports the same pMcode that can be used in comments and blog entries within ExpressionEngine. (pMcode is special code that can be used when you're entered text in ExpressionEngine;

it's similar to HTML, but uses brackets for common HTML-like commands.
See http://expressionengine.com/docs/general/pmcode.html for details.) So, for
the basic text formatting, you can use codes such as [b]bold text[/b] and
[i]italic text[/i]. If you choose to Allow Safe HTML or Allow All HTML
when configuring the wiki, you should also be able to use HTML tags to format
text in your blog entries. In fact, you can have a mix of HTML and pMcode under
those circumstances, so that markup like this:

```
<b>Welcome to Jackpedia</b>
Jackpedia is a [b]wiki[/b] for Jackson, Mississippi that's powered
by the [[http://www.jacksonfreepress.com | Jackson Free Press]].
Take a look around, browse by categories and, once you've gotten
your bearings, feel free to add to the content.
```

will render just fine in a browser window:

Jackpedia: The Jackson, Mississippi Wiki	View - Edit - History
Welcome to Jackpedia Jackpedia is a **wiki** for Jackson, Mississippi that's powered by the Jackson Free Press. Take a look around, browse by categories and, once you've gotten your bearings, feel free to add to the content.	

To create a new page or link to an existing one, you can simply surround
the name of the new page in brackets, as in [[music]] or [[restaurant
guide]]. You can also offer different link text than the name of the page,
as in [[music | The City's Guide to Music]]. Once the page is
rendered, clicking on that link will either take you to the named page (music or
restaurant_guide) or it will create that page and enable you to begin editing it.
That's classic wiki behavior.

And, you can link to external sites using the same approach, as in [[http://
www.expressionengine.com]] or [[http://www.expressionengine
.com | The Home of ExpressionEngine]].

ExpressionEngine's wiki offers the ability to assign pages to categories,
which can be handy for searches or for using the hard-coded Categories link
in the sidebar. To assign a page to a category, enter the tag [[Category:
CategoryName]] on that page. If the *CategoryName* doesn't exist, it will be
created. For example, you could put [[Category:Music]] on a page to assign
that page to the music category, and if the Music category doesn't exist, it's
created.

TIP   *Once you've defined categories, you can view pages by category by
clicking the Categories link in the wiki's Navigation section.*

While you're editing the page, you have some options at the bottom of the entry page. Those include

- **Notes**   Here you can enter a note about the page that doesn't appear when visitors view the page.

- **Redirect**   Enter the URL for the page that you'd like this one to redirect to, if you desire. This can be a handy way to link back out to your blog for instance, by creating a page that redirects to your blog's URL or to a particular permalink on your blog.

- **Rename**   Enter a different name for the page in this entry box if you want to rename it. This can be particularly handy if you have user-generated pages that aren't named the way you'd like them to be.

- **Lock Article**   If you're an administrator within the wiki, you can lock a page so that only you and other administrators can edit the page.

- **Moderate Article**   If you'd like to approve changes to this article before they appear live on the wiki, click this box. Messages will be sent to the e-mail address that's specified for wiki moderation.

- **Delete Article**   Check this box if you'd like to delete the page when Submit is clicked.

When all your choices and changes are made, click the Submit button. You should be returned to the page, where you'll see your page in action.

Upload Images and Files

The wiki module will allow you and your users to upload images and other files to the system and then link to those files using simplified syntax. To upload a file, click the File Upload link that appears in the Navigation sidebar on any wiki page. (You may have to be logged in before you'll see it.) That launches the Special: Uploads page shown in Figure 8-16.)

NOTE   *If you don't see a File Upload link and you're logged into ExpressionEngine, it's likely that you haven't chosen an Upload Folder in the wiki's setup preferences. Load your ExpressionEngine admin interface, click the Modules tab, click the Wiki module, and then click to open the wiki you created. Now, locate the File Upload Directory for Wiki option and choose Main Upload Directory from the menu. Click Update to make the changes and now you should see the file upload tools in the wiki.*

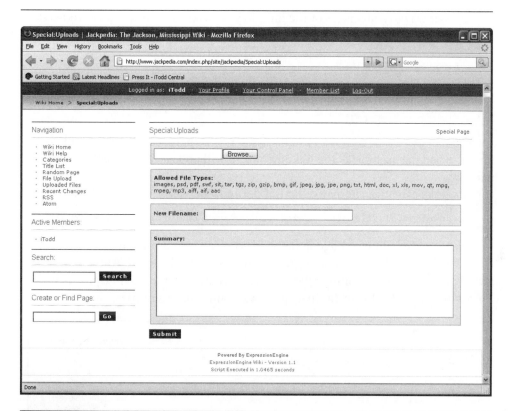

FIGURE 8-16 The Special:Uploads page enables you to upload files to the wiki installation.

On the Special:Uploads page you can click the Browse button next to the entry box at the top of the screen to bring up an Open dialog box so that you can locate the file you want to upload on your PC's hard disk. Select the file in the Open dialog box and you're returned to the Special:Uploads page, where you can change the name of the file, if desired, and give it a short description. Then, click Submit to upload it.

> **TIP** *You need to pre-size your images before uploading them to the wiki; the wiki doesn't process images and create thumbnails in the same way that the ExpressionEngine blog tools do for images.*

Once the file is uploaded, you'll see a page that displays either the image file (if it's a recognized image type) or a sample link to the file if it's not an image. Below that, you'll see an entry box labeled Quick Link. In that box is the code you can use to link to the image or file on a wiki page. You can copy and paste that code into a wiki page to cause its file link or the image to appear.

Another way to add images or file links to your wiki pages is to type a wiki-style link to that file or image while you're editing a page. For a file, the link will look like:

```
[[file:myfilename.pdf]]
```

For an image that you'd like to display on the page, use:

```
[image:myfilename.jpg]]
```

You can use the `[[file:myfilename.jpg]]` approach to create a link to an image; when the user clicks the link, the image will appear in the user's browser window.

File links can have alternative text, if desired, such as:

```
[[file:downloadthisfile.zip | Click to download the archived file (2MB)]]
```

While you're editing a page in the wiki, you can also browse the most recent files, which is handy if you aren't great at memorizing filenames. At the bottom of a wiki page that you're editing, click the View 10 Most Recent File Uploads link. That will cause a list to appear that shows the names of recent files.

```
View 10 Most Recent File Uploads

Recent Files:
FestivalGuide.pdf - Uploaded: 10 Mar 2007: [Add File]
BandPhoto.jpg - Uploaded: 10 Mar 2007: [Add File] - [Add Image]
CoverArtwork.jpg - Uploaded: 10 Mar 2007: [Add File] - [Add Image]
DirectionsToFestival.pdf - Uploaded: 10 Mar 2007: [Add File]
```

To view the file's page (which includes the Quick Link box as well as controls for deleting the file), click the file's name, which is a hyperlink.

To add a link to that file or image in the page you're editing, click the `[Add File]` link that appears on that file's row. That will cause a `[[file:]]` link to appear in the edited page, complete with the filename as part of the reference.

If the file is an image, you will also have the option to click the `[Add Image]` link, which will place an `[[image:]]` link in the edited page, again with the filename for the file.

Once you've made changes to the page, click Submit to add your edits to the wiki. You should now see those file links and/or images appear on your page.

NOTE   *As of this writing, the ExpressionEngine wiki doesn't offer much in the way of special commands for aligning or floating images. If you have chosen to allow full HTML editing of your wiki pages, you can use `<div></div>` tags around the image calls to align and/or float them, if desired. See Chapter 4 for more on HTML and CSS alignment options.*

Chapter 9

Communicate with Users: Forums, Community Blogs, and Newsletters

How to...

- Enable multiple authors on your blog

- Allow your community of readers to add to your blog

- Offer feedback forums for discussion on your site

- Use newsletters to encourage return visits and participation

Build Community Around Your Blog

There's no doubt that one of the key tenets of the Web 2.0 phenomenon is the opportunity for users of your site to participate in the ongoing discussion themselves. Clearly, one way that happens is using the commenting feature on your site, but even if you don't accept comments from your visitors, other tools—such as trackbacks, social tagging, social bookmarking, rating services, and so on—can offer your readers an opportunity to use your content to participate in a greater conversation that's happening online.

If, however, you see that your own blog is taking a turn toward some in-depth conversation, you might want to consider giving your visitors more options for participating. On my personal blogs (or those about writing books and so on), comments generally suffice. For the Jackson Free Press' blog-based site, however, we also offer community blogging features that enable a number of authorized "authors" to add their own blog entries. And, we offer public forums, so that anyone (or, at least, any registered user) can start a topic and generate some conversation on a topic that interests them.

There are a variety of reasons you might want to build a strong community blog. Some of them may be commercial—in the case of a newspaper or local interest blog, generating a lot of pageviews might translate into participation, reader loyalty, advertising revenue, or a captive market for goods and services. The same might be true of a blog that's of interest to professionals, investors, bookworms, the politically minded, or any other sort of online interest group.

Another reason to create a community blog (or, at least, one with multiple authors) is for a non-profit, charity, or hobbyist group to share information back and forth. Such a blog could be public or private; you might use the blog for ongoing business discussions between the committees of your theater group or service organization, or you might use it as a public blog so that those committee chairs can communicate with volunteers and potential donors or attendees.

In this chapter I'd like to take a look at the options you have for multiple-author or community blogs in the major blogging tools discussed in this chapter, as well as hosted or self-served discussion forums that you can add to your blog.

Finally, I'd like to touch on the use of e-mail lists for communicating with your audience and driving traffic and community for your blog.

Community Blogging

The idea behind community blogging is simply that you allow more authors than yourself to contribute to your blog. Depending on the software you use, you may want this to be a separate blog from the one where you wax poetic on a regular basis, or you might be OK with a limited number of people throwing in and adding blog posts to your community blog. (On the Jackson Free Press site, for instance, we have what we call the "JackBlog," which has a rotating authorship of between 10 and 15 authorized bloggers who contribute. Its headlines appear on the main page of our site to encourage comment and conversation, as shown in Figure 9-1.)

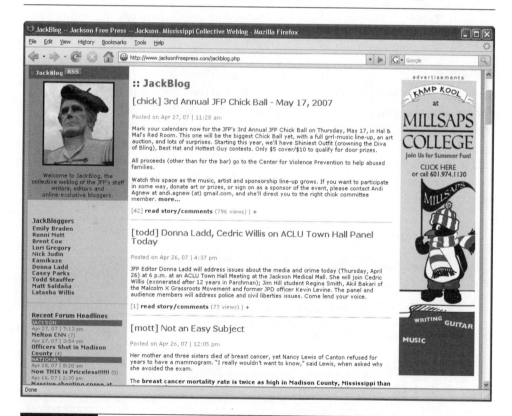

FIGURE 9-1   On the Jackson Free Press website, our community blog (called the "JackBlog") is where a number of our writers and members of the community can post entries.

You may also have a desire to set up a blog and allow anyone to post to it—or, maybe not everyone in the world, but certainly a large number of registered users. As we'll see, a few blogs have been very successful in creating schemes where a lot of their content is user-generated and then incorporated into the blog, making it possible for a great number of updates to take place without requiring all that volume to come from a single blogger. This can be a great way to create a sense of community and belonging among your readers, thus using your blog to build an audience and meet whatever goals you have for it.

Let's start by looking at the technical setup for a community blog in the popular blogging tools discussed throughout this book and how you can either add multiple authors to your current blog or create a second community blog that you can incorporate into the design of your original.

Set Up Multiple Authors

Blogger, TypePad, WordPress, and ExpressionEngine all offer you the ability to open up your blog to multiple authors. Here's a look at how to do that in each tool.

Blogger

In Blogger, sign into your Blogger dashboard and then choose the Settings link for the blog that you'd like to configure for multiple authors. Now, click the Permissions link that appears underneath the Settings tabs.

On the Permissions screen, you'll see the section Blog Authors, where you can add to the people who are authorized to post to your blog. Click the Add Authors button to invite more people to post to your blog. All you do is enter their e-mail addresses and then click Invite.

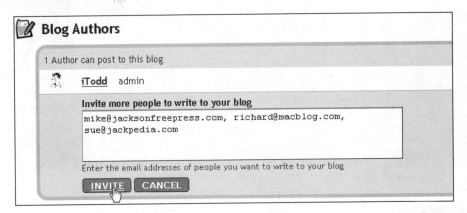

Once the invitations are sent, the recipients will receive an e-mail that instructs them to log in with a Google account (if they have one) or to create a Google account (if they don't have one). Once logged in, your authors will be able to create new posts and edit their own; they won't have correct permissions to change the layout of the blog, edit other authors' posts, or moderate comments.

You can change that, however, by altering the permissions for that author once he or she has logged into Blogger and created his or her account. Once the author is a part of your blog, you'll see a new listing on the Permissions page.

Next to the name of a new author will be the word "guest," which you can click in order to change to "admin." Once the author has an admin setting, he or she has the same access to the blog that you do, with the exception that no author can remove you from the site. (You, as the owner of the blog, can change another admin-level author's status and/or remove that author from your blog.)

To remove an author from your blog, simply click the Remove link next to his or her name on the Permissions screen. He or she will be removed immediately.

TypePad

TypePad (the Pro Level only) enables you to add two different types of co-authors on your blog: a Guest author, who can post (and edit) their own articles on the site; and a Junior Author, who can post (and edit) articles to your site that you then review before they go live. TypePad doesn't give you the option of creating additional administrative users or anyone with the same level of authority on your blog that you have.

To add authors from the TypePad admin interface, click the Configure tab, then click the Authors link. On the Weblog Authors page, you'll see yourself under the Current Authors section. To invite new authors, enter their e-mail addresses in the Invite Authors section and choose the type of author you want them to be.

When you're finished entering e-mail addresses, you can write a short message and then click Send Invitations.

Once you've clicked Send Invitations, the e-mails will go out and you'll return to the Weblog Authors page, where you'll see those newly invited people now in the Open Invitations section. Once they respond to the e-mails and, if necessary, create TypePad accounts, you'll see them listed as Current Authors on the blog.

> **NOTE**   *If you've set someone up as a Junior Author, don't forget that you'll need to check the Lists Posts page to review and publish posts that have been saved as drafts.*

To remove an author, simply revisit the Weblog Authors page and click the small trashcan next to that author's name in the Current Authors list.

> **NOTE**   *With a Pro or Plus account, you can create multiple blogs via TypePad, so one solution might be to create a second blog that can be used for community blogging. You'll have to invite your users to become authors, but if you've got some loyal readers who participate in comments, that could be a nice step. Then, using the Feeds section of the Select Content page in TypePad, you can feed headlines from your community blog to the front page of your main blog, thus creating a relationship between the two. (See Chapter 5 for more on feeds.)*

WordPress

WordPress offers full support for multiple authors as well as support for configuration as a community weblog, in the sense that readers can register themselves with WordPress and then add blog entries if you decide to configure it that way.

To set up new authors for a multiple-author blog, simply access the WordPress admin interface and then click the Users tab. On the Authors & Users sub-tab, you'll see the authors and users who are currently configured for access to the site. To add a new user, scroll down to the aptly named Add a New User section (see Figure 9-2) and enter at least a username, e-mail address, and password for the

FIGURE 9-2   Adding a new user in WordPress

new user. (The other items are optional, but recommended.) In the Role menu, you can choose from a few different roles for this user:

- **Subscriber**   This user has no posting privileges beyond comments if you enabled registration for comments.

- **Contributor**   This user can write and edit his or her own posts, but not publish them. (They're saved as closed for a higher-level administrator to publish.)

- **Author**   This user can write, edit, and publish his or her own posts.

- **Editor**   This user can write, edit, and publish his or her own posts, as well as publish contributors' posts, make decisions about others' posts, moderate comments, and generally take care of the content on the blog.

- **Administrator**   This user has full access to all Editor duties, plus access to themes, plug-ins, user management, and so on.

Once you've made your decision about the new user's role, click the Add User button.

To remove a user, revisit the Users page and click to place a checkmark next to the user you want to delete. Then, choose Delete Checked Users and click the Bulk Update button.

If you'd like people who register for your site to automatically have some privileges for posting articles (making it a community blog), you can set that behavior in this way:

1. In the WordPress admin interface, choose Options.

2. On the Options tab, make sure the General sub-tab has been selected.

3. Scroll down the page to the Membership section. In the New User Default Role pull-down menu, choose Contributor.

NOTE   *WordPress will allow you to set the New User Default Role to any of the predefined roles, but unless your site is password-protected (aside from WordPress' passwords) or otherwise inaccessible to the Internet in general, I wouldn't recommend setting it to anything higher than Author. And even then you might prepare yourself for some spam posts.*

4. Scroll to the bottom of the page and click Update Options.

Now, when new users register, they will automatically have access to the Admin interface as a Contributor-level user. That means they can click the Site Admin link (generally found in the Meta section of the default WordPress templates) and then enter or edit a post, even though it will be held as unpublished until you moderate that post and publish it.

> **NOTE**   *WordPress has another edition, called WordPress MU (available at http://mu.wordpress.org), which can be used for multiple blogs written by different authors. More than a community blog, it's really an open source self-hosted solution that can be used to offer a community blogging service—a bunch of individual blogs written by one or more authors for whatever reason. Of course, using RSS and certain WordPress tags, you could place recent entries from a variety of blogs on a single page, and in that way build a "community portal" of sorts with different bloggers contributing to a larger site.*

Expression Engine

ExpressionEngine can be used for pretty much any sort of community blog—it supports blogs that have multiple authors, and it can be used to offer a public (or members-only) entry form where blog entries can be made without accessing the administrative interface, thus encouraging input from your users without forcing them to learn the ExpressionEngine interface. For items such as event listings, press releases, or just general chat and discussion, ExpressionEngine's community blogging support can be very handy.

> **NOTE**   *Because ExpressionEngine is commercial software, you have to abide by the license of the software. One of the points that is often returned to in the ExpressionEngine discussion forums is that ExpressionEngine's license appears to forbid creating a blogging service (along the lines of what WordPress MU is designed to do), where individuals have their own personal blogs that are managed by a single ExpressionEngine installation. That's not to say that you can't have a community blog, but there are some things to consider if you'll have a large number of people blogging. See the website http://www.expressionengine.com or ask an EllisLabs representative for more details.*

Multiple Authors   Adding authors is easy in ExpressionEngine, although the first step—deciding what privileges those authors will have—is a bit more complicated. The basic installation of ExpressionEngine doesn't really include a "contributor" or "author" class of user the way that WordPress and others do, although all the tools are there for you to create that class of user account yourself.

NOTE *If you fully trust the person you're adding as an author, there is a default user group called Super Admins that you can use for that person. Realize, however, that the Super Admins group is only recommended for someone who knows ExpressionEngine fairly well; even with a trusted user, if they're aren't completely savvy to all of ExpressionEngine's features, you may want to limit their access to modules, plug-ins, templates, admin preferences, and so on.*

Here's how to create a new user class:

1. In the ExpressionEngine interface, click the Admin tab.

2. Click Members and Groups.

3. Click Member Groups.

4. Now, on the Member Groups page, you can edit an existing group or you can create a new one. To create a new group, click the Create a New Member Group button.

NOTE *By default, the Members group can post comments, view other members' profiles, and send messages through the system, while the Guests group can only post comments. For a community blog you could upgrade the Members group definition to include posting to weblogs, for instance, or you could create a new group category.*

5. On the Create a Member Group page, enter a name for the Group and, if desired, a description.

Member Group Name	
Member Group Name	Authors
Member Group Description	Can access the community blog, with limitations.

WARNING: Be EXTREMELY careful assigning group preferences - especially the highlighted ones.

6. Next, you'll page through each of the different group privilege links and make settings for what members of this group can and cannot do.

As you go through the groups of privileges (Security Lock, Site Access, Member Account Privileges, and so on), you'll see that ExpressionEngine places in red text any item that could be a significant security breach. Think carefully before changing those settings.

7. Since the exercise here is to create a weblog author, your first decision is whether or not you want to give an Author access to the admin control panel. If you don't, then you can use the Stand Alone Entry Form discussed in the next section. If you do want the Author to have access to the Control Panel, then click Control Panel Access and click Yes to the question Can Access the Control Panel?

Control Panel Access

Can access the control panel?	Yes ◉ No ○

Update   **Update and Finished**

9

8. Next, click Control Panel Access Area and choose the areas that this user group can access; if you're just giving them the right to post entries, then turn on PUBLISH and EDIT pages and leave everything else off.

9. Now, click Control Panel Administration and see if you want to change any of those options; you don't have to for a basic "author" account. Control Panel Email Privileges is the same; if you want this user to be able to send e-mails to members via the control panel, you can, but it isn't necessary.

10. Another rather important set of privileges is the Weblog Posting Privileges screen; click that link and then you can make decisions about whether or not this user group has access to other users' posts, whether they can delete their own posts, and whether they can create or change categories.

11. On Weblog Assignment, you can determine which of your weblogs this user has permission to post to.

12. Finally, on Comment Administration, you can make choices about whether or not this user group has the ability to moderate comments, delete comments on their own and/or other authors' posts, and whether they can edit comments or simply delete them.

13. With your choices made, click the Submit and Finished button in the Create a Member Group window. Now that group is created and members can be assigned to it when you want a member to have posting privileges.

Member Groups			
Group Title	Edit Group	Security Lock	Group ID
* Authors	Edit Group	Locked	6
Banned	Edit Group	Locked	2
Guests	Edit Group	Locked	3

Now, the issue of creating a new member and assigning him or her to a member group is, as mentioned, pretty simple. Here's how:

1. From the Admin tab, select Members and Groups.

2. Click Register a New Member.

3. On the Register a New Member page, enter a username, password (twice), screen name, and e-mail address for the user.

4. Select the Member Group for this user from the Member Group menu.

5. Click Submit.

That's all it takes; you'll see the list of active members appear. Now that user is ready to take advantage of whatever posting and commenting privileges you've created for them.

Stand Alone Entry Form   The other way to enable your members to submit blog entries in ExpressionEngine doesn't require that you give them access to the control panel. If they have the appropriate privileges, you can make it possible for them to submit blog entries from an HTML form on your site; those entries can then be posted "closed" so that you can moderate them before they're posted. This is an excellent way to offer a community blogging feature on your site, whether it's for a blog-style "open forum" (as opposed to one that uses special forum software, like those discussed later in the chapter), or a way that someone can submit news, press releases, events, reviews, or whatever it is that your site supports.

TIP   *Don't want people adding to your main blog? Then create another one specifically for user input by going to Admin | Weblog Administration | Weblog Management and clicking Add a New Weblog. See Chapter 3 for details on adding weblogs in ExpressionEngine and Chapter 4 for hints and discussion on adding the second weblog to your templates so that its headlines can be seen by your visitors.*

Allowing blog entry input from a web form is done using a special ExpressionEngine tag, called the Stand Alone Entry Form tag. The tag itself is rather complicated, but it can be cut and pasted into a template to give you a running start at allowing your users to post entries from the Web. Here's a look:

1. Begin by clicking the Template tab in the ExpressionEngine admin control panel.

2. Select the appropriate Template Group, and then choose New Template.

3. On the New Template screen, give the template a name ("entry" or "reader_submit" or anything that seems catchy) and make sure Web Page is selected in the Template Type.

4. Next, you have a decision to make. You'll probably find it handy to base your entry form template on a single-page template that you already have, such as a "comments" template. If so, click the radio button next to Duplicate an Existing Template and then choose that template from the pull-down menu.

5. Click Submit.

6. Back at the Template Management screen, click the new template's name so that you can edit it.

7. You're now going to need to open a new browser window so that you can cut and paste the Stand Alone Entry Form code into the template. The full code can be found at http://expressionengine.com/docs/modules/weblog/entry_form.html in the ExpressionEngine documentation. Copy the example code from that page.

8. Paste that example code into the template that you created, taking care to place it in the body of the template, and ideally within the existing design. (If you used a comment template, you can probably replace almost everything between the `<body>` `</body>` tags in the document, although the form might look a little better if you place the entry form code between `<div class="wrapper">` tags if you see them in the template design.)

9

TIP *On the documentation page mentioned previously there's also a link to some recommended CSS styles that should be added to this blog's style sheet in order to make some of the buttons appear correctly. See Chapter 4 for more on CSS styles.*

9. You may need to edit the code for the entry form tag by replacing `weblog="default_site"` in the ExpressionEngine tag with either the name of the blog where entries will be added (e.g., `weblog="jackblog"`) or with a variable (e.g., `weblog="{my_weblog}"`) if you've assigned such a variable at the top of the page. Here's the code you'll need to change:

```
{exp:weblog:entry_form weblog="default_site"
return="site/index" preview="site/entry"}
```

10. Now, save the template and view it in a browser by clicking the View link that is in that template's row (see Figure 9-3).

Using this form, a registered user can add items to the selected blog if the member group that the user belongs to has that privilege, as described in the

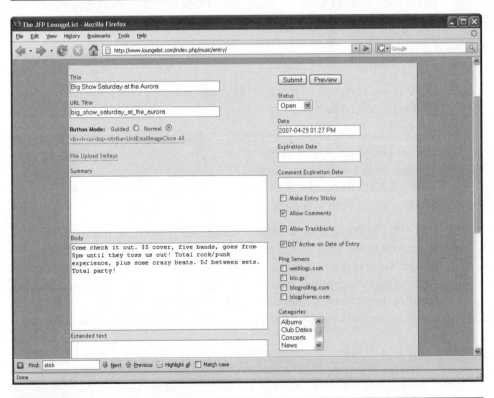

FIGURE 9-3   Here the entry code has been placed in a new template that I can link to and enable my readers to add blog entries.

previous section. If you'd like any registered member to be able to post to the specified blog, then simply edit the default Members category and, in the Weblog Assignment section, assign the weblog to whichever members are allowed to post.

There are a few things you should know about the sample form code that was pasted in from http://expressionengine.com/docs/modules/weblog/entry_form. html. First, that code automatically displays the fields that you've determined are appropriate for that weblog in the Admin | Weblog Administration | Custom Weblog Fields section of the control panel. If you delete, for instance, the Summary field from the field group, then it won't appear on this form, and so on.

Second, it's worth noting that the sample form code we've pasted in offers a full set of options that you may not necessarily want to present to the general public (or to your basic membership) in your form. For example, if you don't want users to be able to select whether or not the entry should be sticky, then you can locate and remove the following line from the template:

```
<p><input type="checkbox" name="sticky"
value="y" {sticky} /> Make Entry Sticky</p>
```

The same is true of items such as whether the user should be able to allow trackbacks or comments. Indeed, if you want to force a particular behavior, you can delete the option from the template and then add a parameter to the main tag. For instance, if you want the entry to be added to the weblog as "closed" (meaning it isn't published and won't be seen by visitors to your site until it's set to "open") so that you can take a look at it before it goes live on the site, you would first delete the status section of the template:

```
{status_menu}
<p>Status<br />
<select name="status">
{select_options}
</select>
</p>
{/status_menu}
```

Next, you would alter the main ExpressionEngine tag to have a new parameter:

```
{exp:weblog:entry_form weblog="default_site"
return="site/index" preview="site/entry" status="closed"}
```

Save the template and, now, whenever someone adds an entry via this form, it will be submitted as a closed entry, so that it doesn't appear until you or another administrator sets it to open.

9

Want to be notified when someone adds an entry to this blog? In the control panel, go to Admin | Weblog Administration | Weblog Management, and choose Edit Preferences for the blog in question. Now, choose Notification Preferences and turn on Enable Recipient List Below for Weblog Entry Notification. Enter an e-mail address (or more than one separated by commas) in the Email Address of Notification Recipient(s) entry box and then click Update and Finished. Now, whenever a new entry is added to this blog, a notification will be mailed to those e-mail addresses.

You've got many, many customizations that you can make to this form; see the URL where the form resides for more information on the various options that you have. The form tag is flexible enough that you can present only the options that you really want the reader to have, while specifying all of the others by using parameters or altering the input fields.

Share Headlines   So you've got a regular blog in ExpressionEngine and you've got a community blog in ExpressionEngine, where any of your registered users can post. How about putting them together on the home page of your blog?

If you've already got a basic two-or-three column blog and you're adding a community blog, you might consider placing the headlines of the later in your sidebar. Here's how:

1. Begin by editing the template for your main blog's index page.

2. In the sidebar, add code for the headlines of the community blog. In my example, the blog is called Reader Notes and the short name of the blog is notes. Here's the code:

```
<div class="title">Reader Notes</div>
{exp:weblog:entries weblog="notes" orderby="date"
sort="desc" limit="5" dynamic="off"}
<div class="link">
<a href="{title_permalink=notes/comments}">{title}</a>
</div>
{/exp:weblog:entries}
```

3. Save the template and view your blog. Here's what it looks like in my example:

In the sample code, the key elements are the hard-coded `weblog="notes"` attribute (since we're showing the headlines from a different blog than the default) and the link to the entry based on its title (`<a href="{title_permalink=notes/ comments}">{title}</a>`), which points the link to the `comment` template with the `notes` template group, instead of the default template group for my main blog. Depending on how you've set up your second blog and its templates, you'll want to make sure those items are all pointed at the correctly named items.

Offer Discussion Forums

Often a community blog can be a great way to bring others into your site's discussions, particularly if you already have a bit of traffic and a common topic or breadth of topics to cover. If your site has a great deal of traffic and you have a desire to give your users more free reign over topics, it might make sense to offer *forums*, which give visitors to your site a section that's distinct from the blog where your visitors can spend time, discuss a variety of topics, and generally drive the discussion a bit more than they can even in a community blogging format.

> **NOTE** *Forums and bulletin boards generally mean the same thing; the name "bulletin board" is a reference to bulletin board systems (BBSs), which were the dial-up precursors to the Internet and Web, where you'd use a modem to call a bulletin board server and then share ideas, discussion, and files with others using that bulletin board system. (That's notwithstanding the obvious reference—the real-world bulletin board, complete with pushpins and notecards.) These days, "Web forum" is a more common way to refer to these discussion-style systems, although "bulletin board" survives in some of the software names such as phpBB and bbPress.*

Why Forums?

Blogging, even a community blog, offers a certain formality to conversations—blog entries just tend to have more "weight" than the comments that follow them. The suggestion seems to be that a blog entry must be some thought or concept that is written and presented to the reader, who can then comment on that entry, often criticizing or appreciating it. With forums, someone might strike up a topic, but the flow is then a bit more democratic, in the sense that you really are supposed to toss in answers, ideas, suggestions, or whatever it is that the forum post seems to encourage.

Which you choose—community blog or forum—will probably depend on at least two factors. First, do you have the traffic to sustain forums? It can take hundreds of regular visitors to sustain web forums, and they need to be willing to come back repeatedly to your site to continue the discussion. If you don't yet have that level of traffic, it might make more sense to create a community blog if you'd like others to be able to offer up their own posts to generate some discussion. You can always move to forums later.

Second, do you have a good reason to separate your content into a blog and forums? If your blog is utterly in your own voice—you're an expert on your topic, or you're a very colorful writer, or the whole thing is driven by your own day-to-day experiences—then a separate forum for your user-generated topics might make more sense. Likewise, if the topic of your blog is technical in some way—for instance, you cover new Apple product releases in a unique way or you do street fashion photography—but you're seeing posts from your readers looking for advice on purchases or troubleshooting or something similar, then that could be a great, synergistic reason to create forums. You might find that you develop both a loyal community of readers and many more pageviews as a result of letting readers talk about what's on their minds.

Hosted vs. Self-Served

Once you've decided to offer forums on your site, you'll be back to a familiar question that was originally discussed in Chapter 2 about blogging software—how are you going to implement your forums? If you're using TypePad or Blogger, you'll need to select a third-party solution. Fortunately, there are some interesting hosted services that offer public forums that you can link to your blog. If you're using WordPress or ExpressionEngine, you'll find that each has self-served forums scripts that are designed to work in tandem with your blogging software, enabling you to give your readers a very compatible experience—all the way down to the fact that logging into your blog for commenting or community blogging also enables them to log into the forums. And that can be very handy, as two different usernames and passwords can be something of a turn-off to your visitors if you want to keep them on your site.

Use Hosted Forums

If you're looking for a quick way to get up and running with forums for your site, a hosted solution might be a good idea. Any number of hosted services are available, running the gamut from free to pricey. For this example, I'll used ProBoards (www.proboards.com), which offers free and paid levels for adding forums to your repertoire.

> **NOTE** *Many other options exist, of course, including runboard.com, bulletinboard .com, forumsco.com, wowbb.com, boardster.net, ezforum.com, wwwthreads .com, and many others.*

To set up your forum, visit ProBoards and click the Sign Up! link. You'll see the typical entry boxes; enter a name, e-mail address, username, password, your blog's URL, and so on, then read the agreement, agree to it, and click Sign Up.

Once you're registered, you'll be told your username and password for ProBoards.com, as well as a username (probably "admin") and password for your actual forums themselves. You can then visit the boards that you've created, as you should have been given a URL such as http://*yourusername*.proboards59.com/ to visit. View that site in a browser and you're ready to do some configuration (see Figure 9-4).

At the bottom of the screen you'll find the Login section; enter your "admin" username and the password that you selected when you registered. That gets you logged in and enables you to finish the registration process, which includes confirming your birthday and that you've given a valid e-mail address. When that's done, you're ready to configure your forums, which you do by clicking the Admin link at the top of the screen.

The first thing you'll probably want to do with your boards is create a few different topic areas. On ProBoards, those topics are broken down into boards, which are specific topic areas where posts appear, and categories, where a number of boards can be collected. So, if your forums are generally about, say, New York City, then you might have a category called Nightlife, that includes a number of different boards such as "Dining," "Dancing," "Live Music," "Broadway," "Film," and so on. So, as you build your forums, you'll use the Categories options to set up

9

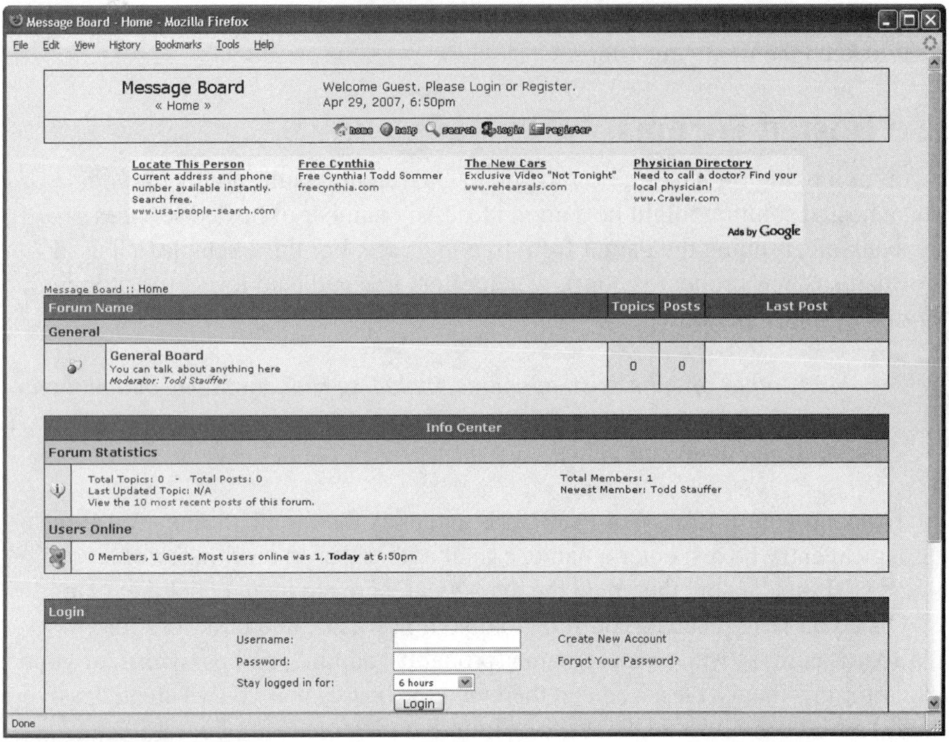

FIGURE 9-4   A default ProBoards installation immediately after registering

the categories and then the Boards options to create, delete, move, and re-order the boards within those categories.

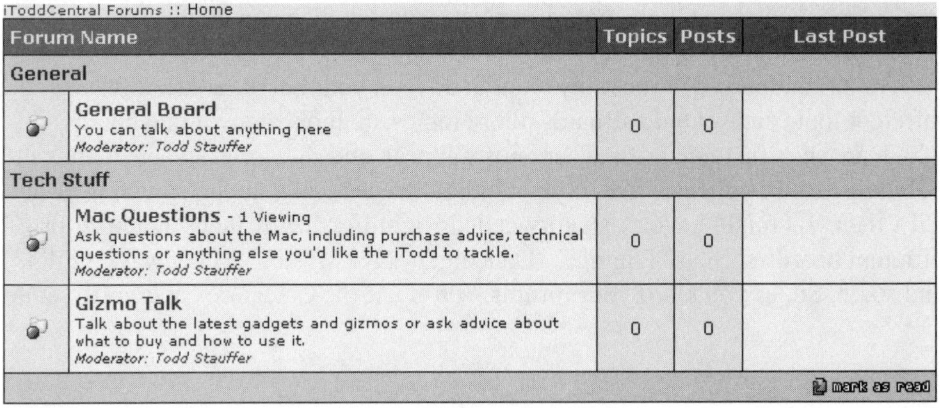

After you've created some boards and categories, the next step is to visit the General Settings, where you can give the board a title, determine whether you want to use the Google search feature, choose where the ads will appear (in the free version), and make a number of other choices including whether or not the "information center" appears on the board (showing how many people are logged in and so on) and how the links appear at the top of the forums pages.

Perhaps more important are some of the security options on this page, including:

- **Disable Signups**   In this case, you, as administrator, have to add new users; they can't register themselves.

- **Disable Account Activations**   This allows people to post without activating their account (by clicking a link in a message sent to their e-mail address, thus ensuring it's valid). This can speed up registration but also open you up to more spam.

- **Limited Registration**   Turn this on if you'd like to moderate all of the registrations on your board. This will slow down participation because your users can't sign up and get instant access to the board for commenting and posting.

- **Guests Must Login**   This option means that a guest can't read the forums without logging in first.

Scan the other options, make changes as desired, and then click Save Settings. As for the rest of your settings, there's plenty to dig into. You can create additional user groups, including moderators and others who don't have full administrative access, but who can create and delete posts or move them around within a particular board (or to another board if a post is made in an inappropriate place). You can also ban users, set up profanity filters, and do quite a bit of the same stuff that you can do with blogging software.

As for integrating it with your blog, a hosted solution can be tough for that. The easiest option is to create a link from within your template to the forums from within the sidebar of your blog, or to use another template element to link to the forums (depending on the template and blogging software that you're using). You can then use the Skins/Forums Colors link in the ProBoards admin interface to alter the look of your ProBoard so that it more closely matches the look of your blog.

Use bbPress

The authors of WordPress have created a forums script as well, called bbPress, which offers some of the same sensibilities as WordPress, with a simplified approach to creating and managing forums for discussions. To use it, you'll need to have access to your own hosting account; it requires MySQL and PHP, with similar requirements to that of WordPress. Note that you don't have to use WordPress at all—you can use bbPress on its own or with other blogging software, if desired. The two do integrate well, however, making it possible for you to require your users to have only one login and access both the blog (for commenting) and the bbPress-based forum for creating posts and responding to them.

Install bbPress

If you have a hosting account, head to http://bbpress.org/ and click the Download link, then choose the type of archive your would like to download. (For Mac and Windows, the .zip archive should work fine.)

Here's how to install the software:

1. Decompress the archive. (You should be able to do that on Windows or Mac by double-clicking the .zip file.)

2. Rename the file config-sample.php as config.php, and edit that file (using WordPad or TextEdit) with your host account's information for a MySQL database connection. (Note that you can use the same database that you used for your WordPress installation, as the bbPress installer will create different tables within that database.) You'll also want to edit the name of your forums, enter your administrative e-mail address, and make choices such as the number of posts to show on a page and your time zone in GMT offset format (U.S. Eastern Daylight Time is -4, U.S. Pacific Daylight Time is -7). When you've made changes, save the file again, making sure you save it as a plain text file.

3. In the Finder or Windows Explorer, rename the folder bbpress to whatever you would like it to be on your host and as part of the URL (e.g., forums, discussions, or something similar).

4. Upload the folder to your host account. If you want your URL for the forums to be something like http://www.*yoursite*.com/forums/, then upload the folder that you've renamed forums to the main level of your public hosting space.

5. Once it's uploaded, you're ready to launch the install page. In your browser window, open the URL to reach the file install.php inside the bb-admin folder inside your forums folder. For instance, you'd enter something such as **http://www.*yoursite*.com/forums/bb-admin/install.php**.

6. Next, the installer will walk you through a couple of steps to get the forums software installed, including the setup of your administrative account, when you'll have a random password assigned to you that you'll need to remember (at least until you change it).

7. When you've been assigned the password, you'll also see a link to the forums; click it and you're taken to them (see Figure 9-5).

Once you've reached the page, you're ready to log in; enter your admin username and password and you'll be ready to go.

Using bbPress

To create a new topic, simply click the Add New link in the Topic section of the page. That launches the Add New Topic page, where you can enter a title for the topic, enter the post and then add a few tags to categorize the post. You can view

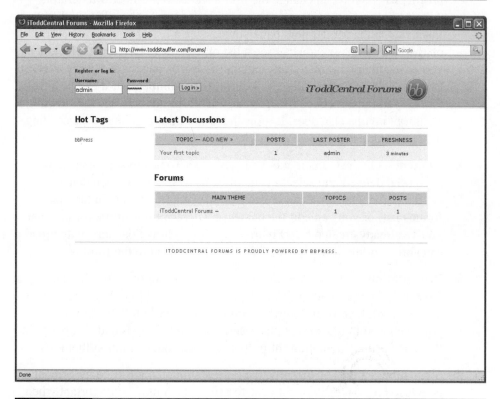

FIGURE 9-5   Here's what a fresh installation of bbPress looks like.

a post by clicking it in the list of forum topics, and then reply to it by entering a reply in the box at the bottom of the post window.

There's also a link to your profile, which you can use to track any discussion threads that you've saved as a favorite, as well as to see what your own activity has been. On the profile page you can change your password and enter more information about yourself, as well.

As an administrator, of course, you have additional options. To access them, you need to launch the path /bb-admin/index.php from the main directory of your forums. (In our example, that would be http://www.*yoursite*.com/forums/bb-admin/ or you can click the small Admin link next to your username when you're logged into the forums.) If you're already logged in as a user, then you'll immediately see the admin interface.

Here are some of the things you can manage in the admin interface:

- **Users**   On the Users tab, you can see a list of the users and edit them on the Find page. When you click Edit you're taken to that user's profile, where you can change the user's status to Member, Moderator, Administrator, Key Master, or to something worse such as Blocked or Inactive. On the Moderators page you can see a list of your moderators; on the Blocked page, you can see a list of users who have been blocked by you or by other administrators, and on the Bozos page you can see a list of Bozos. (A *Bozo* is generally a link farmer or spammer, but it can be a troll, too. By setting someone to Bozo status, it allows them to see their own posts, but no one else does. It fools them into thinking they're succeeding in spamming the site.)

- **Content**   On the Content tab, you can select Topics to see topics that have been deleted and select Posts to see posts that have been deleted. On the Forums tab, you can create a new forum (it appears in the main forums list) or you can edit the names and descriptions of the forums that you've already created (see Figure 9-6). This is how you can create broad categories for the forum posts that your visitors add to the forums.

- **Presentation**   On the Presentation tab, you can choose a new theme if you have one. To work with bbPress themes, you'll need to either create them or download them from elsewhere on the Internet. You then copy them to your web host in the correct place. See the topic Themes and Templates in the bbPress documentation (http://bbpress.org/documentation/themes/).

- **Site Management**   Currently, the only option on the Site Management tab is to recount various items in your forums, which may be important when you upgrade or change servers.

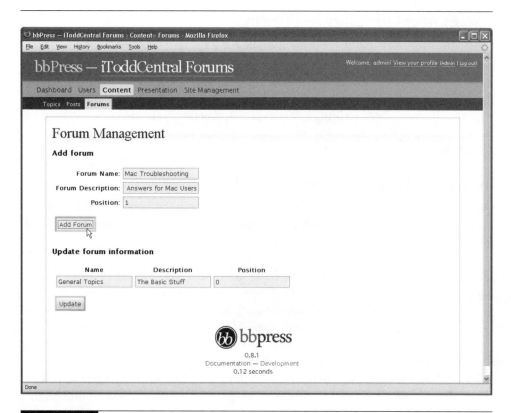

FIGURE 9-6   Use the Forums tab to add a new forum to your bbPress installation.

Those are all the options. In order to make any additional changes, you'll need to create new themes or edit the default theme files, which can be found on your web host in the bb-templates folder inside the main forums folder. There you'll find a folder for each theme that has been installed, and inside that, you'll find both CSS files that you can edit to change the formatting of your forums, and template files, such as front-page.php, which is used to display the main page of your bbPress installations.

CAUTION   *You should back up these files before making changes, as they could affect your ability (or that of your readers) to work with the bbPress forums.*

Use ExpressionEngine Forums

EllisLabs offers a Discussion Forum module for ExpressionEngine with one caveat—you have to pay extra for it. The module plugs into ExpressionEngine with controls accessible from the admin control panel, but only after you've paid the $49 for a personal license or $99 for a commercial license (at the time of this writing). To do so, head to http://www.expressionengine.com and click the Buy Now link; you'll then be guided through the process of purchasing the license and downloading the module's .zip file.

Install the Discussion Forum Module

Once it's downloaded, you install the Forums module in the same way that you install any module in ExpressionEngine, although there are a few more folders and files than in a typical module.

> TIP *You should check to make sure you have the latest build of ExpressionEngine installed before you install the Discussion Forum module. In your admin control panel, both the version number and build number (a date, such as 20070315) are shown at the bottom of the screen. If your build number is earlier than the one shown on the ExpressionEngine download page, you should download ExpressionEngine and update your blog's version first. Visit this page for details: http://expressionengine.com/docs/installation/update_build.html.*

Here's where everything goes:

- Extracting the .zip file creates a folder called forum, which you upload to the system/modules/ directory (remember that you may have renamed your system folder) on your web host using an FTP program.

- The folder forums_themes should be uploaded to your main themes directory online.

- The folder forum_attachments goes inside your images directory online. Its Unix permissions on your web host should be set to 777 or to writeable on a Windows-based server.

- The two files lang.forum.php and lang.forum_cp.php should be uploaded to the directory system/language/english/ on your host.

Once those files are uploaded, you should launch your ExpressionEngine control panel, and click the Modules tab. In the row for the Discussion Forum module, click Install. After the page reloads you'll see that Discussion Forum has become a link; click it and you'll see a list of the default preferences that you can set for your forum (see Figure 9-7). These are only the defaults for newly created forums; once you create a forum, you can change many of these settings as desired.

The settings are rather extensive, but you can begin by opening the General Settings, giving the forums a name, a URL, and the Forum Triggering word. The defaults work fine, but if you want to call your forums something other than "forums" you can change that here. The "Forum Triggering" word is a special setting that tells ExpressionEngine to launch the forums whenever that particular word is encountered as part of the URL. So, the URLs http://www.statedesk.com/index.php/forums.php and http://www.statedesk.com/index.php/forums/ would both launch the Forums module.

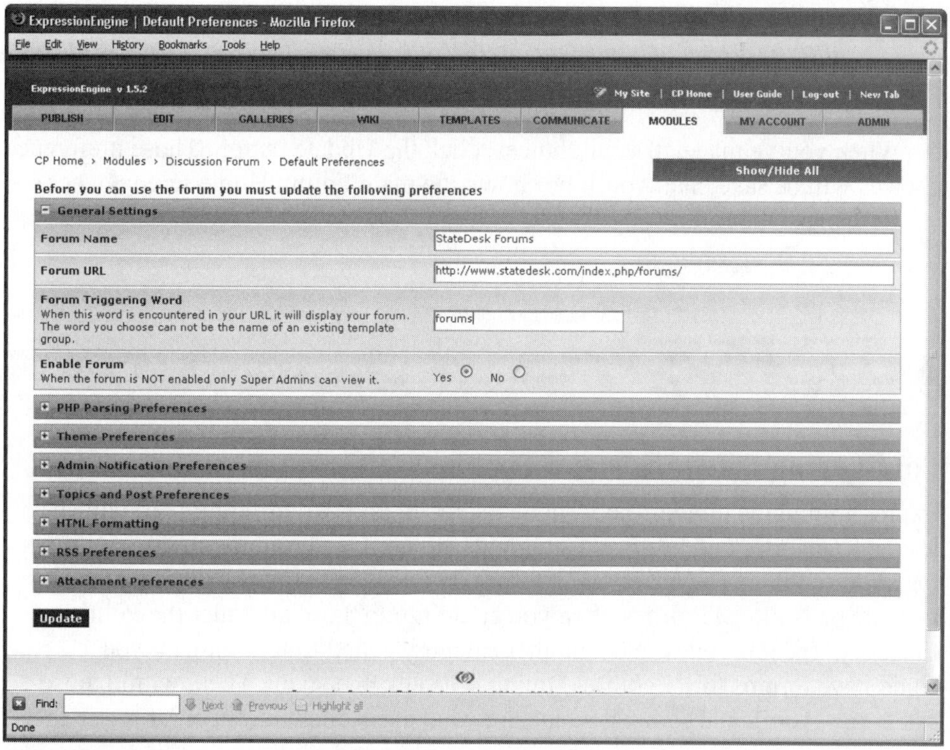

FIGURE 9-7   Setting default preferences for the Expression Engine forums

NOTE   *The Forums module doesn't use the templating system that's built into ExpressionEngine, in part because the dynamic nature of the forums would cause a great deal of server overhead, which would be a duplication of efforts.*

Scroll down and make changes to other settings as desired. The Theme Preferences setting can be used to set the default theme used for new forums; the Topics and Posts settings can determine how many topics appear on each page, in what order topics are displayed, and similar such choices. In HTML Formatting you can decide what level of HTML formatting to allow your participants to use in their posts. In the RSS Preferences you can determine if each forum will have a feed enabled by default and in Attachment Preferences you can determine what types of attachments can be uploaded by your users (images or any files) and what the maximum allowed size is.

TIP   *You can run your Discussion Forum from a subdomain (e.g., forums .mydomain.com), if you have access to some settings on your server. See http://expressionengine.com/knowledge_base/article/run_forum_from_ subdomain/ for details.*

When you've made all your choices, click the Update button. Those preference choices will be saved and you'll be shown the main Forum Home screen, where you'll manage the forums.

CP Home › Modules › Discussion Forum › Forum Home

FORUM HOME	FORUM MANAGEMENT	USER MANAGEMENT	TEMPLATES	VISIT FORUMS

Forum preferences have been updated

ID	Forum Name	Total Topics	Topics Per Day	Total Posts	Posts Per Day
2	My Forum	0	0	0	0

Configuring Categories and Forums

ExpressionEngine divides the forum concept up into two different hierarchical levels: Categories and Forums. Categories are used for grouping multiple forums together, so that if you have, say, a forum on Local Politics, one on State Politics, and one on National Politics, then you could group those all under the Politics Category. Then, if you wanted another category called Entertainment, you could have forums for Nightlife, Dining, Theater, and so on. Then, within those categories, you'll add forums, which are what users click into in order to see the topics that have been generated by fellow readers and create their own.

NOTE *Of course, it isn't necessary to create multiple categories or multiple forums if you don't want to, and I recommend creating relatively few categories and forums at first if you don't expect an onslaught of traffic. The fewer forums you have, the busier they'll look as people start adding to them.*

To create new categories and forums, you click the Forums Management tab within the Discussion Forum module interface. There you'll see the option to Add A New Category that, when clicked, enables you to enter a Category Name, Category Description, and a Status to determine whether the category is Live (so that new posts can be created by your members), Read Only, or Hidden.

Preferences	
Category Name	Entertainment
Category Description	Discuss different entertainment options in our metro area.
Category Status	Live
	Show Preferences

Submit

Once you've entered information about the category, click Submit to create it.

Now, in the category and forum listings, you'll see the option Add a New Forum to This Category underneath each category. When you click that option, you'll see a screen that's similar to the category setup screen where you can enter a Forum Name and Forum Description, choose the category that the forum belongs to, and determine the forum's status. Click Submit and that forum has been added.

Visit and Edit Your Forums

Ever present in the module interface is the Visit Forums link; click it and you'll see the categories and forums that you've created (see Figure 9-8). You can click around the interface as a user and get a sense of how the forums work; click one of the links to visit a forum, then click New Topic to begin a new post.

TIP *By default, there are four different themes that you can use for ExpressionEngine forums. To change to a different theme, click Forum Management | Default Preferences | Theme Preferences. There you can change the theme that's used for your forums.*

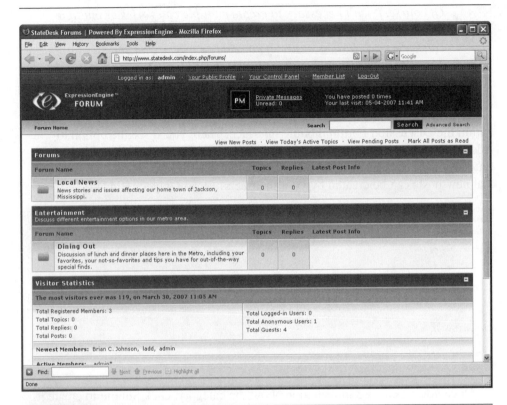

FIGURE 9-8 Here are my forums up and running.

As an administrator, once a post is in the system, you'll see some additional commands that your users don't see.

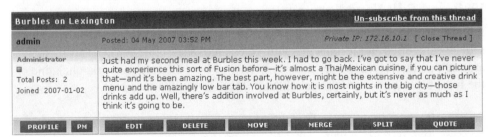

Those include the following:

- **Edit**   Click this and you can dive in to make changes to yours or someone else's post.

- **Delete**   You're the admin, so you have the power to delete other people's rants.

- **Move**   Click this and you can choose to place the post in a different forum within that category. At the same time, you can change the name of the thread if you'd like to.

- **Merge**   You can merge two threads together, which can be handy when two people post about pretty much the same thing. Just click the button and then enter the URL of the thread that you want to merge with this one (you can view that thread in a browser and then copy and paste the URL from there).

- **Split Thread**   If a thread seems to be going off in different directions, click Split and you can choose all of the entries in that thread that you would like to split out into the new thread. After you've clicked Split Thread, you'll see a new thread, with the same name as the old thread, appear as a newer entry. Now, edit that thread to give it a new name.

9

NOTE   *There's a lot more you can do with the ExpressionEngine forums module, including the ability to create additional administrators or assign certain users a "moderator" status, giving them the ability to make changes within a particular forum or category. See http://eedocs.expressionengine .com/modules/forum/index.html to dig deeper into the module.*

Display Forum Posts on Your Blog

Before we end this section, one nice little touch for an ExpressionEngine-driven blog is to post the Recent Entries from your forums to your blog's front page (or elsewhere in the design). Generally speaking, the forums don't offer a lot in the way of ExpressionEngine tags for layout and design. One special tag is available, however, so that you can put your headlines on your blog. The main tag looks like this:

```
{exp:forum:topic_titles orderby="post_date" sort="desc"
limit="10"} {/exp:forum:topic_titles}
```

Between the two tags you have options such as {title}, {author}, {topic_date format="%m/%d/%Y"}, {post_total}, and {views}, such that you could add something like this to your blog to create a "Recent Forum Entries" block:

```
<h2>Recent Forum Entries</h2>
<table>
{exp:forum:topic_titles orderby="post_date" sort="desc" limit="10"}
<tr>
<td><a href="{thread_path=forums/viewthread}">{title}</a><br /> by
<a href="{profile_path=forums/member}">{author}</a> on
{topic_date format="%m/%d/%Y %h:%i %a"}<br />
Most recent reply on {last_post_date format="%m/%d/%Y %h:%i %a"}
<br />by <a href="{last_author_profile_path=forums/member}">
{last_author}</a>
{/exp:forum:topic_titles}
</table>
```

With the variables and attributes available, it's possible to build a very simple reference or a complex one. See http://expressionengine.com/docs/modules/forum/ recent_forum_topics.html for details.

Develop Mailing Lists

Another way to stay in contact with your loyal readers is via an e-mail newsletter. Your blog represents a wonderful way to capture addresses from people who find your content valuable, whether you grab those addresses when you're getting readers to register or afterward. You can then drive repeat visits to your site by communicating with your readers on a regular basis. If your blog is commercial in nature then you can use your newsletter for creating a market for your products or encouraging repeat visits to your site by offering specials, discussion of new products, and so on. If you're blog isn't commercial (or if you're just making a little money from Google AdSense or similar text ad programs), you can still use regular newsletters to create community and build loyalty from your readership. Newsletters don't take that much more effort than blogging, and yet they can be a valuable way to personalize the experience for your readers.

With the exception of ExpressionEngine, none of the blogging solutions we're talking about in this book offer a built-in mailing list capability. That said, there are some great, inexpensive services on the Web that make capturing addresses and sending newsletter content very easy to do. Newsletter-specific services can be very useful for a number of reasons. First, many web hosting companies place limits on the number of e-mail messages that you can send from your account, regardless of the method that you use. (Even if the host account provides "mailing list" software, you may be limited to a certain number of outgoing e-mail messages per hour, for instance.) Second, newsletter services often handle much of the user management features for you, automatically dealing with "bounced" messages, invalid e-mail addresses, and giving you an interface for enabling your visitors to sign up for the newsletter without your interference. In my experience, if you have more than a few dozen e-mail addresses to which you'd like to regularly send an e-mail newsletter, a service is a great way to make that relatively painless.

Send Newsletters Using YMLP

The service I use on a regular basis for sending out e-mails from the Jackson Free Press is called Your Message List Provider, or YMLP for short. (We have a few thousand people on the Jackson Free Press "LoungeList" who receive e-mails from us telling them about music that's playing and upcoming events, and occasionally offering discounts, free tickets, and other radio-style "fourth caller" giveaways.) YMLP offers both a free and a paid service. The free service includes small ads shown to the user when he or she subscribes (it doesn't add advertising to the actual message), while the paid service enables you to send a higher volume of messages and customize the newsletters so that it largely appears to have come from your own domain. The Pro version also offers more options for importing and exporting users and generally managing and "owning" your database of addresses.

NOTE   *Another extremely popular option is Constant Contact (http://www .constantcontact.com). It only offers paid options, but they're impressive, offering pre-designed templates for HTML-based e-mail newsletters, drag-and-drop customization, and a lot of flexibility. Constant Contact can also track the folks who sign up for your newsletter and report back on items they click on, including statistics on whether or not your readers opened the newsletter e-mail and if any of them were encouraged to "take action" by clicking something or visiting your site.*

To get started with YMLP, head to http://www.ymlp.com/ and create an account. If you're opting for a paid plan, you'll need to walk through the registration process and pay via credit card or Paypal; for the free version, you just need to enter some basics for registration.

Once you're registered, you'll receive an e-mail to confirm the account; you can then log in and take a look around the administrative interface (see Figure 9-9).

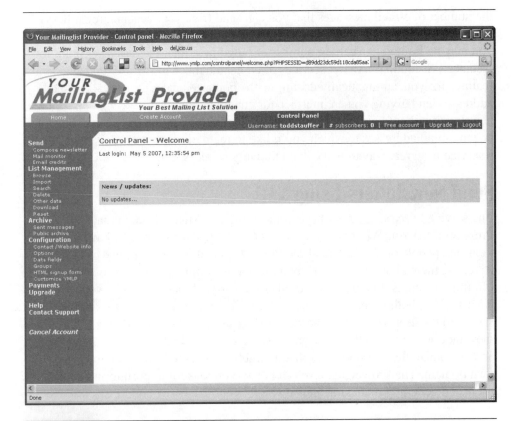

FIGURE 9-9   The basic YMLP administrative interface

For a basic account, you can't add e-mail addresses to the database yourself in order to "seed" your list; instead, you'll need to place the newsletter code on your site, which enables your readers to subscribe to your newsletter. (Of course, once you have even one subscriber you can send an e-mail newsletter; nobody needs to know the size of your list when you're getting started.) Here's the code you'll use (you can click the HTML Signup Form link within the interface to copy and paste this code):

```
<form method=post
action=http://www.ymlp.com/subscribe.php?yourYMLPaccount>
<table border=0>
<tr>
<td colspan=2>Fill out your e-mail address <br> to receive
```

```
our newsletter!</td>
</tr>
<tr>
<td><input type="text" name="YMLP0" size="20"></td>
<td><input type="submit" value="Submit"></td>
</tr>
<tr>
<td colspan=2><a href="http://www.yourmailinglistprovider.com"
 target="_new">Hosting by YMLP.com</a></td>
</tr>
</table>
</form>
```

Paste this code into the sidebar of your blog (note that you would substitute your YMLP user name for *yourYMLPaccount* in the first line of the code) and your users will then be able to subscribe to the newsletter if your blog looks interesting to them.

Once you've added this code to your blog, you may notice, depending on the design of your site, that it doesn't fit quite right in your sidebar because the Submit button it designed to be to the right of the entry box. To put the Submit button below the entry box, you can change the table layout so that the table only has one column per row, and the Submit button is added on its own row. To do that, you'll remove the `colspan` attribute from the first table cell, and then you'll add some additional row tags (`<tr>` and `</tr>`) around the Submit button:

```
<tr>
<td>Fill out your e-mail address <br>
to receive our newsletter!</td>
</tr>
<tr>
<td><input type="text" name="YMLP0" size="20"></td>
</tr>
<tr>
<td><input type="submit" value="Submit"></td>
</tr>
```

Here's the entry form in my WordPress blog:

Get My Newsletter!
Fill out your e-mail address
to receive our newsletter!

[Submit]

Hosting by YMLP.com

Here's a quick look at how to add the newsletter code to the blogging software we're discussing throughout the book:

Add YMLP to Blogger

If you're using the "new" Blogger, then click to the Layout tools and create a new Page Element in your sidebar. Choose the HTML/Javascript element. Give the element a title ("Subscribe to My Newsletter") and then paste the code into the page element's box. Click Save Changes and then, in your template, click Save again. Now, view your blog and you should see the entry box appear in the sidebar of your blog.

SUBSCRIBE TO MY NEWSLETTER

Fill out your e-mail address
to receive our newsletter!

[   ] Submit

Hosting by YMLP.com

Add YMLP to TypePad

To add the code to your TypePad blog, you'll need to create a new TypeList that can hold the code. Here's how:

1. Go to the TypeLists tab in the TypePad admin interface, and then click Create a New TypeList.

2. Choose Notes from the List Type menu and give the TypeList a name such as Newsletter Subscribe; click Create.

3. If desired, entered a label in the Label entry box. In the body of the list, paste the HTML code from YMLP. Click Save.

> **TIP**　*You may want to skip the label, depending on the layout that you're using; often, the name of the TypeList is used for the sidebar element and that may be enough of a label.*

4. Now, you'll need to add the TypeList to your sidebar; click the Weblogs tab, choose your blog, and click the Design link.

5. Under Select Content, scroll to the TypeLists and place a checkmark next to the TypeList you just created. Click Save Changes.

6. Now, back on the Design page, click Order Content.

7. On the Order Content page, locate the TypeList you created and drag and drop it to the location where you'd like it to appear on your blog. Click Save Changes.

8. Now, view your blog and you'll see your new newsletter subscription box.

Add YMLP to WordPress

Here's how to add the YMLP subscribe code to your sidebar in WordPress if you're using a widget-enabled template:

1. Choose Presentation in your WordPress admin interface.

2. Click Sidebar Widgets.

3. Drag a text widget from the Available Widgets section of the screen and place it on your sidebar.

4. Click the edit icon on the widget.

5. When the widget opens, give it a title (such as "Get My Newsletter") and then paste the HTML code into the widget's text area. Click the close box when you're done.

6. On the Sidebar Arrangement page, click Save Changes.

7. View your blog and you should see the newsletter subscription form appear.

Add YMLP to ExpressionEngine

In ExpressionEngine, you'll simply edit the template that contains your sidebar (if you're using a special sub-template for the sidebar) or the index template that is used for your blog. Paste the code in the appropriate section of the template and then click Update. View your blog and you should see the form appear.

9

Send Your Newsletter

Once you've gotten some subscriptions to your newsletter (which you can check by clicking the Browse link under List Management in the YMLP interface), you're ready to compose a message. To do that, click the Compose Newsletter link.

The first step you'll see enables you to set a number of preferences for how your newsletter will be delivered. The options include

- **Test Message**   Turn this option on if you don't actually want to send the newsletter e-mail to your subscribers.

- **Format**   Choose Plain Text or HTML, depending on how you intend to send the e-mail. (To send HTML newsletters, you'll need to generate the HTML in a different application and then paste it in; YMLP also offers the option of sending a plain text version along with the HTML version for e-mail applications or devices that don't support HTML.)

- **Send This Message**   Choose Right Away, if desired, or you can choose Later, and then set a date and time for the message to be sent.

- **Attachments**   You can add an attachment to the message if you're got a pro-level account.

- **Images**   Again, if you have a pro-level account, you can embed images in your newsletter and either have them sent as attachments to your recipients or YMLP can host the images for you, with HTML image links embedded in the newsletter in order to display them.

With those choices made, click Enter Message. Now you'll see the composition window (see Figure 9-10). Enter a title for your newsletter and its content; if you've chosen HTML, you'll need to paste the HTML into the top entry box and then, if desired, paste a plain text version into the Optional Text Part entry box.

When you're done editing, click the Preview button; you can now read through your message and get a sense of what it will look like to your recipients. If you like what you see, click Send Message. You'll then see a confirmation that the message is cued up and ready to go to your recipients.

TIP

There's a link in the YMLP administrative interface called Public Archive, which you can use to display previous e-mail newsletters (or to access them yourself). If you want, you can place a link to that archive on your blog so that people who are new to your newsletter can check out previous versions.

FIGURE 9-10   Editing my newsletter in YMLP

The Mailing List is a module within ExpressionEngine, so you'll need to enable it before you can get started working with it. In the ExpressionEngine admin control panel, choose Modules, then locate the Mailing List module. If it isn't already active, click the Install link in the module's row. Once it's active, you can click the Mailing List title of the module (it's now a link) so that you can manage your mailing lists (see Figure 9-11).

Use the ExpressionEngine Mailing List

Built into ExpressionEngine (in the licensed versions) is the ability to send e-mail messages to a mailing list. The mailing list addresses can be collected from users when they register for your blog, or you can place an entry box on your ExpressionEngine blog in order to collect e-mail addresses.

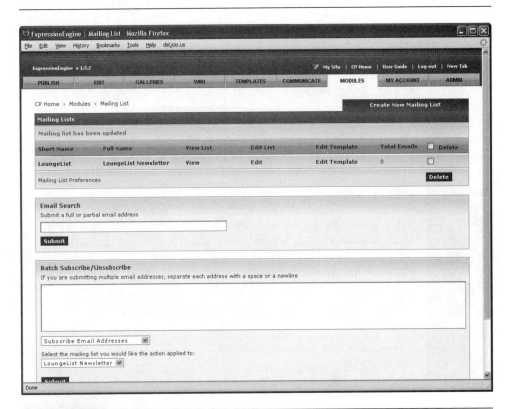

FIGURE 9-11 Use the Mailing Lists module to manage your lists.

Some of the options on this page include

- **View**   See the members of your list.

- **Edit**   You start out with a default mailing list; you can click Edit on that list's row to change its short name and full name.

- **Edit Template**   Add the mailing list template if you'd like to place a footer with information about your blog, links elsewhere, copyright notices, or what have you. The key ExpressionEngine that should be on the page is `{message_text}`; otherwise, you can format what comes before and after that.

- **Mailing List Preferences**   Click this link to enable and disable the mailing list and to determine whether or not administrators should be told when new members join the list.

- ■ **Email Search**   You can enter a partial match to search for a member of your mailing list.

- ■ **Batch Subscribe/Unsubscribe**   Enter e-mail addresses separated by a space or a return and then click the appropriate button to Subscribe or Unsubscribe them to a mailing list. (If you have more than one newsletter, you can choose that from the Select the Mailing List menu.) Click Submit to put that action into play.

- ■ **Create New Mailing List**   At the top of the window, click the button to create a new mailing list that you want to manage via ExpressionEngine.

Now, to send to your mailing list, you simply click the Communicate tab in the ExpressionEngine admin control panel and then enter a title and body for your newsletter. To send the message to your mailing list, place a checkmark next to that mailing list in the Communicate window. (You can also put your own address in the To: entry box, if you like.)

So, how do you get people to sign up for your mailing list? ExpressionEngine offers a special tag that you can place in your templates. Here's the basic look of that tag:

```
{exp:mailinglist:form list="short_name"}

<p>Join our Mailing List</p>

<p><input type="text" name="email" value="{email}" /></p>

<p><input type="submit" value="submit" /></p>

{/exp:mailinglist:form}
```

(Note for the attribute `list="short_name"` you should change short-name to the name of the mailing list you've created.) Once the user signs up via this entry form, the user will be sent an e-mail address to confirm the subscription. The user must respond by clicking the link in the e-mail in order to be confirmed for the mailing list. Once that's done, the user is ready to receive your e-mails.

Chapter 10

Grow and Maintain Your Blog

How to…

- Optimize your blog and increase traffic
- Check pageviews, visits, and other stats
- Make money from your blog
- Back up and maintain your blog

So you've got a solid blog with a lot of the bells and whistles. Depending on the service or software you chose, hopefully you've got some fun stuff going on, ranging from social bookmarking and hooks for rating services to wikis, community blogs, and forums. Now, if you've been at the blogging thing for at least a little while, you may be asking, "How can I get more traffic?" We'll look at some strategies in this chapter.

Once you've added to your traffic, you may want to try and monetize that traffic, at least a little, whether it's just to pay the hosting fees or, perhaps, to make a little more money than that. Perhaps you've heard the stories of people who start blogs and end up quitting their day job—anything is possible. (It hasn't happened to me, alas, but at least I get to write books about blogging!) In this chapter we'll look at some of the different ways that you can make money from advertising, linking, and even begging your users.

Finally, once your blog is up and getting some traffic (and maybe making some money) you'll want to safeguard its data. In the last section of this chapter you'll see how to back up your blog and, for self-hosted blogs, you'll see a few things you can do to maintain those blogs and keep them healthy.

Get Traffic for Your Blog

Something that can be frustrating for a beginning blogger is the relative lack of action. You post, no one comments. Or a few people comment, but not many. You post more, and a few more people show up. Maybe they comment, maybe they don't. What's a blogger to do?

Publicize, of course. There are a few different tactics you can take, from the free-but-time-consuming approach to the paid-but-time-consuming options. The real trick is just to get active by having something to say and then letting people know that you've said it. The more targeted your posts, interests, and insights are, the better chance you'll have of building some traffic, but even very general blogs can build a following if they're entertaining or interesting or enlightening.

Along the way, you can take a few steps that optimize your blog for placement in search engines such as Google, which might get you a few more visitors and pageviews as well.

Let People Know You're Blogging

Once you're up and online, it's a good idea to let people know you're blogging. You can do that in any number of ways, including the old standby—sending an e-mail to friends and family. Generally, the most effective way to build traffic, though, is to get your ideas in front of like-minded people via online interest groups, forums, and social networking sites.

Here are a few tips for getting out the word about your blog:

- *Use trackbacks.* Say you come across an interesting blog post on someone else's blog. If that person posts a trackback URL, then you have the option of copying that URL and entering it in the trackback entry box on *your* blog's entry page. In other words, you blog about that other blog entry, then you link to that other blog entry via trackback. Now, visitors to that other site will see a link to *your* blog entry, which might entice them to visit your blog. **Caveat:** Don't just say "Hey check this out..." and then trackback to the entry. Trackbacks, when used effectively, should continue the conversation from one blog to another.

- *Participate elsewhere.* If your blog covers certain interest areas, you should go to like-minded blogs (particularly those with more traffic) and participate by leaving comments, starting threads, or having conversations in the forums. In your posts and comments, include a "signature" line with a link back to your blog and perhaps a funny quote or saying. **Caveat:** Don't go over the top pitching your blog in other people's forums and blog comments. You don't have to be over the top and you don't have to get pitchy with your blog, especially if you leave most of your references in your signature, such as:

```
-----------------
Todd Stauffer
My blog: http://www.toddstauffer.com
Macs, gadgets and the future of newspapers
"I am not the editor of a newspaper and shall always try to
do right and be good so that God will not make me one."
- Mark Twain
```

10

- *Exchange links.* If you get to know some folks with similar interests or who simply have their own blogs, ask them to link to your blog and/or to comment on posts on your blog using their own. The more links you have to your site, the more traffic you'll get from the people who read those other blogs. Plus, some search engines take into account how many links you have from real-life bloggers and websites when they "weight" search results. The higher you are in Google, for instance, the more hits you'll get. **Caveat:** It's best to avoid spamming people with link requests; choose sites that have some legitimate relationship to yours, whether it's the fact that you're commenting and participating on the other blog often or it's a common topic area.

> **TIP**
>
> *The Jackson Free Press gets 5-10 percent of its new traffic from just a handful of sites that specifically link to local newspapers and newspaper content. So those directories of links that you think are useless might be better than you think.*

- *Post to topical directories.* One of the most reliable ways for me to get an extra few hundred visitors to my blog is to post something interesting about the Macintosh (or Apple-related stuff)—which is a passion of mine anyway—and then submit the story to MacSurfer.com (http://www.macsurfer.com/, see Figure 10-1). That site is a popular aggregator of Mac news links and it's almost guaranteed to boost traffic when they post one of my links. You should seek out similar topical directories that relate to the topic areas that you discuss on your blog and see if you can't get them to link to your stories. **Caveat:** Again, make sure what you submit is relevant and that you're submitting items in ways that don't irritate the editors of those directories.

- *Do some PR.* If your blog truly is a cut above the rest—or if you're covering a topic that would be of interest to your local community—then send out a press release to your local newspapers, weeklies, radio stations, TV stations, and so on. Let them know what you're doing, and then, when appropriate, follow up with links to interesting blog entries or items that show your unique take on the world. **Caveat:** Make sure you're dealing with the appropriate editor or producer and—here's a pet peeve—don't tell those people how to do their jobs. PR is like sales—everything *you* think is important will not be important to other people. Just tell them what you're covering, why, and suggest an angle or two. Then, don't expect anything to happen. (And don't call the paper or station to berate them for not doing a story on you.) But, if you send enough story ideas—and make friends

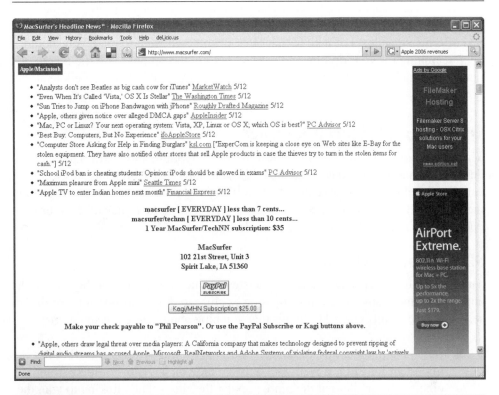

MacSurfer is a popular link site that can generate hundreds of visits from one link to an interesting Mac-related story.

in the process—you may get one bite from a local editor or producer who wants to get something "bloggy" in front of their audience. And if you do good work and play your cards right, you might just get that coveted "local blogger" role on an area radio talk show!

■ *Blog at a bigger spot.* If you're good at blogging, you can drive traffic to your blog by blogging elsewhere, either for pay or for more exposure. A number of different sites offer pay or revenue sharing for bloggers—About. com, 451Press.com, and Weblogs, Inc. (http://www.weblogsinc.com) are examples of places where you can apply and, if accepted, make a little revenue by blogging. The ProBlogger Jobs boards (http://jobs.problogger. net/) can be a good place to start, too. **Caveat:** You'll have to spend some time at your blog-away-from-your-blog and might lose interest in your home blog.

10

Any of these cases assumes that you're passionate about your blog's topics and that you're a pretty decent blogger. If you're aren't posting at least once a day and offering some level of insight that other people will want to read, you should keep searching for your rhythm and passion before you set out to do too much networking and traffic generation, because you won't be able to keep people at your site.

Optimize for Search Engines

There's a whole cottage industry in Search Engine Optimization (SEO) that is designed to make sites float to the top of Google and other search engines when certain related keywords are entered. (If you're exceptionally serious about getting the best results, you can visit any number of websites on the topic and even buy books by the armful at your local bookseller.)

SEO Tips and Techniques

The truth is that you can take a few basic steps to increase your visibility in search engines and make sure that you're floating as close to the top as possible for the search engine results related to topics that you blog about. Here are some tips:

- *Cultivate inbound links.* I talked about this for traffic generation, but it's important for SEO as well. Not only should you have lots of links from others to your site, but the more popular the site is that's linking to you, the higher that link ranks you in search engines. The same is true for sites that are relevant content-wise.

- *Use keywords in your content.* Without allowing it to affect the "voice" on your site, you should endeavor to use keywords in your content that are relevant to your overall blogging topics and that are likely keywords for searches in search engines. You can start with the keywords that you'd like to see your blog do well with. For instance, if you blog about digital photography in Oklahoma, then certain keywords, such as "digital photography in Oklahoma" and "Oklahoma digital photography" should be used frequently and consistently in your writing.

TIP *If your website is regional or local, you should use the name of the town, county, state, or region frequently in your writing. For Jackson Free Press, writing something like "Jackson, Mississippi's music scene" isn't any more difficult than writing "our music scene" and it's much more SEO-friendly.*

- *Use descriptive titles for your entries*. It can also be helpful to have descriptive, keyword-focused titles for your blog pages, blog entries, and for headers within your blog entries (using the XHTML tags H1, H2, and so on). Instead of "My Take on the D-12" as a title for your blog, go with something more like "D-Lite D-12 Digital Camera Review." And, when you're editing templates, make sure the title of your blog's pages is keyword-relevant; I have all of the titles on the Jackson Free Press site begin "Jackson, Mississippi—Music Listings" or "Jackson, Mississippi—Restaurants and Dining" in order to optimize them for people searching for stuff in our town.

TIP *There's a special titling plug-in for WordPress users called Optimal Title. It's available from http://elasticdog.com/2004/09/optimal-title/.*

- *Use friendly URLs*. It's not clear how much non-friendly URLs can hurt search engine optimization (by which I mean URLs such as http://www .toddstauffer.com/index.php?45636=45), but there's certainly some evidence that having friendly URLs with *keywords within your URLs* may help. With the major blogging tools we've dealt with in this book, that can often mean simply titling your blog entries with keywords; with some tools such as ExpressionEngine, you might name your template groups and templates using keywords that make sense for your particular SEO needs.

- *Add outbound links*. Not all SEO experts agree that outbound links are important to search engine rank, but they may be. Plus, having an active "blogroll" not only might help you with search engines, but will definitely help with real people who might be willing to repay the favor.

- *Optimize your posts*. Aside from using keywords within your posts whenever possible, it's also smart to keep your posts to a single topic and write a fair bit—at least a few hundred words—per post. That keeps the search engines from thinking that you're "link farming" or doing other stuff that tends to push you down in the rankings. Plus, the single-topic theory means you can wedge your keywords into the posts more and those individual posts can show up higher in search results.

- *Use META tags*. Different search engines give different levels of weight to META tags, but they're useful to have. These are special tags you place in the HEAD section of your templates. Two different META tags are important in this context—the Description and Keywords tags. Note that

10

with both, an accurate description and set of keywords is important; don't just toss anything in there. Use the keywords that you really blog about. Here are some examples:

```
<META NAME="description" content="News, views and reviews by
book author and newspaper publisher Todd Stauffer.">
<META NAME="keywords" content="Todd Stauffer, Stauffer, Mac,
newspapers, alt-weeklies, Apple, iPod, MacBook, Apple TV">
```

What's a Sitemap?

A sitemap is a special file that tells Google and other search engines more about your site, including where pages can be found and what should be crawled when the search engine's spider comes around. For blogging, a sitemap will generally be an XML document that lists the latest blog entries on your site; it's a little like an RSS feed, but with some specific information that's interesting to search engine spiders.

The leader in sitemap generation is, of course, Google, which offers its own tools for helping you to create your sitemap and learn how Google is accessing your site. For more on Google Sitemaps, visit (http://www.google .com/webmasters/tools/).

TypePad has built-in support for Google Sitemaps, which you can access directly if you're using one of the built-in templates. In the TypePad admin interface, head to Weblogs | Configure | Publicity and turn on the Google Sitemaps feature. If you're using an advanced template, then you'll want to read the TypePad Knowledge Base article on Google Sitemaps, which includes cut-and-paste text that will help you generate a sitemap (http://support. typepad.com/cgi-bin/typepad.cfg/php/enduser/std_adp.php?p_faqid=555).

Arne Brachhold has written a WordPress plug-in that enables WordPress to generate a sitemap on the fly, available at http://www.arnebrachhold .de/2005/06/05/google-sitemaps-generator-v2-final.

For ExpressionEngine, you can visit the ExpressionEngine wiki to get details on creating a Google sitemap at http://expressionengine.com/wiki/ Google_Sitemaps/. You first create a template that generates the sitemap, then you need to force it to appear on the root level of your site, which is a bit tricky with ExpressionEngine and the way it builds URLs using template names. But that entry walks you through the process, including showing you some cut-and-paste text you can use for your templates.

Submit to Search Engines

Perhaps most important with a new blog, however, is to make sure you submit that blog to the major search engines. Submitting to Google, Yahoo!, MSN, and others ensures that, eventually, their *spiders* (the search engine applications that hunt for new content on the Web) will begin to "crawl" your blog and look for content that can then be used for search results. Here's a quick look at the places where you can submit your blog so that it gets crawled by search engines spiders:

- **Google (http://www.google.com/addurl/)**   Enter your URL and a name for your blog, then use the CAPTCHA to confirm that you're a person.

- **Yahoo! (http://search.yahoo.com/info/submit.html)**   You can begin the submission process from here; with Yahoo!, you need to register as a user before you can submit your site.

- **MSN Search (http://submitit.bcentral.com/msnsubmit.htm)**   Enter a URL and an e-mail address, then sit back and hope.

Track Your Blog Traffic (and Increase It)

Something else you'll probably want to get up and running once you've done a little blogging is a tool to track the traffic to your blog. There are, of course, any number of different ways that you can get statistical information about your blog and your website, including tools built into the blogging applications and tools provided by your web hosting company. In this section, we'll start by looking at the stats that are built into the major blogging applications discussed in this book, then we'll take a look at two third-party options: SiteMeter and Google Analytics.

Built-in Blog Stats

The statistics that your blogging software offers are usually somewhat limited; you can get a sense of the number of times certain blog entries have been read and commented on, and sometimes you can get a little more detail than that. Here's a quick look at each of the four tools discussed in this book:

- **Blogger**   Blogger doesn't really have any built-in stats management, but it'll work with Google Analytics and other stats packages discussed later in this section.

- **TypePad**   Click the Control Panel tab in the admin interface, then click Stats. You'll see basic information about the visitors to your blog and, if there have been any in the past few days, you'll see *referrer* links, which enable you to see where those visitors are coming from.

- **WordPress**   WordPress doesn't offer any built-in statistics for blog visitors and pageviews, but there are a number of different plug-ins that can give you some statistical info for your site, including Counterize, which does a pretty good job of putting together the basics about your visitors. See http://codex.wordpress.org/Plugins/Statistics for a list of different plug-ins.

- **ExpressionEngine**   On the "dashboard" of your admin control panel, you'll see some basic stats by default; ExpressionEngine also ships with a statistics module that you can use to place all sorts of items on your blog pages. See http://expressionengine.com/docs/modules/statistics/index.html for details on adding stats to your blog's pages, particularly to note the number of visitors currently on the site, the most visitors ever, and so on.

Add SiteMeter to Your Blog

You've got plenty of choices when it comes to adding a third-party stats solution to your blog, but SiteMeter tends to be pretty popular with bloggers. Not only does it offer a free version, but it also (particularly in the free incarnation) has a "full disclosure" sensibility to it, because it tracks your stats in the open; you add it to your blog by placing its icon on the page (often in the sidebar) in such a way that anyone can see your blog's stats.

To add SiteMeter to your blog, visit www.sitemeter.com and register for the service. When you do, you'll see the option to visit the Manager section of the site, which you should do. You then can navigate to the Instructions pages that will walk you through adding the SiteMeter code to your page. The free version of SiteMeter works by having you embed some JavaScript invocation code in your page design; that creates a small image link on the page that can be clicked to see your sites. It's also invoked every time a new visitor comes to your site, so that the script can learn what page referred that visit and track how many pages that visitor views. That's how you get the statistics.

SiteMeter is pretty full-featured in its free incarnation, although it does show you (and anyone who visits your stats) advertising on the stats pages. The Premium (paid) version's most significant feature is that you can hide the link, so that your stats aren't necessarily public. The Premium version offers a number of other improvements, such as tracking thousands of recent visits, giving more information about the search keywords used to find your site, and generally offering more information geared toward Web-based advertising.

Here's the HTML that SiteMeter typically uses:

```
<script type="text/javascript"
src="http://s36.sitemeter.com/js/counter.js?site=s36yoursite">
</script>
```

In most cases you'll want to paste that into a portion of your template that is loaded with every page view. For most blogs that will be the sidebar of the template; for some you may want to use the footer instead, if you don't have a sidebar on every page. (In ExpressionEngine you may need to copy the code to a few different templates if you don't have a single sidebar that's embedded in all of them. Likewise, if you use the Pages feature in WordPress and you've changed the layout so that it doesn't include a sidebar, you may need to embed the code in that page as well.

In any case, once you've got that code embedded, you'll see a new SiteMeter image on your page, which you can then click to see the full SiteMeter interface, shown in Figure 10-2.

In the top half of the screen you'll see information about the visits that your blog has received, including a total, a daily average, how long visitors stay on average, and how many visitors you've had in the last hour, last day, and recent week. Below that, you'll see the Page Views information, which shows a similar breakdown of how many times pages on your blog have been viewed.

On the left-hand side of the display you'll see quite a bit of interesting information that you can use to learn more about who is visiting your site and how they're getting there. Here's a quick overview of some of those options:

- **Summary**   This is the link back to the summary page that opens when you first click the SiteMeter link.

- **Who's On?**   Click this to quickly see information about your most recent visitors and what pages they've viewed.

10

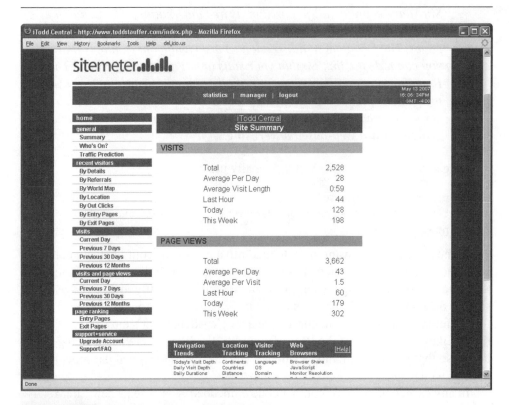

FIGURE 10-2 The SiteMeter stats for my blog

■ **Traffic Prediction** On this page you'll see a matrix of "predictions" that show you what your upcoming traffic may be like, based on different averages over the past hour, day, week, and month. If you've had a good day of traffic, for instance, then you might find that you'll get a spike in traffic if you can keep it up by writing interesting stuff and getting folks to return to the site. In this example, we've had a few great hours ... and you can see what traffic would be like if it kept up:

Based on the site traffic during the last ...	The site will have this much traffic over the next ...			
	Hour	Day	Week	Month
Hour	67 Page Views	1,608 Page Views	11,132 Page Views	48,240 Page Views
	42 Visits	1,008 Visits	6,978 Visits	30,240 Visits
Day	4 Page Views	91 Page Views	630 Page Views	2,730 Page Views
	2 Visits	45 Visits	312 Visits	1,350 Visits

■ **Recent Visitors**   Under the Recent Visitors heading you'll see many different links that enable you to get a sense of who is visiting you and how they're getting to your site. In particular, you may want to check the By Referrals section every so often to see where new visitors may be finding you; every once in a while you'll see a new site or an interesting traffic boost from a particular site. When you do, you might want to track that site down and/or consider building a relationship with that site to keep the traffic going. The By Entry Pages option can also be interesting, because you'll find if your visitors are coming for a particular page or blog entry, or if they're mostly visiting your home page.

■ **Visits and Visits & PageViews**   These two sections enable you to take a look at a graphical analysis of your recent traffic so that you can quickly get a sense of any trends you're seeing in terms of the days of the week or the response to certain types of entries.

■ **Page Ranking**   Click this entry to see which of your pages is most popular. The page rankings may help you hone your site a bit, as you can see what blog entries people are responding to and, perhaps, the topics or types of entries you could concentrate on if you're looking to increase traffic. Note that you can view both the most popular Entry Pages and the most common Exit Pages. Is there some reason that people are leaving your site when they get to a certain page?

TIP

People may not be leaving your site on a particular page or entry because they're offended or tired of reading you (although those are possibilities). It may be because you're linking to something that many of them are finding interesting and so they leave your site. One option if you decide that's the case is to use the `target="_blank"` *attribute when you create a hyperlink in your blog entries. For instance, this link:*

```
<a href="http://www.toddstauffer.com/" target="_blank">Todd
Stauffer's incredibly popular blog</a>
```

will open in a new browser window when the link is accessed. That way, visitors might still come back to your blog and continue reading after they've spent a few hours (ha!) on mine.

SiteMeter has even more options along the bottom of the main interface:

- **Navigation Trends** Here are a collection of different graphs and charts that give you a visual look at how much time your visitors are spending on your site and how many pages, on average, they're viewing. If they're not spending much time on your site, you might try to place "recent comments" or "related entries" or similar lists on your site to see if that improves; whenever you make changes, you can check back here to see if they seem to be helping.

- **Location Tracking** Learn where your visitors are coming from and what time zones they're visiting from. That could give you a hint about your audience; if your New York blog is getting a lot of traffic from Europe and Africa, you might want to add some additional travel information in your blogging or your ads. Conversely, you may find that most of your traffic comes from close to home, which might—help you pitch the local media on covering you as a hometown blogging sensation. Or you might go sell an ad to a local boutique.

- **Visitor Tracking** With these links you can learn about the people coming to your site, including the default language on their computer, the operating system they're using, and the domain and organization from which they're visiting.

- **Web Browsers** Learn more about the web browsers that are being used to visit your site, including information such as screen resolution and color depth that may help you make some design decisions.

Use Google Analytics to Track Stats

If you're interested in moving beyond SiteMeter, one full rung up the ladder is Google Analytics—and, as an added bonus, all of its features are free. Google Analytics can be used to track your blog's stats, learn more about your users, and, in conjunction with Google AdWords and other online advertising programs, you can use Google Analytics to set and attempt to reach certain "goals," most of which revolve around getting additional traffic to your site.

To sign up for Google Analytics, head to www.google.com/analytics/ and register for the service. If you already have a Gmail or Google account, you should be able to sign up quickly for Google Analytics; if you don't yet have an account, you'll need to go through the process of creating a Google account.

Once you're logged in with a Google account and you're accessing Google Analytics, the next step is to create a new Analytics account. You'll do that by entering your blog's URL, a name for the blog, and information about your local time, and then clicking Continue.

Please enter the URL of the site you wish to track, and assign a name as it should appear in your Google Analytics reports. If you'd like to track more than one website, you can add more sites once your account has been set up. Learn more.

Website's URL:	http:// ⌄ www.toddstauffer.com	(e.g. www.mywebsite.com)
Account Name:	iToddCentral	
Time zone country or territory:	United States ⌄	
Time zone:	(GMT-06:00) Central Time ⌄	

Cancel Continue »

Now you'll enter some contact information and accept the Terms of Service. That will create the Analytics account and move you on to the tracking instructions.

Google Analytics works in a way that's similar to SiteMeter; you'll need to paste some special JavaScript code into your blog template so that every time someone loads a new page from your blog, that Analytics code is also invoked. Again, for most of the blogging tools discussed in this book, that means placing the Analytics code in the common sidebar template that is used on your blog; if you have a more complicated or customized design, then you'll need to account for that and place the Analytics code wherever it needs to be (perhaps in the common footer, perhaps in a number of different template pages) so that it's loaded each time someone accesses a page on your site. Here's what the code looks like:

```
<script src="http://www.google-analytics.com/urchin.js"
type="text/javascript">
</script>
<script type="text/javascript">
_uacct = "UA-00000000-1";
urchinTracker();
</script>
```

You'll have a unique user account number assigned and, from the Analytics: Tracking Instructions page, you'll be able to copy that code to your Windows or Mac clipboard so that you can paste it into your templates.

Once you've got the tracking codes in your template, you can move on to your Analytics home page, which enables you to change settings, view different reports, and, if you have them, set up tracking for multiple sites. You'll also see periodic updates and helpful information about Analytics on this page.

10

For now, locate the link to your website's reports. (You may find that you have to wait a day or so before stats for the website you're adding kick in and has information.) Click the link to a report for your site and you'll see the Analytics Dashboard for that site appear (see Figure 10-3).

The Google Analytics Dashboard displays a number of stats about your sites in one quick visual overview. Starting at the top of your site, you can view the number of visits to your site in the graph at the top of the page; mouse over a day to see the number of visitors that day.

Below that you'll see the Site Usage statistics that include the number of visits, information about the number of pages viewed per visit, the number of pageviews, the average time spent on the site, and so on.

Below the Site Usage area are a series of overview graphs that correspond to the main sections of reporting information that Analytics offers; you'll see corresponding entries on the left-hand side of the interface. Those areas are Visitors, Traffic Sources, Content, and Goals.

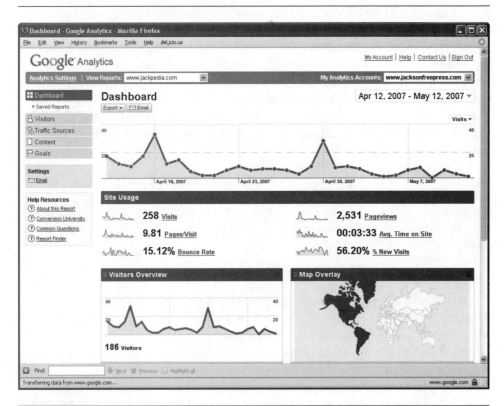

FIGURE 10-3   The Google Analytics Dashboard for one of my sites

Visitors

In the Visitors Overview on the Analytics Dashboard, you can learn more about the unique visitors to your blog; mouse over the graph to see how many people visited on a given day, or click the View Report link to see a more in-depth look at who has been visiting your site, including information about their browsers, bounce rate (how many of them leave from the same page they arrived, meaning they didn't click into the site to view anything else), and other interesting stuff (see Figure 10-4).

The visitor stats can get pretty involved, measuring things like visitor loyalty (what percentage of your users return multiple times to your site), new vs. returning visitors, the length of their visit, the depth of their visit (how many pages did each visitor check out while on the site), and many other interesting options, including information about their browsers, their installed scripting capabilities, and even what sort of Internet access (broadband, dial-up, etc.) they have.

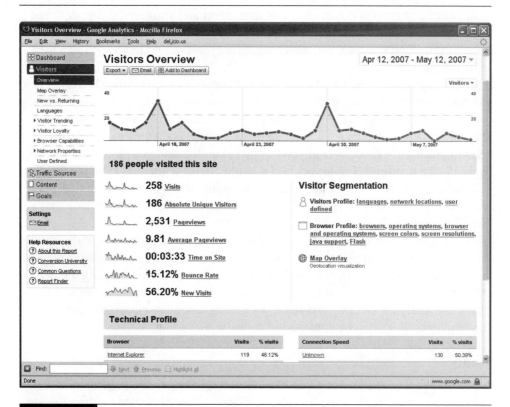

FIGURE 10-4   The Visitors Overview page goes into greater detail about the people who are visiting your site.

Traffic Sources

On the Dashboard you'll see a Traffic Sources overview that shows you who is coming to your site directly, who is coming from links outside of your site, and who is coming from search engines. Click into the Traffic Sources report and you can get a good deal more information, such as what external sites refer the most people to you and what keywords are being used to search (and find) pages or entries on your site. You can also learn about the Referring Sites that are sending people to your blog and find out what specific keywords are getting results on your site. If you're signed up and using Google AdWords to drive traffic, then you can use the AdWords and Campaigns links to learn more about whether your AdWords purchases are giving you good results for building traffics (see the section "Analytics and AdWords" later in this chapter).

Content

Again, the Analytics Dashboard shows you a basic overview of the content on your site that is most popular; click into that report and you can dig deeper to see which pages have the most page views, which pages are the first page viewed by visitors (the "Entry" page), and which pages are most often viewed before a user exits the site (the "Exit" page).

The Content section also offers another interesting feature—the Overlay. Click this and a new window appears with the home page of your blog or website. What you're shown in the Overlay is a graphical representation of which items receive the most clicks on that page. Where are people going when they visit your site? (See Figure 10-5.) This can help you not just to understand your traffic, but to also make design decisions. For instance, if you notice that a link way down on your sidebar seems to be getting a lot of clicks, it might make sense to move it closer to the top. Or, conversely, if you don't seem to be getting traffic to something that's buried in your site's design, maybe it'd be best to move it around.

In fact, the Overlay is probably best for gauging the effectiveness of design and organizational changes that you make to your site. If you don't think enough people are clicking your RSS feed's link, perhaps you could try creating a more prominent icon and placing it at the top of your sidebar. Now, after a few days, check the Analytics Overlay and see if it's getting any more clicks than the old feed link was. If so, maybe your design decision was a success.

Goals

Google Analytics enables you to do more than track visitors and pageviews—you can also create and track goals that can be measured and presented by the software. A goal can actually be quite simple—it's usually a specific page on your site that is

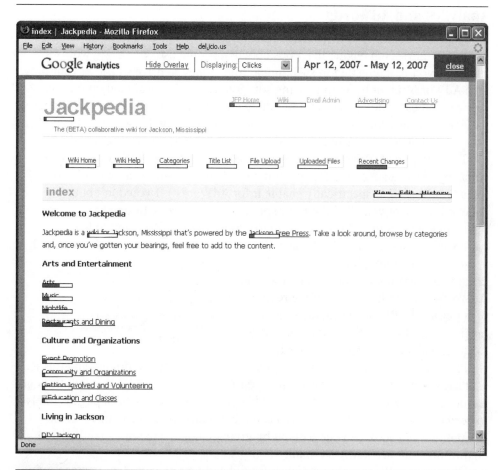

FIGURE 10-5   Here's a graphical overlay of my wiki-based site, Jackpedia.

only shown to your user when they've done something such as make a purchase or complete a registration. The Goals feature in Analytics can be set up to count how many people reach a "Thank You" or "Registration Complete" page of some kind on your site and then present those numbers to you as a percentage of your visitors.

Of course, if the goal that you have for your blog is people reading your stories, then the Analytics goals aren't that helpful. But, if you're looking to get people to sign up for your newsletter, or view a certain story, or download a particular file, then you can use the goals within Google Analytics to track that sort of behavior—just click the Goals icon in the left-hand sidebar, then clink the Learn How to Set Up Goals link. You'll be walked through the process of setting up a goal and getting Analytics to track it for you.

Analytics and AdWords

Google AdWords is Google's system for enabling you to buy text advertising on the Google search engine that pops up when people use certain keywords to search. If you're interesting in spending a little money to drive traffic to your blog, then AdWords might be an interesting solution. Once you're signed up for the service, you can "bid" on keywords, telling Google how much you're willing to pay for each click-through to your site. The more you're willing to pay, the higher your ad will appear in the queue of ads that match that particular keyword.

To sign up for AdWords, you'll need to head over to http://adwords.google.com/ and create an account. (By default, your Google login is *not* an AdWords login; you'll need to specifically enable it for AdWords.) If you don't have an AdWords account yet, click the Begin button and then walk through the process of creating an account. (You may want to choose Standard account to have a variety of options, but the Starter account works as well if you want a simplified approach.) Step through the process of creating the account and choosing how your AdWords will work in terms of the regions or countries they'll appear in, the search languages, and so on. You'll then be asked to create a short ad to get you started.

Create an ad

Example short ad:

iTodd Central
News and views on the world of
Macs, Web 2.0 and the news online
www.toddstauffer.com/

From there you choose keywords, and then move on to the pricing and traffic estimates. You tell AdWords how much you're willing to spend for a click-through to your site and AdWords will tell you what your rank on the search page is likely to be and how many clicks the search is likely to turn up. You can then decide to Continue and activate your account by giving Google a payment method and confirming your account via e-mail.

Once your AdWords account is confirmed and you're signed in, you can set up a billing preference and begin putting your AdWords out there on the Web. You can also link back into Analytics and use the two together. In the AdWords interface, click the Analytics tab. On the Getting Started page, click I Already Have a Google Analytics Account. If you're logged into the same username in AdWords that you used for your earlier Google Analytics account, then you'll see that account appear on the page and you'll have the option to link to that account; click Link Account. Now you can access the Analytics interface via the AdWords interface. Explore Analytics and you'll see that it reports to you when your AdWords choices successfully turn into visitors for your site.

Make Money from Your Blog

Becoming a "full-time" blogger isn't probably something you dreamt about when you were a kid—unless you're really young. (And, if that's the case, then you're also an exceptionally advanced reader for a five-year-old.) It's a new thing, but professional blogging is a true vocation. If your ambition is to spend all of your time blogging and make a living at it, I'm more than happy to encourage you, with the following caveat—only few people *actually* make a living at it. Of course, few people make a living directing films or writing novels or singing for a living, but that doesn't make it impossible.

If you don't want to blog professionally—but you do like to blog—then there's some middle ground to explore. With a popular enough blog, it's possible to make a few dollars per month—or week, or day—and conceivably, at the very least, get your blogging to pay for some of your hosting fees or for a few cups of coffee per week. If you're very lucky and diligent and a good writer and blogger, you might end up making even a little more than that, or using your blog to break into the "big time" on some other level, like a speaking or writing gig.

In this section, however, I'd like to explore the "slow trickle" of money into your blog in three different "bloggy" sorts of ways to make or solicit money from your readers—donations, Google AdSense, and Amazon links. You'll find many others out there that you can experiment with, but if you just want to pay your blog's "rent," these approaches might get you started.

10

NOTE   *No, I don't make enough money off my blogging to live, although I have had my blogs cover their expenses in the past. (And, hey, I get to write a book about blogging, so it ain't all bad.) Somebody who claims he does make money from blogging is ProBlogger (http://www.problogger.net/), whose site offers some interesting tips for making money from your blog. He not only encourages you to try and make money, but he covers the multitude of ways you can go about it if you're serious about adding affiliate ads and other options to your blog. Of course he's making his money by blogging about making money—which may be the trick!*

Accept PayPal Donations

One approach that some popular bloggers take is to hang out a shingle (or an icon) and encourage readers to donate to the cause if they like what they read or the podcasts they hear and view. If you've got good content that seems to encourage or uplift people, this might be the approach to take.

Obviously, donations aren't for every blog. If you're offering a service that others find valuable for whatever reason—it's diverting, informative, your advice is freely given and professional, etc.—then you may find that soliciting donations works.

The most common way to accept donations on blogs is via the PayPal Donate button, which you can add to your blog by signing up for a PayPal account and then heading to Merchant Services on the site. On the Merchant Services page, locate the Donations link. Now you'll be asked to fill out some information about the donations you want to receive, including the option to choose the button you want to use for your donation. (Note that, if desired, you can choose your own image for the link.)

You then see some HTML that you should copy and paste to the sidebar of your blog. When you're done, you should see a button on your blog.

When a visitor clicks that button, he or she is taken to a PayPal donation page, where they can enter (or edit) the item name and the amount of their payment, then use a PayPal account or a credit card to give you that donation that you so richly deserve.

TypePad Tip Jar

If you're using TypePad and you have a Pro-level account, there's a built-in "Tip Jar" option that does much the same thing as PayPal Donations, except that "tips" are processed through the TypePad system and credited to your account. To turn on the Tip Jar, head to the TypePad admin interface for your blog and then click the Design tab, followed by the Select Content link. On the Select Content page, turn on the option Tip Jar.

Tip Jar
Earn tips on your weblog or gather donations for favorite causes.
Configure

Below that option, click the Configure link and you'll see a new window that enables you to choose the look of the Tip Jar button, the text used to entice people into clicking it, and the suggested amount. You can also paste in the URL to a post on your blog that discusses the donations (just in case you want to explain to people that they're going to a good cause or whatnot), and you can determine whether or not you want to get an e-mail whenever someone leaves a donation.

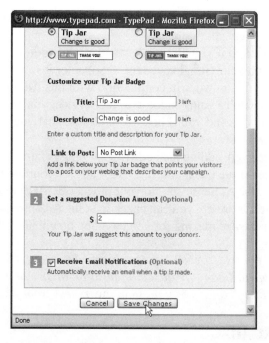

Back on the Select Content page, save your changes and then, if desired, you can click the Order Content link on the Design page in order to decide where, exactly, your Tip Jar will appear.

Google AdSense

Perhaps one of the more significant changes that the world of the Web has brought about is Google AdSense. AdSense is the program whereby you can run ads from Google on your blog and get paid for them, generally when your users click the ads in order to view the sites behind them. You can configure the ads in a multitude of different ways, from vertical and horizontal ad blocks to ads that are just a few words in length. The Google servers look at your blog and try to serve ads that seems to have some contextual relationship to what you're blogging about; it often works, and sometimes it's hilariously funny.

Another things that's significant about AdSense is that the ads are fairly ubiquitous, and not terribly likely to cause too much of a stir among your readership; they're not exactly *expected*, but they're generally unobtrusive. And adding them to your blog's sidebar is just as easy as any other item.

If you'd like to use Google AdSense on your blog, head over to http://adsense .google.com/ and sign up for the service. (If you already have a Google login, you should still click "Sign Up Now" so that you can complete the application form and then attach it to your existing Google account.) Now, walk through the registration process, read the rules and regulations, and click Submit Information to move on to the next page.

Now, you'll be asked if you already have an e-mail address and password that's associated with your Google account. If so, enter it so that your Analytics and other Google tools can work in conjunction with this AdSense account. Once you've chosen how you're going to log into the service, you'll see that you're signed up for the service and you'll hear from Google that you're accepted or not within the next few days.

Once you're accepted, adding the code to your blog is fairly straightforward. Just sign into the service, locate the appropriate sized ads for your blog and then cut-and-paste the HTML for the AdSense ad into your blog's sidebar or elsewhere in your templates. Once the ads are up, you can check in at the AdSense home page to see what sort of money they're making for you based on how many clicks you get.

TIP   *After you've created your AdSense block, don't forget to freshen it up every so often. Changing the color, position or size of your AdSense block can sometimes cause an increase in awareness from your readers.*

TypePad Text Ads

If you've got a Pro-level account with TypePad, you can use the built-in service for generating revenue from text ads. To do so, click the Design tab in the TypePad control panel and then click the Select Content link. There, on the Content Selections page you'll find the Text Ads option; before you can activate it, you'll need to click the Configure link. In the window that appears, you can choose Easy Setup or Customize.

Choose Easy Setup and click Continue if you want a basic ad setup. Choose Customize and click Continue if you want to select the look-and-feel of your ads and if you'd like to customize the keywords used in the advertisements. When you do, you'll be walked through a number of choices, including the number of ads that you want to appear in your text ad bar (Step 2), the categories that you want to advertise (you might want them to be related to the topics that you tend to cover on your blog; that's Step 3), and the fonts and color used (Step 4). If you like what you see in Step 5, choose Yes, Use this Configuration and click Continue.

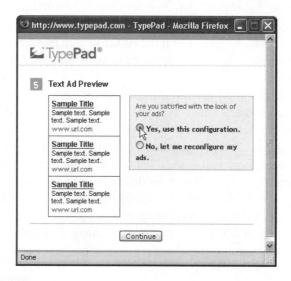

Click Save and, back on the Content Selections page, you'll see that the Text Ads are enabled. Scroll down to the bottom of the screen, select Save Changes and you'll now have ads in your sidebar. Choose Order Content from the Design page if you'd like to move the ads to another location on your sidebar; otherwise, view your site and you should see the ads appear. (Actually, you may see stand-in ads for the TypePad service appear for a while until your account is approved.)

Amazon Associates

One of the longer-running and most successful *affiliate programs*—Web ads that pay you when someone orders from the advertiser, instead of simply when the ad is viewed or clicked—is Amazon.com, which pays associates for the books, electronics, or other products that readers click to and then order from the online store. Amazon is interesting in that you can not only make money from the products that you link to directly, but you can also make money off of other products (albeit a lower percentage) that a person surfs to if they started their trip to Amazon from your site.

Again, you'll probably have the most success with Amazon when you're looking to sell a particular product or when those products are particularly complementary to your blog's content. Random Amazon ads haven't done me well in the past, but I certainly use Amazon links to my own books, since I'm a bit more likely to sell a book to someone who enjoys my blog. If you blog about cooking or clothing or computers, you might consider targeted links to specific products that you recommend.

To sign up as an "associate" (which is what Amazon calls people in its affiliate advertising program), head to http://affiliate-program.amazon.com/gp/associates/join? (or click the Make Money tab on the Amazon.com home page and then locate the Join Associates link) and register as a new associate. You'll be walked through the process.

Now, once you're signed in as an affiliate, you'll have a lot of different options, including the ability to view various reports (earnings, orders, and referrals) and to see, in general, how your pitch for products is doing.

To build ads and links to new products, click Build Links in the main Associates interface. There you'll see a list of the different types of links and ads you can build. Amazon offers all sorts of different links and services, from links to specific products to "Omakase" links (links that fit the topics of your blog) to "context" links that can literally look at the content of your blog and create links from within that content that lead to Amazon products. If people buy the products, then you get a percentage.

With nearly any of the link types, you click into it, make some configuration choices, and then copy and paste the HTML that's created for you into the sidebar (or elsewhere in the templates) of your blog. For instance, using the Omakase style of ad, I've gone in and selected a 120×600 ad (it's best in your sidebar to use the vertical orientations) and make some alterations to the look of it (I've chosen text at the top instead of a logo) . Then, after pasting the provided code into the sidebar on my blog, I get a nice-looking ad that even tends to include my own book on it (since I'm writing about that book on my blog), along with other books that are related to what I'm writing about.

Other Affiliate and Ad Programs

Aside from Amazon you'll find many other affiliate programs out there that will enable you to make a little money if people click an ad and then buy the product or sign up for the service that's advertised. You'll find affiliate programs all over the place; what I'd recommend is that you surf the sites that tend to interest you (particularly e-commerce and paid service sites) and then see which ones you might want to sign up for and create an affiliate ad. Particularly if you can recommend a product or service on your site (without compromising your integrity), then a link to that product or service may make a lot of sense.

NOTE   *For some affiliate programs, you may need a minimum amount of traffic on your site before you can be approved; if you're just starting out with your blog and don't have more than a few hundred page views per month, you may not be ready yet for an affiliate program. Text ads and Amazon may be the way to go in the short run.*

A few different affiliate services and other advertising and commission-based options include

- **Commission Junction (www.cj.com)**   Commission Junction is a network for affiliate programs. Sign up as a publisher and you can then peruse and select the advertisers that you'd like to place on your blog. In some cases, you'll need to apply to join an advertiser's group, after which you'll be able to choose the ads that you want to run, get the HTML code to add them to your site, and then paste them into your templates. Most of their campaigns are CPA (Cost Per Action) payouts, meaning you get paid when someone orders something or fills out a form, not just when they click the ad.

- **ClickBooth (www.clickbooth.com)**   Similar to Commission Junction, offering mostly CPA campaigns.

- **LinkShare (www.linkshare.com)**   Also similar to ClickBooth and Commission Junction, and it offers some big names in online advertising.

- **Microsoft Small Business AdCenter (www.microsoft.com/ smallbusiness/) and Yahoo! Publishers Network (www.yahoo.com/ publishers)**   Microsoft and Yahoo! offer their own take on Google AdSense-style ads, most of which are Cost Per Click (CPC).

- **BlogAds (www.blogads.com)**   These ads are aimed specifically at blogs, particularly if you fit into certain categories. (The best blogs in these networks tend to be political or geared at pop culture and/or gadgets and shopping.)

10

- **CafePress (www.cafepress.com)** A popular option for creating digitally-printed products and clothing that you can sell from your site and profit from the markup.

- **Zlio (www.zlio.com)** Create your own online shop. You can choose the items that go into your shop and anything that's sold through it earns you a commission.

- **Lulu (www.lulu.com)** Got a book in you? Sign up for Lulu and you can publish eBooks for free. Lulu takes a commission from eBooks that you charge for, and it offers a digital printing service that enables you to sell hard copies of your booklet or book.

If you find you're getting a lot of traffic, there probably isn't much harm in signing up for a few different advertising schemes and testing them out; your readers may decide to support your content by clicking the ads and checking out the products.

Even better, though, is to have your own products—if you're a highly prized blogger in a topic area or offering advice, I'd suggest you look into writing eBooks (or regular books!), generating written reports, or doing other things online that can be sold for $5 or $10 a piece in order to "monetize" the market you're creating.

Back Up, Restore, and Maintain Your Blog

Once you've gotten serious about blogging, you need to get serious about that content up there. After all, you've probably spent a good bit of time creating that content, you may have it well-positioned in search engines or hyperlinks all around the world—and, well, it'd be a pity if it disappeared in a puff of web server smoke. The solution to backing up your blog depends on the software that you're using and the way you're hosting your site. Let's take a look at the different options.

NOTE *In an ideal world, your hosting company should be doing regular backups, and if you don't know if that service is offered, you should check immediately with your provider. If it isn't part of the basic package, you may be able to add it. In addition to backups by your hosting company (and you can assume that sites such as Blogger, TypePad, and WordPress. com are doing those backups), you can use the techniques in this section to back up your blog for archival purposes, as a safety net in case your hosting company goes out of business or in order to move your blog to another host.*

Back Up Blogger

If you're hosting your blog on BlogSpot (the free Blogger hosting service), then there's an argument, at least, that your content is pretty safe, as you're relying on Google's servers. (Things should be fine at least up until the moment that Google decides to flip a switch and take over the world; at that point, your blog may be the least of your worries.)

If you want to copy your content to a safe place, Blogger recommends an interesting approach: Set up your Blogger template so that you can get all of your content into one long page; you can then save that to have your posts (and, if you want, your comments) all in one place. Visit http://help.blogger.com/bin/answer.py?answer=41447 in the Blogger Help system so that you can cut and paste the template and make the settings changes that you need to make.

If you post your Blogger-based blog to your own hosting account, then you should be able to access your web hosting account with an FTP client and copy your files from the hosting account to your hard disk periodically. Because Blogger doesn't use a scripting-and-database approach, all of your files are actually HTML documents that are "published" by Blogger to your account. Copying those documents to your hard disk saves the blog entries that you've created (see Figure 10-6). Note that you may also need to locate and copy the images stored on your hosting account, if you have any, in order for your pages to be complete.

10

TIP   *Want to automate the process of backing up the full look-and-feel of your HTML-based blog? I found these applications recommended by the popular blog LifeHacker (www.lifehacker.com): WebGrabber for Mac OS X (www.epicware.com) and HTTrack Website Copier for Windows (www.httrack.com) can both be used to back up a blog such as those created by Blogger and TypePad, where pages are stored as HTML documents. Those files will grab the associated images, too. Unfortunately, they won't work for dynamically served sites such as WordPress and ExpressionEngine.*

Back Up TypePad

In TypePad, you can use the Export feature to back up your blog periodically. Here's how:

1. In the TypePad control panel, choose the blog that you're going to back up (if you have more than one).

2. Under the Manage tab (which should be selected), click the Import/Export link.

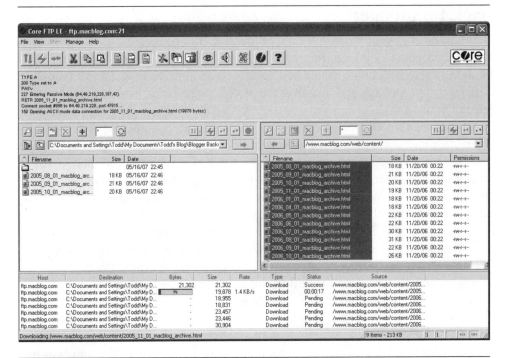

FIGURE 10-6 Here I'm copying Blogger files to my hard disk using an FTP application.

3. At the bottom of the Import/Export Posts page, click the Export Posts From Your Weblog link.

4. Now you can copy and paste the contents elsewhere or choose File | Save (or File | Save As) from your browser and you can save a text file that includes the contents of your blog entries in plain text.

> **TIP**
> *TypePad also stores blog entries as HTML documents, so you can use the same applications discussed in the Blogger section to download the full pages, including formatting and images.*

Back Up WordPress

The easiest way to back up your WordPress installation is to periodically export your posts using the Manage | Export feature. This will export your posts, comments, custom fields, and categories. Even better, if you ever need to move your blog or re-create it, you can import all those same items using the special

WXR file that WordPress creates by going to Manage | Import and choosing WordPress from the list of blogs from which you can import entries.

The second easiest way to back up your blog is to back up the entire WordPress database using the WordPress backup plug-in, which you can download from here: http://wordpress.org/extend/plugins/wp-db-backup/. Here's how to use it:

1. Download the .zip file and expand it, copy the file wp-db-backup.php to the plugins folder (inside wp-content) on your host account.

2. Next, open the WordPress admin interface and click the Plugins tab.

3. Scroll down and find the WordPress Database Backup plug-in; click Activate.

4. With the plug-in active, click the Manage tab, then click the Backup link.

NOTE *On the Backup page, you may get warnings that certain directories aren't writeable; you'll need to use your FTP program to set the permissions on those directories to writeable for the backup to work.*

5. First, you'll see that the plug-in automatically schedules certain tables within the database for backup; if you have any optional tables (created by plug-ins or bbPress, for instance), you can click to place a checkmark next to those that you want to save.

6. Scroll to Backup Options and choose the option you want for storing the backup; Download to Your Computer is probably the one that makes the most sense.

7. Click Backup.

8. You'll see the Backup Progress page. When the backup is finished, you should see your browser's Downloads window appear so that you can save the backup files to your hard disk.

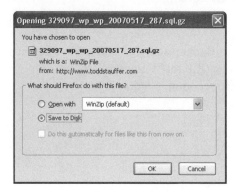

NOTE *The plug-in will also enable you to set a Scheduled Backup, which can be zipped and e-mailed to you on a regular basis.*

Backing up the database is the easy part; restoring from the backup is a little tougher. Fortunately, this is a standard MySQL database export, so you can restore the same way you would for ExpressionEngine; see the section "Recovering a MySQL Backup."

Along with the database that WordPress uses, you may also want to log into your host account via FTP every so often and back up any files that you change to the WordPress installation. In particular, you should consider backing up these files and folders:

- **wp-config.php** This file shouldn't change often (unless you change it manually) but it's good to have its current settings stored somewhere convenient.

- **wp-content/** This entire folder is well positioned to make it easier to back up most of the stuff that's likely to change, including the plug-ins that you install, the images you upload, and even the additional themes that you've installed or tweaked.

Back Up ExpressionEngine

As the most complex blogging system covered in this book, you'd expect ExpressionEngine to have the most complex backup system. Fortunately, EllisLabs has built in some backup features that you can use relatively easily.

As with WordPress, though, *recovering* a backup can be a bit more involved. Here's how to back up your ExpressionEngine database:

1. In the control panel, click the Admin tab.

2. Next, click the Utilities link.

3. In the Utilities menu, locate the Database Backup link.

4. On the Database Backup screen, choose Save Backup to Your Desktop and choose a file type (Zip for Windows, Zip, or GZip will work for most Mac users, with GZip recommended.)

5. Click the Submit button and your browser should display its Download
window. You can now save the MySQL backup to your computer.

Aside from backing up your database, it can be important to back up the files
that are installed to your host computer; to get at those, you'll need to fire up your
FTP application and copy those files down to your computer in a safe place. When
you do, you're able to back up image files, file uploads, and any changes that
you've made to your ExpressionEngine configuration file or any files that you've
added in the form of themes, modules, or plug-ins.

Of course, these files aren't *as* critical as your database backups are,
since you could conceivably reconstruct your blog from a new installation of
ExpressionEngine and a new installation of any modules that you've downloaded
in the past. (And since your templates and many other customizations are saved
in the database via the ExpressionEngine control panel, you've got those secured
at the same time that you back up other data that's in the database.) So, if you just
want to get the bare essentials, here are the files and folders from your installation
that you should consider backing up periodically:

- **system/config.php**   This folder is important, although you should realize
  that if you have to recover a crashed database (or if you change hosts),
  you may need to change some of the settings in this file to reflect the new
  database's name, server, and so on.

- **system/templates/**   Back up this folder if you've added any new
  templates or themes.

- **system/modules/, system/plugins/, system/extensions/** Back up these folders every so often if you've added new items and you prefer not to be forced to install them again in case of trouble.

- **system/language/** Modules come with their own language files and often won't work without them installed, so you'll want to back up this folder if you've ever installed an additional module.

- **/images/** It can take a while to completely back up your images folder, but it isn't a bad idea; unless your web host promises full backups and restorations, these images could be lost if you have a serious failure for your site, and they're tough or impossible to recover, particularly if you've built them up over months or years of blogging. Just set your FTP program to download them at some point and then head out for a bite to eat!

- **/themes/** If you've added to the default themes or done any tweaking to the HTML, you should back up this directory periodically so that you don't lose those changes.

Recovering a MySQL Backup

As mentioned, both WordPress and ExpressionEngine offer a tool that enables you to create a backup of your MySQL database painlessly. Hopefully, that will encourage you to conduct the backup frequently, because it can be a very valuable thing to have your blog's database backed up—in the case of a serious problem recovering with your Web host may only be possible if you have a good backup.

Fortunately, the standard MySQL backup that is created by both WordPress and ExpressionEngine is, ultimately, a plain text file that includes not only the data that's stored in the database for your blog, but also includes the MySQL *commands* that are necessary to restore the database. It's all right there in a single, human-readable file. In fact, you can open up your MySQL backup file in a text editor and see the commands and structure of the database (see Figure 10-7).

So, to restore a database, you simply feed the backup file onto a new database (or an existing one, if you're simply adding these tables to it) and the file itself will populate that database with its commands and stored data.

NOTE *This approach can be used for moving your database-based blog as well. Just copy all of your blog's files from one host to another, create a new database on the new host, and then pour the data into that database using the MySQL backup file. You'll then need to make sure the config.php file (for ExpressionEngine) or the wp-config.php file (for WordPress) is edited so that it is pointing at the new database's URL, username, and password.*

```
statedeskdb_070519.sql - WordPad
File  Edit  View  Insert  Format  Help

#
# TABLE STRUCTURE FOR: exp_actions
#

DROP TABLE IF EXISTS exp_actions;

CREATE TABLE `exp_actions` (
   `action_id` int(4) unsigned NOT NULL auto_increment,
   `class` varchar(50) NOT NULL default '',
   `method` varchar(50) NOT NULL default '',
   PRIMARY KEY (`action_id`)
) ENGINE=MyISAM DEFAULT CHARSET=latin1;

INSERT INTO exp_actions (action_id, class, method) VALUES ('1', 'Comment', 'insert_new_comment');
INSERT INTO exp_actions (action_id, class, method) VALUES ('2', 'Comment_CP', 'delete_comment_notification');
INSERT INTO exp_actions (action_id, class, method) VALUES ('3', 'Mailinglist', 'insert_new_email');
INSERT INTO exp_actions (action_id, class, method) VALUES ('4', 'Mailinglist', 'authorize_email');
INSERT INTO exp_actions (action_id, class, method) VALUES ('5', 'Mailinglist', 'unsubscribe');
INSERT INTO exp_actions (action_id, class, method) VALUES ('6', 'Member', 'registration_form');
INSERT INTO exp_actions (action_id, class, method) VALUES ('7', 'Member', 'register_member');
INSERT INTO exp_actions (action_id, class, method) VALUES ('8', 'Member', 'activate_member');
INSERT INTO exp_actions (action_id, class, method) VALUES ('9', 'Member', 'member_login');
INSERT INTO exp_actions (action_id, class, method) VALUES ('10', 'Member', 'member_logout');
INSERT INTO exp_actions (action_id, class, method) VALUES ('11', 'Member', 'retrieve_password');
INSERT INTO exp_actions (action_id, class, method) VALUES ('12', 'Member', 'reset_password');
INSERT INTO exp_actions (action_id, class, method) VALUES ('13', 'Member', 'send_member_email');
INSERT INTO exp_actions (action_id, class, method) VALUES ('14', 'Member', 'update_un_pw');
INSERT INTO exp_actions (action_id, class, method) VALUES ('15', 'Member', 'member_search');
INSERT INTO exp_actions (action_id, class, method) VALUES ('16', 'Member', 'member_delete');
INSERT INTO exp_actions (action_id, class, method) VALUES ('17', 'Trackback_CP', 'receive_trackback');
INSERT INTO exp_actions (action_id, class, method) VALUES ('18', 'Weblog', 'insert_new_entry');
INSERT INTO exp_actions (action_id, class, method) VALUES ('19', 'Search', 'do_search');
INSERT INTO exp_actions (action_id, class, method) VALUES ('20', 'Gallery', 'insert_new_comment');
INSERT INTO exp_actions (action_id, class, method) VALUES ('21', 'Gallery', 'delete_comment_notification');
INSERT INTO exp_actions (action_id, class, method) VALUES ('37', 'Forum', 'display_attachment');
INSERT INTO exp_actions (action_id, class, method) VALUES ('36', 'Forum', 'delete_subscription');
INSERT INTO exp_actions (action_id, class, method) VALUES ('35', 'Forum', 'move_topic');
INSERT INTO exp_actions (action_id, class, method) VALUES ('34', 'Forum', 'change_status');

For Help, press F1
```

FIGURE 10-7   A MySQL database is really just a long text file of instructions for restoring the database's data.

To populate a MySQL database, you'll need to access that database using PHPMyAdmin, an application that you should be able to access via the control panel of your web hosting account. With the application up and running, use it to log into your host's database server (using the same username and password you used to configure your blogging software to access the database).

Once you're logged in, here's how the import process works:

1. To begin, select the database you want to import your data into; you do that by clicking the name of the database in the left-hand sidebar.

2. Now, click the Import tab.

3. On the Import page (see Figure 10-8), click the Browse button to open a dialog box where you can locate your MySQL backup file. (Note that it can be a .sql, .zip, or .gzip file that was created by your blogging software when you did your backup.

4. Select the format of the file (SQL may be your only choice) and then choose any compatibility needs from the SQL Compatibility Mode menu. (You shouldn't have to do anything here unless you specifically set up your blog to work with MySQL 4.x level databases because your host required it.)

5. Click Go to make the import process begin.

Once the upload has finished, your database should be restored. Depending on what you're doing (moving to a newly restored database on the same host or moving to a new database on a new host altogether), you'll want to make sure that your blog's configuration file (config.php for ExpressionEngine or wp-config.php for WordPress) is pointed at the correct database server and that that config file has the correct database username and password. Once it does, you should be able to view your blog and log into your blog's control panel with full access to all of the entries and comments that you had backed up.

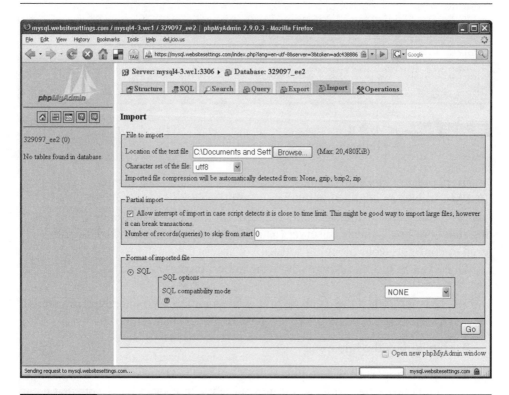

FIGURE 10-8   The Import Page enables you to upload your backed up data file to the new database.

Blog Maintenance

Again, with hosted solutions, there isn't too much you need to do to maintain your blog beyond, perhaps, cleaning out the spam comments (if you allow "open" comments that sometimes invite spam) and, when appropriate, cleaning up your sidebar and/or checking links on old, popular blog entries every so often.

> TIP
>
> *Since Blogger and TypePad both create HTML pages when your blog is "published" by the tool, you can use a link-checking application to visit your site every so often and make sure you don't have broken links. Try WebLight (http://www.illumit.com/Products/weblight/), which offers versions for Windows, Mac OS X, and Unix variants, or visit a site such as Download.com or VersionTracker (www.versiontracker.com) to search for many more options.*

In WordPress, there's relatively little maintenance to worry about. You should, for instance, every so often go through your plug-ins list (Plugins tab in the admin interface) to make sure that you're using all of the plug-ins that you've activated; if not, you can deactivate any unused plug-ins to save a resource or two for your installation.

ExpressionEngine offers a few more maintenance features. On the Admin tab of the control panel, choose Utilities. There you've got a few different options, such as:

- **Clear Cached Data**   You can clear the data that ExpressionEngine caches for a variety of different purposes, including cached templates, cached database requests, and so on. This can be important when you change servers, update your version of ExpressionEngine, or in some instances where you're having trouble with slow responses from ExpressionEngine or when you have some other odd problems (such as data not updating or templates not appearing to save correctly). You'll occasionally find that the tech folks ExpressionEngine forums (http://expressionengine.com/forums/) suggests you clear the caches to deal with some sort of issue.

- **Data Pruning**   You can use this utility to systematically delete old items from your database in order to keep things lean and mean. The smaller your database, the faster it should respond; and a smaller database definitely makes it easier to back up and move your database file. You can clear out old members (particularly those who are banned or who remained "pending" because they didn't click a verification link), old entries, old comments,

10

old trackbacks, or old forums. Just choose the option, enter the number of days that the items should be older than, and then make the specific choices for that type of data (choose from the member type, specific blog, and so on), and then click Submit.

Weblog Entry Pruning
Delete weblog entries that are more than X days old
☑ Only delete entries that have no comments

(365)

Delete only within the selected weblogs
You must select at least one
☐ Headline Roundup
☐ Mississippi Political Events
☐ Mississippi StateDesk

Submit

- ■ **Recount Statistics**   Again, this is generally used for getting accurate statistics after you've moved your site to a new host or recovered (or moved) your database. In Recount Statistics, you can recount your members, weblog entries, forum stats, forum topics, site stats, and perhaps others depending on the modules that you have installed.

Index